WORLD HISTORY OF THE DANCE

CURT SACHS was born in Berlin, Germany, in 1881 and took his Ph.D. at the University of Berlin in 1904. He taught there from 1919 to 1933 and was concurrently curator of the Museum of Musical Instruments in Berlin. In 1930, the Egyptian Government appointed him their adviser on the preservation and classification of oriental instruments.

Dr. Sachs came to America in 1937 as a visiting professor at New York University; he also served as consultant to the New York Public Library from 1937 to 1952. In 1953 he was appointed adjunct professor at Columbia University, a post he held until his death in 1959. He was a member of the American Musicological Society and served as president from 1948 to 1950.

One of the world's foremost authorities in the fields of ethnomusicology, the history of the dance, and the history and classification of musical instruments, Dr. Sachs was the author of more than 28 books, among which are: *World History of the Dance* (1937); *The History of Musical Instruments* (1940); *The Rise of Music in the Ancient World* (1943); *Commonwealth of Art* (1946); *Our Musical Heritage* (1948), and *Rhythm and Tempo* (1953). Two renowned series of phonograph records were issued under his direction: *Two Thousand Years of Music* (Berlin, 1930) and *Anthologie Sonore* (Paris, 1934-38), the latter winning the Grand Prix each year.

Books by Curt Sachs

THE RISE OF MUSIC IN THE ANCIENT WORLD

WORLD HISTORY OF THE DANCE

THE HISTORY OF MUSICAL INSTRUMENTS

THE COMMONWEALTH OF ART

RHYTHM AND TEMPO

WORLD HISTORY OF THE DANCE

by Curt Sachs

TRANSLATED BY BESSIE SCHÖNBERG

The Norton Library

W · W · NORTON & COMPANY · INC ·

PUBLISHERS · NEW YORK

W. W. Norton & Company, Inc. is the publisher of current
or forthcoming books on music by Putnam Aldrich, William Austin,
Anthony Baines, Philip Bate, Sol Berkowitz, Friedrich Blume, How-
ard Boatwright, Nadia Boulanger, Paul Brainerd, Nathan Broder,
Manfred Bukofzer, John Castellini, John Clough, Doda Conrad,
Aaron Copland, Hans David, Paul Des Marais, Otto Erich Deutsch,
Frederick Dorian, Alfred Einstein, Gabriel Fontrier, Harold Gleason,
Richard Franko Goldman, Noah Greenberg, Donald Jay Grout,
James Haar, F. L. Harrison, Daniel Heartz, Richard Hoppin, John
Horton, Edgar Hunt, A. J. B. Hutchings, Charles Ives, Roger
Kamien, Hermann Keller, Leo Kraft, Stanley Krebs, Paul Henry
Lang, Lyndesay G. Langwill, Jens Peter Larsen, Jan LaRue, Maurice
Lieberman, Irving Lowens, Joseph Machlis, Carol McClintock,
Alfred Mann, W. T. Marrocco, Arthur Mendel, William J. Mitchell,
Douglas Moore, Joel Newman, John F. Ohl, Carl Parrish, Vincent
Persichetti, Marc Pincherle, Walter Piston, Gustave Reese, Alexander
Ringer, Curt Sachs, Denis Stevens, Robert Stevenson, Oliver Strunk,
Francis Toye, Bruno Walter, J. T. Westrup, Emanuel Winternitz,
Walter Wiora, and Percy Young.

ISBN 978-0-393-00209-6

PRINTED IN THE UNITED STATES OF AMERICA

4 5 6 7 8 9 0

Contents

AUTHOR'S ACKNOWLEDGMENT

THIS BOOK should not be presented to English-speaking readers without the author's heartiest acknowledgment to the translator, to the publisher and his staff, and to Mr. Lincoln Kirstein who kindly placed his rich collection of dance pictures at my disposal.

C. S.

New York, Nov. 1937.

TRANSLATOR'S ACKNOWLEDGMENT

THE TRANSLATOR wishes to thank Mr. Charles B. Anderson and Mr. J. B. C. Watkins for their invaluable assistance in the preparation of this book. The poems not otherwise credited have been translated by Mr. Anderson.

B. S.

Illustrations

Introduction

ὁ μὴ χορεύει, τὸ γενόμενον ἀγνοεῖ.

Whosoever danceth not, knoweth not the way of life.

CHRIST IN A GNOSTIC HYMN OF THE SECOND CENTURY

THE dance is the mother of the arts. Music and poetry exist in time; painting and architecture in space. But the dance lives at once in time and space. The creator and the thing created, the artist and the work are still one and the same thing. Rhythmical patterns of movement, the plastic sense of space, the vivid representation of a world seen and imagined—these things man creates in his own body in the dance before he uses substance and stone and word to give expression to his inner experiences.

The word art does not altogether express this idea. Indeed, one almost fears to use the word, for its present-day significance, exaggerated and at the same time circumscribed, is not sufficient to explain what the dance in all its richness really is. The dance breaks down the distinctions of body and soul, of abandoned expression of the emotions and controlled behavior, of social life and the expression of individuality, of play, religion, battle, and drama—all the distinctions that a more advanced civilization has established. The body, which in ecstasy is conquered and forgotten and which becomes merely a receptacle for the super-human power of the soul, and the soul, which achieves happiness and bliss in the accelerated movements of a body freed of its own weight; the need to dance, because an effervescent zest for life forces the limbs from sloth, and the desire to dance, because the dancer gains magic powers, which bring him victory, health, life; a mystic tie binding the

3

tribe when it joins hands in the choral dance, and the unconstrained dance of the individual in utter devotion to self—there is no "art" which includes so much.

Repressed powers are loosed and seek free expression; an innate sense of rhythm orders them into lively harmony. Harmony deadens and dissipates the will. Delivered then from his will, the dancer gives himself over to the supreme delight of play prescribed by custom, gives himself over to the exhilaration, which carries him away from the monotony of everyday life, from palpable reality, from the sober facts of his experience—thither where imagination, fancy, and vision waken and become creative.

In the ecstasy of the dance man bridges the chasm between this and the other world, to the realm of demons, spirits, and God. Captivated and entranced he bursts his earthly chains and trembling feels himself in tune with all the world. "Whosoever knoweth the power of the dance, dwelleth in God," cries the Persian dervish poet Rumi impulsively. The dance, inherited from savage ancestors as an ordered expression in motion of the exhilaration of the soul, develops and broadens into the search for God, into a conscious effort to become a part of those powers beyond the might of man which control our destinies. The dance becomes a sacrificial rite, a charm, a prayer, and a prophetic vision. It summons and dispels the forces of nature, heals the sick, links the dead to the chain of their descendants; it assures sustenance, luck in the chase, victory in battle; it blesses the fields and the tribe. It is creator, preserver, steward, and guardian.

From its deep and far-reaching influence it will be apparent that in the life of primitive peoples and of ancient civilizations scarcely anything approaches the dance in importance. It is no art that disregards bread; on the contrary, it provides bread and everything else that is needed to sustain life. It is not a sin, proscribed by the priest or at best merely accepted by him, but rather a sacred act and priestly office; not a pastime to be tolerated only, but a very serious activity of the entire tribe. On no occasion in the life of primitive peoples could the dance be

4

dispensed with. Birth, circumcision, and the consecration of maidens, marriage and death, planting and harvest, the celebrations of chieftains, hunting, war, and feasts, the changes of the moon and sickness—for all of these the dance is needed. But it is not a question here of display and festivity in our sense. We know that in New Caledonia the merchants in the market house dance out in turn to show off their wares, and that the inhabitants of North Queensland pick lice off one another in a festive round dance. We read that the American Indian divorces his wife in the dance and when he is ill, dances himself to dispel the disease; further, that a chieftain in the Cameroons, condemned to death for revolt, walked up to the gallows singing and dancing, and that once, in front of the Turkish soldiers, sixty Greek maidens and mothers with children danced the old *romaiika* as they threw themselves one after another into an abyss. Only when we take into account such examples do we begin to comprehend that the dance in its essence is simply life on a higher level.

The dance is life on a higher level simply—this statement points out its all-inclusive character and its ultimate significance. Yet while it might extend the scope of a scientific consideration, it is nevertheless not a definition upon which to base such a consideration. Such a definition is not easy to formulate; indeed, in the last analysis, perhaps impossible. For all human activity eludes hard and fast classification; work and play, law and liberty, merge and the imperceptibility of the transition may be its chief characteristic. Thus from a positive approach it is almost impossible to define the dance more narrowly than as "rhythmic motion." What is lacking in this definition is that it does not exclude other rhythmic movements, such as running, rowing, turning a handle, working a treadle. These may be excluded only if we adopt a negative approach. For no positive expression is valid. "Playful" would exclude all the religious dances; "purposeless," the magic dances. That which is to be excluded might perhaps best be designated as anything having to do with work. By this we would mean everything which we describe in everyday life as "practical"; all kinds of rhythmical handwork, but also walking and marching, the playing of a violinist as well as the gestures of the orchestra conductor. The rhythmic features of sport and of gymnastics are, to be sure, included in the work motif, and there is a gap here. But we shall leave this gap open deliberately; otherwise we should be ruling out the important power dances, skill dances, and war dances, thus cutting into the whole elastic organism of the dance. Therefore let us consider as dance all rhythmical motion not related to the work motif.

This is still not art in the usual sense. But art is included in this concept, provided it means the re-creating of things seen and heard, the giving of form and substance to the intangible and irrational perceptions of the half conscious, and the experiencing in the creative process of the divine rapture of another world and of self-forgetfulness. As early as the Stone Age, dances become works of art; and on the threshold of the Metal Ages, legend seizes the dance and raises it into drama. But when in higher cultures it becomes art in the narrower sense, when it becomes a spectacle, when it seeks to influence men rather than spirits, then its universal power is broken. It disintegrates. Play and physical exercise renounce rhythm and break away, the drama itself denies its father, and the new religions become estranged from rounds and dances. What was left to the higher civilizations, especially to the European, was divided between guild art and social enjoyment. To pray with the feet like Gottfried Keller's little Musa, like the beautiful gypsy Preciosa of Cervantes, and like the old juggler who knew no Latin quotation to say to the Mother of God—all that is lost to us. But every high culture still has as a spiritual inheritance from a distant past, the lofty conception that all supermundane and superhuman motion is dance. Turning about in divine rhythm, Siva creates the world; for the Chinese, cosmic harmony originates in the dance; planets and gods swing through the universe in the dance; and late Jewish theology, indeed even Christianity, ever hostile to the dance, cannot visualize the lot of the redeemed except in a picture of an ethereal round about the shining throne of God.

Part One

DANCE THROUGHOUT THE WORLD

1. Movements

THE historian of the dance is in the fortunate position of not having to dispute empty and obvious theories as to the beginnings of the dance. Rather, he is able to distinguish, on the basis of established facts, innate from acquired characteristics.

These facts are established by the well-known dances of the higher animals. In the Roroima district of British Guiana, Appun saw a "group of some twenty mountain chickens of a brilliant orange-yellow color, gathered together in a kind of dance characteristic of these beautiful birds. In the center one of the cocks executed the dance-like movements, as he hopped about the open place with wings extended and tail outspread. On the branches of the bushes round about, the others sat and expressed their admiration of the dancer with the strangest sounds. As soon as one cock was exhausted, he joined the spectators, uttering a peculiar cry, and another took his place."

In Cape York in northeastern Australia, Maclaren witnessed a dance of the stilt birds. "The birds, of a kind known locally as Native Companions, were long-legged creatures, tall almost as storks, and white and grey of feather; and the dance took place in the center of a broad, dry swamp, from the edge of which, in a place of concealment, we watched. There were some hundreds of them, and their dance was in the manner of quadrille, but in the matter of rhythm and grace excelling any quadrille that ever was. In groups of a score or more they advanced and retreated, lifting high their long legs and standing on their toes, now and then bowing gracefully one to another, now and then one pair encircling with prancing daintiness a group whose heads moved upwards and

9

downwards and sidewise in time to the stepping of the pair. At times they formed into one great prancing mass, with their long necks thrust upward; and the wide swaying of their backs was like unto the swaying of the sea. Then, suddenly, as in response to an imperative command, they would sway apart, some of them to rise in low, encircling flight, and some to stand as in little gossiping groups; and presently they would form in pairs or sets of pairs, and the prancing and the bowing, and advancing and retreating would begin all over again."

The most valuable document, however, comes to us from the laboratory for the study of anthropoid apes in Teneriffe, where a number of chimpanzees with no previous contact with mankind were brought up under scientific observation. The psychologist Wolfgang Köhler, for six years in charge of this laboratory, also maintained in his reports to the Prussian Academy of Science the astonishing fact that the anthropoid apes dance. He tells of a female chimpanzee, who, when he once appeared unexpectedly, began to hop first on one leg, then on the other, in a strangely excited manner. We might, indeed we must, relate this with what investigators occasionally report: that when the natives saw white men coming, they danced in extreme excitement "from one leg to the other." In both cases the dancing is caused by a state of tension and fear. Köhler further observed a rapid whirling with arms stretched out horizontally. Now and then the apes combined with the whirling "a forward movement with the result that as they rotated they moved across the clearing." Finally there was a genuine round dance.

"In mock fighting two of them drag each other about on the ground until they come near a post. Their frolicking and romping quiets down as they begin to circle about, using the post as a pivot. One after another the rest of the animals appear, join the circle, and finally the whole group, one behind another, is marching in orderly fashion around the post. Now their movements change quickly. They are no longer walking but trotting. Stamping with one foot and putting the other down lightly, they beat out what approaches a distinct rhythm, with each of them tending to keep step with the rest. Sometimes they bring their heads into play and bob them up and down, with jaws loose, in time with the stamping of their feet. All the animals appear to take a keen delight in this primitive round dance. Every now and then there are variations. Once I saw one animal, snapping comically at the one behind, walk backwards in the circle. Not infrequently one of them would whirl as he marched about with the rest. When two posts or boxes stand close to each other, they like to use these as a center, and in this case the ring dance around both takes the form of an ellipse. In these dances the chimpanzee likes to bedeck his body with all sorts of things, especially strings, vines, and rags that dangle and swing in the air as he moves about."

Thus on a level lower than that of man, a series of essential dance motifs has already been developed: as forms, the circle and ellipse around the post, the forward and backward pace; as movements, hopping, rhythmical stamping, whirling, and even ornamentation for the dance.

In view of this testimony we should accept with caution the occasional reports about "danceless peoples." According to early sources the Charrua in Uruguay and the Guarani in Brazil had no group dances. But we know today that the Guarani, at least, have ecstatic gourd-rattling dances, which surely do not appear to have been recently adopted. Often the apparent absence of dance may be accounted for if we remember that the dances are too sacred to be exhibited or even mentioned to a casual traveler who may be regarded with mistrust; or that, as is often the case, dancing is limited to the winter months.

Nevertheless, even trustworthy investigators report that there are a few danceless peoples: the dwarfs of the Malaccan forests, the Kenta and Bateke, and the remnants of the oldest inhabitants of Indonesia, the Redan-Kubu of Sumatra and the Toala of Celebes. Subsisting on the fruits they can find and the animals they can capture, they eke out their existence in the forest without a thought beyond the needs of the day and the propagation of their kind. Social life, play, festival, and music are lacking, as well as a belief in and conception of higher powers. But may we not here be dealing with the phenomenon of a lost culture?

Still we must not allow ourselves to be led to the hasty conclusion that because the anthropoid apes dance, man must have been destined by nature from the very beginning to dance. What we are concerned with here can hardly be regarded too seriously. If the dance, inherited from brutish ancestors, lives in all mankind as a necessary motor-rhythmic expression of excess energy and of the joy of living, then it is only of slight importance for anthropologists and social historians. If it is established, however, that an inherited predisposition develops in many ways in the different groups of man and in its force and direction is related to other phenomena of civilization, the history of the dance will then be of great importance for the study of mankind.

Such a history must necessarily begin with purely physiological facts, with the movements themselves. But we must not be guided by the separate movements of the dance. For the dance is not composed of isolated movements. The whole make-up of an individual and his central motor innervation first determine what each part of the body is to do.

For this reason we shall start with a complete description of two early dances, one of them a dance of a remote branch of the Vedda in Ceylon, the other of the Andamanese. Both these peoples are still in the protolithic stage of development, and hence are reckoned with the most primitive of the races of man. A description in the noteworthy volume about Ceylon by the Sarasin brothers gives us a picture of the arrow dance of the Vedda:

"Only the men dance. They form a circle around an arrow stuck into the ground, and do not touch one another as they move slowly around the arrow. Each one now executes strange movements, of which we will first observe those of the legs. Each dancer makes a turn to the left and comes to a stop on his right leg. He pushes his left leg forward in time convulsively and moves his body backwards. Then, after he has completed a half-turn, he stops on his left leg and makes the same trembling, jerky movements with his right. Continuing thus to make these half-turns and using now the leg which he has just moved as a support after the half-turn, the dancer circles slowly backwards around the arrow. In making his turns the dancer pays no attention to the one next to him; his only goal is to get around the arrow in the prescribed manner. Thus the dancers do not make exactly the same movements at the same moment. If one dancer, for example, turns on his left leg at the same time that his neighbor is turning on his right, it often happens that they incline now their heads, now their backs toward each other, though to be sure they do not take directly confronting positions.

"When a dancer is not jumping or hopping, while he is dragging his foot backwards on the ground, his legs do not move much but his arms play a more important part. While the body is making the turn, they are swung around and at the end of the half-turn they are still swinging vigorously. Then after the completion of the half-turn, the dancers whack their bellies with their hands as a substitute for musical instruments. Their heads, thrown backwards at the end of each half-turn, are swung down forwards in the direction of the dance movement, just as the arms are flung out to the side while the turn is being made. When their heads are thus swung downwards, their mane-like bush of hair is thrown over their faces like a horse's tail; after the completion of each half-turn the bushy hair is thrown back again as the head is flung backwards, with the result that it is swung through the air continuously, from backwards to the right, then forwards to the left and vice versa, depending upon which direction they are moving around the arrow. We are not certain whether they dance both clockwise and counter-clockwise. The above is a description of a dance moving counter-clockwise. As the dancers howl and pant a monotonous song and keep time with it, they work themselves in this way into a state of extreme nervous excitement. Sweat streams over their bodies. They slap their bellies more and more vigorously and the noise becomes continually louder. Then after a time one after another of them falls to the ground exhausted. They remain for a while in a prostrate position, panting and gasping out their cries and at the same time trembling convulsively in all their limbs. Suddenly they all rise at once and the dance is at an end.

"The sight of this drama is painfully moving. The ever increasing excitement of these people dripping with sweat, finally their falling to the ground, and their convulsive trembling, as they lie there stretched out on their backs; all of this together with the howling which grows ever louder and more spasmodic, excites the spectator, too, and he must needs check himself from interrupting the wild dance before it has reached its convulsive end."

This is the description of the Sarasin brothers. And now let us take as our second example an ancient dance of the Andamanese. Each dancer circles in whatever direction and executes whatever movements he pleases regardless of the others, although he always keeps strictly in time with the music. He hops lightly on his right foot, raises his left, lowers it bowing, then hops again on his right foot.

	hop	*scrape*	*hop*	*hop*	*scrape*	*hop*
	r	l	r	r	l	r
2/4	♩.	♪	♩	♩.	♪	♩

This is accompanied by swinging, clapping the hands and stamping on a board.

2/4	♩		♩	♩		♩

A step may also be added:

	step	*hop*	*scrape*	*hop*
3/4	♩	♩.	♪	♩
	♩	♩		♩

The trunk is flexed at the hips, the back is somewhat rounded, and the knee bent. The arms are stretched forward shoulder high and both thumbs and pointer fingers are hooked—a motif that the Greeks at some time learned from the Persians. With this movement and posture they dance a short while in one place, then move on around the circle. Now and then a dancer adds of his own accord another variety of step to his dance.

MOVEMENTS

The women dance on the North Andamans according to this scheme:

step	*flex*	*hop*	*step*	*flex*	hop
l	r	l	r	l	r
♩	♩	♩	♩	♩	♩

Every now and then the dancer stops, bows with knees bent together, and swings her arms against each other.

In comparing these two dances we may have overlooked a few unimportant details of the movements. But we cannot fail to recognize this striking phenomenon: on the one hand, among the Vedda, the most difficult contortion and distortion; on the other hand, on the Andaman Islands, balance, measured action of the tightener and the bending muscles, termination, according to set rules, of the progression of stepping, sliding, hopping, and flexing. There it is an interruption, here a quickening of the ordinary motor activity. There the dancing is tortured, joyless; here it is liberating and joyful. If an Andamanese is asked why he dances, his reply is that it gives him pleasure. He dances after a successful hunt—never when the day has brought disappointments. One calls to mind the Egyptians, whose dance word *ḥbj* means also "to be joyful," and the Greeks, who thought, though mistakenly, that their word for the dance *chorós* derived from *chará,* "joy." The Vedda, on the other hand, almost never dances for pleasure.

The distinction is so great that in the case of two peoples almost equally primitive it can hardly be ascribed to the level of culture but rather to a difference in natures. The Andamanese must dance, not so the Vedda. The contrast of dancing and non-dancing peoples becomes clear, the contrast between persons whom every unusual circumstance forces to motor-rhythmic expression and those who labor to arrive at a state of ecstasy through the dance.

In this comparison one further observation should be made: the Andamanese is familiar with animal dances, the Vedda is not. Should the animal dances and all imitative, mimetic dances then be ascribed to peoples of the same basic natures? Father Schmidt has emphasized that the remarkable difference between the pygmies of Africa and Asia is that in representing people, animals, and natural phenomena in the dance, the Africans are very happy, whereas the Asiatic pygmies have never been described as finding pleasure in their dances.

The African pygmies are decidedly a dancing people. They dance a great deal, in diverse forms and with great variety of movement, which according to one explorer is a pleasant change from the tiresome monotony of most of the Negro dances, a statement supported recently by the dancing scenes in the motion picture *Congorilla*. As early as the third millennium B. c. the Egyptians recognized the artistic gifts of the dwarfs in the dance and brought them into the service of their gods. It was the highest mark of esteem for an Egyptian subject to bring the king a dancing dwarf from the south, from the land of "Punt." The pygmoid Bushmen are masters of the whole field of the dance, from the purely religious standing dance to the wild and passionate one-legged, jump, and convulsive dances of young fellows drunk with love. They are so transported in the dance that in the Boer War they could be surrounded and shot down in droves while dancing. On the other hand, there are the dwarfs of Malacca: one explorer reports of the Kenta in the primitive forest of Malay that he never saw them dance; the Semang dance, though the men do not take part, and the women scarcely do anything more than move about with their knees and bodies flexed and bent, the upper parts of their arms next to their bodies, the parts below the elbows stretched forward. This is a very early stage of development.

We have an especially fine example of the interrelation of animal dance, dance joy, and dance capacity in the comparison of two California tribes, the Maidu and the Shasta, especially as the dances of both have been described in great detail by one and the same investigator. The Maidu, who also have a whole series of animal dances, have a large group of varied movements: jumping, slowly marking time, stamping, swaying, turning of the trunk, lifting, a sideward pulling and swinging of the arms, waving of branches, swimming, and touching. It is possible that also the Shasta execute one or more movements which obviously are not to be found in the animal dances. But our authority credits them only with stamping, kicking tufts of twigs sidewise, and touching. The Maidu dance for every occasion: healing of the sick, consecration of maidens, harvest, fire festivals, scalping celebrations, and countless other ceremonies; they have, in fact, a regular "season," which lasts from October to May almost without interruption and includes an imposing number of dances of great variety. The Shasta, however, perform their dance duties at the consecration of maidens, of women shamans, and at funerals; and in addition, there is a war dance. No more. Again the conclusion is the same: The peoples influenced by the animal dance have a variety of movements and dance with enthusiasm; those who do not know the animal dance have few movements and show little zest for dancing.

The impression is confirmed and strengthened if comparisons are extended further. Why the result can scarcely be otherwise is clear, so clear that later the relationship will appear as a fundamental truth. There can be no doubt that all peoples are not in like measure talented in the dance. And then the next conclusion is irrefutable: an interest in the motor activity of one's own or of another's body, an ability to comprehend the movements of the animate and inanimate world round about, a capacity to use the distinctive and expressive features of gesture and rhythm, must rest with those who are gifted in the dance. Every strong impression activates them, forces them to join in doing, to become sympathetic, to imitate, and to re-create. Out of "passive imitation" ("when in looking at a movement the compulsion to move and the feeling of power overcome us") comes the activity which stands ahead of all calculation and reflection—"active imitation."

DANCES OUT OF HARMONY WITH THE BODY

Pure Convulsive Dances

In considering peoples attached and peoples indifferent to the dance we have found a fundamental contrast between dances which are in harmony with the body and those which are not. Perhaps it is this contrast, weakened and somewhat obscured in the Hellenic world, which Plato referred to when he distinguished two types of dance, one ennobling the motions of the more beautiful bodies, the other parodying with distortion the motions of ugly bodies. Beginning with this contrast let us attempt to comprehend and to put into order the many dance movements.

Opposed to the meaning and nature of the body is the out and out convulsive dance, as we found it in the arrow dance of the Vedda: the legs are moved "convulsively, jerkily"; the song is "panted out"; the dancers work themselves "into a state of extreme nervous excitement, and the sweat streams over their bodies," they fall exhausted to the ground and tremble convulsively in all their limbs.

Such descriptions are very common. The Chukchi of northeastern Asia jump up and down in time, roll their eyes, and throw themselves to left and right with convulsive movements. There are similar reports of many African dances.

When the secret society of the Wayeye in Unyamwezi meets under the full moon, the members form "a closed circle, in the center of which from three to five drummers and several skilled dancers take their places. The drummers squat in a row and tirelessly beat upon their instruments in sharp rhythm. The dancers within the circle turn about several times, keeping time with the drums by stamping on their heels. The eyes of the drummers are fixed on the dancers. Suddenly the dancers swing into violent motion. All the parts of their bodies begin to shake, all their muscles play, their shoulder blades roll as if they no longer were a part of their bodies. The drums resound louder and louder. The movements of the dancers become wilder and bolder. Their bodies are bathed in sweat from head to foot. Now they stand as though changed to statues. Only the weird jerking of the muscles over their whole body continues. Then when the excitement has risen to its highest point, they suddenly collapse as if struck by lightning and remain for a time on the ground as though unconscious. After a short while the play begins anew."

We have just as graphic a report of a dance on the Solomon Islands:

"Imagine an open village square, surrounded by the low huts of the natives, the darkness intensified by the palms and other mighty trees of dense foliage. In a wide circle the naked figures squat and lie, lighted up by the flickering glow of a fire. Four or five older men walk noiselessly into the center with spears, bows, and arrows in their hands; the younger men soon join them and arrange themselves in rows, like the spokes of a wheel with the old men in the center; the half-grown boys take places in a circle on the outside. Now the old men in the center begin their monotonous howling; gradually the young men and boys join in and at the same time the entire throng begins to move slowly around the central point. Soon the pace is quickened and the dancers on the outer edge must make long jumps to keep up with the rest. As they turn the dancers whistle shrilly; they rattle their weapons and toss themselves into the air; and the excitement gradually reaches such a point that individual dancers, bathed in sweat, break away from the rest and roll on the ground in wild ecstasy. This dance and the howling song accompanying it have something so indescribably wild about them that they often give the onlooker gooseflesh."

Even among primitive tribes of the highest level we find the same characteristics. On the Marshall and Gilbert Islands the dancers run and jump with abandon to and fro, throw their bodies as though in convulsions, roll their eyes, wave their arms and legs about, shake their hands; the song, accompanied by a drum, is wild and at certain demoniacal words they all cry out.

The old Malay dances are less wild but just as ecstatic. We know of strangely fantastic night ceremonies in Bali, in which two maidens dance in a charmed sleep, as singers nestle close to one another in a circle and move continually. They either sway right and left in time with the melody, or they shake, as if overcome by a great trembling. But then suddenly they all throw themselves at the same time with a loud outcry to the left in the circle, then again to the right. After an especially intense increase in the excitement of the singing, they often throw themselves all the way backwards. Since they have been huddled together so close within the circle, they are now lying on top of one another like a giant flower opened out in full bloom. Or finally with a weird "hoo," which sounds like the long stroke of a gong in a cavern echoing slowly in the distance, they throw themselves forward into a heap, their heads close together. *The Isle of Demons,* a recent German talking picture of the island of Bali, had photographs of this dance.

All these dances correspond to the description of clonic convulsions —the state of forceful flexion and relaxation of the muscles which may lead to a throwing about of the body in wild paroxysms. The will has completely or to a certain extent lost control over the parts of the body; consciousness may likewise completely disappear. This condition is therefore not an activity, but a suffering.

Although such pathogenic dances are limited to certain peoples, they are nevertheless widespread. If we trace very carefully the extent of their diffusion, we have in Asia a triangle, the apex of which is the northeastern part of the Chukchee peninsula, with the base extending from Ceylon across the Malay archipelago to eastern Micronesia. In addition there are the east and west Bantu tribes in Africa, and in Europe we have examples in ancient Greece, in Bulgaria, among the Slavs, and during the Middle Ages among certain groups in the west and center. The picture is clear. The convulsive dance is a characteristic of shaman cultures. It makes its appearance where priestly dignity and magic power are in the hands of the witch doctor or the medicine man, where as a result of a peculiar racial tendency or of a cultural influence, religious experience and its cult formation rest solely on the rule of hypnosis. In Bali we find a clear example of the borderline type. Here Buddhism is still merely superimposed on animism and we can often see with great clarity what is underneath. De Kat Angelino watched a priest in a very ecstatic state go through convulsive ceremonial motions. In the garb of the Buddha priest we find the ecstatic shaman. And in Bali the convulsive dance reaches into the temple.

If the convulsive dance is bound up with shaman culture, we should not include America in our summary. But Hauer in another connection has shown that the North American Indians in general have progressed beyond the frenzy stage. There are, to be sure, also among the Indians traces of a tendency to convulsive dancing. While the Californias, in general, remain altogether apart from convulsive phenomena, we have one report of dancing frenzy and bleeding mouths, in the dances of the so-called Kuksu worship. This is a cult ceremony, which together with the slit drum was taken over late by the California Wintun when a younger cultural group was absorbed. It is therefore a result of cultural influence. True; but such an influence presupposes an innate propensity or receptivity.

From this example it may be seen that the question of "intransmissible blood traits" or "transmissible cultural possessions" must be posed with caution. For after all, a sharp contrast would exist only if there were pure blood on the one hand, and on the other, a culture separate from everything pertaining to race—in other words, if somatic anthropology and ethnology were in no wise intermingled. But every people, no matter how primitive, is the result of incalculable interbreeding. Though cultures may be carried to any territories whatsoever, they are in most cases taken over only by those peoples who are predisposed to receive them. Thus in the question of racial or cultural influence every dogmatic assertion does violence to the infinitely fine ramifications of the problem.

Weakened Convulsive Dances

That which has developed in the first place, involuntarily and forcibly, out of frenzy and extreme neuropathic disturbance, may continue to live on as an art form among peoples of lesser or of hidden ecstatic tendencies under changed and quite varied conditions. In such cases control over certain groups of muscles develops generally from the clonic convulsion.

We find weakened convulsive dances most widespread in the territory of the Bantu. The black man rattles, pants, and kicks like a steam engine. Ceaselessly his necklaces and skirts rustle. For hours at a time his posterior springs up and down over his bent legs. Fidgeting and see-sawing are to such an extent African that one is tempted to designate the Bantu dances in general as fidget dances. Yet they frequently cross the border line of the pure convulsive dance. At the start the participants generally zigzag to and fro in short steps with their feet dragging, or walk forwards and backwards with short, stamping steps. Soon, when they have become warm, they throw off their light top dress and tie their underdress tighter. As yet they show no sign of fatigue. On the contrary, the tempo becomes more lively, the dance wilder and more passionate. From the circle of dancers a skilled artist now steps forth, comes to a stop in the center, and begins to make very convulsive contortions with the upper part of his body, bringing especially his abdominal muscles into play. Then two men break away from the group of dancers, step into the foreground, and dancing toward each other, execute wild and erotic pelvic motions. At the close these two dancers, one playing the part of the woman, carry out highly repulsive love scenes. The more extreme the portrayal, the greater is the applause of the spectators. Then the same dance scene is executed by two young maidens. All these are the well-known features of the convulsive dance. But they are subordinated to the will, and the dancer does not wait until he collapses to stop dancing.

Even the ecstatic shaman of the Malay Islands has learned how to control his frenzy artistically. The medicine man of the Sakai tribe in Sumatra in healing a sick person "tests a knife on his forehead and breast, as his assistant, the Junko, sits on crossed legs, with his arms bent at right angles resting on his legs. His fists are clenched lightly and move in time with the music. Gradually his whole body takes up these movements, which become more and more convulsive, more and more automatic; his eyes close and he is transported, as it were. Both the shamans murmur prayers and incantations continually. . . . Now the witch doctor arises and begins to dance with his eyes closed. The dance is graceful and lively. His whole body dances—arms, legs, hands, and feet. In his left hand the shaman holds a fan or sword, oddly enough a bow and arrow too, oftentimes. On his left arm he has a bracelet with little bells, by means of which he gives the time to the drummers. He swings the fan gracefully, makes pleasing movements with his forearm, and dances sometimes toward the sick man, sometimes away from him. He stamps lightly, with his feet turned at the ankles, his legs bent at the knees. He often crosses his feet, sometimes in front, sometimes behind. Frequently the dance takes the form of a genuine round dance in polka step to the right or left. The drum beats faster, the dance becomes wilder, the contortions of the squatting Junko become more convulsive. Then suddenly the dancer falls to the ground, or at least pretends to do so. The drummers cease to beat their drums, the witch doctor opens his eyes. . . ."

Often only a single convulsive movement is incorporated into a dance that is otherwise non-convulsive. No part of the body has been overlooked. Women of the Malay island of Wetar move their hands in time convulsively. Women dancers of southern Australia make the muscles of their thighs quiver; the Arunta of Central Australia, their thighs, trunks, and hands; the tribes of the Torres Strait between Australia and New Guinea, their heads; the Kiziba of East Africa, the larynx; dancing players of India, their lips; and the natives of Yap and Hawaii, center of the hand dances, their fingers. The really classic example of this type is the trembling and undulatory motion of the trunk: movements of the breast and back muscles and the well-known movements of the *rectus abdominis,* common among the tribes of northern Africa as well as among the Canela of northeastern Brazil. Authors have grouped these movements together under the heading "abdominal dance," usually with the pelvic roll, which is an entirely different type. The abdominal dance is the art of the old Gaditan dancing girls of whom the poet Martial wrote:

> Tirelessly the lustful move
> In gentle tremor eager limbs.

Today the Arabs consider this type of dance Egyptian. In the Celebes, where the natives recently took the abdominal dance from the Arabs, it is called *messeri* or *másseri*, obviously a form of the Arabian word *maṣri*, meaning Egyptian.

These locally restricted convulsive-like movements can be again extended. Like a rapidly swung rope which no longer shows each single vibration, but is crossed rather by a wave-like up-and-down motion, the motif of the simple hip or breast vibration grows in the course of the dance into a snake-like motion running through the entire body. Only the women appear to do this type of dance. Two dance cultures so diametrically opposed as the East African and the Cambodian offer the best examples, and especially the Cambodian show quite clearly their kinship to the old convulsive dances. Right in the midst of a formal mythological dance it may happen that the maiden pauses, relaxes her leg muscles, and trembles with a slow undulatory motion seeming to start at one of her hands, which are held with the palms upwards. Gently the snake-like movement slides along her arm, passes on to the other shoulder, lifts her breast scarf, goes over to the other arm, and disappears in the fluttering vibration of the other hand. At this moment her hip is arched. Her abdomen recedes beneath the flood of the heavy glistening folds of silk and metal which stream out over her knees. When she opens her eyelids one can see her eyes roll and turn in her mysterious white face.

DANCES IN HARMONY WITH THE BODY

Expanded Dances

From the convulsive dance out of harmony with the body let us seek to understand its most direct opposite, the dance which originates in an irrepressible delight in motor expression and which has the value of an enhanced feeling of life for the dancers as well as for the spectators, regardless of whether or not they are in the service of a cult and are carrying out its prescriptions.

MOVEMENTS

Exhilaration and ecstasy are a part of this stimulation just as they are in the convulsive dance. In both types of dance the corporal limitations of man are conquered and the subconscious is freed, the difference being that in the inharmonious dances this is accomplished by means of a mortification of the flesh, in the harmonious dances by an exaltation of it, by a release from gravity, by motion upwards and forwards.

The most essential method of achieving the ecstatic is the rhythmic beat of every dance movement. As anyone can testify from his own experience, it is an effective unburdening of the will. "The movements are executed automatically without the intervention of the self. Thus the consciousness of self disappears completely and is lost in the primitive consciousness. Rhythmic motion has become therefore the carrier and creator of almost every ecstatic mood of any significance in human life." The harmonious dance, therefore, not only progresses in rhythm, but calls the movements of all parts of the body into the service of the beat, with the result that the rhythm is strengthened and the exhilarative character of the dance is intensified.

Stamping is universal. From the lowest levels of mankind, indeed from the apes, it reaches into the rustic dances of higher cultures and into the round dances of our children. It represents, to be sure, not only rhythmic motion. A heavy stamping of the leg is a motor expression of exceptional intensity, or a light rebounding from the ground an effective levitator in the battle against gravity.

Just as universal is the bending of the knee. It appears in two forms, in stationary position and in rhythmic movement. Here too the resilience of the half-loose joint seems to be the essential characteristic. The squat dance, originally perhaps an animal dance, is still preserved in Frankish, Rhenish, and English folk customs, the low bending of the knee in the Swiss dances.

We shall speak later of several other kinds of positions and movements, which although not universal are to be found in dances of the most varied motor character. For the present we shall mention only one movement, that known as the *stretta*, the intoxicating development of speed in the course of the dance, the increase of gesture from quiet and reserve at the beginning to the most reckless abandon.

Although they have these qualities in common, the number and variety of the harmonious dances are so great that one would despair of making a satisfactory survey of them, if it were not that there are two principal types of movements which stand out with impressive clarity and which separate, as we shall see more and more, sexes, peoples, races, and personalities. We shall call these types "expanded movement" and "close movement."

The expanded dance is characterized by the stronger motor reaction. It is almost a form of battle, a wild rebellion against the law of gravity. Every muscle is stretched taut and does its utmost to be the bearer, not the burden, in the upward surge of the body. The heel and the ball of the foot are lifted off the ground and the considerable task of support is left to the toes. One leg is held so high in the air that the foot is above the knee of the leg that is on the ground and the dance proceeds on one leg. The trunk is curved backwards, the face looks into the sky, and the arms stretch upward. The last weak connection with the ground is dissolved—timidly in the short skips, boldly in the leap. We are often reminded of that European style of architecture which more than any other grew out of the ecstatic soul—the Gothic. It too is a conquest and denial of the terrestrial burden, a defiant triumph of the vertical, a single, irresistible pushing aloft.

The high point of the expanded dance is the leaping dance in which dissolution of the bonds of gravity is brought about by force. In Europe this dance has become rare. Only the pastoral peoples in the mountain districts still have it: the Basques (*aurrescu*); the Bavarians (*Schuhplattler*); the Morlaks (*kolo*); the Scots (*fling*); and the Norwegians. The Greeks of antiquity were skilled leap dancers. Elastic high leaps of rare beauty, without stiffness and without the passivity of the catchball, are depicted on a Greek vase of black-figure style in the Berlin Museum of Antiquity (Plate 12). The game here pictured, the leap in turn of two dancers, may still be found on the coast of Tanga in East Africa.

A dance of the Georgians should be mentioned at this point. In a solo dance in Cachia the man walks slowly at first, one hand flat on his breast, the other stretched out to the side. As the drum beats faster, he leaps back, crossing his legs in the air in so doing and whirling his body to all sides. An essentially ecstatic quality clings to this dance: the steady increase of speed, the stirring *stretta*.

In Hindustan the Bengali do the leap dances; in Indo-China, the Naga. And the Naga have this peculiarity: before they touch the ground again, they cross their legs in the air three times. Thus the *entrechat* of our seventeenth-century dances is to be found also in the Far East.

But Africa is the continent of the leap dance. The Wanyamwezi and the Wasiba in the east make "gigantic leaps into the air," the Yoruba in the west, one might believe, "have no bones," and in central Africa hundreds of Angoni leap all at one time in their war dances. In southwest Africa the Herero walk out together to the circle. "Two dancers and a singer take their places in the center. The latter sings the praises of their old chieftains, perhaps also of their favorite oxen, and beats the time with his hands, as the two dancers do their leaps. The men of the circle stamp so hard with their feet that the ground trembles."

We find especially appropriate illustrations in the dances of the Mangbettu tribes and those of the Nilotic Suk of the Uganda protectorate. The important movement is the leap. The body is tensed, the arms are crossed and held tight against the body, and the hands are placed on the hips. The conclusion is obvious that similar leap dances which we see in old Egyptian carvings are likewise Nilotic.

These examples drawn from Africa, like those from Europe, are chiefly from sections where the principal occupation is herding. The same is true of the leap dances of Asia.

The leap dances, on the other hand, constitute exceptions among peoples in the Pacific islands and in America, who are not herders. On the island of Tumleo near New Guinea the man "spreads his legs somewhat to the side and forwards, bends his knees a little, and thus jumps up and down, moving gradually sidewise until he has described a circle." There are descriptions of very high jumps in the dance of the extinct Tasmanians and in the war dance of the Maori of New Zealand. Among American examples we should mention the leap dance of the California Yurok. The hand with its dance basket is raised, then as the knees are bent it is swung to the ground, and from a squatting position the dancer jumps half a foot into the air. These people are not herders. But the inhabitants of Tumleo are totemists and the Tasmanians are reckoned in the forefront of totemism. Together with the African herders and the Maori of New Zealand, they belong to a group of predominantly masculine cultures, of which we shall have more to say later.

Closely related to the leap dance as an unrestricted movement is the *lift dance*. Later we shall speak of the dance-like lifting in the air of children to promote their growth. The classic form is reached in the maiden lift of the East African Negroes and of certain Alpine peoples. Every German knows what an important part the lift plays in the spectacular conclusion of the *Schuhplattler* and in the May dance of the Franks of the Main valley, a practice one also finds in the *jota al aire* of Aragon and the *corranda alta* and *sardana* of Catalonia. This is the same *Aufwerfen*, "upward fling," which the German municipal laws punished so severely as late as the seventeenth century.

Let us call one division of these dances the *slap dances*. For so much of them is the working-off of excessive masculine energy, so strong is the urge to vivacity and exuberance that the prescribed movements alone do not satisfy. Movements of the hands and feet are converted into violent commotion, swings and kicks into a noisy clatter. The *Siederstanz* of Swabia and the thigh-slapping dances of New Zealand and of the Caroline Islands belong to this type. Wilder still are the Bavarian *Schuhplattler* and the Ukrainian *prisjádka* with their heel stamping, and the old Greek dances in which the buttocks were slapped. Most abandoned of all is the kicking of the backside, which steatopygous women in Little Andaman do with great zeal and which under the name *rhathapygízein* was the *pièce de résistance* of Hellenic dancers (ancient authors sing the praises of a Spartan maiden who flung her foot against her posterior a thousand times without stopping). This may have been an animal dance originally, for among the Czechs this movement is called *kluk tluče běrany*, "the boy beats the rams."

While the feature of the leap dances is the upward surge, that of the *stride dances* is the surge forwards. Together with the Etruscans, the Egyptians again offer impressive examples among the ancients: in the rattling harvest dancers of Tomb 15 at Giza of the fifth dynasty (about 2700 B. C.) and in the run dances of the king. Among the moderns the stride dancers are especially certain tribes of California—the Diegueño, Luiseño, and Mojave—the tribes of northwestern Brazil, and the Bubi of Fernando Po in Africa. When the Luiseño of California do a jump with both legs and after that take a stride, they are performing a model of the expanded dance.

The stride may also be directed upwards. It then becomes a leg-throw and thus is on the border line of the acrobatic strength and skill dance. Egyptian reliefs of the sixth dynasty in the middle of the third millennium depict whole rows of female dancers, who with the trunks of their bodies extended backwards throw their right legs above the heads of the dancers in front of them at an angle of 135 degrees (Plate 9). There are movements which correspond to this in modern Europe: the Breton peasant women, throwing their legs up to the ceiling in the *triori;* the Basques in the *aurrescu* and the Catalonians in the *sardana* knocking one another's hats off with their feet, and the Parisian women in the *can-can* kicking the hats from the heads of the gentlemen spectators (Pl. 31).

A peculiar example of the leg-throw dance is the *squat-fling dance,* as we shall call it: the body takes a squatting position and the legs are in turn thrown out forwards and drawn backwards. Among the North African Mangbettu an observer saw the dancing king move his legs almost horizontally "to and fro on the ground in the manner of a Cossack dance." The Greeks, who took over this dance from the Persians, knew it as the *óklasma;* carvings show that the Etruscans had it; and Strabo ascribes it also to the ancient Iberians. The Spaniard Caro (1626) is right when he emphasizes the tenacity required in the Iberian dance. What Strabo has to say of the dance of the Iberians may also be said of the dances of his time: in all of them the dancers adroitly take a squatting position and cross and throw out their legs. The squat-fling dance is still the possession of many European peoples. In Spain it is preserved as the *charrada;* in the Ukraine it is known by the term *prisjádka* as a part of the *hopák.* In central and western Europe we have examples in Hungary, in the *rigaudon* in France, the *hornpipe* in England, and the *jig* in Ireland. The *grue* of the sixteenth century may be a weakened courtly bourgeois form.

Skip dances as movements in which either foot is used ought to be distinguished from the jump dances; in the real jump dance the dancer leaves the ground with both feet at the same time. It seems to me that only the Hebrew language discriminates carefully between the two terms. The verb רקד *rāķád* is used to describe lambs and frolicking children, grain poured through a sieve, and a wagon clattering along a rough road. In the Talmud it means skipping with one foot, whereas קפץ *ķāfáṣ* means jumping with both feet. King David's dance before the Ark of the Covenant, described in I Chr. 15:29 as רקד, was therefore a skip dance.

Travel articles and historical surveys scarcely ever distinguish with the necessary clarity between the two concepts. *Hüpfen* and *springen* are used interchangeably by the German writers with the same unconcern as *skipping* and *jumping* or *leaping* by the English. For the most part it is only possible to ascertain what is meant when the author allows one at the same time to discern whether the dance he is describing is a light and playful one or a more powerful attempt to conquer gravity.

This want of clarity interferes with a survey of the diffusion of the two types of dances. Nevertheless, it is certain that the skip dances are the more widespread and the older. Indeed, even the pygmy Andamanese are acquainted with them.

A moderated form of the upward surge is the *knee-lift dance*—the quick, alternate raising of the upper part of the leg, as described especially in the dances of the Indians and often, too, in those of the ancient Egyptians.

Lunge dances appear to be closely related to the stride dances, though this statement must be made with reservations. The very fact that they reached their highest stage of development in the cultures of the Malay archipelago, in the center of restricted movement, shows the character of the lunge: stride without locomotion, retention of the original center of gravity, very rapid alternation of tension and release, in short, unrestricted movement under the control of restricted movement.

Toe dances are characterized by a stretching upwards, a release and unburdening carried to the extreme without the body's leaving the ground. They are not in wide use.

One-legged dances are another expression of the same urge: dancing on one leg reduces the base and diminishes contact with the ground. These are even less widely used. The Japanese one-legged dances, which will be discussed later in our chapter on motives, are danced together with the stilt dance in field ceremonies and are obviously vegetation charms.

The strange dual nature of these last dances, and further the marked contrast between close dances and expanded dances, are caused by physiological factors. There is a fact known to all gymnasts and athletes which is fundamental: the man strives for release, for motion forwards and upwards, and is better adapted to it than the woman. She is in general held down to the ground, and her gestures tend to be directed toward the body rather than outward and upward.

The inference is not to be drawn that the expanded dance is the exclusive province of men, and the close dance that of women. Men may dance the close dance, too: in many cultural groups, in fact, they do so exclusively. With a very few exceptions, however, the expanded dance is left to the men. The women participate without concern for what the men do and do not permit themselves to be drawn from their own true natures.

The Ostyak in West Siberia, whose dances have been described in such detail, leap with elastic knees from the "spread." The women do not do the leaps. Their knees are loosely bent as they dance, and their feet do not leave the ground. Exactly the same thing is true of the California Hoopa: the dancers jump with both feet; when a maiden dances, she may rise on tip-toes, but she does not leave the ground. Among the Apinage: the women remain almost motionless or bend the legs only slightly; the men, on the other hand, leap. Among the Maidu of California: the men leap and exert themselves strenuously; the women dance more quietly and just sway their bodies. Among the Huhuteni of northwestern Brazil: "tripping along eagerly, the painted beauties seek to make their steps correspond to the giant strides of the men dancers." In the Loyalty Islands: the men dance "fast and furiously"; the women only move their arms and hips slowly and stand firmly on the ground. Among the Nicobar: the men sit, rise, bend, and leap; the women follow with a simple step. Among the Herero: the men do leaps; the women bow and touch the ground with their hands. Among the Bullom (of Sierra Leone): the men make "the most labored exertions"; the women are "slow." In the *hopák* of the Ukraine and in other Slavic dances the men jump; the women sway or circle slowly.

Compared to the masculine, these feminine movements are therefore diminutions of expansion. The bold leap, the separation from the ground, is reduced to a stretching on the toes, and the large stride degenerates into a timid tripping. The dance of women almost always and everywhere shows evidence of suppression and diminution. Even where theme and occasion in the truest sense would seem to call for a departure from the usual, a dance of women will return almost certainly to a close form. Thus in Palau in the Caroline Islands:

"From one side came a crowd of women, their naked bodies and legs completely painted red. With frenzied gestures and with lances brandished in their hands, they were moving in the direction of a smaller group, similarly armed and adorned, which was approaching from the opposite side. The two groups walked to within three or four paces of each other, as if they were about to do battle. But then they stopped, formed several rows, and began to sing in unison a very monotonous, though not unmelodic song. After many years I was hearing for the first time here a sound coming from deep in the breast. Meanwhile they did not move from their positions, but as they all set their hips into a strange, swaying motion with a carefully measured rhythm, they accompanied their song with a loud rustling of their skirts of leaves in time with the melody. The pantomime, which I was told represented a scene from the latest war, came to an end with a loud outcry."

All exceptions to the close form are based on motives. The European woman leaps when she wishes to promote the growth of the seed, and the Egyptian takes a big stride when at a funeral she must win eternal life for the dead by dancing. Based on motive, too, are the predominantly sexual "frivolous" jumps of the women of Palau in the Caroline Islands in honor of a feminine divinity, and the short jumps with which in dancing the young girls of Massai entreatingly approach a lover, their meeting in the evening being considered arranged if he leaps likewise into the air. With these exceptions also belong the little girls of Tidore in the Moluccan Islands—and here indeed our statement is confirmed—who at the Djin feast must first be stupefied by incense before they can dance contrary to their nature in leaps.

The contrast of expanded and close is a contrast of the sexes. But more than that it is a contrast of peoples. We have seen that the leap dance is, with a few exceptions, lacking in eastern and southeastern Asia. Or to make a positive statement, the more a people is marked by planter culture, the more closed is its dance; the more completely it is totemistic and patriarchal, the more it will make use of the leap. Thus the principal leapers are, among the basic cultures, the Tasmanians; in the Early Tribal cultures, the totemistic inhabitants of the Torres Straits and of Tumleo; in the Middle Tribal cultures, the pastoral Suk, Herero, Kachian, Abchase, Ostyak, Naga. Those peoples use the leap, in other words, whose economy and society are predominantly masculine.

The recent descriptions by Herbert Baldus of the dances of certain tribes of northeastern Chaco offer further evidence of these relationships and are especially valuable for us because the investigator knows nothing of the connection between the dance and the form of economy. "In the wild dance leaps, the powerful gourd-rattling, and the loud and boisterous singing, the Chamacoco expresses the tempo which is his by nature. . . . On the other hand the dances of the Kaskiha are a hesitant, listless walking to and fro." In these two tribes living side by side we have an impressive contrast in dance attitude. None the less impressive is the economic contrast. The leaping Chamacoco are hunters; the hesitant, listless Kaskiha are tillers of the soil. This must not be misunderstood. The form of economy cannot determine the dance. "The Kaskiha are slower but more persistent, more serious, more quiet, perhaps more thoughtful, always disinclined towards gesticulation"; for this reason they dance in a closed manner. And for this reason, too, they are farmers. But here we come upon the question of the relationship between motor character and cultural development, any answer to which it must be the business of anthropology to give.

Close Dances

The chief characteristic of the close dances is not so much a diminution and narrowing down of masculine movements, steps, and leaps; more than that it is the starting from a fixed center of motion, the whole body or its parts swinging in both axes or in a narrow circle. These dances are swinging, swaying, and suspension; the rhythm flows with measured symmetry and suppleness through the limbs. Contrasted with the expanded dances, they are often surprisingly calm and composed. For unruly power they sometimes substitute charm and grace, even daintiness; for dynamic release, the static ideal, the striving for quiet, steadfastness, and harmonious balance.

MOVEMENTS

Common swinging movements are:

Bending of the head forwards and backwards and from right to left	Waving movements
	Swinging of bundles of brush
Rolling of the head	Bending and stretching of the arm
Bending of the trunk forwards and backwards and from right to left	Bending and stretching of the hand
	Bending and stretching of the finger
Swinging of the pelvis forwards and backwards and from right to left	Bending and stretching of the knee
Rolling of the trunk	Bending and stretching of the foot
Rolling of the pelvis	

These are essentially the movements that in gymnastics are called limbering exercises. Indeed, in descriptions of such dances it is often emphasized that the arms hang loose or dangle. At the same time they are movements which to a considerable extent facilitate or bring about a state of ecstasy. All Orientals at prayer rock and sway rhythmically. Swinging of the arms belongs also in this outline. But this is not less a characteristic of the expanded dances, and as is so often the case, it is not the single movement alone but rather its relation to the whole which determines whether a dance is dynamic or static.

Although the close dances may be executed differently, indeed in direct contrast to the expanded dances, they still have in common the struggle against the oppressing pull of gravity, and again the urge to be light, to be free of the earth, to fly, that is the yearning of mankind and that is fulfilled only in the dance.

Especially characteristic of restricted movement is the maiden dance of the East African Barundi: "Their arms are stretched out sidewise, their flat hands are moved gently and gracefully at the wrist. Smiling, the dancers move into rows facing one another, their heads sway in various directions, their gestures become increasingly vivacious, their whole bodies bend forward and sideways and backwards in fantastic turns and reels."

From among countless examples let us choose the pygmies of Uganda as our second. They sit on the ground, strike it with their elbows or with their thighs, roll their heads, turn and swing their little round bellies, and rock their whole bodies forwards and backwards—all this with irresistible rhythm and beaming pleasure.

The rolling of the pelvis as practiced in this dance is especially significant. For as the seat of all sexual and child-bearing activity the abdomen, which is emphatically accentuated in the dance, is a very important part of the body. When it is thus stressed we shall call such movements *belly dances,* although this term may not always be accurate.

The *belly dance* is no uniform phenomenon, to be sure. The later form—swinging movements of the *rectus abdominis*—has already been discussed. The older form consists of rotating motions of the entire pelvis, which travelers describe as belly dances, posterior dances, or hip dances. In the South Seas we know of examples of such dances in Namoluk and Tuk of the Caroline Islands, on the river Sepik in New Guinea, the Shortland Islands of the Solomon Archipelago, and East Polynesia. The remaining examples are in Africa—from the north coast to Loango in the west and Zanzibar in the east—though we have a record of such a dance from ancient Hellas. The dancers in practically every instance are women.

Frequently these arts may have only the purpose of sexual stimulation. But the original goal was magical: coitus movements, like all other sex motives, promote life and growth. The pelvic dance of the Bafioti in Loango is "ancestor worship, directed towards past and future generations. It glorifies the transmission of existence to those who are yet to come."

Clothing which veils, obstructs, and rounds out the contour of the body has a definite place in the close dance. The dress that is allowed solemnly to fall in the Japanese Kagura dance, and the mantles covering the hands and feet in certain ancient Greek women's dances offer classic examples.

SITTING DANCES. From the static swinging of the close dances, we come directly to the standing dance and to the sitting dance. When the center of the swing is above the legs, the inactive lower part of the body is almost necessarily reduced to a state of inertia in order not to dissipate energy unnecessarily.

Ceremonies in which the dancers remain seated on the same spot and make use only of the upper part of their bodies are rooted even in the early cultures. In the "lightning dance" the Andamanese medicine man sits down on a rock in the middle of the dance place and swings his arms in time with the music of the singing chorus. In the more highly developed form sitting dances are danced mostly by women. The inhabitants of the Ratak Islands in the Marshall Archipelago, according to the German poet Adalbert v. Chamisso in an account of his trip around the world, "perform their sitting song dances mostly in the evening, gathered in a circle around a crackling fire. An intoxicating joy then lays hold of all of them and the voices of all join in the chorus." In Micronesia and Kalahari the women sit on their heels, in Samoa they sit crosslegged. The dance is made up of movements of the upper part of the body, of the arms, and of the hands, as well as clapping and the skillful striking together of little wooden sticks. In Butaritari of the Gilbert Islands, Krämer, a German investigator, observed a hand-slapping game with which our children are still familiar: A girl dressed in the festive grass skirt goes mysteriously to the loft of the house, followed by three men. The four sit down as though around a table, sing, and sway their hips. Those sitting across from each other strike the palms of their hands together, the right hand of one against the left of the other, and vice versa; then all four in a circle, or right, left, and across—and they scarcely ever miss. The same game is known in Hindustan and Cameroon, in the Allgäu, in Catalonia (*Castaña*), and in Italy.

Generally the "earlier" religious significance of the sitting dances is emphasized. On the isle of Yap the dance is said to center around eroticism; on Ponape, around ancestors, stars, fruits, and animals. In Likieb of the Marshall Islands the chieftain seats himself on a mat in the center of a crowd of women and in the dance turns his trunk, shakes his hands, and rolls his eyes. The direct connection with the Paleolithic motif of women dancing around a man is apparent here, as is also the primitiveness of the Micronesian dance, in spite of the fact that the sitting form is late. J. W. Hauer is probably on the right track when he groups the sitting dance with methods of inducing frenzy that have been spiritualized. For the Micronesian music also shows unmistakable signs of spiritualized ecstasy and frenzy.

The development of the sitting dance culminates in the dances of the Samoan women which are described in most records, though not altogether correctly, as *Siva*. Let us now examine a detailed description of the sitting dance by Krämer:

"As the people crowd around outside to enjoy the spectacle too, someone generally starts a song and the others join in. Meanwhile the village maiden, the *taupou,* walks out of another house where she has been fitted out with head ornaments, necklaces, and breast chains. Thoroughly anointed and wearing a brown mat or perhaps only a *titi* (loin cloth), she approaches the center. As the song nears its end, she sits down in the middle of a row of ten men or women dancers, so that there are five on either side of her. When the song is ended, the striking of the mats, called *ta le siva,* begins as a prelude to the dance proper and may be accompanied by hand movements but never by singing. This prelude is short for the most part and is usually danced in unison. The beating of the mats sounds like the trotting of a horse, the first tone struck with both sticks, the second with only one—a trochaic pattern. The dancers themselves, with their hands hollowed, begin now to clap, the sixth being a double beat. Then approximately the following movements are executed:

right arm stretched half forward, the hollowed hand is turned at the same time inward and upward, then a slap of the right thigh with the hollowed hand;

the same, with the left arm;

the same, with both arms at once;

right stretched forward, backs of the hands upward, the left hand comes close to the right shoulder; at the same time the palm is turned upwards twice;

the same, left;

stretching out of both hands to the right and a double turning of the palm from underneath to the inside and upwards;

the same, left;

both fists, one on top of the other, resting on the right knee, turned twice in opposite directions, as if they were holding a stick vertically;

the same, left.

"After several additional improvised hand movements at the close, the backs of both hands are drawn to the sides of the body and then thrown forwards on a level with the armpits, palms upward. Then with the backs of the hand striking toward the outside, both hollowed hands are thrown forward at the same time toward the spectators and held in that position for a time. Or the hands may be struck together on the mat.

"This is one example of how approximately such a slap dance is executed. The sequence and the kind of movements may of course vary a great deal. The important thing to be observed is that these movements, like our ballets, are all executed with symmetry, and that the symmetry and grace with which the hand movements are done determine the quality of a dance.

"When the slap dance is over, the *taupou* begins to sing in a clear, high voice, usually alone, but only a few measures; then the chorus joins in, singing at first slowly and formally, then steadily faster and more loudly. The mat clappers work along furiously, sometimes with double beats in dactylic rhythm, their arms fly to and fro, their bodies sway sometimes to the side, sometimes forward, and even their legs, stretched out in front of them, tremble. It is a turbulent cataclysm, a raging storm until, with a loud outcry and a sudden lowering of the voice, the dance comes to an end."

This is a fine example of how a strictly regulated spectacular dance, characterized by the play of the hands, may exist alongside "the raging storm" of a genuine ecstatic and convulsive dance with its flying arms, its shrill cries, and its trembling legs.

Hand dances of the Samoan type are comprehensible only when one knows that in the Buddhistic cults the gesture of the hand, *mudra,* has a very definite value as expression and has become a part of an extensive ritualistic sign language. Together with meditation and recitation, it forms the three mysteries, which call forth the qualities of Buddha in mankind. Hindustan is the home of the hand dance. From there it made its way to the East with Buddhism and far beyond where Buddhism traveled, to Japan, to Indo-China, Indonesia, Micronesia, and Polynesia, and may also have migrated from Hindustan westward to Greece, whence it was probably carried still farther. Of the dance of Greece as well as of the hand dance itself, we shall present a more detailed account later. One of the offshoots of the hand dance, the dance of Cambodia, has been described by a poet:

". . . There they were, these dainty little dancing maids, like gazelles metamorphosed. Their long, slender arms as though in one piece drawn through the shoulders, through the slender yet sturdy torso (with the full slenderness of Buddha pictures), as though in a single finely wrought piece as far as the wrists, out of which the hands walked out like players, mobile and independent of action. And what hands! Buddha hands that know how to sleep; that lie down easily when their time comes, finger next to finger, to rest for centuries on their laps, lying palm upward or standing straight up from the joint, bidding ceaselessly for quiet. Imagine these hands awake! These fingers spread apart, open, radiate or turned inwards like the petals of a Jericho rose; these fingers enraptured and happy or anxious, pointing out from the very end of the long arms; these fingers dancing. And the whole body in action—this ultimate in balance dances suspended in the air, in the atmosphere of the body itself, in the golden glow of the Orient. . . ." (Rainer M. Rilke)

WHIRL DANCES. In Cairo in the years 1930 and 1932, the author repeatedly watched the Friday afternoon dances of the dervishes. There is a special house in the cloister courtyard, built like an octagonal baptismal chapel. On the lower story, enclosed by well-turned wooden bars, is a round dance floor, and above, a circular balcony with a section for men, and another, carefully screened off, for women, and a platform for the musicians. Seventeen monks seated themselves in the circle, most of them rather aged, all of them wearing the tall felt headdress. On the platform a splendid old dervish began to repeat prayers from the Koran in a nasal voice. After a quarter of an hour a flute player relieved him with good, continuous improvising, occasionally accompanied by a second, playing a prolonged bass note. After another quarter of an hour the squatting dervishes began to join in with various motions of the body. Now the music becomes more provocative, three flutes and a violin taking over the melody, which shows clearly traces of the old Turkish. A tambourine, a couple of small kettle drums beat out the weirdest rhythms. Thirteen of the monks now rise and move slowly counter-clockwise in a circle. They walk solemnly. When a certain spot is reached, a dancer turns to the man behind him and both make low bows to each other. The music changes the *Maqâm* and rhythm, and now they all throw off their cloaks. Ten of them are standing there in white cowls, one in black, one in greenish blue, one in gray. The last —the abbot—is standing just below me. The others walk up to him, bow, and kiss him. Then the ten soar forth, spread their arms out horizontally like the wings of an airplane, and begin to whirl in such a manner that the many cowls worn one over another form a large bell around them. Four of the dervishes make up a small circle, six a larger one, and as they whirl about constantly, the eldest in the black cowl moves slowly and continuously between the two circles, again counter-clockwise. These old men with outspread arms spun like tops for a full half hour—

an astonishing, inconceivable performance. Here the dance severs the natural bonds of human posture and motion. In dizziness the dancer loses the feeling of body and of self; released from his body he conquers dizziness. Physicians who were present later verified for me the "Yoga" state of the dancing dervishes. The significance of the dance is apparently astral: the sun, the moon, and the revolving stars. There is no doubt that it is something primitive, preserved from a period thousands of years before Islam, inherited from the shamanism of central Asia. And there is no doubt that in the absolute sense it is beautiful and deeply impressive. The verses of the Persian mystic Ğalal al-Dîn Rumi came to my mind:

Sound, ye drums, and echo, flutes!
Allah hu!
Dance, O waving Dawn!
Allah hu!
O Sun that God the master has created
The fiery soul which planets whirl around!
Allah hu!
O hearts! O worlds! Let love your master be,
Your dances else are vain,
Allah hu!
The leader of our round of love goes out
Beyond the sun and dawn . . .

In Europe we have the "loss of self" motif clearly illustrated in the whirl dances of the Russian sects of the Molokani in Armenia; of the self-emasculated Skoptzi, and of those of the Khlisti, who whirl about and lash themselves as they dance around a beaker of water, until they finally become Christ and utter prophecies. Carvings like the round of the angels in divine frenzy done by Agostino di Duccio in the fifteenth century are witness that this ecstasy is felt and understood also in western Europe.

All the countries that bordered the Mediterranean in ancient times, and the less remote sections of Asia as well, appear to have had whirl dances. Frescoes like the one recently excavated near Giza from a burial vault of the ancient Egyptian Empire and that of a Negress ornamented with vines from Tomb 113 at Thebes (c. 1300 b. c.) may hardly be interpreted otherwise. In Assyria in the seventh century b. c. the soldiers are said to have whirled themselves like tops, and women dancers of Turkestan carried the whirl dance as far as China. Likewise the women's dances of the old Jews were probably often whirl dances. For the word מחול *māḥôl,* which is used constantly for women's dances, derives from a verb חול *ḥūl,* "turn," a word used both for a sword swung in a circle and for the whirlwind. This revolving was, to be sure, no dervish-like whirling in the strict sense.

> Return, return, O Shulamite;
> Return, return that we may look upon thee.
> Why will yė look upon the Shulamite,
> As upon the dance of Mahanaim?

When we read these verses from the Song of Songs we are convinced that what is referred to is a facing in all four directions. It is hardly reasonable to read into the lines at this point a sword dance or a round dance.

The division of the whirl dance into classes may best be attempted on a geographical basis. In the majority of cases it is women who dance it. It carries unmistakably the marks of close movement: in Loango, light shuffling, rolling of the pelvis, leaping forwards and backwards; among the Cui of Hindustan, gentle swaying and balancing of the arms; in the Celebes, slow walking; among the Pueblo, pressing together of the heels, sliding, and rolling. Even where men are the dancers, it seems nowhere to proceed in an expanded manner. In the Marshall Islands the legs trip along "shyly"; the Bashkir stretch out one arm "not ungracefully" (*modo che non mancava di grazia*), while the other rests on the hip; the dervish soars steadily; and even the sword dance of the Pamir-Tadjik bristling with numerous weapons consists only of "extremely picturesque rotating patterns." Thus it is necessary to classify the whirl dance as a close one.

Over and above this systematic classification the whirl dance must be acknowledged as the most thrilling expression of the feminine power of conception. The whirling dervish, who extends his arms horizontally and turns his palms upwards, assumes, without wishing to, the gesture of taking, of opening. No fertilizing power streams forth from him, he himself awaits the generative force which takes possession of him, which removes the limitations of his body, extinguishes his consciousness, and pours the divine spirit into him. The whirl dance is the purest form of dance devotion.

WRENCH DANCES. If under this head we have an apparent overlapping with the convulsive dances of the shamans already discussed, we shall limit this group to those dances which have consciously progressed from activity originally harmonious to movements out of harmony with the body. The physiological basis of all distortion dances is probably the pleasurable turning and twisting of the whole body that we know as "stretching"—a defense against blood congestion after an overlong period of uninterrupted quiet. No dance can be executed entirely in two dimensions. Therefore we can in any case hardly be expected to set up a hard and fast division for the distortion dances as such, but especially not in a scientific work which is dependent for the most part on the insufficient descriptions of others.

The participation of both sexes is about equal. But the accompanying movements are almost exclusively short steps forward and backward, standing on one leg, swaying, rolling, and contraction of the body. Only rarely, as in the dances of the Waheia, the Singalese, and the Ostyak, are jumps a part of the distortion dance.

"From a pleasurable expanding to stretching out" does not suffice as a definition of the wrench dance. It must be understood that all seeking after, holding to, and emphasizing of the distortion is by definition contrary to nature, and furthermore that every dance and especially

44

every primitive dance is ecstatic. Ecstasy in the meaning that is essential to our theme, does not search for and produce naturalness. Rather it avoids what has been given by nature and what is near at hand in nature and forms its repertory of movements from the models of the involuntary convulsive dances, and surely also from the fantastically unreal visions of oppressive dreams. We are reminded of Hauer's statement about the "mingling of the genuinely intuitive and the grotesquely ridiculous thoughtfulness" that seems so strange to us. We are reminded at the same time of the statues of Gothic cathedrals. They, too, often show a position and movement that are anything but natural. They avoid the normal posture; indeed, they seem to be relieved of anatomical restrictions. They are twisted and distorted and seem to have no bones. An ecstatic spirit created them, too, and lifted them out of everyday reality. The North American Ute and the Sakai of Sumatra maintain their balance only with difficulty when they cross their feet as they move forward in the dance—a movement that is to be seen in dance pictures of the Gothic period. Here we see activity out of harmony with the natural carried to the point of affectation.

The peculiar stretching motions which are the essential part of the wrench dances often give the effect of an arrested, expanded movement, of an interrupted swing. When they are of three dimensions they can be grouped together and may be described as "bit and brace positions." Like the dances of the later Egyptian Empire in general, the funeral dance of the eighteenth dynasty, depicted in a life-like relief of limestone in the Cairo Museum (Plate 9), offers a good example. A later dance of the Near East (Plate 17) may be regarded as a companion-piece.

In southeastern Asia where the wrench dance has moved into a more restricted artistic province, the limbs are methodically wrenched out of joint. The girl dancers of the Cambodian court, seated by twos in the practice room, bend each other's fingers backward, until all the joints crack. They force back each other's arms, which by nature are already loose-jointed, as one might break off a branch, until they can move them as much as forty degrees backward at the elbow. By constantly bending

45

their supple young bones in the elbow exercise they widen the bone sockets and expand the ligaments. And every joint of the body must undergo a training in distortion like that of the elbow. In Cambodia, as also in Burma, the arms and legs are bent at an angle, the shoulder blades are pushed together, the abdomen is contracted, and the body as a whole is in "bit and brace position."

In this and in countless other non-European dances, the spectator from the West must needs call to mind the marionette. A Burmese child who leads such a maiden dance is "as though moved by another's will, quite like a puppet, therefore, with elastic resilience. Each time she flings out her legs or arms as if they hung from wires." The legs of the dancing women of Fiji are like "puppet's legs attached to invisible wires." Observers of the dances of the West African Fan and the Ostyak of Siberia have also been reminded of marionettes. The movements of the Ostyak are described as being like the craziest and most unnatural that a wooden puppet could be made to do. And the pygmies of Uganda, who are superior dancers, caused an observer "irresistibly" to think of their dance as an unconscious parody of "marionette action."

There is a very conscious relationship to the puppet dance—where according to absolute standard the dance as a high art has reached one of its peaks—in the dances of the Sultan families of Java, and, somewhat degenerated, in those of the Javanese professional dancers, who use the former dances as a model. For the dance of living men and women on the stage of Java and the presentation in pantomime on a white screen of old hero stories by means of dolls cut out of leather, have stood for centuries side by side stylistically and otherwise. If the shadow play has taken from the real dancers the convincing, gripping truth of life, the dance has borrowed from the shadow theater the coercion to move the limbs in silhouette, so to speak. The Javanese dance is almost in two dimensions, and since every limb of the body must reveal itself complete and unforeshortened, it is incomparably expressive.

"As though moved by another's will." In these few words is the entire inner history of this type of dance. At the beginning is the pure convulsive dance in which the will has "completely or partially lost control of the limbs"; at the end is the old Mexican, the East Asiatic, and the European ballet, where the dancers are "as though moved by another's will." The convulsive element degenerates and disappears; but the ecstatic release from the will remains until it is smothered in artistry and automatism.

And yet—are not such automatic, puppet-like dances in themselves of high intrinsic merit? The Hindu might refer to the saying in his country, "The dancer should be like a puppet on strings." The white man would prefer to let the beautiful words of the poet Heinrich von Kleist be his answer:

"And the advantage which this doll would have over a living dancer? The advantage? First of all a negative one, my fine friend—namely, that it would never be affected. For affectation appears, as you know, when the soul finds itself at any point other than the center of the movement. Since the operator with his wire or string plainly has no other point in his power than this, all the rest of the limbs are, as they should be, dead, pure pendula, and follow the simple law of gravity—an excellent quality, which we look for in vain in most of our dancers. . . . Then, too, these puppets have the advantage of being anti-gravitational. They know nothing of the inertia of matter—that force that the dance strives against more than any other—because the power which lifts them into the air is greater than that which ties them to the earth. The puppets, like the elves, use the ground only to glide along, and to add force to the swing of their limbs by the momentary restriction. We need it to rest on, to recover from the exertion of the dance—a moment, which is apparently not dance in itself and with which nothing more may be done than to make it disappear as quickly as possible." And at the end we see that "to the extent that (as in the organic world) reflection becomes dimmer and weaker, grace appears ever more radiant and coercive. Like two lines which intersect, the one after a journey across the endless on one side, finding itself quite suddenly on the other side; or like the reflection in a concave mirror, which, after withdrawing into the endless, steps suddenly right out in front of us again. Thus, when perception has passed through an infinity as it were, grace puts in an appearance again; in such a manner that it appears at the same time in its purest form in that human structure which either has no consciousness at all or an infinite one—that is, in the mannikin or in God."

2. Themes and Types

THE thinking processes of primitive man do not include a comprehension of the natural relation of cause and effect. The natives imagine spirits and powers which influence life in mysterious ways, which bring about hunger and satiation, birth, sickness, and death, and which in turn can be influenced in magic activities that will attract them or drive them away. Man can work magic when dehumanized, transported, lifted by the divine out of the everyday, torn out of the normal path of life, he walks into the void, into that expanse where the self mingles with the infinite. Out of his transport a mastery over spirits grows in him; a power to work in conjunction with the superhuman, to take control over the events of which his daily life is a part.

Transported, disfigured, dehumanized, made into a brute or into a god—all this can be accomplished only in exhilaration. Only in exhilaration are the bonds of everyday loosened, only where joy, sorrow, love, anger, fear, are all-powerful, where willing and thinking are blotted out and the body, slipping from under their command, exaggerates the accustomed movements out of all proportion or arranges them into the rhythmic dance.

Every dance is and gives ecstasy. The adult who puts his arm around his companion in the ballroom, and the child in the roadway, skipping in a round dance—they forget themselves, they dissolve the weight of earthly contact and the rigidity of daily existence. How much more intense the reaction of primitive man, whose unburdened mind offers so little resistance to every stimulus and whose body, unstunted and undisciplined, responds to this stimulus without restraint to an extent

49

that is foreign to us. Again and again travelers report that natives gesticulate in their dance "like lunatics," that their bodies jerk as though in a convulsion; all parts of the body tremble even to the fingertips, only the whites of their eyes show, the throat forms wild, animal-like sounds, until the dancer rolls unconscious on the ground. The passion of the transport can be so intense that during the Boer War the Bushmen of the Kalahari Desert often let themselves be surrounded in the midst of their moonlight dance and shot down in hordes.

If the soul here slips into a twilight state, it often enough crosses the threshold into the darkest world of night. The urge for preservation of self and kind changes to the destructive, the weapon of the dancer tears apart his own body and destroys the vehicle of propagation. Ecstatic dancers of Bali may be likened in their frenzy to the worshipers of the Cappadocian Mâ, who, lashed by the noise of drums and trumpets, spill their blood in a mad dance in front of an idol. The Russians of the Skoptzi sect in a frenzied whirl dance emasculate themselves. Frequently such dances become pure fakirism. In a fire dance the Bulgarian sect of the Nestinari and the Luiseño of California stamp on glowing embers with their bare feet without burning themselves; indeed, chieftains of northeastern Brazil and devil-possessed Negroes of the Sudan form a dance circle and swallow burning coals. Similar things were done by the old German Berserks.

These dancers are possessed in the real sense. They not only undergo a narrowing of consciousness—a spirit, a devil, a god has taken control of their body and has transformed them. Thus primitive men become demons, and members of Christian sects like the Russian Khlisti and Molokan become Christ. Two examples from contrasting cultures may make this state clear to the reader. For the basic cultures let us examine a description of the Vedda:

"As the charm is recited over and over again the shaman dances more and more quickly, his voice becomes hoarse and he soon becomes possessed by the 'Yaku,' and although he does not lose consciousness and can coordinate his movements, he nevertheless does not retain any clear recollection of what he says, and only a general idea of the movements he has performed. Although there is doubtless a certain element of humbug about some of the performances, we believe that this is only intentional among the tamer Vedda accustomed to show off before visitors, and that among the less sophisticated Vedda the singing and movements of the dance soon produce a more or less automatic condition, in which the mind of the shaman being dominated by his belief in the reality of the 'Yaku,' and of his coming possession, really acts without being in a condition of complete volitional consciousness. Most sincere practitioners whom we interrogated in different localities agreed that although they never entirely lost consciousness, they nearly did so at times, and that they never fully appreciated what they said when possessed, while at both the beginning and end of possession they experienced a sensation of nausea and vertigo and the ground seemed to rock and sway beneath their feet.

"Some men, including Handuna of Sitala Wanniya, whom we consider one of the most trustworthy of our informants, said that they were aware that they shivered and trembled when they became possessed, and Handuna heard booming noises in his ears as the spirit left him and full consciousness returned. He said this usually happened after he had ceased to dance. . . . The shaman in fact surrenders himself to the dance in the fullest sense, and it is this, combined with a high degree of sub-conscious expectancy, which leads him to enact almost automatically and certainly without careful forethought the traditional parts of the dance in their conventional correct order. . . ."

A section from a work on the secret societies of the Wanyamwezi will provide an example from the tribal cultures. "When I came upon a member who was not participating in the dance and asked him why not, he would invariably answer 'Natali kusangwa n'iswesi,' that is, I have not yet encountered the spirit, or I have not yet been visited or possessed by the spirit. Accordingly every member taking part in the cult dance and decorated with the characteristic amulets and insignia believes himself possessed by a spirit. No longer does he belong to himself, the spirit speaks through him, the spirit (iswesi) takes control of his entire being. Therefore if you attempt to converse with a Muswezi during the period of his alleged * frenzy, you receive in answer only incomprehensible sounds and twisted and mutilated words. Even the ordinary forms of greeting become meaningless, incomprehensible words. You have the feeling that you are trying to talk to somebody who has escaped from a lunatic asylum. During a dance ceremony one time I took hold of a fine old bow and asked the owner the price to see whether I could entice him into speaking reasonably. I did not succeed. He assumed a wild manner, grunted, and uttered a stream of inarticulate sounds, from which you could pick up phrases now and then like: 'Put it down! The spirit says no!' "

In other cases the withdrawal of willing and thinking takes on characteristics of the hypnotic state of trance. Then the eyes may close, the limbs straighten out, and solemn quiet and renunciation take the place of heated frenzy. Artificial methods are also used to bring about such a state. On the island of Yap the leader hypnotized every single dancer with revolving, stroking motions of the hand and with the magic formula, with which a dying man had empowered him as an inviolable secret. In Bali a writer watched women dancers go into a charmed sleep. "It was dark—only here and there a gloomy, flickering oil lamp. The two maidens got down on their knees in front of a smoky fire, while priests dressed in white muttered charms and prayers and kept throwing fragrant herbs and flowers into it. A large chorus of naked brown women sang weird, monotonous melodies for a long time—and often held single notes an unbelievable length of time. Finally one girl went into a trance. She got to her feet, uttered a confused babble, and swayed to and fro. Then she was quickly fitted out with trappings of a golden color, with clinking foot rings and a tall, showy headdress of gold flowers; after which she was led into the open circle. . . ."

The transcendental stream pours into the dance, even performing the

---

* Dr. Sachs questions the appropriateness of this word (German *angeblich*) in the document from which he quotes. Translator's note.

act of artistic selection and arrangement, which seems to us white men so conscious, so intellectual. In North America, in Melanesia, and in Micronesia, whole dances and series of dances have been manifested in dreams, and throughout the world rounds and dances are thought to be inspired by the divine. Then phantasy takes control of an individual's mechanism of movement in order "to carry the imaginings of the dream-consciousness into external reality."

The superhuman power which exhilaration and hypnosis bring to a dancer is shown especially clearly in his almost inconceivable staying powers in a state of high tension. "In the dance even the weakest can do wonders." For a dance to be continued through a whole night is quite normal. The Lengua of the Gran Chaco eat during the dance, and what must seem strange enough to the European observer, the men stuff food into their mouths without even changing their movement, indeed, without even taking from their mouths the tobacco pipe, an instrument indispensable for ecstatic effect. But already the exhilaration, which comes from the movement alone, has brought "a certain anesthesia: the extinguishing of all feelings of exertion and fatigue." Therefore an early observer can report of a dance of the Indians that "their muscles were so strained that at the last their legs looked more like a bunch of ropes than human flesh." At her first period of menstruation a girl of the California Achomawi dances for ten full nights, and among the Guaicurú in the Gran Chaco a suitor must dance "convulsively" for eight days in front of the house of his maiden.

As early as 1774 a German writer, Georg Wilhelm Steller, in his *Description of the Country of Kamchatka* expressed this phase of the dance in classic words: "Wild as these dances are, their outcries are just as barbaric. They fall so much in love with the dancing that once they have started, it is as if a frenzy had fallen upon them. They cannot stop, though they exert themselves so much that the sweat runs down from their faces in streams. Whoever can hold out longest regards this achievement as a great honor and advances his cause by reason of it with the young ladies, who have been talking to the dancers with gestures.

They may dance for an hour over one sentence, and the circle keeps getting larger, as more and more people inside the dwelling can contain themselves no longer and must join in. Finally even hoary old men crowd into the dance and spend their last powers in it. The dance continues twelve or fifteen hours, from evening until mid-morning of the next day. . . ."

Still the dancers do not always depend entirely upon the exhilarative power of rhythmic movement. Incense and tobacco are frequently used, and intoxicating drinks like mandioca beer and maize beer, palm juice, mead, and brandy. Supernatural aid is not scorned either: before the dance in New Guinea, the limbs are rubbed with the powder of a magic stone.

At this point the dance is shunted from its accustomed course into a blind alley. Ecstasy, active performance under one's own power are no longer the essential element of the magical effect. It can come about, as we wrote above, that a bodily activity may remain out of the picture and that only the fact of a definitely ordered movement may work as a charm. A person can *be* danced, if he is himself unable to dance. When the boys of the California Juaneño become tired at the maturity celebrations, older men walk into the round and take them on their shoulders, and in eastern New Guinea a female attendant carries on her shoulders the girls at their first menstruation and jumps over the fire with them. In all continents the dancers carry little children on their shoulders. "To make them sweat," according to the Yuka of California. Even in our level of culture we have examples of the same custom. In the fourteenth century there was a circle dance around lighted candles with the newborn child. Until as late as 1913 at least, at a high mass dance on Marcellus Day in the church, the mothers of Barjols in Provence lifted up their babies and swung them in a circle. Rumanian mothers still place their children in the arm of the Călușari. It is hardly surprising then that the Mexican Maya should lead animals around in the circle and the Battak of Sumatra should have their dead chieftain dancing with them in effigy.

As an antidote—a backward swing of the pendulum—the sacred frenzy gives birth to a roistering troop of clowns. Beside the divinely inspired dancer walks the jester—a child of the dance. (Is not the German *Narr*, jester, cognate with the Sanskrit *nṛtú*, dancer?) From the America of the Indians, across Oceania and Asia as far as Europe he takes part in the dances and sometimes dominates them. He caricatures the other participants, frightens the spectators, teases the young girls, and dips into the mysteries of life and death. In the scalp dance of the Cheyenne Indians clowns wear the costumes of slain enemies, and in the cloister dances of Tibet besides two jesters appear two other figures carrying skulls and dressed in tight-fitting white suits on which skeletons are painted.

The divinely inspired dancer has become a rarity in the Occidental world. But his counterpart and play-fellow, the bell-ringing fool, as Prince Carnival, as the Villingen *Hansl*, as the jester in the English *Morris Dance*, and as the *gigantone* of Seville remains, through the centuries, the life-giving power of the fertility cults. The sacred frenzy of the Dionysian maenads has been extinguished. But we have an illustration of the earlier significance of the European carnival in the fact that the ancient Portuguese vegetation charm, in which masked men dressed as women still fling themselves about as though possessed, has borne the name *folías*, meaning "lunacy," down to the present day.

The dance of the animals, especially that of the anthropoid apes, proves that the dance of men is in its beginnings a pleasurable motor reaction, a game forcing excess energy into a rhythmic pattern. But in this case, also, man is distinguished from the animal in that he feels and thinks at the same time, that in his play he searches after meaning and content, and that he makes his play inadvertently a purposeful activity. "We dance both for pleasure and for the good of the city," say the old Mexican Zuñi. Whenever the impulse to play or to move is without an objective, the dance joins up with the highly systematized organism of life and takes from it a law of form.

Primitive man dances for every occasion: for birth, circumcision, the consecration of maidens, marriage, sickness and death, the celebration of chieftains, hunting, war, victory, the conclusion of peace, spring, harvest and pork festivals. Still the themes are limited, for the goal is everywhere the same—life, power, abundance, health. Therefore one dance may often be used in place of another, the weapon dance for the marriage dance and for the consecration of maidens, the phallic dance for the rain and funeral dances, or the sun dance for the medicine dance.

All these themes are expressed sometimes in one kind of dance, sometimes in another. In one place the erotic motif is formed by simply dancing around a person of the other sex; in another place a group of men may move toward a group of women; in a third place it may be expressed by phallic couple dances of unmistakable positions and gestures; and in a fourth by the provocative muscle dances of individual women. We see war dances among one people as a simple circling movement with the singing of the exploits of departed generations; among another, as a sham attack between two sides. A colorful variety of dance movements emerges and words used to express what corresponds in the other arts press forward: stylism, idealism, realism, naturalism. Meanwhile it is best at the beginning to avoid these fixed and yet ambiguous catchwords, these terms that must ever be defined anew, and rather to state one by one from the material at hand particular concepts which will give an adequate picture of the many-sidedness of dance forms without arbitrarily relating them to one or another "ism."

The few methods of dancing two themes, given above as examples of the variety, show a fundamental difference of formation. On the one hand the circle dance in which the special content and purpose are not made clear—the same dance with the same movement centering around fertility or battle; on the other hand the most rigid adherence to nature of the movements that is possible to the particular theme; and in between, a middle ground, hard to lay hold of, which hints at the special theme metaphorically, rather, by position, gesture, and ornament without faithfulness to nature down to the last detail. Few themes are treated according to only one or two of these possibilities. The great majority are expressed with all their transitions in each of the three ways.

The clearest, most easily recognizable type is that culture group which fulfills its purpose in the dance by rigidly adhering to nature. A dance of this kind will anticipate events together with the end desired and thus force the occurrence to that end. This dance depicts the flourishing of animals important for sustaining life, the chase with the bringing down of the game, the battle with victory over opponents, the rich harvest, the dying and the resurrection of man. Let us call it therefore the image or mimetic dance.

A contrast to the mimetic is that dance which serves an idea, a definite religious goal, without imitating in pantomime the events, forms, and gestures of life and nature. We shall call it the imageless or abstract dance. It aims simply at ecstasy, or it takes over the form of the mystic circling, in which power jumps across from those on the outside to the one on the inside or vice versa. A gnostic hymn of the second century gives us a most vivid conception of this stream of power. After the feast of the Passover before going out to fulfill his destiny, Christ commands his disciples to join hands and dance around him in a circle. In this sacred union he makes his last bequest: "Now answer thou unto my dancing. Behold thyself in me who speak."

This transformation into another self, which is so clearly the form here, has the same meaning that lies at the base of most imageless dances. The adults circle around the newly matured maiden so that she will become a fruitful member of the tribe; married women dance around the woman newly married to receive her into their class; the people encircle the head of an enemy, the sacrificial buffalo, the altar, the golden calf, the holy wafer, in order that the power of these objects may flow across to them in some mysterious way. Always it is a question of "thyself in me."

The image dance and the imageless dance are thus clearly distinguished one from the other. If the forms and movements stood in close relation to the theme and yet did not really describe the event itself, if they generalized and replaced it with a related event, then beside the mimetic and imageless dance we might speak of an allegorical or a metaphorical dance. An initiation dance would be allegorical which has as its theme the flogging of the novice to promote power. A sex dance would be allegorical in which the men stamp on the ground, while the women respond to each stamp with an outcry. A marriage dance with the characteristics of a weapon dance would be allegorical. But we will do well to leave the words "allegorical" and "metaphorical" out of the picture. Strictly they cover only a modern, Occidental conception; applied to primitive peoples they would always have to be qualified. It would be better not to label arbitrarily a group of dances which have nothing more in common than that they stand more or less to one or the other side of two extremes without belonging to a third category. Such a middle type cannot always be easily differentiated from dances which are similar to it. But this should not trouble us. Life knows no sharp dividing lines and if we wish to represent something living, the boundaries that we set up are at best only scientific aids.

Observation of the apes would lead us to think that the imageless dance came first, and the imitative, mimetic dance followed. Nevertheless we are confronted with the noteworthy fact that in the European Old Stone Age and among many peoples of the lowest cultural level living today there are just as many evidences of the image dance as of the imageless. Since even in earliest times both types of dance are found side by side, the feeling arises that we are dealing here with two contrasting elements, which are evident though at times they each break bounds, but which cannot have been developed from one another. They are completely different as to type. The one has grown from observation of the outer world. What does an animal look like? How does it move? How does it jerk its head and flap its wings? How does it hop forwards? And how can a person imitate it? This imitative dance—quite like the Miolithic rock painting—is of ocular origin; the modern psychologist, following Dr. Jung, would call it extravert. The imageless dance is on the other hand altogether non-sensory in its origin and in its religious aims. It originates in no perception, it imitates no form and no movement. It strives for a magical effect only through the transmission of a definite power from the dancer to the object danced around or vice versa. In contrast with the extraversion of the animal dance it is decidedly a dance of introversion.

The terms extravert and introvert have recently been taken over from psychology into sociology: the mental and spiritual make-up of the so-called patriarchal peoples has been described as extravert and that of the matriarchal as introvert, and the peculiar social relationships have been ascribed to states of mind which have grown out of this fundamentally different mental attitude. Thus we are faced with the necessity of carrying the dance into that uncertain realm which enwraps the profound duality of human life.

Apparently the distinction hinges on little. In the one case the child belongs to the family of the father and is subordinate to the father; in the other it belongs to the maternal family and the mother's brother is its guardian and protector, while the father counts for nothing. Present-day Europe is patriarchal. The wife assumes the family name of the husband and is under his guardianship. A familiar example of matriarchy may be found in the first book of the Bible: Hagar, Leah, and Rachel—not the fathers—give their sons names. But behind these sociological labels there is a large number of contrasting ideas, points of view, religious and moral feelings, economic forms and social institutions. On the patriarchal side the greater influence appears to be exerted by the masculine qualities—violent unsteady nature, nomadic tendencies, herding, worship of the sun; on the matriarchal side the feminine characteristics have the greater influence—cheerful, patient nature, settledness, planting, ancestor cults, and worship of the moon. These antitheses exist side by side in individuals as in peoples in different mixture, and, according to the ratio of their components, determine disposition and culture.

When we occupy ourselves with this contrast so important in shaping destiny, we must use the concepts patriarchy and matriarchy as no more than expedients. The sociological side of the duality concerns us least of all, and if we were to stop there we should scarcely arrive at our goal. In the most primitive relationships the conception of society has not yet reached the stage of a strict family classification, when the tendencies, ideas, and points of view that are the base of such a division have long been formed.

Our task will be to proceed from the purely intellectual contrast and to test it with the contrast of the imageless and the image dance. The former is designated by psychologists as:

matriarchal	patriarchal
introvert	extravert
free of the body	bound to the body
imaginative	sensory
capable of abstraction	empirical

There is no denying that these qualities in exactly the same arrangement are reflected in both the dance types.

The image dance is "bound to the body." It starts with the idea that imitation of gesture and position is sufficient to capture a power and make it useful. "The extravert type is constantly tempted to give himself up to an object and to assimilate with the object." To portray the animals is to be one with them. "But when we transfer this will to activity into another object, we are a part of the other object." Thus can we triumph over the animals. A hunting game brings luck in the chase; to represent the sex act is to achieve fertility.

The imageless dance is "free of the body." The purpose of its movement is to lift the body out of its accustomed corporality, until with the deadening and extinguishing of the outer senses, the subconscious becomes free and increases the spiritual powers in ecstatic ascent. The ecstatic dancer dances to lose his body and to become spirit. In the complete loss of self he works toward a goal which has grown from an appearance into an idea: the rain which he will bring about cannot be embodied in a dish of water, nor fertility in a phallic drama, nor victory in the clatter of swords struck together.

Thus the two types of dance in their sharp contrast enter those great intellectual spheres which in violent and unceasing conflict determine the culture of mankind. Any question of time in this regard is therefore pointless.

The bridge between these two extremes, the broad middle zone, may now be seen in a still clearer light. In it the "materialization" of the imageless dance joins with the "idealization" of the image dance. Such is the case when the ecstatic rain dancers use instead of the blazing fire a bucket of water as their central point to dance around and to drink, or when the Indian sun dancers hang a picture of the sun on the pillar around which they are dancing so feverishly. These changes in the original types lead us right into the midst of that continuous process of transformation which is caused by the constant invasion and transplantation of the two great culture forms. Interbreeding among neighboring tribes and migrations of peoples and thoughts over large distances account for this. Therefore we find scarcely a single tribe possessing only imageless or only image dances, just as we do not meet the rest of the patriarchal or matriarchal characteristics in the intellectual or material domain in altogether pure form. In these contacts the higher culture wins out, and with it the dance must also come under the influence of the growing feeling of personality and the increasing division of society into classes. Even without external influence the dance suffers the fate of all human institutions and forms of existence: it becomes refined; the spiritual and physical power which created and maintained it weakens; the faith which gave it content and form is forced by religious evolution into the realm of uncreative superstition. Though deadened and dispirited, the gifts of delight in physical activity, beauty of motion, the power to unite a community, and sexual freedom remain to it. Thus to a large extent it has already become in prehistoric, primitive civilization what it is today—an object of artistic enjoyment and of social pleasure. New sources of power have no longer flowed to it since with the deadening and dispiriting process the old ones have dried up. The old stock of forms and movements is simplified and reduced and—strange as it may sound—since the Stone Age, the dance has taken on as little in the way of new forms as of new content. The history of the creative dance takes place in prehistory.

General Characteristics

The imageless dance is bound to no special form any more than the mimetic, but in an overwhelming majority of cases its movement is circular. The circle may be without a central point or it may have as its center a person or an object, whose power is supposed to radiate to those on the circle or vice versa.

The magical goal of the imageless exhilaration dance is the attainment of a state of ecstasy in which the dancer transcends the human and physical and, released from his self, wins the power of interfering with the events of the world. The particular goal—rain, health, victory—is thought of only as a pure idea without putting its stamp on the dance form. Thus we have at least in the beginnings a strong uniformity in the dances. First of all nothing is changed, whether the object of the charms in one instance is a sick person, or in another the newly matured girl or the sacrificial animal. The medicine dance, the initiation dance, the sacrificial dance are not differentiated. Thus in the Andaman Islands the dance at the conclusion of mourning or before marching out to attack an enemy is the same in all its essentials as the dance after a successful hunt.

The end of the development is not different from the beginning. The Micronesian women sing of everything that moves the tribe, of fruits, animals, stars, and ancestors, and with all the songs they do the same quiet rocking dance. The imageless dance remains thus uniform, until, deculted and transformed, it becomes the possession of the youngest, until a child appears in a circle of children and the old round dance freed of purpose merges into the elixir of pure delight in motion and existence.

Medicine Dances

In the healing of the sick, the relation of the circle dance to the world of the ecstatic, visionary mental state becomes most impressive. The dancer or dance leader of a whole dance chorus is the shaman, the witch doctor, the medicine man. Demoniac, clairvoyant, prophetic, appointed because of a natural, often a parapsychic predisposition, possessed by a transcendental inspiration, he condenses and increases within himself the ecstatic powers of the tribe to a miraculous extent. Transported far from the physical, he looks at the mythical past and the future. He ascends to the spirits who threaten the well-being of man and struggles with them, until they give up and release their victim. The *medicine dance* is his most direct medium of expression.

The picture of such a dance in pure form is the same in all shamanistic cultures. The sick man is placed in the center and encircled, until the dancers in an ecstatic state have overpowered the spirit of sickness, chased him away, or even drawn him into themselves and conquered him. The Vedda dance described in detail on page 12 may be considered an example, even though the Vedda have only adopted shamanism. It would be difficult to think of anything more impressive than the fact that as late as the end of the nineteenth century the rural population of France ranged itself in unaffected primitiveness alongside these pygmoids whose culture is of the Early Stone Age: in the *département* of Seine-et-Oise a child suffering from a hernia was carried under an oak tree and danced around by the women.

In other cultures wild ecstasy often gives way to grave solemnity. Thus in the Celebes (Neneng) in an unconstrained procession men and women wearing red wreaths of holy flowers on their heads, their hands on the shoulders of the dancer in front, jerk their bodies forwards and backwards and move slowly in measured rhythm around the sick persons, who squat on mats in the middle of the circle. Further up in the scale of mankind, among the Yurok of California and those Vedda of Ceylon no longer reckoned as primitive, the dancers hold branches instead of flowers—the same branches that are so often swung in the fertility dances.

Contrariwise, it may be the sick person himself who dances to get well. The sick Toba women of the Gran Chaco dance faster and faster within the circle of townspeople, who sit and sing, until the sickness spirits escape in perspiration and are driven into the woods by one of the men with a firebrand. There are parallels in North America. The Ute, for example, create healing power against rheumatism by dancing around a sun pole. But even in Europe, in Rumania, there are healing dances for the sick.

Fertility Dances

For the non-hunter the chief concern of his daily life is sufficient rain, regardless of whether he gathers wild fruits or tills his own soil. Therefore in the earliest society the rain charm stands in the forefront of cult activities, and even in the advanced Chinese culture—in the first millennium before Christ—the shaman must make rain in an ecstatic dance. In northwestern Australia this ecstatic dance has the purest form: the rain maker heaps up a pile of stones or sand, places a magic stone on top, and for hours at a time dances around the pile chanting magic words, until he is so exhausted that he must call upon an assistant to continue. More recent offshoots of the weather charm are the solemn procession of the Arval priests in ancient Rome with the magic circumambulation of the fields, and the same custom in present-day Catholic communities. Over and above the more restricted rain charm the imageless dances can also work for field fertility, even telepathically, across great distances. The agricultural Tarahumara of Mexico have a man dance and sing throughout the night in front of a vacant house in order to bless those working out in the fields.

These are still not image dances, when stalks of sugar cane or bunches of fruit like those desired are danced around or when the central post is decked with fresh green, with rice sacks, or many-colored ribbons. The northern Europeans are not the only people who dance around this "maypole" on bright midsummer nights. In southern Europe the Basque sword dancers dance in the same manner around the maypole, and so do the Hindu and the Toradja of the Celebes in Asia, the Indian girls in agricultural northern Mexico and Yucatan, and many, many others. The special motif of this old American round dance is the long variegated ribbons which, with one end tied to the pole and the other held by the dancers, are twisted attractively one over another in the circular course. In exactly the same manner this motif is executed in many parts of the world—in the *Hammeltanz* of Alsace, in the *Bandltanz* of southern Bavaria, Salzburg, Tirol, Steiermark, and Siebenbürgen; in the *ballo della cordella* of Sicily; in the dance of the women weavers of Provence; in the sword round of the Basques; and in the Spanish *bailes de cintas* and *danzas del cordón;* outside of Europe, in the dances of the Santal of Hindustan and those of the Indians of Venezuela; and finally, in the dance of the Indian girls of Central America mentioned above, which is not at all a European importation, since the Spanish conquerors found it there. In place of the pole stuck into the ground, we find in northeastern Africa and all over Europe the living tree, which is sanctified as a fertility center to be danced around. As in northeastern Africa, men and women of Silesia used to dance in couples on Christmas night around the fruit trees and wind a rope about each one. From the fertility dances stems the famous *carmagnole*—the round dance of the French Revolution around the tree of liberty and the guillotine—which takes its name from the city of Carmagnola in Piedmont.

The dancer—and this is the second point in the objectivizing of the dance—makes himself the carrier of the power of growth as he takes living green as an implement of the dance. The idea is the same when the South African Angoni in the rain dance break branches from trees and hold them in their hands; when the Galla in dancing around the sacred tree carry grain and grass in their arms; when ancient Egyptian women dancers deck themselves with grape vines and swing branches;

when the Japanese women wave cherry branches in the *azuma asobi;* or when Jewish women of old hearken to the word of God:

> On the first day go and get
> Fruits from the wondrous tree,
> Palm tree fans,
> Leaves from the thicket tree,
> From the brook poplar,
> And rejoice before Him,
> Before thy God.

The mythology of Papua has given to this idea a special turn: the grass pierces the eyes of the rising sun until it weeps and its countenance is covered with clouds. But let us not forget that even the dancing chimpanzees deck themselves with vines. The need of decoration is primary.

The tree dances of which we have spoken are often given a sexual accent, which is perhaps still clearer in the spring festivals of the pre-Chinese cultures in eastern Asia. Unmarried boys and girls dance in couples, grasping each other by the hips; at the conclusion of the dance the girls are lifted on to the backs of the boys and carried away. The dances of the Itogapuk of the Amazon territory and the Tsaloa of the Rio Yapurá are similar. The men and women dance in couples and then disappear two by two into the dark of night.

In these as in other dances of the same type (page 69), it becomes apparent to what extent this imageless dance is already charged with pragmatic eroticism. It anticipates in temperament and gesture, certainly, much of the sex act, to which it is a prelude; but unlike the image dance, its fundamental motive is not to represent cohabitation. One cannot always divide erotic dances into a reserved first movement and the execution of the act in a second movement. Often the boundary is extended so that moments of sexual intercourse are brought into the dance and combined artistically with it.

In general the great majority of the vegetation rites begin with human fertility—and how could it be otherwise? Yet in the individual dances we can scarcely be sure of the particular subject. Is this a dance for the propagation of the tribe or for abundance of food, which will also assure its continued existence? The question is vain. For fertility of food and fertility of men are identities in primitive mentality, and are no allegories. In every mystic consciousness such distinctions are blended into one, and any analysis here which proposed to keep them separate would carry modern Western patterns of thought into a foreign world to the detriment of our knowledge. Primitive men, who are rooted so inextricably in nature, who are bound by destiny so close to earth and sea and trees and animals, cannot place themselves on the outside in their activity or in their thought. Sowing and copulating, germinating and bearing, harvesting and delivering are under one law.

The fertility rites of the imageless ecstatic dance, however, do not take the outward motor act as a theme. They strive rather after a mystic taking possession of one sex by the enclosing and circling of the other.

An early example of this type is the Miolithic rock painting of Cogul in the province of Lérida in eastern Spain (Plate 1). It shows nine (!) dressed women dancing around a naked boy with a large but not ithyphallic membrum. From this group of nine women we glance across thousands of years to the ceremonial round dances of the nine shepherd girls around Krishna and of the nine muses around Apollo.

The Abbé Breuil and J. W. Hauer are wrong when they assume that the man of the Cogul painting is an idol. For the incident represented has enough parallels even in recent times to need no picture adduced as evidence. The Chaco Indians and the Bushmen, who may be originally related to the Grimaldi Negroids of the Rock of Cogul, dance even today, the women around a man; at marriages of the Wanyamwezi the bridegroom must dance in the center of a circle of women; and in Central Australia four men are encircled by eight women. Contrariwise, among the Negritos of the Philippines a girl stands within the circle of dancing men; among the East African Dinka and Moru a group of women are inside the circle. The parallel of the Bushmen and the Philippine Negritos shows especially clearly that this motif is a part of the basic culture; therefore it would have no connection with idols. The same motifs are preserved in Europe, especially in the Asturian and the Swedish folk dance. And when children dance in a ring, in the center stands the "prince" or the "princess" with her apron pulled over her head.

A Polynesian custom leads us somewhat further. In Hawaii the women sit in a circle around the dancing man; the dancer strikes his staff against that of each of the women until he has chosen the right one; he touches her with a ribbon or streamer. The motif of choosing partners in the Hawaiian dance recurs in the European folk dance; very clearly in the English *Babbity Bowster* and in the Bohemian *Šateček*—the boy encircled by the girls hands a piece of cloth to the girl of his choice. And in these dances we are reminded of a children's round dance in Germany in which the "prince" chooses his partner with the words: *"Springt sie auf die Kette, dass sie klingt"* (Break the chain, that it rings). The border line of the mimetic has been crossed.

At the close of a section dealing with fertility dances, we must not fail to mention the noteworthy fact that among several Indo-Chinese planter tribes no dancing is permitted between the sowing and the harvest. There may be a relation between this and the taboo of a large part of all primitive peoples against dancing before the harvest. Our own "dance season" from autumn to the end of winter can look back upon a long history.

Initiation Dances

If you ask an Auin Bushman what really happens at the puberty ceremonials, he will tell you, "We dance." In the initiation customs of all peoples the dances play an especially important part, whether the ceremony be one of circumcision, subincision of the membrum, piercing of the ear, filing of the teeth, or something else.

Questions as to the meaning of these dances must be answered differently. In America they seem to be a defense against demons: the evil spirits, which, as in all transitions from one stage of life to another, threaten the young girl at the critical period of puberty, must be chased away. From Africa comes another answer. The chief goal of the ceremonies is the attainment of a certain something which will bring the appropriate power to sexual activity, the power which will assure the tribe of healthy descendants. The means of achieving this power are only secondarily instruction and circumcision; they are primarily the dance—the dance to generate power, to prepare and transfer it to the maiden.

These purposes are served first of all by the abstract, entirely imageless circle dance of adults. The Australian men circle around the fire during the initiation, just as the East African Wayao do during the circumcision of boys. Even clearer: the California Indians dance around the newly matured girl and the Australians around the boys who are to be initiated. It is the same motif of magic transmission of power that we find in the Hellenic *thrónosis,* in which the members in a mystic dance circled around the new Cybele adepts, and—some time later—in that strange circle dance of the dean and the professors around the newly proclaimed doctor of theology, a dance which was part of the ritual of German universities as late as 1700.

The relationship, however, may also be reversed. In Dutch New Guinea the novices must run in a circle around the old men—apparently becoming adult by the magic encircling of adults.

A solo dance of those reaching puberty has the same goal of power. At her first menstruation, and often at each following one through the entire winter, the California Indian maiden must dance forwards and backwards swinging the rattle made of an animal's hoof before all her relatives and friends; when she tires, helpers jump to her aid, for the dance may not be interrupted. Whether she dances forwards or backwards, her face is turned always to the east.

We meet this last characteristic at initiations on other continents also, especially in Central Australia. The meaning of the mysterious custom is clarified by a similar usage of the Sotho in northwestern Transvaal: before the circumcision the novices sit with their faces turned toward the west, but after the circumcision, toward the east. Obviously it is the primitive idea here that the immatured boy dies to wake again as a man. The west is the direction of the dead (the early Miolithic Tardenois buried skulls facing the west), and the east is the direction of the rising sun, of birth, and regeneration. Motivated by this idea the Miwok, the Luiseño, and the Juaneño of California have the newly matured girl lie as quietly as possible in a pit on the floor of her hut for three or four days during the maturity ceremonies, while the dancers circle around her. The uninitiated, earlier person dies and awakes to new life after a few days of quiet in the grave. Among some tribes of California four is a sacred number; but the moon remains invisible for three days before it shows itself in the sky again as a tiny sickle; therefore throughout the world three is the number of lifeless days before the resurrection. Often in these California menstruation dances, as in the dances at the ripening of fruit, there are no restrictions on sexual intercourse. The meaning of the celebration is the transition to the age which shall bring an abundance of descendants to the people.

But whatever their content, the dances must continue without stopping. The girl of the California Indians at her first menstruation must dance ten entire nights without rest (in the last days she is so weak that two men must hold her up), and among the Atxuabo of Portuguese East Africa the women relieve one another, so that the dance is never interrupted. The theme is extended to initiations in general—as when a Pawnee Indian is exhausted in the dance, he is not eligible to be received into the circle of braves.

Marriage Dances

The dance is the center of wedding festivities; the ancient Germans referred to them simply as "the bridal round." Unless symbolical in character, the marriage dance is seldom to be distinguished from the ordinary round dance which has no special purpose. For like other marriage customs, it frequently arises merely from the idea that the bride and groom are in particular danger and that measures must be taken to protect them. Only three individual motifs need be considered here. The first is rooted in the idea of transition from one stage of life to another, the second in the idea of the transference of power, and the third in that of purification.

The transition motif is seen most clearly in the old German custom of "dancing the bride out"—out of the group of the unmarried. A double circle of dancers surrounds the bride, the girls on the inside, the young men on the outside. The groom forces his way through the circle, followed by the married women shrieking. The meaning is clear. Similar to this is the "dance of the old wives" at weddings in the district of Vorsfeld in Brunswick. Here the married women dance with their new sister. It would be impossible to think of a more effective rite for initiation into the state of matrimony, and here if anywhere is the place to speak of what van Gennep calls "passage rites." The bride may herself have to take possession of her new home. On the island of Ceram in the Moluccas, for example, the bride skips nine times around the ladder leading to the new house before she is allowed to climb up into it. Many examples of this kind of marriage dance are found in Germany, some of them even as late as the nineteenth century. In Bramstedt, near Geestemünde, every bride who came from outside the community had to drive around the Roland statue three times with all her dowry. The custom of circling three times around the fireplace or the pot-hook was common in western Germany. In Krems on the Danube every bridal couple danced three times around a certain linden tree and in Westphalia around an oak tree. To this order belongs also the Greek Orthodox custom of considering a wedding ceremony complete only after the officiating priest has solemnly led the young couple three times around the pulpit.

The second motif has been preserved in Java. At the wedding of an oldest son the grandparents, and perhaps even the great-grandparents, dance with fire-fans in their hands in order to transfer their strength to the young couple.

The third motif was the leaping together around the fire or through it. This motif is often falsely ascribed to the Indo-European civilizations, but actually it is older and more widespread.

The pagan Germanic custom of jumping through the warning bonfire, and the Christian Quadragesimal, Chain Festival, and St. John's Eve fire-jumping had another purpose, that of protecting the people from fever for a year. Indeed, this custom spread throughout Asia and the South Seas, and even to America. King Ahaz of Judah "made his son to pass through the fire, according to the abominations of the heathen." In curious contrast to this quotation, Ludwig Börne tells how the Rothschilds of Frankfurt, "as little fellows, stuck small lights in the ground at the feast of Hanuka and jumped back and forth over them in childish glee, as is the custom in Israel." Moreover, the dance of the children around the fire on the eve of the feast of Lag Beomer seems to be common in Palestine at the present time. At Bukaua in New Guinea today, a girl in her first period of menstruation, led by an attendant, jumps through a great fire. Even in so early a civilization as that of the Shasta Indians, the witch priestess is consecrated by a ceremony in which four men carry the young girl head first, with a peculiar left-footed gait, around a fire, or swing her ten times to and fro across the fire, as she hangs by her knees from a taut rope with her head downwards and turned towards the east. In England the motif of young girls jumping over candles was known as late as 1686. At the funeral rites of the Guahibo of Venezuela and Colombia, the medicine man leaps through the fire, blowing with all his might. The youths of the primitive Canella tribes in northeastern Brazil do the same. The old Nahua of Mexico had a custom quite similar to that of the Indo-Europeans. With clothes sewn together, their bridal couples danced seven times around the fire.

The general significance in the marriage rite is a charm for strength; the specific meaning is a charm for fertility. The important thing is the circumambulation; that which is danced around may vary. In Ille-et-Vilaine, for example, girls desirous of marrying dance thrice around a bramble of three branches, and in Auvergne the newly married couple dances three times around the sacred stones. To conclude the cycle, we might mention the dance of the Australians around the stone heap to bring rain.

The reverse was the custom in pagan Prussia: the bride was welcomed with fire on the threshold of her new home. A young man ran three times around her carriage bearing a torch and a jug of beer. Apparently this custom also belongs to a transition rite.

In connection with the fire dance, we must consider the torch dance, which was last performed at the court of the kings of Prussia as the concluding part of the wedding ceremonies and still lives in popular memory in one of Meyerbeer's compositions. Twelve ministers of state, carrying lighted wax torches, marched two by two, to the festive sound of trumpets and cymbals, in front of the bridal pair as they circled about, until after the last turn the couple was escorted to the bridal suite by all the princely personages. Here pages took the torches from the dignitaries and lighted up the bridal chamber. In this torch dance the first turn was made by the couple alone; next the bride invited the king to dance, and after that the other princes. Then the groom danced with the queen and with the princesses. A similar ceremony exists in German folk custom, the bride dancing first with the oldest relative and then with all the other men, and the groom with all the women. The corresponding ceremony at the French court was but slightly different; there the first dance was performed by the royal couple.

The torch dance has presumably two different roots: the token of esteem and the wedding torch. Up to the sixteenth century the honor of bearing the torch ahead in the dance belonged, except at weddings, to the highest princely dignitaries, and even in classical antiquity the wedding torch was a well-known symbol of life and love. In Greece and Rome a boy carrying a torch marched in front of bridal couples, and Eros himself was a torchbearer. A similar custom has survived among the Polabs, the early Slavic inhabitants of the Elbe basin. After the noon meal young maidens wearing wreaths dance with lighted candles.

73

Light or candle dances are not entirely restricted to these two motifs, for the torch may represent a variety of concepts. In the Holy Land men danced with torches at Yom Kippur in the women's court of the temple. In ancient China the plague was charmed away with torch dances. At one of their feasts the Eskimo of Alaska perform wild round dances with torches, and in East Africa the file of dancers approaches slowly with lighted candles. And finally all church processions belong to this cycle.

Funeral and Scalp Dances

Imageless funeral dances have almost the form of a round dance with a central point. Often this central point has only a remote connection with the occasion being celebrated. Dancers may encircle the shaman, the drummer, the figure of an animal, or a table of food; or they may dance directly around the corpse on the post, around the funeral pyre, around the bones of the deceased. In northern Europe the custom has been maintained down to the present: in the Faeroe Islands and in Denmark the coffin is danced around. The Dayak of Borneo have worked out a motif of their own. Before the tree destined for the coffin is cut down, a feeble-minded old slave woman must dance around it eight times. In many matriarchal cultures eight is the perfect number (Plate 16).

Often the meaning of all these circle dances may be the protection of the dead and the living from attacks of hostile spirits. But in the planter cultures the idea behind them is probably for the most part to form a tie between the living and the dead by means of the ecstatic dance and to make it possible for the soul of the dead man to find his ancestors. This is illustrated most clearly where the religion as a whole is rooted in ancestor worship, in China, and also in much earlier cultural levels: in California, among the Shasta, the Karok, and the Yurok, the dancers, who circle around a woman, begin after a while to dream of the dead. The mystic dance at the death of young girls has been preserved longest —even into our own civilization. In 1846 in Galilee at the burial of a

74

young girl, her playmates were seen to dance solemnly around the grave with their hands joined. In olden times in Holland the young girls used to sing:

> Up in heaven there is a dance,
> Alleluja.
> There all the little maidens dance,
> Benedicamus Domino,
> Alleluja, alleluja.
>
> This dance is for Amelia,
> Alleluja.
> We dance around, we little girls,
> Benedicamus Domino,
> Alleluja, alleluja.

The heaven dance of the maidens, to which the song alludes, is a theme of hymns of the Catholic Church.

An unusual example of the dance around the corpse is the skull or scalp dance of the late planter and head-hunter cultures. In this dance, too, the purpose is the creation of a bond between the living and the dead and the incorporation of the power of the former owner. This is accomplished at the close of the head hunt by a dance in a circle. Men and women paired off in a chain, or often only the women alone, are the dancers. I know only a single apparent exception to the usual circle form of this round. In the Sepik district of New Guinea the men and women who have stayed at home go in boats to meet the returning head hunters. As they dance in their boats, they sway their hips with knees flexed, wave the long oars, and poke their spears into the water. This is not in any sense a head charm, but rather a festive dance of welcome.

The dance around the skull of a captured enemy carries us into the war dances of the next section.

War Dances

The imageless war dance has no need of weapons. The Andamanese formerly executed their usual dance before a battle. From the sixteenth century we have an example of the war dance without weapons
among the Tupi Indians of Brazil. A copper engraving of the year 1593,
in a German edition of the *Historia Navigationis in Brasiliam,* shows
naked warriors without weapons in a circle dance moving to the left
around the chieftains, who amidst the rattling of gourds blow tobacco
smoke at them from long cigars. "Take unto yourselves the spirit of
strength," they call to them, "that you may conquer your enemies."

The war dance may even be taken over vicariously by the women
and girls remaining at home. Examples of this type of dance are
furnished by North America, Madagascar, and western Africa. The
power which they produce unceasingly day and night in the dance
travels telemagically to aid in the war and to protect the lives of the
men. It is the same idea which we have already met in the fertility
dances of the Mexican Tarahumara.

Though weapons are not commonly used in the imageless dance,
they are not necessarily excluded. The women of the Thompson Indians
of northwestern America used to point them in their telepathic dances
toward the land of the enemy. "If a squaw saw a hair or a piece of scalp
on the weapon, then she knew that her husband had killed an enemy.
But if a drop of blood appeared on it, she was certain he had been
killed." There is a very similar example of a telepathic weapon dance
in Australia which we shall discuss here, though it must be reckoned
with the image dances. While the men are away hunting, the women
and boys left behind draw pictures of animals in the sand, dance around
them, and stick spears into them. And once again modern Europe, in
this example untouched by thousands of years of development, ranges
itself alongside the Australians of the Early Stone Age: in the middle
of the eighteenth century the women of Normandy would dance

around the holy Menhir in order to bring about a safe return of their husbands from the sea.

This use of astral motifs in the dance is discussed in its proper place in another section. There it will be noticed that the sun and moon themes in individual cases seek an expression that is almost imageless.

THE IMAGE DANCE

General Characteristics

Two basic types stand at the beginning of dance history, as we have already demonstrated, just as two types stand at the beginning of cultural history in general. The one, formed and carried by an incorporeal, transcendental, introvert attitude of mind, is frequently directed against the body, although achieved by physical means. The other basic type is created by the extravert, who has faith in his senses and in sensual perceptions, in his strong limbs, and in the power to cause the metaphysical to become physical.

We may regard as the distinguishing religious action of the image dance the analogy or formation charm. The essence of things—this is its meaning—adheres to what may be perceived, to form and motion. It is sufficient, therefore, to reproduce in painting or in dancing the wished-for events, the victorious battle, the successful hunt, in order to be certain of them, in order to have control of them. *Similia similibus.*

But behind this mentality (how could it be otherwise?) is a predisposition for pantomime. Persons and peoples of strong sense perceptions are born actors; and this talent is lacking in those who are not sensual. The contrast is very striking in two tribes of the northeastern Gran Chaco district, described in detail in a recent work. The lively Chamacoco have more distinctive movements of expression than the phlegmatic Kaskiha. "The gestures for rejoicing and for love are numerous, as are those indicating people, animals, articles of food, or other objects.

The transition from gesture language to the dance becomes clear, particularly among the Chamacoco. One might say that these Indians give expression to every powerful mental stimulus in the dance, whether it is joy, a tender longing, a favor asked of the demons, or a bristling defense against them, indignation or mental anguish. . . . On the other hand, the dances of the Kaskiha are a hesitant, weary pacing to and fro."

What is important in this contrast is not the difference in behavior of two neighboring tribes, but rather the fact that the phlegmatic Kaskiha are planters, and the gesticulating Chamacoco are hunters. It is the heritage of roving, hunting peoples which produces the contents of this section of our book.

Extravert persons of the Chamacoco type do not simply wish to, they are forced to represent whatever a definite impulse directs. An investigator recounts that when the Marutse of South Africa on a journey began to sing a boat song, they drifted involuntarily into the motion of rowing—the idea was converted into action. From this point, perhaps, we may also trace the beginnings of those handicraft dances which are rooted in the harvest and hunting dances and have survived down to the present day in playful forms like the weaver dance, chimney-sweep dance, scissors-grinder dance, and so on. Out of the work grows the work song; the work song, apart from the work, forces the corresponding work motions to be imitated. Their transition to the work dance is intended magically to increase the output of work by a form charm.

Such image dances need not be less ecstatic than imageless dances—Wundt's contrast of ecstatic and pantomimic dances is not valid. In the section of this book devoted to the Middle Ages we shall speak of handicraft dances in which the dancers are incapable of stopping until they collapse, unconscious, at the end. The image dancer is possessed by his part. The person, the animal, the spirit, the god which he represents, takes control of his body. The dancer becomes the animal, the spirit, or the god. He must act like what he has become; he must work, give, bless.

But it is most important that in the image dance the frenzy be a part of the dance form. Not the fact of the dance, not attrition through over-exertion, or the uniformity of the rhythmic activity produces the ec-stasy, but rather the assumption of an outward form perceptible to the senses—a form not merely in the sense of pantomime, of ordered, imita-tive movement, but also in the sense of the observed or imagined char-acteristics of the being or object. The dancer is possessed when he depicts an event, and he is possessed when he disguises himself. The Javanese dancer who puts on a horse effigy has himself fed with stalks of grain (Plate 3). Among the ancient Germans the ecstasy began at the moment when the dancer put on an animal skin. The skin was sufficient to blot out the self and to admit the animal spirit. This ecstasy of mummery accompanies religious life through all the stages of its development to the belief in gods. Osiris, Dionysus, Siva, and the deities of old Mexico—God has descended upon the earth and becomes flesh in his dancer. And out of the deified dancer is formed retrogres-sively the beautiful conception of the dancing god who creates the world and keeps it in sacred order (Plate 10).

Animal Dances

Of everything capable of being imitated the animal must be a model of peculiar interest for the dancer. Ever in motion, on the search for food, in attack and in flight—and in this motion different in a thousand ways—related to human motor activity and yet strange enough to charm and to captivate again and again. And among all peoples the mobile image dancers, delighting in the senses, are those for whom the hunt propagates life and for whom the entirely sensual, affectionate activity with animal life is a matter of course.

Thus we comprehend the special position of the dance which imitates the animals. Among the Berg Damara of South Africa alone, one inves-tigator counted twenty-two different animal dances. Many tribes believe that they first learned to dance from the animals, from the bear, the stag, the eagle, the turkey. And they have learned well. Authorities on primitive peoples and especially on the African dwarfs admire the almost inconceivable talent for observation and representation of these people of Early Stone Age cultures.

They imitate not only every movement of the animals familiar to them, but they can reproduce deceptively even their footprints. It is the same talent that we admire in the striking faithfulness to reality of the Paleolithic rock paintings; it is the same talent that we admire in the ability of Bushmen to reproduce to the point of illusion on the single, weak-toned fiber chord of the musical bow with the little rod, the gaits of the native animal world. A few examples follow.

TURTLE DANCES. At the initiation of the Andamanese the dancer bends down so far that his back is almost in a horizontal position. His hands are raised to the nape of his neck and two bundles of leaves rest on his back. In time with the stamping board—about 144 beats to the minute—he hops on both feet with knees flexed. After every eight jumps, approximately, he brings his hands forward, downward, and back, and sweeps the ground next to his feet vigorously with his bundles of leaves, then places them again in the first position. After fifteen or thirty seconds, he rests for a time. It has been assumed that this is an imitation of the swimming turtle.

The women dancers of the Katherine and Victoria River districts of the Northern Territory of Australia hop in a straight line forwards and backwards, heels together and toes pointed outward. They jerk their bodies forwards and let their thigh muscles knock together. The trail which they leave behind in the sand is said to be like that of the mother turtle, which comes on land to lay its eggs.

The boys of Samoa crawl around the ground with their heads down until somebody pushes them over. Then they lie on their backs and move all four limbs in the air.

The RHINOCEROS BIRD DANCE of New Ireland, where the totem is the rhinoceros bird. The dancers range themselves by twos in a long row.

Each one holds in his mouth a carved and painted head of a rhinoceros bird; his hands are generally folded over his back. The rhinoceros bird is a rather shy patron who consumes the fruits that he likes in the quiet of the treetops, but never becomes careless of his own safety and moves his head continually in all directions to assure himself that there is no enemy at hand. Should an enemy appear, he utters a peculiar cry and with a loud flapping of his wings flies away. The dancers represent all these actions very realistically. They bend their heads to right and left, forwards and backwards; they keep one eye half closed and the other fixed in a certain direction; they execute each movement deliberately and calmly, quite as the bird itself does it. At the end they utter the cry and imitate the flapping of the wings.

The TREE-CREEPER DANCE of the Maidu of California. About a dozen men come from the dressing room, move counter-clockwise around the fire, jump first to one side and then to the other, and swing their hands left and right. After one time around they continue the circle until the first dancer is at the door and the others are standing behind him, facing the fire. In this position they dance for a while, moving their hands, with the palms downward, slowly up and down in front of their bodies and flexing their arms sharply. Suddenly when the first dancer cries out "Yo hohi!" all of them dance again, and raise and lower their elbows, as if they were flapping their wings.

The BUTTERFLY DANCE of the village maiden of Samoa. "She sees a butterfly, dances toward it, catches it, and hides it in her hands. Opening her hands a little, she looks to see whether it is really there; then it escapes and the chase begins anew. The colorful game continues and grows more frenzied. Sometimes she falls on her knees, sometimes she jumps up and dashes away, fluttering like the butterfly itself. Then finally she cowers down, bending her knees and turning in a circle in so doing."

The dance of the Samoan maiden is the common property of all the Japanese dancers. They, too, play the same dual role. Now they are butterflies delicately fluttering their wings; now captivated observers and hunters reaching out in vain for their prey. Is it coincidence, or is it not rather a heritage of the ancient Indian dance art which Japan as much as Polynesia has taken over? Do not the striking hand dances of Polynesia point clearly to the artistic kingdom of Brahma and Buddha?

The SEAL DANCE of the Yahgan of Tierra del Fuego. The men in a squatting position rock to and fro, sniff to right and left, scratch themselves on the chest and under the arms, and grunt.

MOUNTAIN COCK MATING. In the *Nachsteigen* of the *Schuhplattler,* "the young man does not simply dance with his maid, but with wooing movements, clicking his tongue, hissing, and clapping his hands, he jumps along behind her or, if space is lacking, next to her, stamps on the floor, takes a couple of leaps, or perhaps even turns a somersault. Finally, with his arms outspread or hanging close to the ground, he rushes towards his partner or leaps suddenly in a curve towards her, after he has struck the ground hard with one or both hands."

Four ideas motivate the animal dance. The first is the hunting charm. To imitate edible animals in their distinctive character and gait, in their crying, howling, yelling, and roaring means to win power over them, to entice them into the net or trap or within shooting range. Fishes, birds, bears, buffaloes, kangaroos, turtles, and other animals that are hunted may all be brought to the hunter by the animal dance, just as the Paleolithic painter brought the animals to his cave by making lifelike reproductions on the walls. Other methods are used for the same charm. After the hunt—this is the second idea—the soul of the slain animal is propitiated in the dance.

The third idea: certain animals have in their own right magic power, have control over rain and sunshine. To imitate them in their distinctive characteristics means taking and rendering useful their magic power.

The fourth idea: the animal dance brings about an increase of useful animals, especially when it represents their mating. The Kalahari Bush-men give an inimitable picture of the antelope buck making the most comical leaps before the female, and the Papua depict the wooing of two birds. Here the basic motive is never a wish to "put on a show."

Mating is not the only theme that is represented in pantomime. Countless other incidents from animal life are danced: animal fights, tigers breaking into a sheep corral, turtles laying eggs, the baby rhinoceros bird being fed by the older birds, woodpeckers and monkeys climbing trees—"all strictly in time with the accompanying music."

Within a totemistic world of ideas, the dance must serve to increase not only the edible animals, but often enough those animals in particular that are taboo as food. For in totemistic cultures the individual groups of men feel that they are related by blood and bound by destiny to definite animal types. When these animals flourish, their own well-being is assured, and to promote the life of the animals becomes a matter of human existence pure and simple. Such totemistic animal dances are executed especially at boys' initiations. Only in the dance is the mystic union between man and animal consummated.

A counterpart from the Early Stone Age of Europe has been found in the cave of Tuc d'Audubert (Département Ariège in France) with delineations of Franco-Cantabrian style. The heel-prints of young people make a circle in the ground; it is supposed that these are the tracks of boys and girls. Five outgoing tracks lead to phalli made of clay, and on the walls are pictures of bisons jumping. Thus through good fortune there is preserved for us information about an initiation dance in which the novices renounce human motion and reproduce by walking on their heels the tracks of the bison.

It may be said that in general within the basic cultures the animal dance belongs to the pygmies and within the tribal cultures to those peoples of the South Seas designated as patriarchal and totemistic. Where animal dances are found in fully developed matriarchal cultures, they are to be regarded as vestiges of an earlier cultural stage.

Animal dances are executed almost exclusively by men. Women take part very rarely, probably only when female animals, or those which for any particular reason are allegorically close to the woman, are to be portrayed. In this category belong the dance of the egg-laying turtle in northern Australia, the grasshopper dance at the initiation of girls among the Atxuabo of East Africa, and the cattle dance of the Nilotic Dinka. The girls' dances of Malay in imitation of the animals belong in the category of late art dances.

Finally the animal dance comes to children. And it has been preserved by them in Europe down to the present day—in the "Marmot," "Bunny in the ditch," "Wolf and Geese," and in the cat and mouse game in a circle, which is reflected in the rabbit spirit dance of the Šipaya of northern Brazil. "The dancers, joining hands, formed . . . a narrow circle around the rabbit spirit, Nakurú, who sought in vain to escape from the circle by trying to slip through their hands. Finally with great adroitness he darted through and escaped into the hut amid the laughter of all."

And let us not forget that like the *aceridanza,* the fox-round of the Basques, the *fox trot* is also an animal dance.

From these examples we may see that it has been the fate of the animal dance to grow continually away from nature. The urge to compose the movements into a stylized dance, therefore to make them less real, has taken more and more of the natural from the steps and gestures. All too quickly the duck walk becomes a simple squatting step; the remarkable hither and thither movement of the tree-creeper becomes a regular jumping from left to right; the head motion of the turkey, a rhythmic throwing back of the neck; and the scratching of chickens, an ordinary shuffle of the foot. Besides, there is a gradual incursion of the animal dances into celebrations of the most varied kinds, especially into fertility rites of all forms. Here the dance must lose so much that it is often difficult for us to find justification for applying the name of an animal to the dance.

On the other hand, perhaps motions of purely individual motor origin have been considered mimetic and animal-like and given a new interpretation. If a definite raising and bending of the arms in the dance of the Barundi and the Dinka women is understood as representing the horns of cattle, we might assume that the natural expression of a strong, feminine impulse to movement was original and that the idea of horns was adopted later. Nevertheless, in the drawings on Egyptian vases of the fourth millennium the women dancers round their arms above their heads like handles, so that the tips of their fingers touch their shoulders. These are the same handle-like cow horns which appear in every picture of the goddess Hathor. And during the entire period of the Old Kingdom the dancers have the same pose. The ancient Egyptians and the Negroes of northeastern Africa, however, have more than one cultural relationship. Yet L. Séchan may not be wrong in thinking of the arm gesture in old Greek funeral dances as originating in a stylization of hair plucking.

There are therefore in the animal dance exactly the same relationships which are familiar in the history of the decoration: have we to deal with the abstraction and geometrization of an animal theme or with the zoomorphic naturalization of an abstract and geometric theme?

These questions, too, probably belong to those which cannot be answered because there is no strict "either-or."

Fertility Dances

The extinct Tasmanians, who are counted among the Late Basic cultures, had a thunderstorm charm of an obvious kind: they threw themselves down, rolled on their bodies, and struck the ground with their hands and feet. Thus lightning and thunder are imitated with their own bodies and by analogy are brought into being, and at the same time power is transmitted out of this ecstatic tension into the earth and subjugates it. For stamping is to primitive man an act of taking possession—in the myth of the creation of the Uitoto of Colombia, the "father" took the "ground" into his "possession and stamped on it repeatedly." And when the idea of possession degenerates, stamping becomes an act of exorcism. The women of the Kol of Hindustan bend to the earth in their dance and strike it with their hands.

The old Tasmanian thunderstorm dance lives today in a certain sense in the Germanic *Siebensprung*. Seven times the ground is struck, with both feet, both knees, both elbows, and the forehead. In the Heligoland version a large circle of dancers changes direction every four beats. After the eighth beat comes an interpolation with two pauses; at the first eight beats it is brought in only once and the dancers stamp with one foot; after each succeeding eight beats, it is brought in twice and the dancers stamp first on one foot, then on the other; and so on. They sing in accompaniment: *"Det es jan mol—det es tau mol—det es sében mol"* (that is once, that is twice, that is seven times).

Two prominent scholars regard the *Siebensprung* as a new "discovery," not to be dated before 1732, and see in it a mockery of the old-fashioned bowing of the nobleman. Rationalism is not always a trustworthy counselor. They bow—well and good. But what German nobleman stamps before his lady? And this fashionable motif of mocking a custom is supposed not to have chosen, as one would have to grant, the frame of a minuet—though the minuet has been taken over often enough into the folk dance—but rather that of the very ancient round? It is supposed to link up with the venerable seven, the number of the cult? It is supposed to win popularity over a large territory, to endure for two hundred years, and to determine the dance through the period of fertility worries? A dance, which at Pomeranian harvests is danced, very characteristically of the Stone Age, only by men—such a dance is supposed to mock the conduct of men before the other sex?

To aid in dancing the wind mimetically, the purely totemistic Arunta of Central Australia wave rubber branches in rhythm. An advanced dance culture on the other hand will represent at the same time the effect of the wind and thus extend and deepen the originally restricted motif. On a wall painting of the twelfth dynasty of the Middle Kingdom at Beni Hassan in southern Egypt (c. 1900 B. C.), three women

86

dancers do a pantomime entitled in hieroglyphics "The Wind." One, in upright position, seems to be waving her outstretched arm above the trees, the second is bending underneath this arm like a palm, the third like a pliant reed is making a "bridge"—a weather charm in a non-magic art form which must have been preceded at some time by a genuine form. Strangely enough, almost four thousand years later, in the winter of 1849–50, when Gustave Flaubert was traveling in Egypt he could write thus to Louis Bouilhet of dancers disguised as women: "Sometimes they throw themselves to the ground on their backs, like a woman lying down, and with a movement of the hips get up again quite like a tree which straightens when the wind has passed by."

In calling up the beneficent forces of nature, in the enchanting of storm, wind, and rain, the dancer keeps to the general, to the super-human. It is relatively seldom that he represents his own activity in connection with food gathering and planting. To be sure, the Maidu of California dance the gathering of acorns, and the people of the Torres Islands the bringing in of crabs; the ancient Mexicans represent catching fish and gathering roots; and the Kai of New Guinea execute their fruit harvest in the dance. But these are exceptions, almost. Is the reason that in contrast to the hunt, so often and so enthusiastically depicted, the business of gathering and planting was at the beginning in the hands of women, while the mimetic dance belonged to the men? It is a fact that most reproductions of planting stem from the actual peasant cultures, in which indeed the man has taken over the principal work in the fields. An example, the English bean-planting *Morris Dance,* is discussed in Chapter 7.

More frequent and much closer to the nature of primitive thought is the identification of the dancer not with the planter, but with what is planted. The leap dance presents one of the most popular motifs. The higher the leap, the taller the corn will grow. This idea exists in the German sower tradition, as well as in the English, the Bohemian, and the Bulgarian. From it we may understand why the Kayan of Borneo at their sowing festivals bring the high leap of an entirely different dance world into the decidedly calm dance world of Indonesia, and why, according to reports we have, the Moluccas do the same. Similarly in the dances of old Mexico the people used to lift their children high to make them grow, and the Kurnai of southeastern Australia do it at the present day.

The stride seems also to be a motif of growth. The best evidence for this statement is its use at harvest dances and dances for renewal of life, which have already been discussed. Until a short time ago, in the *Langaus* at marriages in Baden "such long strides had to be made that the dancers almost flew."

Accordingly, it is scarcely to be doubted that the rare motif of the stilt dance, vestiges of which occur in the play of our own children, aims at nothing other than fertility. This dance may be found in Africa, among the Negroes of western Cameroon, and among the western Akamba and Makonde; and in the South Seas, among the Maori of New Zealand. It appears again in present-day Japan and in classical Greece, with the satyrs and fauns of the drama. In Japan it is used, like the Indonesian leap dance, at field festivals; and the other occasions of which we have any information are just as close to the fertility idea: in Cameroon, at full-moon and funeral festivals; among the Makonde, at initiations. The meaning of the satyr dances is clear.

The arch dance as a fertility rite is discussed on page 162.

But for the most part, in the realm of fertility also, man creates according to his own likeness and expands his own sex life into cosmic incidents.

Human fertility dances in their purest form are drawn from two different phases of sexual intercourse: the meeting and wooing, and the act itself.

In Java the man dancer is supposed in former times to have kissed his partner, a strange report which is confirmed by a custom of the Blackfoot Indians. The Blackfoot woman throws kisses to the man of her choice and dances toward him. When they are together, somebody places a piece of cloth over their heads, under cover of which they kiss each other as they dance along between the rows of men and women. The Dakota even kiss one another openly, and the Akamba of East Africa at least press their cheeks together.

The kiss has played a part even in the late European dance—and not only in the folk dance. A kiss before and after the dance was the usual custom in the fifteenth and sixteenth centuries, and a little "caressing" during the dance was not forbidden—though the moralizers did inveigh against "licking."

Earlier cultures form the motif in other ways. When Preuss watched the Uitoto of Colombia dancing, "each man was armed with a long, thick stick, to almost every one of which the people of the other town had fastened a knee-rattle. With this they strike rhythmically on the ground (*harikina dutai*) 'he strikes quickly'; at every stroke the women respond with a cry." We are reminded of the once obscene dance of the Uzume priestess of Japan who stands on a tub turned upside down and knocks on it ten times with a pole. Each time she strikes the tub she utters a long-drawn-out cry, "Oh! oh! oh!"

The motif is even more apparent among the Watchandi of western Australia. In the middle of spring they begin to "celebrate their great, semi-religious Caaro festival in preparation for the important duty of producing offspring. . . . On the evening of the festival the women and children withdraw from the company of the men . . . and now the latter may not look upon a woman until the close of the ceremony. . . . Those left behind dig a large hole in the earth. . . . Crying out and singing they dance around the hole and continue doing so throughout the night. . . . Every figure of the dances, every movement, and the refrain of all their songs are intended to kindle their passion. The hole is dug and decorated with bushes in such a way as to resemble the sex parts of a woman. In the dance they carry in front of them a spear to represent a phallus." Circling around the ditch, they poke the spear inside as a symbol of generative power, and sing continually, "not the pit, not the pit, not the pit, but the vulva!"

Spear and arrow, because of their shape and their function of piercing, are unmistakable phallic dance attributes—Eros, like Kama, the Hindu god of love, is an archer. The Baining of the Gazelle Peninsula take an ornamented spear (*vingal*), beneath which projects at an acute angle the stub of a branch covered with the penis capsule, and pull it through two folds cut into the skin of the back so that the penis part protrudes between the legs. In other instances the phallic character of the dance spear is less exaggerated but apparent enough. When the men and women of the Usíai of the Admiralty Islands do a circle dance, the men hold spears, but the women hold mother-of-pearl shells, the symbol of the vulva. In this dance only, the men carry a penis capsule, the familiar symbol of the patriarchal totem culture. In this the cultural level to which the dance belongs can be determined. The phallic signifi-cance of the weapon, then, accounts for the fact that the Somal dances with a spear at his own wedding, and perhaps also that the Shasta of California do a war dance at the initiation of girls.

Though the sex act is, to be sure, never really completed on the dance place, the various phases of the act are depicted here and there very fan-tastically. It would be difficult to imagine the motions of onanism and cohabitation, the suggestion of enormous sexual organs, and the ex-posure of their own, the frenzied shrieking of obscene words, and the chants of unprintable verses which the dancers of both sexes in the various cultures alone or in couples bring to their dances.

Not long ago Couchoud was able to point out a strange parallel with the exhibition theme in Greek and Japanese mythology. Amaterasu, the Japanese goddess of the sun and fields, is insulted by her brother and withdraws into a cave. Darkness and sterility reign upon the earth. The gods hold a conclave and finally decide to send forth the goddess Ama-no-Uzume. She ties up her hair with creeping plants, seizes a bunch of bamboo leaves, and climbs upon a tub that is turned upside down. She stamps on it in dance, and amid the resounding laughter of the gods who are standing around her, uncovers her breasts and privy parts. Curious about what is happening, Amaterasu steps from the cave. The entrance is quickly sealed behind her, and the sun shines once more.

There is the same motif in ancient Greece. Demeter, goddess of the fields, incensed over the abduction of her daughter Persephone, which has banished growth from the earth, leaves the sky and is not placated until Baubo jokes with her and shows her his sex parts. Both incidents are to be found in late rituals, in the final act of the Hellenic mysteries, and in degenerate form in the autumnal full-moon dances of the Sarume priestesses of Japan. In drawing this parallel, Couchoud recognizes that the myth in essence is a vegetation charm. The French scholar might have added a third example to his comparison. An Egyptian myth, recently published, tells how one time the sun god (the Japanese Amaterasu is also a sun divinity) became angered and lay on his back in solitude for a whole day until his daughter Hathor found him and showed him her privy parts. The great god had to laugh, and returned into the world.

Even in the unmythical present, disrobing dances play an extensive part in increasing fertility. Negresses dance at the harvest festival "naked and intoxicated around the stacks of wood"; on the Isle of Yap dancing women must show their bodies by swinging their grass skirts; women of New Caledonia after a birth lift their skirts high in the dance; and Indian women fold their dresses in such a way that when they are dancing only their sex parts are visible. And in the Middle Ages in Germany, in a genuine peasant dance (the artistically indiscreet spinning of the girls was a favorite motif), dresses were supposed to fly.

Yet it will not always be easy to decide whether the allegory is specifically that the bosom of the earth shall open to receive the new seed, or whether it is intended as a defense in general against hostile powers. In letters written on his Nubian journey, Gustave Flaubert throws light upon the "defense" motif: Coptic monks swim to his Nile ship to beg alms, and immediately, *pour chasser les moines chrétiens* (to chase away the Christian monks), one of the Mohammedan boatsmen takes off his clothes, dances, and turns up his backside at them.

A good example of the degeneration of Stone Age motifs in our civilization is the ceremony of child baptism in the Eifel, which may be ranged alongside the customs described above. This is a matriarchal institution "to which men are not admitted, but are made sport of, especially the father of the child. . . . The women pick up their skirts at the hem in criss-cross fashion, jump around in a circle and sing." This motif of picking up the skirt at the hem is nothing other than exhibition degenerated.

In this form it has been maintained in the higher civilizations of Europe. In the early period of ancient Greece it appears thus, and is particularly striking and characteristic because the skirts of the temple dancers did not reach the knees and the upper parts of their bodies were entirely bare. The final form of its degeneration is the affected rococo fashion of taking up the skirt.

The male dancer on his side exaggerates the natural potency by putting on a phallus, frequently of gigantic size, wound of bast or carved. Almost every Dionysian dancer of Greece attached one to his body. Among the present-day survivals of the old custom many have been hushed up out of prudery; yet the phallic dances of the Altai Turks and those of the Cobéua of northwestern Brazil have been especially well described. To illustrate, we quote from a report of the Cobéua:

"The dancers have large phalli made of bast with testicles of red cones from the low-hanging trees, which they hold close to their bodies with both hands. Stamping with the right foot and singing, they dance at first in double quick time, one behind another, with the upper parts of their bodies bent forwards. Suddenly they jump wildly along with violent coitus motions and loud groans of '*ai (ye)—ai (ye)—ai (ye)*'. . . . Thus they carry the fertility into every corner of the houses, to the edge of the wood, to the nearby fields; they jump among the women, young and old, who disperse shrieking and laughing; they knock the phalli one against another. . . ."

The final step of the fertility idea is the hermaphroditic dance, in which the woman herself ties on a phallus. This dance, too, survives in the advanced civilization of Greece, in the festival of Artemis Korythalia.

Examples from primitive cultures are furnished by the Nuba of north-eastern Africa and again by the Altai Turks. In the case of the latter the phallus is even inserted into the vagina of the dance partner.

White men have often become excited over the "shamelessness" of such dances. But the words which they use to describe their reactions— "indecent," "unbridled," "obscene"—are not objective. For to the primitives it is not a matter of sensation and pleasure, but of life and unity with nature.

In Negro Africa, to be sure, the mimetic form of the mating dances seems to have lost all religious sanctification and to have become an out and out dance of lust. As an example we shall cite the nightly dances of the Suaheli women, in which the young men look on and criticize the sexual artistry of each dancer. "The whole thing is only a presentation of the functions of the female in coitus." How different are the dances of the ancient Jewish maidens, which are described thus in the Talmud: "There were no other holidays for Israel like the fifteenth of Ab and the Day of Atonement, on which the daughters of Jerusalem went out in white dresses which were borrowed, so that no one need be ashamed if she had none (!). And the daughters of Jerusalem went forth and danced in the vineyards. And what spake they? Youth; lift up thine eyes and behold her whom thou hast chosen!"

At last the erotic dance dies away in the solo performances of professional and in no wise distinguished dancers whose chief performance is the "belly dance."

Does this form of the fertility dance, we may ask ourselves, belong in the category of the mimetic dance? Are there not in this dance so many ecstatic moments, so much of the exhilarative and frenzied that we ought rather to place it among those dances which are a mixture of imitative and non-imitative ecstatic motifs? It is an open question. No answer would be satisfactory, except that in respect to the phenomena of life no classification, no matter how complete, is ever anything more than a lode star for knowledge as it gropes its way ahead.

Courtship has enriched the dance more than the sex act. Its motifs still exist in the social dances of the present time.

Within the realm of these dances the oldest theme is probably that of a row of men and a row of women moving towards one another without quite coming together. There are examples even in Australian culture. When it is individualized and reinforced mimetically, it may become a group wooing or robber dance. In the Gilbert Islands of Micronesia two men rush upon a woman and fetch her to their side—the European "robbers and princess"; or the reverse, two women go over to the men's side and with the fly brush pick one man and sit down by him. Togo has a dance game that is quite similar: the men sit in a semi-circle, while the women stand in a line at the open side and clap their hands; one or two men keep dancing in the direction of the women, or one or two women, in the direction of the men. The same dance is done by the Eskimo, the Moapa of North America, the Argentine (*el palito*), and the Nahua of old Mexico in the front court of the Huitzilopochtle temple: one woman, hand in hand with two men, or the reverse. In view of the extraordinarily protective nature of all dances, I cannot resist thinking of this motif as a survival of early group marriage, particularly of polyandry.

The strange custom of this two-one group is to be found also in Europe. It is the theme of early Greek satyr dances which are depicted on vases of the sixth century B. C. We meet it in the folk dances of all countries, in the *Dreisteyrer* of the Alpine peoples, in the *Vingåkersdans* of Sweden, in the Norwegian *Krossadans med tri,* in the *galletta* of the Reno valley and of Romagna in Italy, in the Asturian *pericote,* in the whirl dances of Hungarian peasants, and in the *hopák* of the Ukraine. We shall find it again in the western European society dance, from the courtly dance of the Middle Ages through the *basse danse* down to the *ecossaise-triolet.*

Down to our own civilization a second form of the courtship dance has also been preserved, the "Prude." In New Ireland (North Melanesia) the masked males dance trippingly toward the masked female, withdraw, approach once again, seek to win favor and to oust their rivals; the female appears cool to their advances, turns her back toward one, pushes another roughly aside, but finally accepts one of the masked males and takes the consequences, while the others withdraw. A description of the Wadegerenko of East Africa is similar: The woman is very calm and her features are immobile; with a lighted cigarette in her mouth and her hands behind her, she looks on as the men in turn try to win her favor. The same motif exists in the year 1500 in the German *Schmollertanz* and even down to the present day in the *Hierig* of Appenzell.

At this point we are on the threshold of the important *couple dance:* the transition to the couple dance is the necessary final step in the mimetic reproduction of courting. The usual motif is the dance around the girl by the lover. One has the impression that this motif is directly connected with the ancient theme of the girl encircled by the chorus. A growing feeling of individualism together with a stronger sense of reality would then have substituted the individual lover for the general, more abstract chorus. The mimetic quality is indeed still insignificant when among the Pueblo Indians the encircled woman spins like a top. Since Mexico lies on the outer border of the territory in which this motif is to be found, we must suppose that we have in that country the oldest form. In Asia, which we may regard as a middle ground, the situation is clearer, more direct, and more interesting. The woman dancer still moves only in one place and lets the man carry the action. The Kundur of the Caucasus sings as he jumps around his girl, who never moves from her place. But out of the passivity of the *stand dance* may develop the resolute, fashionable reserve of the well-bred woman: on the island of Seran in the Molucca group it is the girls of highest class who call out the man; while he dances around them, they cast their eyes to the ground, bob lightly from the knees, and move one or the other arm rhythmically; and it is theirs to decide when the dance shall be over. Finally the girl plays her part—dramatically, too: in the *lezghinka,* the dance of the Lezghians which has conquered almost the entire region of the Caucasus and of which there are counterparts on the coast of Upper Guinea in western Africa, the man and woman circle around each other, now approaching, now withdrawing, now calmly, now excitedly. Attack and flight, beckoning and retreat alternate, as in the words of the poet:

Unto thee did I spring: then fledst thou back from my bound;
And towards me waved thy fleeing, flying tresses round!
Away from thee did I spring, and from thy snaky tresses:
Then stoodst thou there half-turned, and in thine eye caresses.

Nietzsche, *Thus Spake Zarathustra*. The Second Dance Song.

The dance of the *zamacueca* or *cueca* among the Chile Indians is witness that the man on such occasions does not become the mere plaything of the woman. The male dancer whose partner turns her back on him must have the presence of mind to whirl about at the same moment or he becomes the laughing-stock of the crowd.

In Greek antiquity—at least in the realm of Dionysus—and even in contemporary Europe this dance of courtship and coquetry may be found. As danced on the coast of the North Sea in Germany, it was somewhat heavy and wooden. The dancer of East Frisia used to labor with wild movements of the legs in front of his partner, who would stand motionless and sing: "Upon my word :/: stand still!" And he would answer, "Why should I stand still? What harm have I done to you?" After a time he would stand still and it was the girl's turn to dance before him. But the best performances of the courtship dances in Europe are those of the Spaniards, the southern Germans of the Alpine districts, the Russians, the Poles, and the Hungarians.

The Hungarian forms are especially close to the Caucasian, particularly the tease dance (*csalogatás*) at the hay making and the *magyar kör*, from which the better-known *csárdás* (innkeeper) was derived scarcely a hundred years ago. In structure it is divided into two parts: the slow dance of the men in a circle, *lassu*, and the violent couple dance, *friss;* in execution, the spurs beat out a sharp rhythm, the feet are turned inwards and outwards, and they dance with a proud, martial air and lofty zeal. "Steps, turns, movements, attitudes," wrote a connoisseur a hundred years ago, "are arbitrary and left to the genius and taste of the dancers. They do not walk in regular, measured steps, one, two, three, four as in the minuet; it is not the monotonous turning about of the waltz; it is a free dance, which may be enlivened by any sort of idea. The people never make stupid faces as when they dance the minuet or waltz, and that is natural; you never see livelier, more spirited countenances than you do in the Hungarian dance, and that is again quite natural, for the Hungarian dance is poetry, the waltz and the minuet are mechanical occupations. The mechanic can make an automaton that could dance the minuet superbly and the waltz divinely, but he never could make one that could do the Hungarian dance."

The Alpine form of the courtship dance, the *Schuhplattler* of the southern Bavarians, the Tirolese, and the Salzburgers, with all its suppleness emphasizes power more than the Hungarian dances.

"It is a Ländler only for a couple of steps. The girl with modestly lowered eyes continues to turn quietly; the boy meanwhile circles around her and in every possible manner expresses his joy and his love in pantomime. He stamps his feet, slaps his thighs, his knees, and the heels of his shoes in time with the music, does a somersault, too, perhaps, or turns a few cartwheels. He jumps over the girl or lets her whirl under his arm, then in turn whirls under hers. But only rarely does he take her into his arms, though he is ardent when he does. At the last, if he wishes to observe the time-honored tradition and has strength enough for it, he swings her into the air, high over his head and lets her flutter gracefully down again. This is wooing in gestures."

Its composition is usually as follows:

Vorspiel: a prelude in which the couples swing their arms forward and backward for four beats.

Einlaufer: the boys slap themselves six times:

  1. on the right thigh with the right hand

2. on the left thigh with the left hand
3. on the right thigh with the right hand
4. on the left thigh with the left hand
5. on either foot with the right hand
6. on the left thigh with the left hand.

Then they jump and fall to their knees while the girls spin in their places.

Ländler: a slow waltz in couples.

Nachsteigen: pantomimic courtship dance (mountain cock mating).

Plattler: as the boys slap themselves the girls spin in a continual circular movement.

Auslaufer: like the *Plattler*, with the boys and girls changing direction only at the end as they come together again.

Nachsteigen.

Ländler.

Schlussfigur: at the close, lifting of the girl and falling to the knees.

In the individual dances there are local variations.

Emphasizing grace of motion more than muscular power and owing far more to an old, advanced culture than to prehistoric or primitive tradition, the courtship dance of Spain reaches a perfection which never fails to enchant the spectator anew. The *fandango* with its variations, the *malagueña*, the *rondeña*, the *granadina*, or the *murciana*, which came into Europe only in the course of the seventeenth century, acknowledges its origin in the *Reinos de las Indias* of the American Indians. But even if this attribution is justified, it has nevertheless a heritage of two thousand years on Spanish soil, going back to the Phoenicians, which aided in its formation. In the provocative rhythm of the castanets

in which 3/8 and 3/4 time are mixed with such charm, the courtship dance rushes on deliriously.

"The fandango is always danced by only two persons, who never touch each other even with the hand. But when one sees how they challenge each other, now moving away, now approaching again; how the woman at the moment when she seems about to surrender, slips suddenly away from the victor with renewed vivacity; how he pursues her, then she, him; how in all their glances, gestures, and positions they express the various emotions which enflame them both; when one sees all this, one cannot help confessing with a blush that this dance describes Cytherea's battles as truly as the final cannonade of a fireworks display describes the actual thunder of cannons before a besieged fortress."

Casanova used the most fiery words to give a picture of the *fandango* which he saw in Madrid in 1767. "Each couple, man and woman," he writes, "never move more than three steps as they click their castanets with the music of the orchestra. They take a thousand attitudes, make a thousand gestures so lascivious that nothing can compare with them. This dance is the expression of love from beginning to end, from the sigh of desire to the ecstasy of enjoyment. It seemed to me impossible that after such a dance the girl could refuse anything to her partner."

In the nineteenth century it was scarcely danced any more; it was entirely too exuberant and sensual. The *jota* in the north, the *sevillana*, and the *bolero*, supposedly "discovered" by the dancer Zerezo in 1780, take its place. The *bolero*, executed in 2/4 or 3/4 time with castanets, guitar, and tambourine, also depicts the woman slipping away, approaching, and escaping again, but the violence of the *fandango* is here calmed to a gentle flattery; it is the "triumph of tenderness."

Let us conclude the series of examples from Europe with the *furlana*, the folk dance of Venice. It is a wild courtship dance in 6/8 time with one or two couples, in which men and women approach and withdraw, touch and let go each other's hands and feet, wave and whirl their arms —similar to the *tarantella* but more ragged and irregular. "No national dance is more violent," says Casanova. The great adventurer danced it in 1775; indeed, Ungarelli in 1894 lists it among the living dances. The statement that it was danced only until 1760 is therefore incorrect.

99

It is in no wise necessary that the couples who are mystically united in the sex dance or the courtship dance be actually a man and a woman. In many cases a man plays the part of the woman. A well-known instance is, of course, the masquerade of the European Mardi Gras. Its dissemination outside of Europe indicates a cultural stage which extends essentially farther back than that of the actual man-woman dance. At the mandioca-beer festival of the Brazilian Parecí-Cabixí a man represents the wife of the snake demon, and in the Australian subincision festival, a man plays the ancestress of the tribe. In earlier cultures the man is disguised as the woman lover; often it is a young man of feminine appearance with false hair and a false bosom, with neck pearls, bracelets, and feminine adornment in his nose and ears. Among the Tadjik of the Pamir the remarkable couple "first do the usual rhythmical figure dances without touching each other. Gradually the man makes various attempts to draw closer, which result in his wife's running away. She jumps up among the spectators on the terrace, hides herself usually beside one of the most distinguished guests, kissing him and putting her arms around him. The man meanwhile looks desperately for his wife, finally finds her in the arms of another—and receives a tip."

There are countless examples. The ancient custom is maintained in the advanced cultures of America, in Guatemala and in old Mexico, where dancing and singing "in the manner of a woman" were a part of the festivals; nor is it lacking in old China or in Europe. It is known in ancient Greece; in later Spain, which preserved the prehistoric custom in spite of the prohibition of the Council of 572; in the island of Mallorca in the folk dance *els cossiers;* in Portugal in the *folías;* in England in the *Morris Dance;* and throughout the Continent in carnival merrymaking. There is a direct relationship between the man of the masked dances dressed as a woman and the parts of women played by men in the theater of eastern Asia, Siam, and ancient and medieval Europe (Plate 14).

Contrariwise, though much less frequently, the women may dance in men's costumes. Again there are examples from all parts of the world

—the Mandan Indians, the Blackfoot Indians, the Klemantan of Borneo (at the harvest!), and the Sissianu women of New Guinea, who with wigs and breastplates and with their faces blacked burst forth from the bushes and throw lemons at the men.

If we would understand this motif, we must not confine ourselves to the dance. We must examine corresponding concepts and customs that are not directly connected with the dance: the disguise of newly married couples in Denmark, for example; or the old woman who in Silesia used to be brought first to the bridegroom, before the real bride came from the cow-stall; and further, the artificial beards of Argive brides, the bearded Venus of Cyprus, the priapic Artemis of the Scythians, and many others. The Saturnalia of Rome and the later carnivals must not be forgotten. Women dancers of the Nuba on the White Nile, of the Altai Turks, and the Greeks, dressed as men, even dance with large phalli. J. W. Hauer interprets such phenomena much too loosely as deceptions of evil spirits at a critical time or as a change of personality under the influence of a supernatural power.

This is not sufficient as an explanation; the intricate custom may have several roots of various kinds. The most superficial is the general exclusion of the woman from spirit dances and related rites. We must look for more basic causes, especially since neither one sex by itself is kept at a distance. Before harvest or marriage it seems to be concerned with increasing fertility by lifting and bursting the bounds of sex; otherwise, its purpose is simply increasing power. Among the Koryak of Siberia, those shamans who dress as women are supposed to be the most powerful. It may be the same idea which leads the dancer to put on women's breasts. When we take examples from peoples so far apart as the inhabitants of the Bank Island of Melanesia and the ancient Greeks, we may get a notion of how extensively this idea has been diffused. I regard as the Greek example the bearded dancer of a black-figure Capuan vase in Attic style from the Berlin Collection of Antiquity, for which an ithyphallic, ejaculating aulete is piping (Plate 11). To make the motif of the fertility charm clearer, a large butterfly, symbol of immortality, is added. Recently Ida Lublinski made credible the idea of the androgynous unity of power as the quality of the mother of all who produces without a spouse.

Initiation disguises are obviously quite apart from the previous discussion. Among the Nilotic Nandi the boys who are to be circumcised dance in women's clothing, the girls in the costume of boys or warriors. The basic idea here is doubtless that in becoming man and woman the remoteness of the earlier life, the life that is to be blotted out, is thus intensified.

The survey of the couple dances presents a delightfully clear picture: couple dances of both sexes are not to be found in the South Seas; there and in the characteristic diffusion through northwestern Brazil and the advanced cultures of America, they may be grouped with the twelfth of the instrument stages, which I have designated in *Geist und Werden der Musikinstrumente* as "West African-Indonesian." "Most of the instruments [of this stage] are closely related to the conceptions of the late planter cultures." This is the stage which is on the border line between middle and high cultures and is essentially identical with "peasant culture."

Marriage dances are only an application of the sex dances. Especially beautiful is the *tudeschina* of the Bozen district, in which the bride is pursued by her partner but is never caught. Singular motifs, like the initiation of the bridegroom and the abduction of the bride, are only rarely encountered. The first of these exists among the Shortlanders of the Solomon Islands; the bridegroom may climb a tree and from there watch the secret dance of the women—the only man permitted to do so. The motif of abduction is at the base of the old Scandinavian *Bortdansingen* (dancing away): men and girls try to contend with the women for the bride.

Initiation Dances

In the same general category within the image type are the initiation dances, including those which are danced for tattooing. The power of generating and producing is not transmitted to the novices in a magic and ecstatic circling, but in a mimetic representation of the sex act or lascivious movements.

At the circumcision of boys in Central Australia, the women dance with their arms flexed and make inviting movements and beckon with their fingers to the men. We are reminded of the *beckon dance* (*Winktanz*) in Germany in which the women say:

> Come to me, come to me,
> I am so lonely!

In degenerate form the Apalaii boys of northeastern Brazil dance with arrows and flutes, the phallic instruments, or the men may dance with spears. This is not an introduction into their future profession of warrior, for such an explanation will not hold water in view of the fact that battle dances are executed at girls' ceremonies.

A further sex motif is the public display. Not the disrobing, perhaps: at the initiation of girls among the Makua of East Africa the majority of the participants suddenly divest themselves of all their clothes, and that may well be the definite form of ecstasy which is described under entirely different circumstances in the Bible. Saul was seized by the spirit of God, stripped off all his clothes, and prophesied before Samuel. But the motif is probably nakedness and the exposure of the sex parts. At the initiation of boys among the California Juaneño a woman dances in the nude, and at a corresponding occasion in Rhodesia all the men and women are naked. In Nauru (Marshall Islands) at a dance celebrating the first menstruation of the chieftain's daughter, men and women raise their grass skirts in front and behind and exhibit themselves to each other.

If the goal of these dances becomes more and more one of instruction rather than of magic, we may seek an explanation perhaps in the growing rationalism and temperance of the mimetic dance peoples, and perhaps also in the gradual and inevitable decline and alienation of the sacred and the mystic. At maturity (though it is not necessary for either the boys or the girls) the young people are "instructed in matters of sex" and are taught the required movements. Particularly among the nations of the African coasts, again, the profanation is at its greatest. In many sections of East Africa the dances at the initiation of girls are simply a training in the rhythmic movement of the belly and the posterior.

But sexual intercourse alone still does not make the man. Much is demanded of the youth taken into the company of adults. Therefore the men of the Monumbo Papua of Potsdam Harbor in New Guinea "depict in the dance what is expected of the boys in the years to come: (1) they must often excite themselves by inserting a liana stalk in the penis; (2) they must steal diligently and not let themselves be seen by the women; (3) they must catch fish diligently with the fish-spear; (4) they must diligently fetch down cocoanuts and drink the milk from them; (5) they must diligently fetch down bread-fruits with pickers and foot-slings; (6) they must delight in women; (7) they must secretly watch the women bathing."

But it seems to me that these are individual characteristics which must be used cautiously in passing judgment on primitives—if the word "primitive" may be applied at all to degenerate peoples.

Funeral Dances

The extravert cultures oppose the life charm to the power of death. In sight of the Great Conqueror they dance out continued generation and new life. It is the same idea which once led Europeans of the Old Stone Age to bury corpses in red ocher, so that the ban of dying would be broken by the magic color of the fluid of life. The funeral cults become erotic. Dance leaders of the Pangwe of Cameroon must whirl their loincloths in the air to show their sex organs, and in the dance at the death of a young girl in the Island of Yap, the women must throw their grass skirts in the air with a violent motion to uncover their sex parts. The dances of Yap at the bier of a chieftain have been called frankly a choreographic Kama Sutra, and dances of more or less abandon follow the funeral ceremony—often, indeed, only at this time—in later cultures from South America across Polynesia, Micronesia, and Africa to the Canary Islands. The motif even passed into the advanced culture of the New Egyptian Kingdom: a lifelike relief from Saqqâra in the Museum of Cairo shows two young girls with rattles leading the funeral procession and about them in a circle the round of women in transparent dresses with tambourines in their upraised hands—all of them in passionate sex movement (Plate 9). The out and out phallic funeral dance also has parallels in the old Egyptian culture of a later period.

In 1800 Degrandpré observed funeral dances on the Congo with an enormous priapus moved by springs. After Egypt was Hellenized, the women carried the same type of priapus at the festival of Dionysus, though, to be sure, nothing is said of the dance in this connection.

On the other hand, early Egypt (before 2000 B. C.) creates the motif of its funeral dance from another concept: life charm by the long stride and leg throw. Life is treated like growth: just as children and grain flourish when the normal stride is exaggerated in the choral dance, in like manner this exaggeration must also break the life-destroying power of death. In the sixth dynasty of ancient Egypt (c. 2500 B. C.) the women dancers who are accompanying the coffin throw their legs in a wide spread over the heads of the dancers in front of them (Plate 9), and their descendants in the Middle Empire dance toward each other in two rows with a long tilting step. In Cameroon the theme is exaggerated to the point of a stilt dance.

If the idea of renewal of life is in these examples embodied in the movement, in other cultures it is embodied in the form of the dance. The Alfuro of the Moluccas walk in pairs in front of the house of mourning. A child walks over a bridge that they have formed by locking their hands together; when the child has walked across the hands of one pair, this couple goes to the front part of the line to extend the bridge. This is continued until the house has been encircled eight times: life, by renewing itself eternally, has no end.

But the funeral dance may be executed also in altogether direct form:

in the Torres Strait each individual dancer, wearing a mask, imitates the appearance and motion of a person who has died in the course of the year. This seems to represent the first step towards being possessed by the spirit of the dead, a motif which is treated on page 132 in the section on the mask dance.

When a Yoruba Negro dies, "a wooden mask is carved before his funeral, which one of the men puts on together with the shroud. Now he begins to dance and speak in a falsetto voice as the spirit of the dead man, uttering consolation and admonishment. The mask is then stored away and is from that time on Orisha, a supernatural power. The spirit of the dead man has imparted to the mask life and power, so to speak, which again and again may jump across to the wearer and make him possessed." At funerals of the Volga Cheremiss a person in the clothes of the deceased dances and speaks in his name: "This is my last festival with you. I shall drink, I shall eat. Afterwards I shall come no more." For the historian of music a younger custom stands alongside this old one: as late as the nineteenth century at funerals in Germany, the best of the choir boys walks to the grave and sings words of admonishment as the spirit of the dead man. In the fifth movement of Brahms's *German Requiem,* "Now are ye sad" is the last echo of this recantation. Related most closely to the primitive death mask bearer is the Roman *archimimus,* who walks in advance of the funeral procession in the mask and clothing of the deceased, imitating his gait and gestures. The same usage is still to be found in France of the fourteenth century at the funerals of princes.

There is an older European custom for which primitive parallels are still extant. In the seventeenth century at Hungarian funerals, one among those present had to fall to the ground as though dead; men and women danced around him singing, prepared him as they would a corpse, and then danced with him:

"Some time ago I saw a strange dance at a funeral in a Hungarian city also. In the middle of the room a man lay down with his hands and feet stretched apart. His face was covered with a kerchief. He lay there and did not budge. Then the leader called for the death dance with the bagpipe. As soon as it began, the men and women walked around the fellow in the center singing and half crying, folded his hands on his breast, bound his feet, laid him sometimes on his back, sometimes on his stomach, and did every manner of thing with him. Finally they stood him up slowly and danced with him, which was frightful to behold, because this fellow of his own accord did not move in the least, but let the others move his limbs for him. I stood there dumfounded, so to speak. But I am told that once God punished such a player and that he really died as the dead do and never did come to life."

Is the circle dance with the corpse the motif, perhaps, of that sport in which a group sitting close together in a circle push back and forth a person who stands in the center and holds himself stiff as a corpse to keep him from breaking through the ring at any point? The account of the Hungarian dance does not discuss the meaning of the dance around the corpse: at the end the "dead man" stands up and they all join in a dance of joy—the whole procedure is a resurrection charm. In this form it is used at weddings in Hungary and also in Silesia and Brandenburg; in 1674 at Cleve it was executed even at a Jewish wedding. In Germany and Bohemia, the motif of the Sleeping Beauty has latterly been added: the dead person is kissed to life and the ghastly funeral ceremony changes into a lively society game. One or the other of these motifs is at the base of the Italian death dances which spread among the people from Tuscany to Sicily under various names, such as the *mattacino, baraban,* or *lucia.*

As a resurrection charm this group is connected with the folk dance of the Sardinians. To the shrill sound of the triple clarinet, *launedda,* the men form a circle and dance with heads bowed, eyes cast down, and with every appearance of sorrow. Their excitement grows continually greater, until a boy breaks away from the circle, twists his limbs, stiffens, and falls to the ground. The round dancers stamp more excitedly, strike their foreheads, and throw themselves on their knees in despair. Then the *launedda* starts to play a lively and cheerful melody, the boy jumps up hale and hearty, and all unite in a dance of joy. Sardinian folklore interprets this dance as the death and resurrection of Adonis; it is the ancient myth of the dying and awakening of nature. In this manner Egyptian priests may once have executed those dances which represented the departure and return of Osiris, and the first Bacchantes may thus have danced the fate of Dionysus before Attic tragedy was formed out of the choral dance and pantomime.

The motif itself—a defense against death by death and deliverance dances—is very ancient. It has already been formed by a hunter people as primitive as the Toba of the Gran Chaco: when a pestilence threatens they all join in a circle; one after another of them sinks down as though dead and must be called back to life by the medicine man's singing, exhaling, and inhaling, as the others dance around him in a circle. One after another comes to his senses again and takes part once more in the dance until all are joined as at the beginning.

Weapon Dances

To the imageless war dance, which magically infuses the power of victory into the warrior, mimetic culture opposes the analogy charm. By depicting a victorious fight in the dance, it aims to compel the happy outcome of an expedition. The imageless dance has no need of weapons, which for the image dance are practically indispensable.

The weapon dance is extremely widespread: handling a weapon is still man's favorite sport. A swinging forwards and backwards, a protected position and a hasty jump, an attack and a running for cover, a heavy stamping, and an impassioned thrust, throwing and striking with a smooth swing motion—battle action and the dance meet in the fight. If the Greeks saw in the dance a training ground for battle, on the other hand battle has furnished a colorful group of very fertile motifs of movement.

For the sake of expedience we shall distinguish the two principal forms of the weapon dance—the choral round and the solo dance. The dancers may be on one side or divided into two sides:

> One group against invisible enemies
> Two groups against each other
> One dancer against an invisible enemy
> Two dancers against each other

Melanesia offers some fine examples of group encounters with invisible enemies.

In New Ireland the dancers form "a double row or several rows. Each one holds in his hand the usual battle spear. His whole body is in continual motion from start to finish: legs and feet make quick, tripping movements or flex at the knee joints or are thrown to right and left, forwards and backwards." Swinging of spears, thrusts against invisible opponents, ducking of the head—these movements have been rehearsed so carefully that they are executed simultaneously by all.

We come now to those mammoth presentations in which the fighting games are formed around carefully regulated and dramatically constructed processions to and from the village square. The magnificent weapon dances of the Fiji Islands, which are presented at the most varied occasions after months of practice under special dance masters, are the most impressive since the decline of those in Japan. As many as six hundred painted and decorated dancers move forward in parade formation singing and stamping their feet; after a dramatic pause the fighting begins; at the close they march solemnly off the field in a manner resembling the Greek *embaterion.*

If in the Fiji dances it is not known who the opponents are supposed to be, the motif of two hostile groups is brought out clearly in other lands—in Ruanda, for example. We must look to the Malay Archipelago for noteworthy formations of the motif of single combat. Borneo and Sumatra in particular have a wealth of hand-to-hand fight dances against visible and invisible foes. Only among the Circassians do we find comparable perfection in this type of dance. Individual dances develop later in the history of the weapon dance than the group dances, though, to be sure, the preliminary motif of slaying an enemy has already made an appearance in Australia.

Joining the hand-to-hand combat with the chain round, on the other hand, is no doubt a later development. Among the Haussa the motif was executed somewhat as follows: walking forwards within the dance circle, "each dancer attacks the man in front of him, then in the next moment turns around to defend himself from the blows of the one behind him." This is obviously nothing other than the *pyrrhichē,* portrayed in a wonderful relief belonging to the Vatican Museum. We have here, perhaps, the peak of the European weapon dance. The *pyrrhichē* was notable not only for its detailed working out of the artistic, but also for its strict adherence to nature: it was rhythmic training, rhythmic preparation for war; the leading warriors were at the same time the leading dancers, and it used to be said of capable soldiers that they had developed their ability in the dance. The God Priapus, said the Bithynians of Asia Minor, had "made a profession of giving instruction in fighting and when he was ordered by Hera to give lessons to her son Ares, who was indeed still young but unusually tough and virile, he taught him to fight with sword and lance only after he had made an accomplished dancer out of him."

Already we have slipped from the more restricted territory of the battle dance into that of the skill dance. For fighting in the dance requires the uttermost presence of mind and accuracy of aim, if one does not wish to wound or be wounded. The battle of weapons as such may be entirely forgotten, and the pure dance element stands out so clearly that now and then the Malayans throw down their weapons and fight with empty hands. Or—in a further development—the dancer jumps about among blades stuck in the ground. This remained a popular motif of professional jugglers in medieval Europe: in several pictures one sees them doing very dangerous somersaults from one space to another. This recalls a parable of Democritus: "If they are untrained, the children of miserly people are like the dancers who do jumps between swords. If the latter, in making a jump, miss the place where they are supposed to land, they are lost; but it is difficult to get to this place, since only a tiny spot is left clear for their feet. Thus it is also with the former: if they are not the cautious and frugal type like their father, they generally fail."

The antithesis of this deliberate stylization of the dance is the frenzied devotion to the ecstasy of battle and the fever of victory which all too often pervades even high cultures. In the year 1486 the city of Vitoria in Spain was forced to prohibit the sword dance because it involved too much bloodshed. Particularly among the Malayans the games used to develop into bloody fights, and even today in Bali the kris dancers frequently inflict severe wounds upon themselves. But this motif also is often weakened and transformed even by the Malayans. When sticks are used instead of swords, the weapon dance often becomes an out and out strike dance. Brandts Buys describes the Javanese *gitiqan* as a torture dance, in which the theme is no longer fighting and defense, but rather an even-tempered, smiling suppression of pain. In this dance also there is an old relationship between the sword and the staff of life, between the weapon dance and the fertility charm. This is the more unmistakable as the most primitive weapon dance that we know, the spear dance of the Australian Watchandi, is interpreted by the dancers themselves as an imitation of cohabitation, the spear representing the phallus.

But behind this relationship is the emotional make-up of man. For him the battle impulse and the sex impulse are as closely intertwined as they are for the stag that battles when in heat. The ecstasy of blood and of love flow together in life as well as in the dance, which here, too, uses life itself as a model: an erotic dance is often added to the war dance, or in taking part in a war dance, women become sexually aroused. This motif is indicated in a strange manner in the former German colony of New Guinea: at the victory celebration the wife of the chief warrior, wearing no covering whatsoever (unthinkable except for this occasion), dances around the circle of men.

In the light of the very ancient relation between battle dance and love dance, between victory charm and life charm, the deep significance of the weapon dance at sowing and mowing, at girls' rites, weddings, and funerals is crystal clear. Almost every fertility charm is at the same time a defense charm—even the weapon dance. A twofold analogy is apparent: first, if weapons and blows chase away hostile men, they will surely have the same effect upon hostile spirits; second, if noise puts fear into men, it will do the same to demons. Good examples illustrating the first idea are the apotropaic sword dances of the Borneo priestesses, the naked sword dance of the northern Hindu at the end of a year in which a relative has died, and above all the funeral ceremony of the East African Makonde: in a war dance the young boys attack the hut of the deceased. The neighboring Angoni illustrate the second of the two ideas of analogy: hundreds of warriors leap into the air simultaneously, then strike their spears against their shields. The leap, which forms part of the weapon dances of the Alfuro of Molucca, shows clearly that these are not war dances but fertility charms. In this category the ancient Japanese "rhythmic shield dance" *tate-fushi-mahi* may belong. But classical antiquity offers the best-known illustrations. In the Zeus legend of Crete the young god is protected from the destroyer Chronos-Saturn by the priestly *curetes,* who circle around him striking their shields with their swords; and likewise the *Salii* of Rome dance around the altar, striking their swords on the clanging metal of their shields: Saturn, who stamps out all life, is the destroyer of seeds, and the Salian priests like the *curetes* are also guardians of the seeds.

In our next section, in the discussion of the later European sword dance, we shall probe these relationships still further.

General Characteristics

Our investigation thus far has established the imageless and image dances as the two basic dance types and has related them to the two opposing types of man's spiritual life and cultural forms. In our survey we have now and then been forced to stop and ask ourselves whether an example under discussion still really reflects the basic type purely or whether one or another foreign element has not intruded and marred its purity. But does not every people, every individual, carry in the bloodstream something of the extravert and the introvert, of the physical and the metaphysical, of the rational and the irrational, and out of this duality, out of the constantly shifting balance, do we not draw our highest powers? Just as there are no races in existence today which have been able to live to themselves and to block off all contact with the outside world, there never have been such races among the primitives or in prehistory. Complete purity of the blood, of the spirit, and of culture is a condition that has never existed anywhere so far as we know. This intermingling has been accomplished automatically by the diffusion of entire cultures through contacts with neighboring peoples, migrations, and conquests, and no member of the human family has been able to resist it.

In the same manner the fate of the dance is determined. The rational, objective tendency of even the introvert peoples, and the irrational, spiritualizing and idealizing tendency of the extravert peoples must lead to a mixed type, in which the predominance of one or the other trend is as impossible to distinguish in the dance as in other expressions of culture.

The mimetic dance in particular cannot remain purely rational and bound to the body, because all dance, like play, raises a person by its very nature from his accustomed state into another world. As a child playing in the street is run over because he does not see the approaching car, or as he does not hear his mother's call because it does not penetrate his consciousness, so in the dance the capacity of perception is weakened and even snuffed out completely. Every dance, including the mimetic, is ecstatic. And this ecstasy pushes it more or less powerfully away from mere corporal imitation, away from the sober and rational toward the imageless dance of the introvert peoples.

113

Fertility Dances

The Sioux Indians dance four times around a vessel of water, fling themselves to the ground, then drink up the water. And in New Guinea among the Monumbo Papua, two masked men dance around a vessel of water, then the women crowd around and sip it out greedily. Both dances are rain charms—different from those we have encountered in introvert or extravert cultures. The rain-makers of northwestern Australia had danced around a magic stone; the totemistic Arunta had caused the rain-bringing wind to blow by a fan dance. Both had pursued the same goal, the former in an imageless circle dance, the latter in an imitative action. In the dances of the Sioux and of the Monumbo, the two methods are united: the imageless circling remains, but the central point of the circle is objectivized by the pantomime. A vessel of water as a rain magnet is from this point of view a solution not easily surpassed in freshness and insouciance. Later the vessel and the cruder act of drinking are also dispensed with in favor of the motion of scooping, which has been more productive from the point of view of the dance; the girl bends gently to the ground, and as she rises again her hands are brought together in lifting the dish—a dance form in use today by almost all women dancers. Plate 8 brings a charming illustration from ancient Egypt. But there is a new crossing in the scoop motif: the concept of religious fertility power in the chaste maiden.

The motifs come together in ever new relationships: imageless circle, decoration with fresh green, nudity in cult ceremonies, pouring water to bring rain, the power of girls, the whirl dance as a wind charm, and even phallic rites as a magnet for fertility in general. Standing beside the pit of a well, the Fuegians move their heads, which are ornamented with long fringes wound from tufts of grass, and the women pour cold water on their naked backs. The beautiful old earthen dish of the Mexican Hopi Indians (Plate 6) shows an ithyphallic round, in which the participants are drenched with water as they dance.

With the exception of the phallus, all the motifs are made use of today in the rain dances of southeastern Europe: in times of drought a troupe of young girls moves from house to house. One of them, naked but decked with grass, leaves, and flowers, whirls continually within the circle of the others and lets the housewives pour water on her. The custom is known throughout the Balkans, among the southern Slavs (as the *dodola*), the Bulgarians, the Rumanians, the Aromuns, and the Greeks; but it extends also to Siebenbürgen, Moldau, Germany, and even to England; and Berthe Trümpy tells the author that as a child in Glarus, without knowing their significance, she took part in such dances in which only the pouring of water was lacking.

Initiation Dances

BOYS' INITIATION DANCES of the middle type most frequently adopt the form of *flagellation* and *stamp dances*. The flagellations themselves are familiar as the principal part of many secret society rites and boys' initiations. They are interpreted for the most part by European observers as tests before reception into man's estate, a category requiring courage and skill with weapons. But this is only a half-truth and surely does not explain the original significance of these usages. For we also find exactly the same customs outside initiation rites. The Aruak in Guiana whip one another at their funeral dances until the blood flows, and the Koryak of Siberia on returning from a funeral walk between two rods and have the shaman beat them, so that the soul of the deceased will not carry them away. Likewise, it would seem to be inadmissible to explain the flagellation dances by reason of such customs as a defense against demons, which indeed are especially feared in the transition from one stage of life to another. When in southern Australia self-castigations belong to the rain charm, it is clear that the blow itself has not, or at least has not only, a defensive but also a vocative significance. Here as at initiations and funerals the meaning is the magic consecration with the staff of life, a blow from which brings fertility and power and counteracts death. This becomes still clearer when we consider that in Baden deaths used to be announced by blows of the rod on house-doors and the driver of the hearse carried a rod instead of a whip.

Flagellation as an initiation rite is preserved indirectly in the dubbing of knights and in the box on the ears perpetuated in Richard Wagner's *Meistersinger* by which the apprentice is welcomed into the guild. But it has been maintained directly into our time in the staff of St. Nicholas or Santa Claus—not without its complements among the primitives: in New Britain among the Sulka, a dancer in an old man's mask moves from home to home followed by a procession yelling wildly and brandishing rods. The "old man" squats down, then jumps up again and dances. As he is in a squatting position, the people push their children towards him so that they may prosper through contact with him. But the adults stand upright and allow themselves to be flogged in order to grow stronger. Santa Claus in the South Seas! Thus it becomes clear why certain California tribes, celebrating a first menstruation, touch the cover beneath which lies the newly matured girl, with a rod split into nine sections, and dance in time with the strokes.

For boys' initiations, there is the idea of "running the gauntlet," just as in the funeral ceremonies of the Koryak. The Nor Papua in New Guinea form a line one behind another with their legs spread apart and also stand their lances in a line, one resting obliquely on the other; the boys must go through this line three times and let themselves be whipped with thorn rods. We have the same picture on the island of Tami near New Guinea, among the Babali of the Ituri, and among the Scymo of Hindustan: the novices crawl on all fours as fast as they can through a double row of adults and receive blows from cudgels. In Ovamboland the newly matured girls must force their way through a rhombic opening which an old man makes for them by spreading his legs and bending apart a staff that is stuck into the ground and split lengthwise in the center. Strangely reversing this procedure, the old men of the Pangwe (Cameroons) dance their way through a line of novices with arms and legs outspread. To crawl through is to assimilate: in the alligator dance of the North Australians, the one who represents the crocodile ancestor crawls underneath the legs of the tribesmen, and in Morocco the bride crawls under her bridegroom's legs so that she will become a good wife.

Somewhat on the same level are the customs which symbolize the sex act in order to bring the power of generation to the novices. One of the most widespread symbols of cohabitation is stamping, as we have already seen in the example of the Uitoto. Therefore special stamp dances on appropriate bases are here and there prescribed for those to be taken into the company of men. Among the Papua and in the secret society of the Kuksu of California such a base is a large slit drum symbolizing a woman, and among the Yaunde of West Africa it is a heavy tree trunk on two high forked sticks, regarded as a penis.

GIRLS' INITIATIONS. An excellent illustration of how the imageless circle dance becomes pantomime is a dance of the Lengua in the Gran Chaco of Paraguay: the women enclose the young girl in a dance circle to protect her from attack by the evil spirits, just as in the imageless dance described in the preceding section. But here the evil spirits are not imagined; they are represented mimetically by masked boys, who are attracted, then repulsed—as a lightning rod, instead of driving away the lightning, catches it and renders it harmless.

Is it a reshaping of the same motif when the Bushmen of the Kalahari Desert depict the evil spirits as rutting animals and, with a background similar to that of the dance above described, use it as a fertility rite? "The old women stand in one place and compose the band; as they sing, they clap their hands and rattle iron sticks. The young girl lies on the ground at their feet. The younger, married women now walk single file in figure eight formation around the girl, stamping their feet in time with the music and moving their outstretched arms rhythmically up and down. They coquet and show off with their uncovered buttocks, which by the way, like those of the Hottentots, are amply developed. Thus the dance proceeds for a while, then suddenly a Bushman approaches slowly, likewise stamping his feet according to the rhythm of the music, and beating the time with his upper arms and clenched fists. On his head he has fastened a pair of horns and a piece of hide. Supposedly the horns are real eland horns. But our Bushman had tied to his forehead a pair of carved wooden horns about a finger in length and blackened with charcoal, and in addition, a piece of goatskin. The horned Bushman is the bull, the women the cows, a relationship which is very apparent. The bull approaches and runs several times around the cows, who continue to stamp and coquet. Suddenly he jumps behind a woman and carries her along with him. The motions of the bull and the cows are then so extreme that one recognizes immediately that they are imitating animals in heat. Thus the procession goes for a while back and forth, with the bull darting in and out among the dancers. Finally the music stops and the line breaks up amid joking and laughter, but after a pause the game begins again."

I am convinced that the same dance is pictured in a rock painting from South Africa recently brought back and exhibited by Leo Frobenius. In it, too, is the same figure eight formation with a person lying in one of the rings; in it, too, the women are naked and the men dressed as animals.

Weapon Dances

The Khasi of Upper Burma trip along slowly and very unnaturally from one foot to the other in a circle around an open place. From time to time they shout jubilantly and come to a halt; separating into pairs, they jump at each other and strike swords; then with a loud cry they move back into line and continue circling. In this dance, therefore, the pantomime of battle is superimposed upon an imageless background. Quite in the same way in the Loyalty Islands of Melanesia, where so many cultures mingle, we find the circle and other formations, the non-mimetic and the mimetic united in the same dance: first the men decorated for battle turn quickly in two circles; then with a yell they pounce upon one another.

In our historical section we shall show to what extent this alternation of imageless and image, of circling and pantomime, has determined the forms of the later European dance—and also of music, for the principal root of the suite is here. Its classical form is the *sword dance.*

The *sword dance,* which entered European folklore as a strict conception, was in flower between the fourteenth and eighteenth centuries. There is an appreciable gap in its traditions between then and its sources in ancient Rome. In the nineteenth century it decreased so much in importance that since 1850 it has lived on only in relics. Every year, or sometimes less often, perhaps on Shrove Tuesday, a group of young bachelors, for the most part members of a particular trade guild, came together in an open place for the sword dance—at least six men, but often as many as forty, and in old Nürnberg over two hundred. Among their numbers were one or two dance leaders and a "fool." Occasionally their faces were blacked and they were almost always dressed in white with bells on their suits and swords in their hands. Fife and drum were the most common music. The dance was opened by a ceremony of homage; it was composed of artificial step figures, rotations, figure eights, chains, snake lines, bridges, arches, and jumps over the sword. After that came the middle part, the battle dance proper. The conclusion was the "rose," which takes its name, by the way, not from the flower, as Meschke still believes, but obviously, like the "rose" of the old lutes, from Middle High German *râz,* meaning "braid"; the dancers "braided" their swords artistically into a figure of tightly woven mesh which was placed on the ground and danced around or lifted up —at least in its later form—to carry the dance leader as a kind of conquering hero. Occasionally they added the "killing" of the fool and often his resurrection. The entire ceremony ended in special tricks in fighting, in a round dance, and in "salute."

The meaning of the sword dance is no longer known anywhere. Still it may be determined with little difficulty from the separate motifs. We have seen that the weapon dance is not only a dance stylization of the battle, but that it unites the two powers of furthering growth, the negative (defensive) and the positive (phallic). In addition, the white of the garments and the blacking of the faces, the hanging of bells, the figure of the "fool," the scenes of death and awakening, and finally, as we shall see, the intertwining of the rows of dancers are all unmistakable characteristics of a vegetation ceremony.

This fact alone places its origin in prehistoric times. At the same time it crushes the notion that the sword dance is a special Indo-Germanic or even European phenomenon.

Such a narrow conception has been due especially to a misinterpretation of elevating the leader. We read that in the town of Bilk in Westphalia the sword dancers walked under the large opening in the ceiling of the farm house. "In doing so, they laid the four swords crosswise one on top of another to form a star-shaped design. . . . At a signal from the drum, the dance leader now jumped on the crossed swords. To the beat of the drum the sword dancers then raised and lowered their dance leader several times. Then again at a signal from the drum, they threw him with a mighty heave into the air through the opening in the ceiling up to the cross beams of the house. A big jump. From the cross beams hung several sausages, a side of bacon, or some other article of food. . . . If the dance leader were adroit, he grabbed something as he jumped. Sometimes the dance leader stayed up in the beams for a while, as the others danced around on the floor below, always in time with the drum. Not until they had taken their places under the opening again did the dance leader let himself down through it, to be caught by the sword dancers." Meschke is certainly right when he calls this figure "a typically rustic formation, an expression of unrestrained wildness and genuine daring." But the real key to what is actually formed is found in the primitive usage of jumping as high as possible in the weapon dance. In the previous section we cited the African Angoni and the Indonesian Alfuro as examples, and to these two we might add the Baronga of South Africa as a third example. The high jump of the primitive peoples is, therefore, as we have shown, an emphatic growth motif. The round dance in Bilk is evidence that the elevation of the leader is nothing other than this: the jump was executed only once; but when a "birth had taken place, the dance leader did the dance in the air also a second time." We have further evidence in the elevation episode of the Biscayan and Slovakian sword dance: the dance leader "dies" as a vegetation spirit and is lifted by the dancers horizontally, as though he were a corpse, high over their heads; when he is lowered, life is restored in him.

Like the raising of the leader, other characteristics of the European sword dance have their parallels outside of Europe. First, as a superficial example, the solemn part played by the salute in Sumatra. Then, at least in early stages, the "rose." With different emphasis but with the same meaning, the motif may be recognized in the weapon dance of the South African Baronga: after the battle (here also!) all the dancers form a circle and join their shields together in such a way as to make a giant ring. The braiding of swords as practiced by the European people is more closely related to customs of Borneo in which the motif of swords placed together and danced around is used. Among the Dusun the solo dancer places sword and sheath on the ground in the form of a cross; among the Sea Dayak two dancers cross their swords on the ground.

But a round of the Singhalese of Ceylon is most closely related: "Each dancer has two sticks, something like our drumsticks, which are struck together with a skillful twisting of the dancers, to and fro. Very accurate as to form, with an accomplished technique, unbelievably exact, powerful, and yet graceful. The figures keep getting more complicated, more frantic, and the dance more frenzied, but the dancers do not fail to execute their figures and they never strike against one another. Finally one sees only whirling bodies and hears the very rhythmical and skillful rattle of the resonant sticks of wood." Six men (Morris!) and two women dance here around a man decked with bells, who is on his knees; in the sword round of Europe, too, there is the same dance around the kneeling dance leader. In conclusion, as in Europe, we have the salute.

The division of the weapon dances into a non-mimetic circling and a mimetic battle, however, is quite general. This is the arrangement in

Fiji, among the Khasi, and in Ruanda. The figures come from another source, the *stick dances*.

In the *stick dances* short sticks are struck against each other rhythmically. They are to be found in Lower California and northeastern Brazil, in the South Seas, Australia, and Asia, and as far west as Togo and western Europe.

With this mighty territory, which points to great antiquity, an important distinction as to type is apparent: either both sticks are held by one person, or two persons each hold a stick and strike them one against the other. Two stages stand out in marked contrast: the first type— both sticks held by one person—is the older because of its greater diffusion and its attachment to lower cultures. The other type—each of two people holding a stick—is the younger; it is not to be found in America, but is limited to the Late Tribal cultures of Hawaii, the Micronesian Islands, Malay, Pamir, and Togo, and to European folk dances (Plate 15). With great skill, relates Semper, eight dancers of the Micronesian Island of Palau wind in and out with the most varied figures and strike with the most accurate harmony the two ends of their short sticks, which are grasped in the middle, on the sticks of their two neighbors.

Judged on the basis of European examples, such stick dances might give the impression of fighting games. But this would be a gross delusion. For we must keep in mind the older "one man" sticks, which exclude any idea of a weapon fight: they are intensifications of the rhythmical, and to a certain extent also, skill, element; they are outgrowths, as it were, of clapping hands. In Micronesia, the center of the "two man" stroke, the dancers often strike not their own hands together, but those of other dancers in turn, while going through a complicated series of forms.

But already we have connections with weapons: the Australians strike not only sticks together, but in exactly the same way and for the same purpose, their javelins; in Yap the sticks serve as weapons in the war dance; the New Irelanders strike their hatchets one against another; and the Cameroons and the Dagbama in Togo strike swords together instead of sticks, yet intend no allusion to battle. This is perhaps like the German fraternity students who strike blades together at the *Landesvater*. The weapon beats out the time. It is a substitute for the stick when the latter is not at hand or when one looks for a stronger effect from it because it is of metal. It is a question of stronger effect when the rhythmic beat abandons what is purely emotional and like all regulated noise joins the defense against the spirits.

Now it is clear why in the European sword round the wooden stick and the sword may be interchanged at will. At the same time it becomes apparent that elements from the most varied cultures have been brought together in the sword dance. The following may be listed as the principal motifs:

1. the battle game;
2. the weapon as a defense against spirits;
3. the weapon as a phallic fertility charm;
4. the stick game;
5. the figure dances.

Of these motifs 1 to 3 are the older, judged by their meaning and their extensiveness; 4 and 5 are appreciably younger, 5 at least in the form that is common here. The pygmies have already developed mimetic battle games; these belong, therefore, to the Protoneolithic stage or the Middle Basic cultures. The beginnings of the stick game belong to the same level. The growth charm must be reckoned with the Miolithic stage and the totemistic cultures. Then there is a large gap: figure rounds and the stick game with two persons belong to the Full Neolithic and the Late Tribal cultures. Thus two sources have joined, the one proceeding from the weapon, the other from the stick. We may assume that they came together at a point at which the weapon had somewhat the shape of a drumstick. The bow, the lance, the spear are nothing like the short stick; the sword alone can be considered. Thus their meeting ground is somewhere in the Metal Age.

That round dance of the stars, the positions of the planets in relation to
the fixed stars, the beautiful order and perfect harmony in all their movements—what is all that if not a picture of the primeval dance! (VARRO)

Astral Dances

Astral motifs are to be found in very many dances, especially in
circle dances. The strictly regulated direction of movement—with or
against the course of the sun or shifting between the one and the other
—may not be easily explained otherwise. The astral influence becomes
quite apparent when dancers must face a particular direction. The circumcision dancers of Central Australia, the sun dancers of the Arapaho,
and the newly matured girls of California face the east; the dance
houses of California and the dance rings of the Blackfoot Indians open
toward the east; and the mystic *Chassidim* of the Rabbi Lurja Circle
alternate between west and east before the approach of the Sabbath.
The Cágaba in Sierra Nevada, although each dances for himself, turn
their faces in the same direction at the same time. The bull dancers of
the Mandan represent the four sections of the world by male couples.
On a field laid out from north to south or from east to west, the Mexican Cora execute riding dances toward the four sacred directions. And
the Pawnee of North America paint themselves half red, half black for
the dance, and turn the red side to the east, the black to the west.

Yet in all these cases the astral motif is more or less subordinate. It
dominates the dance only when the course of sun and moon is represented by appropriate figures and movements with the idea that life and
growth are thus assured.

SUN DANCES. The sun is less interesting from the point of view of both
the cult and the dance. For unlike the moon, it does not change its
shape, if one may speak of this blazing object as a shape, and its path
remains uniform. Therefore it brings to the dancer no inspiration other
than the circle movement "sunwise" or clockwise, east-south-west-north
in the northern hemisphere and the reverse in the southern hemisphere;

as a dance motif this is older than sun worship. To what extent the ordinary dances around a fire may have been influenced by the sun is difficult to say. The solar content of dances becomes clear when as among the prairie tribes of North America they definitely move around a sun pole. Nevertheless, even here the imageless circling predominates. The Mojave of California kneel down in rows toward the east, their eyes fixed on the sun, and get up at a signal from the dance leader—the sunrise. And of the old Hindu, Lucian reports that in the morning they prayed facing the east, and in the evening, the west, and they imitated the dance of the sun god.

In ancient Egypt the king, as representative of the sun, had to walk solemnly around the walls of the temple as a guarantee that the sun would continue its daily journey across the sky without interruption from eclipse or other misadventure. In time of eclipse the Chilote of Chile, both men and women, tie up their garments, "as they do when they are on a journey, and wander around in a circle, leaning on staffs, as if they were bearing heavy burdens, until the eclipse is over."

MOON DANCES. The lunar cults have been far more productive. The course of the moon is multiform; it moves clockwise, but each day the point where it rises is a certain distance farther in a counter-clockwise direction. Besides interest in the moon's course, there is interest in its shape. It increases until it has the form of a circle, then diminishes to the point of disappearance. But at the same time the visible completion of the circle sharply set off in black from the white—this outline which decreases as the light grows greater and increases as the white decreases; which is crowded out and absorbed when the white part has attained its round shape, but which itself becomes a circle when the white has thinned out and disappeared—what a world of potential ideas! What a wealth of motifs! How many new forces for the dance!

But here, too, there is an imageless type. Among the Brazilian Cayapó, on the day of the new moon there is a "strange excitement in the village. About eight o'clock a long line of women decked with leaves approaches, singing. The three in front have banana leaves tied to their heads and shoulders, the others have palm leaves resting obliquely on their heads like a halo. At the end are a couple of little girls. Singing, they all form a large circle; the first two women take the lead in the song and the others join in from time to time. Then they begin in dance fashion to stamp with their right feet and to move the lower parts of their arms up and down. The dancing and singing become livelier and more excited. Two children bring up some dry palm leaves and light two blazing fires, one in the middle of the circle, the other on the outside. Only a few men look on. The dance lasts almost an hour, then the women separate. With glowing sticks of wood they walk diagonally over the clearing to their houses." The only mimetic element here is perhaps the lighting of the fire to bring about a return of the moon.

The mimetic moon dance may be identified first of all by certain attributes. Let us consider the pit and spear dance of the Australian Watchandi already described which they themselves call a moon dance. It is based probably on an analogy somewhat as follows:

Pit = seed-bearing bosom of the earth = vulva.

Spear = fertilizing moonbeam = phallus.

The Greeks were still familiar with a circle dance known as *óklasma* or *hygrá órchesis,* in which the dancers carried shields in the form of crescents and by turns sank to their knees and rose again; they called it a Persian dance. The Uitoto and Tama of Colombia stamp upon a felled dance tree until it breaks; the moon fades. But the same Uitoto form their rounds of the new moon according to the course of the moon: a few dancers start a segment of a circle, and this is gradually rounded out by the addition of new dancers.

Mimetic moon dances in New Ireland have been described in greatest detail by a missionary named Peekel who observed them over a long period of years. If we use this report as a basis, we find that there are the following principal motifs:

    I. Course of the moon:

        1. Circle formation.

2. Walking forwards and backwards in such a way that the whole group gradually moves out to the edge of the dance ground.

II. Phases of the moon:
    1. Congemination.
        (a) Two solo dancers or two choruses in rows or in concentric circles, which in the course of the dance sometimes become separate circles.
        (b) Turning toward one another by couples or by rows.
    2. Waning and waxing.
        (a) Stooping down in a squatting position at the beginning, then gradually rising, crouching again, and falling over in a faint.
        (b) Raising and lowering of the arms and dance attributes.
        (c) Walking forwards and backwards.
        (d) Counter-movement of both rows to represent the shifting of the two halves of the moon and their alternate light and dark.
        (e) The rows in light and dark clothing.
        (f) Languid movements at the beginning with a gradual quickening to a vibrant trembling and confusion.
        (g) Circle form for the full moon, oval (Uitoto: segment) for the half moon.

According to this scheme a large number of dances may with certainty be classified as lunar. First, a dance of the Gazelle Peninsula made up of two to four rows of dancers, who walk forwards and backwards, squat, stand, hop, and swing their arms, carrying bundles of feathers or flowers. Or a dance of the Monumbo Papua: in a circle with "complicated figures, in which half the dancers squat and the other half continue to dance." The Sissianu of New Guinea: two concentric circles in counter-movement around a staff, men on the inside, women on the outside. The Nicobars: four hundred men and women in two concentric circles moving counter to each other; alternately raising and lowering their arms, they face now to the right, now to the left, and contract and expand the circle; the dancers of the inner circle get down on their knees with their heads touching the ground, and those of the outer circle, upright, step over them. A dance of the Dagbama in Togo is quite similar: two concentric circles are in counter-movement around a drummer; after a few steps the dancers change place so that those who have been on the inside are now on the outside. Again among the Nicobars: the men's dance is successively a sitting, standing, flexing, and jumping. Then in New Ireland: the dancers are in fours, one group behind another; at the start and at the end the dancers squat; then they begin to sing and in turn the first, second, third, and fourth dancers, obviously representing the phases of the moon, rise and bend down, with their arms and heads forward and with bundles of green in their hands. As the dance progresses a couple in front move backwards to the end of the procession, change places (*"chassez-croisez"*), then jump to the front of the line again— "As in our modern contre dances," the observer comments.

A circular round of the middle Angola is also certainly lunar. The dancers join hands and whirl around in a circle; sometimes they take dainty steps toward the dancer opposite, as in the quadrille, and sometimes they sink to their knees, bend to right and left, and lean backwards. Then after a pause of a few seconds, they let out a deafening roar and rush to the center, throwing their arms high in the air and standing on their tiptoes. The entire group is charged with the highest ecstasy; then as though slowly tiring, as a result of their overexertion, they sink to the ground with their eyes closed and touch the earth with their foreheads. Is there any doubt? Circling, facing one another, forming a crescent by bending right, left, and backwards, rising suddenly with a loud yell, and sinking down together—all these are familiar motifs of the moon dance.

The moon theme has been maintained in the European dance also. In the year 1400 (?) a round dance of both sexes was executed in Berlin under the name of *Zwölfmondentanz* (twelve-moon dance). Twelve couples danced in a circle first with their faces toward the center, then toward the outside (wax and wane!); they divided into four groups (phases or seasons?), formed a circle once again, and ended the dance with loud shouting. Perhaps the unexplained *Treialtrei*, which itself was danced by twelve couples at the time of the minnesingers, is related to this twelve-moon dance.

And we must consider still another motif. In the mythology of almost all peoples there appears the idea of the limping god. Limping, according to mythological conceptions, means "to be still weak, to begin." The great nature gods who live through the year, die at the end, and then come to life again in the spring with renewed youth, are without power at the beginning of their cyclical life and walk with a limp. The Greek god Dionysus, and also the Egyptian Harpokrates, son of Osiris, may be this type of god—like the waxing, young bright moon, which is to win out over the dark moon.

The limping dances are found, therefore, in the most far-flung sections of the world. In southern Australia a single dancer limps along supported and commiserated by companions; then he suddenly laughs loudly and jumps into the air. Similarly the Samoans dance around a cripple. The Ute women of northwestern Utah do a lame dance: they arrange themselves in two rows, ten yards apart, move in a parallel line, then turn towards each other; each dancer drags her right foot. But in Jewish history there is that mighty struggle of Elijah against King Ahab and four hundred and fifty prophets of Baal and all the people, when in time of drought he had a sacrifice to God placed on one side and a sacrifice to Baal on the other; and the sacrifice to God, three times drenched with water, was consumed by the heavenly fire, but the heathen sacrifice remained dry and untouched by the fire, although the faithful "limped" around the altar in a round dance. One might for a moment think of the possibility of a knee-bending dance, for the Greek translation has the people limping "on the hollows of both knees." But philological information shows clearly that the word represented limping. This motion is not at all surprising in view of the lunar attributes of Baal. Yet it appears that the Mosaic religion was also familiar with the limping dance: the name "Passover" comes from the verb *pāsah* and Passover, the Jewish Easter, is a spring festival, a celebration of resurrected nature which has just begun to move and is still weak.

The motif of the limping dance enters ancient China. (Or does it proceed from here?) Yü, the god of fertility, who has obviously lunar characteristics, drags one leg as he hops in an ecstatic dance; and it is reported that the two boys who sing the song of Chang-Yang dance by twos on one leg with each boy trying to pull his partner towards him. This motif is in no sense erotic, as Granet believes. I can see in it only lunar characteristics: the two sickles of the moon which in eternal battle endeavor not to push an opponent away but to bring him close, to absorb him.

The same motif is maintained even in Europe, in the Chiemgau of southern Bavaria, in the "dancing in of marriage": the bride limps— once more an appropriate rite for the transition of the still incompleted person into a new life. We are reminded of the crawling of the bride among the dwarfs of central New Guinea, which is in no sense an expression of humility, as the observer believes, for the same practice is to be found elsewhere at ceremonies celebrating the maturity of girls. Do we have in this conception of a new life an explanation of the funeral ceremony of the Norwegian Lapps of the middle of the seventeenth century, who "cried, limped, and took many other positions like senseless people"?

COMPOSITE ASTRAL DANCES are rare, as far as we know. The Mexican Cora have beginnings, or more properly relics inherited from a high culture. Their "Christian" Easter dances, in which they take off their loincloths and make obscene gestures, are pure fertility rites. The "Jews," dancing naked in their places in a circle and bending their heads as if they were about to fall, are for them the white stars which fall from the black sky, come into the world as spirits of spring, and by coitus movements serve the growth of plants and animals. Into this cycle of themes the death of the star demons, caused by the sun, also enters. The battle of the morning star against the night stars brings another common theme to the Cora.

We have already discussed in detail the triple-circle astral dance of the dervishes of western Asia and Egypt. The high point of such representations was reached at the turn of the sixteenth century by the painter Leonardo da Vinci in his composition of a ballet in which the entire astronomic system was depicted in the dance.

The idea itself, in all its purity and magnificence, uninfluenced by worldly exhibition and corporality, was formed by Dante in his *Paradise.*

The Masked Dance

In the preceding section we have shown how strongly the non-mimetic dance moves in the direction of the mimetic, and how great is the need of representing and objectifying the non-physical concept in a physical way. But we have also shown how the mimetic dance forms, by reason of their magic goals and of the ecstasy inherent in all dance, open the way for that inspiration and spiritualization which carries the image dance beyond the purely mimic into the super-mimetic.

When these two tendencies cross and give way to each other, the result is oftentimes nothing more than a deterioration or degeneration. But when time and place are favorable, they may come together in a third type and be lifted to a plane which alone they could never attain. The masked dance has its origin in a realm where a deep mystical and ecstatic experience can split the consciousness of self and where a powerful exhilaration disembodies and releases the human part of this consciousness but molds the spiritual part into a new existence that is perceptible to the senses and based on the physical.

Even without masks the dance is able to transport a person into ecstasy, to restrict or release his consciousness, to obliterate completely or almost completely the feeling of self, and to implant in him another self, a spirit self: the dancer is "possessed," as we have shown earlier in the example of the Vedda shaman and of the Wanyamwezi. But the possession of the Wanyamwezi is "animistic"; for them, all things are bound essentially to the spirit; the form which the spirit assumes, in which it works and manifests itself, is a matter of no importance. The reverse is true of the masked dance, which like the mimetic dance in general is non-animistic: the outward form is of prime importance; the form draws into itself the appropriate spirit, no matter where it may be. Masked culture, one of whose roots lies in the physical, conceives its spirits in perceptible, often in animal form; and the full achievement of possession and the complete repulsion of the self are bound up with the loss of one's own shape and physiognomy, with a visible transformation.

The loss of one's own shape is vitally important for the success of the charm. He who is recognized causes the charm to be destroyed and endangers his own life, unless one can hush up the incident by quickly covering the exposed person and calling out that he is dead. Even in a stage of transition from the maskless to the masked dance, the participants attempt to effect a release from their own personality: in a girls' initiation of the California Shasta, friends and relatives come from nearby villages, arrange themselves in a line, dance toward the local participants who are also dancing, and carry bunches of leaves in front of their faces "to conceal their identity."

To conceal their identity—even the ordinary dance releases the sensitive primitive from self, whether he seeks to loosen the corporeal ties in ecstatic circling or to imitate an animal in a mimetic dance. But how much more effective when he puts aside his human countenance! And how much more effective still when he borrows another! For the face especially is the seat of the spirit. To put on another face is to admit another spirit. We call this other face with all its costume and decoration a mask.

Although it is often newly made and after use destroyed and burned, the mask not only bears the characteristics of the demon, but it is his face. The first priests—according to the Cágaba of Colombia—made "treaties with the demons, in which the latter make known by what songs and dances they may be induced to apply their useful qualities to the benefit of mankind and to keep in check their harmful ones." And the priests "removed the faces of the demons or the demons themselves did it of their own free will, so that men could wear them in dancing as a mask." That is why in a masked dance culture as degenerate as the Siamese-Cambodian the sick dancer may still pray to her own mask.

Whoever wears a mask gives up his own identity and takes on that of another. The wish to be a part of the other self in every way is so strong that the Javanese sews a piece of leather in his mask and bites on it with his teeth to intensify the spiritual act of taking possession. But no matter how the assimilation of the new identity is achieved, the dancer acts and talks like the spirit which the mask represents; indeed, the relatives recognize in him their departed one. "That is my husband, that is my child," they say, not "that represents my husband."

The beginnings of the mask may be traced back to the early period of dance decoration. Dance decoration is not simply a matter of course. Many dances are executed in the dress of forefathers, many naked. But for the festive occasion it is obvious that the dancers will make their toilet carefully, that they will shave and paint themselves and put on beautiful clothes and gleaming ornaments—even Wolfgang Köhler's Teneriffe chimpanzees liked to hang "all kinds of things to their bodies, best of all swinging and dangling strings, vines, and rags": the dance as an exhilarative force, as a means of achieving another state, brings festive ornamentation along with it.

This ornamentation may be very strange: often only a few lines painted across the body; or something like glasses; sometimes a tuft of feathers which looks like a bird's tail; a helmet which may be more than three feet high; or the clothes of white men.

But wherever the dance still carries with it a religious significance, this adornment—which it is not the province of this book to discuss in detail—serves one or the other of the two basic powers with which we are familiar, in order to intensify the magic charm by means of color, form, and material. On the one hand, it assists the dancer in lifting himself out of his everyday consciousness of self, in freeing him from himself, and in bringing him to a state of exhilaration. On the other hand, the ornamentation emphasizes the mimetic character of the image dance: in the animal dance clothing and attributes must take over the traits of the animal imitated. The duck dancers of the California Maidu wear on their heads a net cap covered with down, the totem dancers of New Ireland hold in their mouths carved and painted heads of rhinoceros birds, and the Cobéua of Brazil carry light wooden figures of birds, fishes, or lizards, which are fastened by strings to thin sticks; every pair of dancers carries the sticks under their arms, so that the figure swings in front of them. We still find the same kind of representation on European soil: in England, for instance, and Mallorca, southern France, northern Spain, the dancers gird themselves with little cardboard hobby-horses, and in Mallorca, with eagle figures also.

The mask also has a double meaning. As far as we can see, it bears in the extravert, image cultures the mimetic features of the animal or other creature which is being imitated. Australia provides our illustrations of this point. In the introvert cultures it represents no form of reality, but rather a spirit which the shaman or the mask-maker has seen in a dream transport. If the mask in its wild and licentious fantasy often seems in no sense sacred or elevated, but distorted rather to the point of the ridiculous, let us recall J. W. Hauer's remark that the "mixture of really intuitive and of grotesque and ridiculous ideas which is so strange to us" is characteristic of subconscious experiences.

The high point of the grotesque and fantastic, with an attendant richness of color and artistry that is most impressive, is to be found, no doubt, in northern Melanesia. What a world! Unfettered, free of all physical ties, the creative fantasy molds into new formations what nature has divided strictly into types and classes. From a countenance that otherwise appears almost human, the mighty beak of a frigate bird protrudes; from an enormous mouth with the teeth showing, an insect more than a meter long shoots out instead of a tongue; in place of a tail a greedy goose's neck or a cobra sticks out. Other parts of the body, too, are distorted to the point of unreality. The goggle eyes of a mussel stand out; the head is stuck to the trunk without a neck; or a neck without a head rises from the trunk, tilts over, and seems to divide and open like a mouth; or where neck and head should be, a pointed cone may stick out. An absurdly vaulted forehead is perched above an otherwise flat face; two faces stare out one above the other; a man has become a pillar with two eyes in the middle and a mouth above the feet. All proportion ceases; the head structures may rise over fifty yards in the air. Even in the museum, on racks within glass cases, altogether apart from the dancers and from their native surroundings, the masks preserve something of their mysterious and demoniacal character. But out in their own world, worn and looked upon by the credulous and supersensitive, rushing forth menacingly from the forest and moving nearer with rhythmical and unhuman walking, bending, and swaying to unreal, ghost-like sounds—what a frightful drama! What chills must run up and down the spines of the boys at their initiation when they first cast eyes upon the horror masks! And we have all of us set foot upon that kingdom where the masked dance had its real beginning: that dream world in which our horrors and our fears, quite apart from logic and reality, lump themselves into irrational apparitions.

In later cultural stages the mask becomes smaller and smaller until only a narrow eye and nose mask is left. This development may be seen especially clearly in the history of the Japanese mask. The end of the development may be the transition in eastern Asia to "masklessness," which forces the painted face itself into the rigidity of a mask, which forbids to the danseuse any physiognomic expression and makes of the pantomime, as E. Guimet has expressed it so nicely, *une élégie à froid.*

With the use of the mask the movements of the mimetic dance often depart from a strict adherence to nature. As in our dream visions, they slip away from the real, the earthly, and the comprehensible and follow the irrational laws of the creative fantasy of the subconscious. Out of the mimetic dance there often develops a distortion dance.

The themes and contents of the dance have scarcely changed at all. The big events in the life of man and of nature and the important incidents in the existence of the tribe form the occasions, and just as before, the dancers anticipate future happenings and depict them as coming to pass in the best interest of the individual or of the tribe. The point of difference is that in the masked dance what is peculiar to the cultures of the image and imageless dance comes together. When the dancers of New Ireland show how their totem, the rhinoceros bird, looks about shyly for enemies or how the totem dove is pursued by the snake, when fertility and life are exhorted by means of phallic rites, these representations derive entirely from the territory of the mimetic and extravert dance. And at the initiation of Lengua girls in the Gran Chaco, the wicked demons beneath masks come running out of the forest and circle threateningly around the maiden, until the women defend her by dancing around her and chasing the demons away: with a slight interplay of mimetic motifs this is the imageless, magical circling of the introvert culture. And it is almost symbolic that the Cobéua of northwestern Brazil after a maskless period professed to have learned their masked dances first from the god Cúai, protector of the fields: the world of the extravert hunter and totemist and that of the introvert tiller of the soil have grown together in the mask dance.

No basic culture has masks, and they are likewise lacking in a number of Middle and Late Tribal cultures such as the Polynesian, the Micronesian, the Ainu, and others. This confirms internally the relative dating of the anthropologist: the mask is so typical of the so-called "exogamous and matriarchal" or "matriarchal two-class culture" that Graebner could give it the title "mask culture." It is the Miolithic stage of tribal culture which in the second part of this book we call "Early

Planter, Coup-de-poing Culture," after Menghin. We must add, however, that it is not this culture in the purest sense, but, as it seems always to be, crossed and mixed with totem culture.

Two principal lines of development lead from the mask dance into Europe of the present day. The one, a descending line, shows a steady degeneration and profanation down to the carnival of Catholic countries, which has preserved nothing of the old fertility ceremony so deeply moving to the participants, except mask, disguise, and sexuality; and also down to the world of the children, who in mask and disguise satisfy the ancient human impulse for exchange of personality and the "incessant longing to make believe."

An illustration from southern Bavaria shows how direct even today is the connection with the Early Stone Age in particularly settled regions, and how clear and vivid the substratum appears beneath thousands of years of later stratification. Notice here in spite of all degeneration what precautions are used to keep secret the everyday personality of the mask-bearer.

"Beginning at eight o'clock on 'Nonsense Thursday' and on the three last nights of carnival, the males of every age in Partenkirchen went *maschgeren* (masquerading). . . . Every man wore a *Gsichtl* or mask carved from wood and painted lifelike. This was tied tight yet so that it could be moved with strings running crosswise over the head, the hair was covered with a white cloth, and over the *Gsichtl* and cloth the headdress was fastened. By skillful manipulation the heavy *Gsichtl* was raised from time to time to make way for the beer mug. The masquerader would cover the exposed part of his face with both hands, then after drinking would lower the mask quick as a flash. For the first condition of going masquerading was the concealing of one's identity, and it was considered bad form to attempt to penetrate obtrusively the disguise of another. But if through leading questions from the group anyone was in danger of being discovered, he would change his *Gsichtl* and costume with unbelievable rapidity. The rest of the masked men protected him as he slipped away to a little room which was kept in readiness; after several minutes the same figure would return, but another man was inside, and this deception was repeated several times of an evening if need be."

The second, ascending line leads, as we shall see, from the mask dance to the drama.

3. Forms and Choreography

Individual Dances

ALL dance is originally the motor reflex of intense excitement and of increased activity. Thus from the very beginning, the unorganized individual dance must stand next to the choral dance, which represents the organized excitement reflex of a community. Studies of animals, which we have already discussed, and experiences with primitive peoples confirm this statement. When the primitive man offers peace to an approaching visitor by hopping and waving his fist at the entrance to the village, or when in extreme fright at the unexpected appearance of a white man he hides the women and children in the rushes and does a war dance in the shallow water, we have examples of the simplest type of individual dance.

The gradual replacement of the impulsive and instinctive by something planned and organized comes about whenever an individual activity of definite purpose adopts the dance as a form of expression. The young Guaicurú of the Gran Chaco in ceremonial dress dances for eight days with convulsive movements in front of the hut of his girl before she is promised to him; among the Gajo of Sumatra the bridegroom must dance from midnight until morning; the Usiai (Admiralty Islands) who has received a pig takes lances in his hand and hops to the sound of the slit drum; and the merchants in the markets of New Caledonia dance as they display their wares.

On the border between an individual personality and a representative of the community is the girl at her first menstruation. When the newly matured girl of the California Indians dances forwards and backwards for ten nights with her face turned toward the east, she is creating for herself, by dancing, all the powers needed to make her a complete woman, and more than that, a complete and productive member of the community. If her creation of power in the dance were no community affair, the people of the village and even her relatives in other towns would certainly not be attracted to the festival place as active participants at her maturity celebration.

To what extent the young virgin is a representative of the community, especially in the dance (we have already discussed this in detail), is evidenced in the rain charm and similar fertility rites. In seeking examples we need not leave Europe, nor even Germany. In Prussian Lithuania at the spring festivals the virgins used to dance facing the sun; in the Slavic countries young girls must bring about rain in a whirl dance; in Bohemia and the Palatinate only virgins were allowed to take part in the May dances; and the Spanish church dances are boys' or girls' chorals. In this sense we may also understand the dances of virgins outside of Europe: the six girls of the Celebes who in a narrow circle turn slowly about on their own axis; the maiden of the Khasi who dances in the early morning in front of the drink offering and is carried with swaying motions by two men to the village square; the girl of Tasmania decked with leaves, who dances in front of the men with her hands behind her head, her feet together and her knees spread apart and clicked together with a snap—to excite "the passions of the men," says Bonwick, but this is an entirely false explanation as far as the original sense is concerned. It is nonetheless a fertility charm when at funeral ceremonies on the island of Yap very young girls dance with slow, un-erotic movements of the arms and trunk; or when also on Yap at the new moon the men sit around in a circle with a girl in the center and make gentle motions of a sensual nature with their arms and trunks; and when in Seran only girls, not women, are allowed to dance. The view is indeed very widespread that girls and boys also who have not had sexual intercourse are particularly endowed with religious powers, and even the history of early Christianity tells us of the rain prayers of the children. The motif appears in weakened form in the Cambodian court ballet: a dancer who has become a mother may dance no more. In a different form it emerges once again among the Plains Ojibway Indians when the participants must have remained abstinent before a certain dance or receive a black mark across one cheek.

From this it becomes clear why in Egyptian dance pictures of the New Kingdom (after 1500 B.C.), small, that is to say young, girls are again and again depicted, even when there is apparently no longer any question of devotional dances.

But more important for the history of the dance as representative of the whole tribe is that highly excitable man of ecstasy, so full of imagination, who has the power to slip away temporarily from what is human and in a state of exhilaration to assume the power of the spirits—the medicine man, the witch doctor, the shaman. His duties are to banish evil spirits, to ward off misfortune, to heal the sick; and his principal medium is the ecstatic dance. With his knees flexed, his body bent over, his eyes closed, hopping from one foot to the other, he jumps around in a circle until he has achieved a state of ecstasy. The dance becomes more rapid, the movement wilder and more convulsive, until finally the dancer collapses and thus regains consciousness.

Descended from the shaman after thousands of years of development are the Jewish and early Christian prophets, who found the spirit of God in the ecstasy of the dance, and the priestly chieftains and kings of the old monarchies. This heritage is impressed on the dance in the particular form of the chieftain's and king's dance. In the Polynesian culture in Tonga, there are difficult dance movements which only the chiefs and leaders learn how to do, and for the African Negro monarchies we can do no better than to read the description by Schweinfurth of King Munsa of the Mangbettu, who jumps around in the huge festival hall before all his wives and warriors "in a furious dance, throwing his arms out in all directions like one possessed."

Nor have the high cultures allowed the king's dance to languish. In old Mexico the princes dance every four years. "They form on the outside; Motecuhçoma, leading the dance, comes followed by the others; the two great kings, Naçaualpilli, King of Tetzcoco, and Totoquiuaztli, King of Tepaneca, come up to his side; the spectators are gripped with fear as the dance proceeds."

In ancient Egypt the Pharaohs with a long and measured stride danced around the temple walls, so that the sun would continue in its course; on the day of Mithra, the King of Persia danced; and in Israel, King David whirled before the Ark of the Covenant.

The priestly heritage is like the kingly. In the post-biblical Talmud period the rabbi with a myrtle branch in his hand danced at weddings, and in the eighteenth century in central Germany the rabbi and the Christian priest as well would have the first dance with the bride. Even at the present time on the Faeroe Islands the parson in the dress of his office takes part in the bridal dances.

CHORAL DANCES

Classification

It will be best if first of all we set up only a general and somewhat loose classification for the choral rounds in order that we may not choke what is living in the dance by too tight a net. Yet the important pictures ought to be arranged systematically so far as possible, so that historical work may stand on sure footing.

The most striking difference exists between the simple and complex forms of the choral dance. In the simple choral the dancer keeps his original place, in the complex he leaves it temporarily or permanently. Whether the dancers move in a circle, in a straight line, in figure eights, or in spirals, they remain in line and are led by the dance leader like sheep by the oldest wether. In the crossing, chain, bridge, arch, or star, on the other hand, they must act independently; they change places. We should like to give to this form, therefore, instead of the ambiguous designations "complex" or "figure choral," the name "place changing choral dance."

Within these large groups we may distinguish a whole progression of forms with increasing richness of movement: the circle to the spiral, the snake line to the meander, the double circle to the chain. The double circle already points to a second type of progression, the increase of the element of form. A third type would make these elements independent: counter-movement in the double circle and in the double front. But for the present let us avoid forcing observations of this sort into a classification. We must be the more cautious because most of the dances outside of Europe and most of the extinct dances of Western culture are insufficiently described, especially in respect to form.

In this discussion belongs finally the more or less close relation of the dancers one to another, their joining together by grasping hands, hooking arms, or otherwise. In the earliest cultures any tie between the dancers is slight; everyone dances for himself without touching his neighbor, without making his motions or even the directions of his movement correspond. This stage extends even into the higher cultures. In Colombia the Cágaba, in Indo-China the Khasi, in Togo the Adele, all dance for themselves without touching one another and thus establishing that tie which makes the dance a social activity in the full sense. The Shasta of California, who touch one another only rarely, really have no community dances, as A. L. Kroeber points out. When they dance, it is with a special purpose, for a single person or a single group. They dance to prepare themselves for battle, to assist a girl in the critical period of her maturity, to achieve the power of the shaman, to heal a sick man, and that is about all. No genuine victory or scalp dance is credited to the Shasta, and the lack of such dances is characteristic of the culture of northwestern America.

In a higher level the choral dancers almost always touch one another and thus force themselves into the same stride and the same movement. The closer the contact, the stronger is the social character of the choral.

They hold hands, they place their hands on the shoulders or hips of their neighbors, or they lock arms; the pre-Chinese Li in Hainan, like the Polish *Krakowiak* dancers, even cross their arms over their chests and give the left arm to the man on the right and the right arm to the one on the left; and the children of New Guinea, Greece, and Romagna hold one another by the ears.

Rounds

The oldest form of the choral dance is the circle. Even the chimpanzees dance in a circle, and people of every continent still do it. The front, row, or line dance, which as its counterpart must be touched upon here, originates in a later period. Many traditions confirm this statement. The Nahua of old Mexico used to dance their solemn ceremonial dances in a circle, but their profane dances in two rows. The myths also have the dance beginning as a circle. The Caingang of eastern Brazil, who are at an early cultural level, tell the story that once a marriage was to be celebrated, but the people did not know how to sing or dance. Then while they were hunting in the jungle they saw a clearing with a tree trunk in the center and several sticks leaning against it. These sticks began to move in rhythm, and at the marriage these motions were imitated. "Thus it came about that we learned how to sing and dance."

The circle later takes on a spiritual significance. This is not the result of a development of understanding but rather of the connection between an idea and its motor reflex—to encircle an object is to take it into possession, to incorporate it, to chain it, or to banish it ("ban circle"). The captured head or scalp which is encircled must give over the power of its late owner; the shamanistic circling banishes the sickness spirit of the sick man; it makes the matured youth a complete member of society; it forces the growth power of the living tree into all natures and causes the bleeding sacrificial animal to die for them all. This incorporating, giving, and receiving of power which is achieved in circling is reflected in a beautiful myth of the Melbourne Australians:

their god forms two men out of clay; he lies down upon them and blows his breath into them; when they begin to move, he jumps up and dances three times around them; then their tongues are loosed and they start to speak. Yet the Sanskrit Rig Veda regards the creation of the universe as a wild and magnificent circular dance of the gods, who whirl into the air the dust of chaos.

The round dance form did not originate, to be sure, in a spiritual conception no matter how obvious; for the apes, as we have seen already, possess it. Before all spiritualization was the clearly felt need of traversing and molding space with the body.

When men were no longer content to seek out caves or overhanging rocks or to set up simple windbreaks to protect themselves from rough weather, when they set about building huts, it was a circular room which they made for themselves. The dwellings of primitive man look like bee-hives; no perpendicular wall, no square grew from his hands: the space conception of the basic cultures and of a large part of the early levels requires the circle. This noteworthy fact stands convincingly beside the other fact that in dancing, also, the circle is the earliest space form. In the dance, indeed, it is infinitely earlier: before man expresses his space requirement objectively with foreign material, with wood, and stalks, and stones, he must satisfy it with his own body, with the impulsive movements of his limbs and trunk. How strong this inner need is, how inseparable is the formation of movement and of construction is illustrated by a further fact: in those cultures which depart from circular building and set up rectangular huts—and quite exclusively in such cultures—the choral dance also takes on the form of the straight line. The formation and development of the circular dance coincide essentially with the formation and development of the circular hut; the front dance is connected with the formation and development of the rectangular hut.

This conformity is shown most clearly in North America. Where the circular round prevails, there we find, also, the round hut and the round dance house. Only in the northwest, where the rectangular house of planks has made its way, and in California, which under the influence of this house builds rectangular huts and dance houses, together with the round hut and dance house for ceremonial dances—only in these sections does the front dance turn into a circular round. Indeed, in this mixed hut territory, the circular choral dance very often becomes a front dance.

Just as the circular hut turns about a fireplace or a center post, as it were, so does the circular choral dance move around a fire, a pit, or a post. Even the round of the chimpanzees has a central point. Let us compare the following descriptions. The first concerns the construction of the round hut in New Caledonia: "In the middle of a hole which they dug into the ground, they set the trunk of a tree, and around the outside they stuck poles, which they bent at the top and tied to the middle of the trunk. Between these poles they inserted branches, then covered the whole structure with leaves and grass." Compare with this the myth of the Caingang of Brazil about the origin of the dance to which we have already referred: "One day the men of the Cayurucre went hunting and when they came upon a clearing in the forest, they noticed a nice open place around the trunk of a high tree. Leaning against the tree trunk were several sticks with leaves, one of which protruded from a hollow gourd. . . . Shortly afterward the little sticks began to move rhythmically from the bottom to the top."

Whoever dances around the fireplace dances around a hole in the earth. This may be the reason that in many parts of the world a pit without a fire is the turning point of the round. Then in the predominantly feminine cultures with leanings toward the matriarchal the pit in the ground is given a clearly defined magical significance as a symbol of the generating maternal bosom and of the fruit-bearing earth itself.

The slit drum and the dance tree which precedes it are sometimes placed over a pit at initiation dances and similar rites, and in California the Miwok and the Pomo do one of their spirit dances by climbing out of the pit and stamping on the drum. It is the same motif of climbing out of a dead world into which the novice has been lowered that we have already encountered at girls' initiations among the California Indians. The pit is therefore in no sense a place selected because of its acoustic properties—even outside of California and America. For when the masked Cumang dancers of the Bosso emerge from a pit, we have the same motif again on African soil. Thus we have explained the pit dances of three continents.

The highly important question as to the direction of the circular movement—where the dancers do not remain in one place—cannot be answered in most cases: only a few investigators have recorded this phase of the dance. Wherever we have this information we speak of a movement to the right, that is, clockwise: the dancer, following the line of the circle, must keep to the right. Movement to the left, accordingly, is counter-clockwise.

The occasions of movement to the right are so varied that no one principle becomes apparent. The Navajo use it for the sun dance, the Maidu for girls' rites, the Tupi of South America for the war dance. The Siusi of Brazil "set their pace leftward" when five of them blow the large flute and each of them places his hand on the right shoulder of an accompanying girl; the neighboring Huhuteni have a similar tradition. Among the southern Slavs movement to the right is used for a sun dance, and the "horse races" of the Alar and the Burjate, which are danced to the right, are also sun cults. Examples of movement to the left are less frequent and their meaning is not clear. Among the Toradja of the Celebes the direction of the death cult dance is understood as being leftward, and among the Indians of Puget Sound a dance moving to the right is regarded as endangering life. In other cases the dancers may turn about and proceed in another direction.

The number of the rounds and of the steps, as of the dance days, songs, and repetition of songs, is frequently determined by sacred numbers. The number four is sacred to the California Indians, for example, and this number is therefore a guide in the dances of the Maidu, the Yuki, the Hupa, and the Mojave. Five, on the other hand, governs those of the Yurok, the Wyot, the Sinkyone, the Modoc, the Achomawi, and the Atsugewi. Four also predominates in Puget Sound. Elsewhere eight or nine is preferred; eight, for example, among the Dayak, and nine in Ceram.

Double circles (inner and outer circles). In hut dances the occasion of such formations is simple enough; where there are a great many participants, one circle is not sufficient to contain them all. Another occasion is the participation of both sexes with the desire to avoid mixing them. In such cases, for the most part, the women are on the outside, the men on the inside. This is easily explained: it is quite clear that such a form will come into being when the women, excluded from the ring of men, nevertheless succumb to the dance impulse and begin to join in timidly outside the circle. Wherever the women dance on the inside, there is apparently the idea of the magic enclosure, to which we have already devoted attention. The mixing of the sexes in the same circle is essentially a much later development: first, the separation into segments; last, as in the Celebes, the men and women in a row in alternate positions. Counter-movement of two circles is often attested; in New Ireland it represents the moon.

Three-circle rounds are to be found in the primitive world among the Toradja of the Celebes and in western Melanesia—in their dances, also, women and children are on the outside. There are occasional examples of the triple-circle dance in Europe. One of the most remarkable examples comes from Florence where in 1497, after a sermon of Savonarola, the wildly enthusiastic listeners danced in a three-way circle in the square in front of St. Mark's: "on the inner circle the monks of this cloister alternated with the choir boys, in the second circle were the young clergy and layman, and finally on the outside, old men, citizens, and priests."

It may have been such a picture that inspired Dante's splendid vision of the round dance of the sun:

And ere it turned full circle, a new throng
Within a second circle closed it round,
And motion matched with motion, song with song.
Paradiso, XII, 4-6.

Then both signs in such fashion to revolve
That till the first has started, the second stays.
XIII, 17-18.

And lo, around us grew another light,
In lustre even as those already there,
And like the horizon which is growing bright.
And as at rise of early evening new
Appearances enter upon the heavens,
And to our vision seem, and seem not, true,
So new subsistences were gathering,
It seemed, before mine eyes, and round about
The other two were forming a third ring.
XIV, 67-75.

The counter-moving dance of the dervishes also had an astronomical meaning.

Dances of four circles and more are to be found especially in eastern Melanesia. We have examples in the Solomon Islands and in New Caledonia. They also place the younger dancers on the outside—only in the concentric women's dances of the Kiwai of New Guinea is the reverse the case. Ten circles moving in opposite directions alternately are said to have been achieved by the Yurok and other California tribes, and at the great festival of Quetzalcoatl, the ancient Mexicans used to form almost as great a number of circles.

When we consider the concentric circling, it becomes clear that the significance of the movement in the round dance is not constant, and that any scheme which classifies the circle dance as simply the opposite of the line dance is but superficial. We recall a *pilu pilu* of the New Caledonians: the inside circle takes only short steps, the middle circle must turn more rapidly, and the outside one flies around in a mad whirl. What a long way as a form of motion this is from the simple turning in a line of most circle dances! It is as far removed from them as the whirling propeller designs and the wagon wheels with spokes characteristic of mature ornamentation are from the lifeless line of the simple circle of decoration.

Special forms of the circle dance have been discussed in various parts of this book. At this point we shall describe only the game of the Assiniboin of North America: inside a group of sitting tribesmen the dancer hops in a circle, holds his fists in front of each participant, seizes one of them suddenly by the hand, lifts him up, dances for a while with him, and has him stand in the middle of the circle; then he takes a second and a third and so on, until all of them are standing. This type of dance has special interest for us because it has been handed down to our children: in games like "Going to Jerusalem" the circle is broken up in the same manner.

The figure eight round leads to the serpentine dances described below: the double S, which finally arrives at its starting point. We found it among the Bushmen of the Kalahari Desert and we meet it frequently again in the sword rounds and other figure dances of Europe.

The actual starting point of the serpentine dances, however, is the free round which developed from the circle. The ordinary form of the round is, as we have seen, a tightly closed circle with a center which the dancers face or which they move around. The dancers form a circle. But it may also be that the dance floor forms the circle, not the dancers. The latter, whose numbers may be insufficient to complete the circle, form only a segment and describe a circle as they move. The dancers *walk* in a circle. When they walk around in this fashion and connect this march with the circle movement, the circle, ring, or wheel form has become a free and open continuous movement, in which the original circling has lost value and meaning and which finally may disappear altogether. Then the row of dancers becomes a kind of snake, which winds through the whole house upstairs and down, among the nearby dwellings, and through the streets of the town, always following the leader and always imitating his steps exactly; the charm of its movement is the colorful and surprising variety of the direction in which the dance may lead. Open rounds like the Germanic *Langtänze* and the Provençal *farandoule* live on in the ballroom in our *polonaises* and *cotillons*. Now we have used the word "snake"—every open round becomes a serpentine dance. In the next section we shall discuss its peculiarities of form and its meaning.

Serpentine Rounds

In later Greece the legend of the labyrinth, drawn from various sources, is pieced together: Theseus leads the boys and girls of Athens, who are a tribute to Crete, through the passages of the labyrinth at Knossos, kills the minotaur, finds a way out with the help of the threads of Ariadne, daughter of the King of Crete, escapes and brings those entrusted to his care back to Athens.

It is doubtful whether this labyrinth actually existed; the one at Lemnos has disappeared, and the Egyptian labyrinth near Hauwâra, built in the nineteenth century B. C. by King Amenmês III and described exactly by Herodotus and Strabo, was indeed so tremendous in its massive proportions and its three thousand rooms that a stranger could not find his way in and out without a guide, but we have no report of people being purposely led astray in it.

Even in pagan antiquity ground plans of labyrinths are represented by concentric lines as *sgraffiti* or floor mosaics. The custom was then taken over by many Christian churches: those unable to make the journey to Jerusalem might here make a pilgrimage from space to space on their knees or on foot, and by seeking for the path experience for themselves how men are ensnared by sin and error. The cathedrals at Sens and Amiens are said to have had labyrinths of a thousand spaces. Only a few of these mosaics have been preserved. In Germany there are none at all; there is one in the cathedral at Lucca and one in San Michele of Pavia; there are several in France, the best known in the cathedral at Chartres. Transformed into amusements for the courts, the labyrinths are found again in the Italian, French, and English parks.

The labyrinth as a form of Christian procession has already led from a stationary structure into movement. The myth of Theseus itself mentions an earlier relationship: after their release the Athenians land on the isle of Delos and there do a round dance with many twists and turns in representation of the fatal paths of the structure on the island of Crete, and as late as Plutarch's time the inhabitants of the island are still doing the same dance. Van den Leeuw has rightly asserted that movement through a labyrinth is older than the labyrinth itself. I should like to defend this argument in the paragraphs to follow.

The essence of the labyrinth is movement. The building has no meaning by itself—it takes on meaning only when people walk through it. It presupposes the snake movement, but the snake movement does not presuppose the building. The movement can exist without the building and actually does in places where nothing is known about a labyrinth. Among primitive peoples and in European folk dances the round often develops into a spiral and in certain instances into a snake line. The most impressive illustration is from Nyassa, where as many as four hundred men and boys take hold of one another and dance with a snake movement faster and faster, until after the last *prestissimo* they fall breathless to the ground. All these dances live on in our linear choral dances, farandoules, and polonaises.

One is tempted to include here the many primitive dances which avoid rectilinear movement. The dance group often moves in a zigzag. In the rain charm of Mallorca, the *Ball de la Xisterna,* the girl skips backwards in a zigzag from the fountain. The circumcision procession of the Merina of Madagascar, of which we shall have more to say below, even follows meander lines which have been drawn in advance of the ceremony.

We have no information about the significance of these dances and are therefore dependent upon our conclusions. In these dances we shall look first for a "natural" origin. For neither the contents nor even the occasion of the earliest zigzag and serpentine dance can be the conquest of death, of the underworld, or of the sinful life. The natural origin may lie in an innate impulse to motion or to imitation. There is evidence for both. Dogs and children, who move ecstatically, that is, who give way to a motive impulse that is emotional, are more likely to jump to and fro in a zigzag than in a straight line: movement released of purpose avoids a direct path to a goal. This is the explanation of part of the dance. The other would be "sensory" imitation.

Sahagun relates of an old Mexican dance: "They did not skip nor did they make any motions, they did not move their hands back and forth, they made no dance movements with their hands, they did not bend their bodies, they did not turn around, they did not go in any particular direction, they did not walk backwards—they walked, they danced quietly, slowly, deliberately; their dance was one single big snake. No one made any motion, or disturbance, or confusion. And they grasped the women by their bodies, only the great chieftains and the elder brothers were not permitted to grasp the women by their bodies. And the dance ended when there was little sun, when the sun was about to set. Then they broke the line and walked away. And in every house there was singing, everywhere they sang of their gods 'Two Cane' or 'Seven Snake' [the corn goddess] or the wind god."

There are two noteworthy facts about this dance: first, the form content of the dance is not the attainment of a goal but rather a continuous winding; and then, the corn goddess, in whose honor this dance is also danced on other days, is called "Seven Snake." Thus this dance is unmistakably an imitation of a snake movement. In the serpentine movement of the Gond of Hindustan, Fox Strangways sees the crawling of a gigantic centipede; and likewise, according to Rosenberg's impression, the hundreds of Nyassa natives "represent the movements of a snake." Modigliani says of the latter that it was their intention to represent this movement. Therefore, we shall have to look for one root of the serpentine dance in the animal dance.

The labyrinth motif itself seems to be suggested for the first time in the spirit dance of northeastern Chaco, when the dancers prepare a round place in the middle of the forest and then cut out a scarcely recognizable path with many turns leading to it, thus causing "any unauthorized intruder" to lose himself very quickly. Here, as in the dance festival itself, the motif of mystery, of initiation as another root of the labyrinth is apparent. But it is even more apparent in the circumcision dance of the Merina of Madagascar. The path to the sacred stone of circumcision is divided into five sections by means of strings: on the middle string walks the king in a straight line, on the other four strings, which are arranged in a crooked, meandering fashion, walk the people. The king, who is surely thought of as being divine, has, therefore, a straight path ahead of him to the initiation shrine; the others must dance to it on twisting paths, which lead in a roundabout meandering fashion. The serpentine dance of the Kurnai of southern Australia is also an initiation ceremony. From the circumcision of Madagascar it is perhaps not a far cry to another initiation: admittance into the sacred mysteries of Eleusis was secured by solemnly wandering through dark, labyrinthine paths which had no outlet.

The Buddhistic cult of Indo-China supplies a second connecting link. In Arakan the faithful read the holy *Bana* as they dance through an artificial labyrinth; at every turning they challenge the Yaksha there and drive him away; then at last they come to the divine region. In reading the *Paritta,* which is directed against the Yakshas, the Ceylonese unwind a thread. It is not far from such usages to purification from the sinful life.

In view of the countless allusions to snakes in myth and story throughout the world, it need not be difficult to trace step by step how the snake dance gradually becomes metaphorical, how the animal dance of primitive society becomes a dance of another significance among the high cultures. But this delicate task must be left for the expert mythographer.

Since the writing of this book, Mr. John Layard has read an extremely interesting paper to the Folk-Lore Society of London, showing that in the Megalithic cultures the labyrinth and the maze dances represented the journey of the dead.

Choral Front Dances

While the purely ecstatic, imageless dances are executed for the most part in the circle form, we saw that the mimetic dancers repeatedly form lines or rows. The circle stands for itself; it is closed to the surrounding world and to spectators, just as the ecstatic peoples are closed to the outside and are "introvert." The row, on the other hand, which is open toward the outside, permits the dancers to face one another when they dance mimetically.

The first themes in which the dancers face one another are the love play and the weapon battle. For the weapon battle the men's chorus divides into two hostile groups; in the love play the men and women face one another in a wooing pantomime. In the dances themselves there may be astral motifs; especially the battle of the light moon and the dark moon, which, to be sure, is only a lunar transformation of a war dance. Thus may be explained the two rows in the limping dance of the northern Ute of the Great Basin, especially in view of the fact that only women take part in it and that limping is familiar in many myths as a characteristic of the man in the moon.

Although the circle dance is known throughout the entire world, the front dance is limited to the cultures of which the rectangular hut is a part. In two instances we find the front dance in the territory of the round hut and even of the windbreak—in Gazelle and in Australia. But once again they point to the somewhat forcible engrafting of the mask or rectangular hut culture, in the former case from New Ireland, in the latter from New Guinea.

It must, of course, not be inferred from the fact of this double parallel that the circle dance will always be found in company with the round hut. The circle dance in its development is linked to the round hut, but is not confined to its present-day territory. For as a primitive cultural property it was taken from earlier stages into later and retained in spite of a modified cultural condition. Yet the front dance, as we have seen, not only in its origin but essentially also in its diffusion at the present time is united with its structural counterpart, the rectangular hut.

Especially in more primitive regions the relationship of the rectangular hut and the row dance is shown in the vivid consciousness of direction. Wherever there are four walls, consciousness of direction is far keener than where there is the uninterrupted rotation of a single, circular wall. At the ceremony for the dead among the old Bora of Brazil, a dancer is stationed at each of the four corners of the hut. In the duck dance of the California Maidu twelve or more men form a line in the dance house in front of the fire, but separate immediately into two groups. The dancers stamp and move their hands rhythmically as one group goes slowly to the north side, the other to the south; then the two groups take their first positions. After four movements such as this, the two groups change directions, the original north dancers moving to the south, the south dancers to the north. In the roe dance, the dance choruses form two parallel lines on the north and south sides of the house, and the dance leaders move between them forwards and backwards from west to east. This is a perfect illustration of the rectangular use of space in dancing. In the turtle dance, four men walk together to the north side of the fire, four to the south, while the two dance leaders look for their places along the middle post, the one going from east to north, then south, the other, directly north. Here we have clearly reflected a space consciousness that still fluctuates between a search for the middle of a circle and a rectangular confrontation.

Likewise in California, after a circle dance of several hours' duration at girls' initiations, the dancers form a line which must face the east, join hands, and move forwards and backwards without turning their eyes from the east. In this illustration the dance around a tangible object is replaced by a dance toward an intangible direction. The line formation seems to be the necessary expression of another type of religion which has expanded from the near at hand into the infinite.

The same festival reveals an occasion for the line formation which is apparently independent of the rectangular hut, but which presumably first developed as a dance from a feeling for the rectangular. While the people of the village dance in a circle, the guests from outside the village move forward in Indian file, come to a halt, and wave alternately from left to right the bunches of green which they hold in their hands. From the Indian file they can, to be sure, swing easily enough into the accustomed circle, and as a matter of fact such transitions from the long row to the circle are frequent: the line of march turns about what has been plotted out as the dance place without "encircling" anything, without giving up from start to finish the characteristics of the row in favor of a continuous, closed circle. But the Indian file for the most part becomes a front with the dancers making turns at an angle of ninety degrees.

The front, like the circle, is often composed of two, three, four, or more columns—mass formations which are to be found especially in western Polynesia, in particular the beautiful weapon dances of the Fiji Islands, which are culturally Polynesian. More than eight thousand men are supposed to have taken part in the ceremonial dances of old Mexico. In eastern Asia, the multiplicity of rows has a special significance: the Chinese ceremonial dance, which was taken over by Japan before the year 1000, was arranged in eight rows for the emperor, in six rows for the Chinese feudal princes, in four rows for dignitaries of the crown, and in paying homage to an official it was considered a breach of etiquette to set up more rows than were his proper due.

But the choral front also has a number of special characteristics which are lacking in the round. First, on the island of Yap, a symmetrical arrangement according to size with the little children at the two ends; second, the horseshoe or semi-circle arrangement of several rows; third, the dance bridge several stories high of the Caroline Islands, in which the dancers take up their positions in brilliant costume and execute their dance with uniform trunk, arm, and head movements.

The usual ceremonial dance in Ponape is the *Uin,* "which may be danced at any time and also in honor of the dead or for religious purposes. While the spectators remain silent, the dancers, decorated with wreaths and their bodies anointed with oil, mount in a solemn procession one behind another the dance bridges (*paj*) built with several recessive stories. For the ceremony of homage, they sit down, and the song leader names the person to be honored, not forgetting at the same time to call out by name the other important personages present. The dancers rise. The song leader begins the song in a coarse, deep voice, the chorus joins in, the singing continues, shrill and dissonant, but overpowering in its volume. As soon as the song is struck up the dancing commences. The dancers stamp their feet rhythmically on the floor boards and move their hands artistically in the manner of a Siva of Samoa. The *Uin* is without doubt one of the most impressive of the South Sea dances."

Europeans are especially attracted by that group of dances in which, as in the Spanish figure dances and particularly in the English contres, the dancers face one another in two rows and calmly or otherwise join together in simply moving forward and retreating or in executing more complicated figures. In these dances not only the basic position of the contre is anticipated, but the greater part of its figures as well.

The Ute of North America, as we have already shown, have a "lame dance" of two long rows which move forward in Indian file, then at the same time wheel inwards, and after a short interval march back. On Cape Nelson in New Guinea, writes Pöch, a popular dance figure is "the wheeling of the outside rows into the inside." Obviously this is a variation of the same form.

Among the Boloki of the Congo, the Ba-ila of Rhodesia, and the people of eastern Turkestan, one couple after another breaks away from the columns to dance together, and the Papua of New Guinea, the New Caledonians, and the people of Yap dance complicated forms with the greatest accuracy. In the rounds of the Orokawa of New Guinea one may find figures of great variety, and even chains. The counter dances of the Quoiren tribe of the Naga have six turns, exactly like the European double column dances: (1) crossing of the two columns; (2) turning backwards; (3) chain; (4) snake line; (5) large circle; (6) two small circles and return to the original lines. This is the arrangement of a Spanish figure dance of the seventeenth century or of an English country dance.

The dance in which the men form one row, the women another, and dance with and opposite each other in a form of love play, is widely diffused and may be confidently assigned to a Protoneolithic culture level.

"Two hours after sunset," writes Schimper in 1835, of the Bedouins of the Sinai peninsula, "the main ceremony began in the bright gleam of the stars. Men and women formed in groups linked themselves together amid singing and clapping of hands. The women, dressed in dark costumes and closely veiled, danced forward in an arch from both ends of the links without particular artistry, as in the contre dance, but with a natural grace; their dance was modest, serious, and truly beautiful. They moved forwards and backwards along their places and opposite, bending up and down in many curtseys. Two women outside the link are occupied in doing special dance turns, which, like the whole ceremony, are very solemn and dignified; these dancers continually alternate their movements with those of the dance chorus and develop in their positions a grace that is ever new."

Place Changing Chorals

The preceding section leads to a group of dances in which the dancers no longer remain linked but change places independently. There were mentioned a number of *double column dances* which correspond more or less to the European contre. The principal place changing figures in these dances are the crossing, the bridge, the arch, and the chain.

The place changing chorals at their best are found in the Caroline and Palau Islands. In Palau the natives dance "in the most varied figures, winding in and out between one another"; and likewise in Yap "the figures are extremely varied" and the dancers do "twists and turns in ever new artistic figures." On the other hand, in Togo the Ayuti have "notable figure dances." The cultural level of Micronesia, like that of Togo, is Full Neolithic and patriarchal and must be reckoned with the Late Tribal cultures.

CROSSING ROUNDS. When two columns dance toward each other, usually either the two fronts approach alternately or one moves forward while the other moves backward. Besides this pure *counter dance* there is a *column dance* in which the purpose is for one front to break through the other. A dance of this type is the *medicine dance* of the Guarani, of which we have a good description. "From the front the two groups walked through each other and ran to the ends of the wings where they immediately turned about and rushed toward each other once again. As the three dancers of each group had to run in a line together, not behind one another, and as the space where they crossed was rather limited, a certain agility was necessary for one group to move easily through the other. The dancers accomplished this smoothly by making a quarter turn of their trunks with their right shoulders forward at the moment when the one group was to pass the other."

There is a similar illustration in a dance of the Dagbama in Togo which falls within the framework of the circle dance. Two concentric circles are formed around a drummer, and the dancers move rhythmically in opposite directions in such a way that after a couple of steps those who were on the outside at the beginning now stand on the inside and vice versa. As they cross they strike short sticks against each other. This play has a lunar significance. We meet it again in the Spanish figure dance of the seventeenth century: "run on the inside and on the outside and intersect," is the instruction. In the Nicobar Island instead of this formation the dancers of one circle climb over the others, who have bent down on their knees.

QUADRILLE. The French *quadrille,* the *cotillon,* and the *counter dance* of four couples in a square have already been anticipated among the

160

primitive peoples as a fertility charm. An early form may be seen in a dance of the Naga of Upper Burma: in the center of the dance circle two men and two girls dance in couples with the girls continually changing places—*changez les dames!* In Sumatra we find four girls *en quadrille,* and the cross arrangement of two men and two women is mentioned in the seventeenth century as the only dance of the East Frisians, a dance which was already extinct at that time. "Thus the old East Frisians, besides this one song, also did have one East Frisian dance all their own, which was danced by four persons, two men and two women or maids, in accord with the rhythm; they did make very strange movements of the trunk, the arms, the legs, the head, and all parts of the body; which dance was of such difficulty that it did pass out in the manner of the old speech and was laid to rest (because so few might be found who could dance it in the old way), and the sweat which often did cover the dancers' bodies was allowed to dry. But one might see in this difficult dance the agility and nimbleness of the Frisians, who according to their own feelings could move their limbs masterfully in rapid or slow time without instruction from any French dance master; and the women had to take the same positions as the men and to imitate them in everything; and they did strike their hands together in the dance, sometimes in front of them, sometimes behind their backs, sometimes between their legs, all of which the women did do and had to do, and which, as I saw it, did seem to me comical but not awkward." The *moulinet* or the whirling star is a formation in the dances of Yap, as well as in the maturity dance of Lungau and in other European folk dances.

The Spanish *seguidilla* is a parallel from a high culture: "the four couples stand in the four corners and as they dance in front of each other, imitate the principal turns of the fandango. In the dance the señorita, dressed in national costume, accompanies the music with her castanets and beats time with the heel of her shoe with unusual accuracy; altogether, she is one of the most seductive figures in the service of the God of Love."

ARCH DANCES. We are all familiar with this formation in the dance and in gymnastics: the couple in front stops and the couples following crawl underneath the arms of the first in order to take up their positions in the same manner and let the others pass through. It is somewhat like the London Bridge of our children: "London Bridge is falling down, falling down." It still lives in the folk dances of most European countries. The *farandoule* of Provence is the classic example; but it is found likewise in the *ramelet* of Foix, among the Basques of Bayonne, in the Romagna, in the Abruzzi, in England, on the Rhine and the Bodensee, and in Bavaria (especially in the initiation dances of the guilds), in Bohemia, the Austrian Alps, and modern Greece.

We discover the same formation among the primitives. In the Torres Strait between Australia and New Guinea the men move forward in two groups: the first couple, facing the spectators, forms an arch; the next couple walks between these two dancers and takes a place behind them; the following couples do the same until all have taken new positions.

The *arch dance* of the primitives and of the common people and children of Europe is linked with the *interwoven dance* of the Middle Ages, which has its most beautiful painted memorial in Lorenzetti's fresco of the "Good Regiment" in the town hall of Siena and its best poetic monument in G. B. Marino's epic *Adone*:

> Sotto la treccia delle braccia alzate
> Per filo or quella, or questa il capo abbassa,
> E torcendo le mani inanellate
> Altra se n'esce, altra sottentra e passa.
> Canto XX.

> (Under the bridge of upraised arms
> The maidens lower their heads,
> Each one moves and twists her hands
> As she slips through the row in her turn.)

The BRIDGE DANCE is closely related. The Hallein Dürnberger *Salz-knappen* (salt journeymen) and other sword dancers jumped over a double row of swords which was constantly extended by moving the end pair forwards. Here, also, the primitive parallel is not lacking: at the funeral ceremonies of the Alfuro in the Molucca Islands, Halmahera and Seran, a child decked with ornaments must walk over the linked hands of the girls and boys, who keep moving in turn to the head of the line until the child has walked eight times around the house.

It is quite clear that the arch and bridge dances in conjunction with funeral ceremonies are symbols of a life that is constantly renewed. Any cause for doubt must disappear when we hear that the English perform the arch dance on Shrove Tuesday, which is associated with vegetation magic, and that farmers of central France say that it makes the hemp grow better. Among the Basques it is supposed to chase away evil spirits.

The CHAIN DANCE. This dance is widely known as the *chaîne anglaise*. Each gentleman turns to the left, takes the right hand of the lady nearest him, moves to the left of a next lady and gives her his left hand; then he winds past her on the right side to the third lady, to whom he gives his right hand; the dance continues thus until the dancers return to their own ladies again. This figure is rare among primitive peoples; we have already referred to the example of the Naga of Upper Burma and that of Papua. But it is common in the folk dances of Europe. It lives on in particular in the Swiss *Allewander* or *Aliwander:* in the Zug canton the boys form a circle and the girls dance through the chain with every other girl skipping through in an opposite direction. The people of Appenzell make a real *chaîne anglaise:* all the dancers reach out their hands to one another as they pass through the whole circular chain. This motif cannot have been taken from the courtly dance. For in Appenzell during this figure the women are sent away—proof enough that a bit of an ancient initiation rite adheres to their dance. The name *Allewander* seems to be a corruption of the word *Allemande* under the influence of the verb "wind." Alongside the Swiss dance are ranged the classic *reel* of the Scots and the *motovidlo* of the Czechs, both of which names mean "winder" or "windlass."

THE BRAID MOTIF. After all we have seen, it is impossible for us to believe that the place changing dances, for the most part, originate in a spirit of play and have no intellectual or religious relationships. If we are in doubt about the simplest forms, we surely cannot entertain similar doubts when we consider the advanced formations which have grown far away from the direct motor impulses of the primitives. None of the sources available to us contributes anything to our information in this regard, neither the travelers who have seen such dances among primitive peoples, nor the historians of the great nations of antiquity. We are compelled, therefore, to formulate explanations of our own.

When we attempt to describe the movements of the chain and crossing dances, we choose quite naturally such obvious expressions as "work through," "interlace," "interweave." If we give ourselves over to them, we find ourselves in the realm of the braiding and weaving art. If we can find symbols here which are linked with the fundamental movements of these handicrafts, then we must apply them also to the dances which have the same movements. As early as 1845 a mythographical source supplies the information to us that such symbols actually do exist: "in the hieratic speech weaving is synonymous with generating." Fourteen years later J. J. Bachofen wrote a booklet about the symbolic significance of the rope braiding theme on ancient gravestones. We extract from it the following statements:

"Rope braiding is a symbolic activity which recurs frequently and is based upon the same notion as the spinning and weaving of the three Fates. . . . In the picture of spinning and weaving is represented the shaping and forming power of nature. . . . When the activity of nature and its artistic shaping and creating came thus to be represented in spinning, braiding, and weaving, men recognized in these handicrafts still other relationships with the work of tellurian creation. In bringing together two threads they could see the duality of power and the penetration of the potencies of both sexes requisite to generation. This relation is still clearer in the technique of the loom. The crossing of the threads, their alternate emerging and disappearing seemed to present a picture that corresponded in every way to the perpetual work of nature."

Bachofen's well-founded interpretation may be applied to one phase of the place changing dances. It must be clear, however, that the cultures in which they make their appearance have a spiritual relation to such concepts. The three Fates, the shaping and forming power of nature, tellurian creation, the perpetual work of nature—these are ideas which can have penetrated only to that half of humanity dependent on planting. They are of necessity foreign to the people of acquisitive economy, especially to fishers and hunters.

If we bring together the examples we know of the place changing dances, we have the following picture. All the illustrations but two are from thoroughgoing planter cultures. The exceptions are the southeastern Australians (Port Stephens) and the Nicobars. But both may be easily demonstrated as immature, early stages. In Australia two rows of warriors run through each other from a great distance, then begin their dance proper; in the Nicobar Islands no actual interpenetration takes place, the dancers of one row simply climb over the others, who are on their knees—the essential element of weaving is lacking entirely.

DANCE AND ORNAMENT. Meschke has brought the characteristic figures of the European sword dances with their interlacing and unraveling into close spiritual relationship with the Germanic braided ornament. The fantastic, metaphysical mentality which is revealed in the ornament, he says, expresses itself in the weapon dance. Meschke's case is not proved, since he knows nothing of the fight and interlacing dances outside of Europe. The same relationship between the braided dance and the braided ornament must be demonstrated in other cultures, if such a relationship exists at all. Further investigation does not support his case. The lands where the most refined figure dances are to be found—the Caroline Islands and Palau—content themselves with elementary themes of ornamentation, for the most part with simple straight line arrangement; their braiding or interlacing themes are extremely primitive in form. In the South Seas the Maori have a truly mature braided ornamentation similar to that of the Germans of the migratory period; yet so far as is known, the Maori have no figure dances whatsoever.

To seek relationships between dance and ornament, as Fritz Böhme first proposed, is very enticing. Both art types are almost purely motor—ornament more than any other plastic or graphic art: as they are born of a definite impulse to motion, they must surely reveal forms that are related. But more often than not we do not find what we expect, and it is not difficult to discover why. First of all, the making of an ornament is in many ways conditioned by the technique of the maker and the material he uses; the design is altered according as a braider, a weaver, a potter, or a carver shapes its lines. Second, it must be remembered that braiding, weaving, and pottery making are almost exclusively women's occupations; and the woman, as we have seen, reacts to the dance in a fundamentally different manner from the man. Third and most important, the question arises whether the ornamentation and the dance of a people were not developed or taken over at different times. If this is the case, then one may be perhaps a lively witness of the motor activity of this people, while the other may simply have been carried along without any real inward relationship. Or one may be an ancient and cherished possession, and the other, on the contrary, a late importation, perhaps not yet assimilated to the motor characteristics of its new home. These are grounds enough for approaching the problem with the most extreme caution.

One point in particular must be considered: according to immutable law every new style must first impress itself upon that form of art which is most closely related to it by virtue of its peculiar quality. A style which is calm, solid, and static will begin its triumphal march with architecture, as Greek classicism and the Italian Renaissance bear witness. On the contrary, a style of accelerated movement, a dynamic style, will announce itself first in the motive art proper, which is the dance. While this variation of stylistic origin is often accomplished within decades in the later history of the Western world, in the slower course of prehistory it may be a matter of centuries or millenniums. Accordingly, we must not assume that ornaments and dances indicating vigorous motion put in an appearance simultaneously. It is to be expected rather that a new tendency will find expression much earlier in the dance than in decoration. And this has indeed been the case: the figure dances of intense movement belong mainly to the Full Neolithic period, the ornaments of intense movement, to the Metal Age.

Yet one scarcely need weigh all of these considerations to be aware of the fundamental fact that in ornamentation straight line forms are older, while in the dance the curved line is developed first.

Nevertheless we believe that spiritual relationships do exist between ornament and dance. Everything that men feel, think, and create comes from one source and must be in some way related. But here also we shall do better to concern ourselves less with what the elements are than with how they are employed, less with the single themes of the ornament and the dance than with the composition as a whole. For the theme as such can be carried from people to people without difficulty; but its application and execution demand individual performance and reveal the characteristics of individual talents. Thus instead of discussing single forms—bands, circles, and spirals—it will prove more profitable to speak of the whole picture, of the manner of filling in a surface.

The first observation which comes into the foreground is the contrast between simply filling up space and constructing organically, of composing in the more narrow sense. It can be established that the Australian likes to form groups of zigzag lines, that the Melanesian, on the other hand, in most of his ornamentation divides a surface into two symmetrical halves by making a vertical middle line; that the Micronesian likes to decorate the edges and leave the inner surface open, while the Samoan prefers a checkerboard arrangement with equal spaces. It must impress one that the arrangement of the Samoans gives the effect of calmness and stands in contrast to the quick movement of the Melanesian linear order, which is, to be sure, a strictly regulated composition, but at the same time expressive of an inward tenseness and frenzy. Whoever feels this contrast must see in it the same difference of temperament which has determined their dances: the extremely restrained and static nature of the Samoan sitting dances and the dynamic and at the same time rigid quality of the Melanesian dances. He will also feel then that a spiritual relationship exists between the uncomposed zigzag lines of the Australians and the columns of the Korrobori, which move eternally forward and backward with knees flexed. Any profitable comparison of style must proceed from generalities such as these.

Return Dances

The two basic forms of our systematic section, the choral round and the column dance, have developed in a certain sense through external influences—from a conception of space, from materials, and many other sources. Two further basic forms, owing far less to outside influence, are rather the result of an inner and dynamic quality of man, of his particular cycle of tensions and releases, which are the essence of every artistic style. We shall refer to them as "the continuous dance" and "the return dance."

In the continuous dance the same movement, whether forward or backward, to right or left, is maintained. This is true of most circle dances. The return dance shifts: a few steps forward, then a return to the starting point. It is not important whether the line of movement is in a circle or in a straight line. What is essential is that it comprises only a few steps. The larger return dances are outside of rhythmic consciousness and do not come under this head.

In these forms again we see contrasting impulses and creative powers. In the one there is a restless movement onward, a rolling and flowing ahead which we are once more tempted to describe as "dynamic"; in the other a "static" swinging, which nullifies every movement and every tension, as the contracted muscle is released, or the lung which breathes in the air sends it out again, as in all human activities and processes the harmonious, satisfying, restful norm is sought.

If we can with a certain justification apply the terms "dynamic" and "static" to these forms, it will be clear to anyone familiar with the history of the mind, or especially with the history of art, that the contrast of the continuous and the return dance has to do with the original creative power.

Most of the return dances are to be found in southern Asia. The natives of Cabaena in the Celebes take four steps forward, as do likewise the North American Ute; the Li of the Chinese island of Hainan in a narrow circle take two steps toward the center and two backward; and the women of the Chiriguanó and Chané tribes of the Gran Chaco move one pace forward and return. If we make a survey of the territories over which this form has been diffused, we find them to be planter cultures, who thus again give evidence of their sense for a static and symmetrical arrangement. And let us note that in these cultures the same tendency to multiples of two, to 2, 2×2, 2×4, dominates both the rhythm of the steps and that of the music. This point we shall discuss in the next section.

One of the strangest examples of the forward and backward movement is the so-called "pilgrim step," best known in the "leaping procession" at Echternach near Aix-la-Chapelle; taking three or five steps forward and one or two steps back, the procession makes its way ponderously to the sacred bones of Willibrord, and then circles around them. In other Catholic processions, also, the incense-swinging ministrants walk according to a definite "reverse" pattern.

L forward	R forward		R forward	L forward
		L back		R back

The left foot is brought forward, then the right is drawn after it, then the left is moved back, after which the steps are reversed. This old pilgrim step is older, indeed, than ministrants, pilgrims, or the Catholic Church. In the territory of the Roroima near the Orinoco the participants in the festival formed a single line with the dance leader at the head and the men followed by the women; each dancer placed his left hand on the shoulder of the dancer in front and the procession moved slowly ahead—always two steps forward and one back. The same or similar step patterns have been reported in North America, Indonesia, India, and Denmark, and the *branles* and *pavanes* of the sixteenth and seventeenth centuries are late offshoots. Quite recently Hellfritz discovered the pilgrim step—three forward, one back—in the *sibwâna* dance of southern Arabia.

The origin of this form of step is not clear. Yet we can scarcely believe that it developed purely in play and independent of any spiritual meaning. It would not be amiss to consider astral themes. These we have in New Ireland: the forward and backward movement of the dancers signifies the rising and setting of the moon—but the dancers must make a steady progress forward in representation of the course of the moon.

Left and Right

The preference for one side of the body as a problem of culture history was first observed and discussed by Bachofen: the left side of the body is given preference over the right in the cultures in which women occupy an important position—in matriarchies, earth and moon religions, and agricultural societies. On the other hand, the right side is favored over the left in the cultures in which males have the more important place— in patriarchies, sky and sun religions, and among hunters and nobles. In addition to his illustrations we can add a Chinese counterpart: in old China the peasants give preference to the left side, the nobles, to the right.

In view of the extraordinary diffusion, continuance, and ultimate effect of such conceptions, this fact seems also to have a certain importance for the history of the dance. In it, perhaps, we may find an explanation for the strange phenomenon—which cannot be ascribed to pure physiological reaction—that in many dances, according to rule, the left foot begins the dance, in others, the right. Thus the *bacubert,* the sword round of southern France, calls for the left foot, but the *basse dance* of the fifteenth century for the right. The former is a vegetation charm and consequently rustic; the latter is a dance of the nobility.

But for want of trustworthy observations we can carry this poin. no further.

COUPLE DANCES

The *couple dance,* which has been maintained as the most important form of the dance down to the present day in Europe, is not at all unknown among primitive peoples, as is so often asserted. Even in the cave of Combarelles (Dordogne), representing the Early Stone Age, there is a reproduction of a male phallic mask following a female in the dance.

The couple dance is based on two motives, one of which is astral. Among the Cora of Mexico, a little girl representing the earth mother and a boy representing the morning star dance in the church, and elsewhere we may see in an impressive manner that in many moon dances there is a transition from the choral to the couple dance. For here we are dealing with a double concept: the light and dark moon are represented by each row of dancers and also at the same time by each individual dancer. Thus it comes about that in northern New Ireland, in the middle of the choral row dance, every two dancers turn toward each other and continue to dance "until finally one sinks to his knees as though unconscious, while the other, with arms lifted high in the air, dances more vigorously than before." How frequently the double shape of the moon is the basis of the couple dance is difficult to say, in view of the fact that astral motifs more than others are overlooked by travelers and forgotten by the dancers themselves.

The second motif—pairing of the sexes to promote growth in the tribe and in nature—is more important and more diffused. We have already spoken of it in detail. But the couple dance is not limited to the mimetic, creative cultures. When imageless dancers make use of the couple form, they come together purely and simply with no intention of representing a definite phase of the sex act. In a circle dance of northwestern Brazil, each man places his right hand on the shoulder of his woman partner and blows the phallic, fertility-bringing traverse flute; in the rain dance the Mgogo hold both hands on the shoulders of the women dancers; and the women of the Kenya of East Africa in a slow procession around the fire stand on the feet of their men partners and hold them in close embrace.

The special form with three dancers—a man between two women or a woman between two men—has already been discussed.

We have also attempted in an earlier section to date the couple dance in its pure form—executed by man and woman. Our conclusion was that it must be placed on the border line between the middle and high cultures, whereas the couple dance among men exclusively goes back to the primitive cultures of the Pareci of Brazil and of the Central Australians.

Almost all these couple dances are "open": the dancers either have no direct contact with each other or they may touch each other at the most with one hand. "Close" couple dances, where there is contact with both hands, are very infrequent and come late. We have just referred to the Mgogo and the Kenya, to which we might here add a third example, the Lamba of Rhodesia, representing an even earlier cultural stage. Close turning dances, like the European, seem not to be executed by the primitives.

THE SEXES

The couple dance, which finishes by placing both sexes on a par, poses the general question of the status of men and women in the dance in general—apart from the couple dance.

Men's dances far exceed women's dances in number. Men alone execute hunting, war, and sun dances, and nearly always the animal, spirit, and boys' initiation dances. Besides, they have the rain and medicine dances in those shamanistic cultures in which the shamanism is in the hands of the men. In totemistic and exogamous-matriarchal societies, the men's dances, like certain tone instruments (the bull roarer, flutes, and tubes), are so peculiarly the property of men that women may not so much as look upon them. It is not the custom to inflict the death penalty on an infringer; at the most, the "animal" in the center "eats" the intruder. In border cultures like the California Maidu, the men are so tolerant as to permit the women and children to see what they can of the dances from the outside of the dance house, and the Arunta of Australia demand of their women simply that they pretend to be asleep. Yet in only a few instances do these dances have a sexual significance.

Women have little or no part, then, in hunting, war, and sun dances and are permitted only rarely to join the animal and mask dances. Women's dances are based on the particular concepts of the predominantly feminine collector and planter cultures. Within the framework of these cultures, women are often the only participants in the fertility dances—rain, harvest, consecration of girls and female shamans, birth, and moon worship. They often have exclusive charge of mourning rites and head-hunter dances, for mourning and head hunting are matriarchal, pre-agricultural traits. We are still reminded of these ancient prerogatives of women in the *Grastanz* of the Harz and the baptismal dance of Eifel.

Like the men, the women also have dances from which the other sex is excluded. A male who trespasses may be punished by being blinded or even put to death. As one might expect, our information about such dances is meager. Nevertheless, we do have a number of useful descriptions which unite in pointing to them as fertility charms which may go as far as to represent the sex act and often as far as *introductio phalli*. In certain high cultures in Cambodia and parts of Islam, for example, only women are permitted to become professional dancers. In many countries, on the other hand, in Central and South America especially, women's dances have become less important. Tribes like the Cayapo and Cágaba, of which this is not true, are exceptions.

In the beginning it is chiefly the man who dances. The Vedda (at least those who have not been influenced by other cultures), the Meo of Indo-China, the Veddoids of Sumatra, and the Yurok of California do not allow women to dance. Among the pygmy Negroids the women may dance, but never with the men.

The territory of the mixed dance has no hard and fast boundaries. In general we may say that the mixed dance is not found in basic cultures and is not common in the tribal cultures that are predominantly masculine, like the totemist. It is found principally in the predominantly feminine planter and later in the peasant and noble cultures up to the high cultures.

Meanwhile, the high monotheistic religions—Judaism, Christianity, and Islam—have either forbidden the mixed dance or strongly disapproved of it. The rabbis of the Middle Ages permitted only husband and wife, brother and sister, and father and daughter to dance together; at Jewish weddings as late as 1700, men and women danced separately. It was a deliberate break with tradition when at the arrival in Smyrna (1665) of the iconoclastic Sabatai Zewi, the false Messiah, men and women danced together "for the first time in ages."

4. Music

TIME beating and melody are not the first sound accompaniments of the dance. Imitation and the involuntary expression of emotion precede all conscious sound formation. Animal dances, which have the sole purpose of reproducing in a lifelike manner the characteristic bearing and movement of an animal, are accompanied—almost as a matter of course—by sounds which are appropriate to this animal. Every primitive hunter has the gift of imitating convincingly the growling, grunting, howling, whistling, yelling of the wild animals and the barking of his dogs. The fact that he makes application of these in the mimetic dance is due not only to a wish to represent, but also to a feeling of being completely at one with the animal which he is dancing. The genuine animal dance has need of no other music.

But the imageless dance is necessarily in many instances accompanied by nature sounds. Ecstasy in the broadest meaning of the word dominates the throat as well as the limbs. The introvert dance employs those dull aspirated and humming sounds of dark coloring and with few overtones which, with mystic power, seem to lead away from every-day life. The Buddhist worshiper forgets the world with his *om* sound, the Samoan sitting dancer with his *mm*. The dervish forms the sound *oo;* the ancient Cybele priest and the charmed sleep dancer of Bali, *hoo;* and the Indian of northwestern Brazil, *poo.* Perhaps the hum dances of the southern Maidu of California belong also in this category.

Contrariwise, the ecstasy of the wild leap dances is expressed with powerful cries: the Asturian dancer flings his *hee-yoo-yoo* into the

danza prima, and in the Bavarian *Schuhplattler*—right in the midst
of the regulated music of violin, zither, and accordion—the man gives
vent to his exuberance in wild yells.

RHYTHMIC ACCOMPANIMENT

One might suppose the unity of dance and music to be something
inherited from prehistoric times. Yet here again we must accept such
a generalization with extreme caution.

Plato denied to the animals a feeling for rhythm. This is largely
true, but not entirely. Köhler observes that in the stamping of his dancing chimpanzees "they produce what approaches a distinct rhythm
with each of them tending to keep step with the rest." And Pechuël
Loesche describes a gorilla which during a dance slapped its chest and
clapped its hands with childlike boisterousness. The same slapping of
the breast among the gorillas was recently pictured in the film *Congorilla.* Man has tendencies to rhythm, no doubt, in his blood; but he
is the first animal to dominate rhythm.

How far he proceeds with the domination over rhythm may depend
upon his talent and disposition. The Bahua Dayak, for example, are
said not to have exact rhythm; the Bafioti in Loango keep their hopping quite independent of melody and time; and the same is reported
of the modern Greek *tratta.* Among the Eskimo the rhythmic accompaniment is not the same as the song (it may be 9/8 as against 4/8, or
otherwise), and the East African Wassegeju dance more slowly as the
tempo of the accompaniment increases. It is hardly possible to do much
with the scanty information now at hand. Only when we have at our
disposal more testimony from investigators trained both in music and
in psychology will we be in a position to draw definite conclusions as
to the relationship of dance and music. Meanwhile it appears almost
as though an actual unity is not a natural heritage.

Nevertheless, entire dances may have originated in the germ cell of
a rhythmic motif. Otherwise the Orokaiva Papua in British New
Guinea might not have come upon a beautiful story which they tell

about a dance. Once an old man sat gazing at the waters of a river when suddenly something lifelike appeared on the surface. A crocodile? No, it was a tree trunk which kept rising from the waves, then disappearing, at definite intervals. The old man reached for his drum and softly beat out the rhythm, and as he struck the drum, the picture of a new dance took shape in his mind.

The original time beater is the stamping foot—with the elbow and knee sometimes taking over the same task. To the dull stamping sound is added the sharper sound made by slapping the hand on some part of the body; thus the upper arm, the flanks, the abdomen, the buttocks, and the thighs become musical instruments. Not often, to be sure, in the more advanced cultures, for the increasing use of clothes renders these parts of the body less effective as sound producers. Besides stamping, therefore, only hand clapping is found among all cultures at all periods. A careful classification would here distinguish between clapping the hollow hand and the flat hand—a contrast which enables the Polynesian women especially to create some charming effects.

Most of the basic cultures are in the stamping and slapping stage. The accompanying instruments of the pygmoids of southeastern Asia and the Veddoids which apparently refute this statement are a late importation from Malay.

A second stage, which appears in the so-called Late Basic cultures at the close of the Protolithic period, "intensifies" the stamping of the foot and the striking of the body. The dancers strike not only their bodies but aprons or folded skin garments; they use poles for stampers and often set up a base that is more resonant than the bare ground. They sometimes attach rattle ornaments to their bodies. Stamping and rattling are more effective when the rattle ornaments are tied to the knee, the calf of the leg, or the ankle; and if a pole is used for stamping in place of the leg, the rattle ornaments may be attached to it. Even so mature a culture as the Micro-Polynesian makes use for the most part only of hand clapping and the simplest noise makers in the dance. Nothing is altered fundamentally when the purely rhythmic noise makers of the later cultures (which frequently influence the lower cultures) are replaced by more advanced instruments such as gongs, bells, cymbals, and the like. Nothing except that the increasing number and use of such instruments betrays the fact that the ecstatic powers are diminishing. On the other hand, as in ancient Egypt and Greece, rattling may lead back to finger snapping, though we never find finger snapping among peoples not using rattles.

In the Early Tribal cultures there is a further extension of clapping and stamping. For the hands struck together are substituted rattling sticks; but what is most important, the matriarchal early planters invent the drum.

We have discussed up to this point percussion instruments of rhythmical and hence ecstatic nature. They produce regulated noise. They remain an integral part of the dance from its beginnings to the present day.

But at a definite stage of development new noise instruments are brought into the service of the dance, which reflect clearly the dual nature of the dances as well as of the cultures. They may also produce regulated noise. But more than that, they have magic power—in their shape, in the material of which they are made, or the manner in which they are played—and they add this power to the dance for the achievement of religious goals. Since I have already discussed the general nature of these religious goals, I now proceed directly to the examples.

Scraper. "Scraped diagonally with an appropriate object, it produces a clicking, scratching noise that is musically unattractive." The instrument is not a time beater in the strict sense, for the noise it makes lacks the necessary precision. Throughout the world it is used as a fertility charm; I have listed detailed examples in my book *Geist und Werden der Musikinstrumente.* Only in this sense can its use in the dance be understood. The Ute of North America play it at the bear dance; the Tonkaway of western Texas at the women's dance; the

Cheyenne at the love charm dance; and the Matto Grosso people at the *cururú*.

Struck Rod. "A rod-like bamboo stick split into sections through the greater part of its length, sometimes struck against the body of the player, sometimes against another stick." We have already spoken (page 115) of the life charm with which the rod is associated; it might be mentioned here that the rod plays a special role at the girls' initiations of the California Indians.

Slit Drum. "A tree trunk hollowed out and split lengthwise." In the beginning the dancers stamped on the wood with their feet. At a later stage they used poles, and finally, drumsticks. The hollow and the slit symbolize the feminine; stamping and striking, the sex act. In California, the northeastern outpost of the slit drum, it may be beaten only in the "house of the spirits" and only for dances of the secret societies.

Flute. More than any other instrument, the flute is the symbol of phallus and fertility. In this magic sense it is used to accompany countless dances in which the fertility idea is obvious—especially the animal, harvest, and love dances.

There is an apparent contradiction when K. T. Preuss reports that among the Cágaba of Sierra Nevada the flute may be played only for the gay and never for the religious dances, while among the northwestern Brazilians, living at no great distance from the Cágaba, the large flutes are always used at the fertility dances of the cult. The contradiction may be accounted for in this way: the Brazilians use old ceremonial flutes with no finger holes, but the Cágaba have later flutes with finger holes, which they use to play melodies as a dance accompaniment, but which they keep apart from the cult dances for the very reason that they are a late importation.

The Middle Tribal cultures add nothing apparently to the older equipment, aside from perfecting the rhythmic instruments and laying the foundation for a melodic dance accompaniment.

This type of melody probably has two roots. The first is the pleasure in the different tones of the various large time beaters. In Samoa, in the Gazelle Peninsula, and in Javanese Madoera, five cane tubes of graduated pitch are stamped in turn like paving rammers and are brought into a short *ostinato* theme. The Semang of Malacca have a similar arrangement, which is an importation from Malay. In the western Archipelago blocks of rice husks on wooden poles are stamped in place of cane stalks. By means of these the natives produce "noises of varied coloring, the dominant intervals of which form a kind of melody in the confusion of high and low, light and dark within a poly-rhythmic setting which is often rather complex." We find an earlier stage of this stylized stamping with articles of food, where the musical element has not been fully developed, in a custom of the Melanesian Solomon Islands, where at festivals taro roots are stamped in large mortars not only rhythmically but in a ceremonial fashion with dance movements. On the same level with the Javanese rice block stampers are the gourd rattles of West Indonesia (*angklung*), the stone music of the Micronesian preparation of the Kawa, and the xylophone in the Archipelago and in Africa.

Southeastern Asia especially works on the refinement and melodizing of the early rhythmic and ecstatic time beaters. With body striking and the dull, cracking noise makers as a starting point, this high Bronze culture has created the gong. But the development does not stop here. The gong makes a contribution to unity and harmony, and out of the individual gong music, whole orchestras grow. With a varied development, with a different training in Burma, Siam, Cambodia, and the Archipelago, and again with various gradations in each country, the orchestras nevertheless all share the distinction of a unique intensification of the old time beaters: rattles, drums, wooden and bronze strikers are brought together in a glorified form. The simple but dully exciting monotony has given way to seductive richness and splendid color.

This development can be appreciated only when one realizes the extent to which the culture of southeastern Asia is unique, wherein a race, ecstatic to a high degree, reaches the topmost stage among all the nature peoples. At this level it meets with the culture and religion of India and China, which strengthen and develop all its tendencies towards a spiritual deepening of ecstatic experience, but which at the same time awaken the need to create for this experience an impressive and resplendent dress. For it seems to be at once the essence and the contradiction of all high cultures, in their irrepressible urge to unite content and style, to put their most sacred things on exhibition.

A melodic instrumental music in the full sense appears as a dance accompaniment surprisingly late: we find it in the Late Tribal peasant culture which has as its eastern border the old Malay world of Indonesia. It is understood, of course, that we are not taking into consideration developments that may be described as "inorganic," such as those of the Malay dwarfs in southeastern Asia and certain Indian tribes whose instruments are importations from Europe. Where melody accompanies the dance, the sexes are often observed to make use of different instruments: men's dances use wind instruments, women's dances, stringed instruments—the first class being more "extravert," the second "introvert."

Instrumental dance melody is not a development from instrumental rhythmic music but rather—and this is the second root—the instrumentalizing of dance songs. In all probability, the first songs to be instrumentalized are those for which the words have been forgotten.

MELODY AND ITS RELATION TO THE DANCE

Not only rhythmic but also melodic dance accompaniment, to which the concluding remarks above have brought us, carries the dancer with passion and exhilaration, even with intoxication in the strict sense of the word, into the state of ecstasy which is the innermost essence of the dance. Furthermore, the melodic accompaniment, which at first was always sung, tends to create a spiritual connection between the dance theme and the magic purpose of the movement.

This must not be interpreted from the modern Western point of view. The words of such a song need have no relation to the meaning or the occasion of the dance. For the mourning dance the Andamanese compose quite unconcernedly texts relating to hunting or boat-building, while for boys' initiations turtle texts are preferred. Instead of a connected text, the Sakai of Malacca even recite a series of mountain and river names. That meaningless word combinations are also substituted for a real text is an almost inevitable result of the adoption of unintelligible foreign words. One of the best described basic cultures, the Andamanese, will serve to introduce us to the character of the primitive dance song. Here the ordinary dance is always accompanied by song, and all the songs are composed for the dance. Indeed, there are no songs except dance songs. The cohesive force of traditional music is also lacking. Everyone invents songs, and even the children are instructed in this art. While carving a boat or a bow, or while rowing, the Andamanese sings his song quietly to himself until he is satisfied with it and then introduces it at the next dance. His female relatives must first practice it with the women's chorus; the inventor himself, as song leader, sings it at the dance, and the women join in the refrain. If the piece is successful, it is added to his repertory; if not, it is discarded. Nobody sings another's song. The words treat of everyday occurrences such as hunting and boat-carving. They are unpretentious, as for example: "Poio, the son of Mam Golat, wants to know when my boat will be finished; so I must be as quick about it as possible." The melody is limited to three closely related steps. The verse has the freedom of recitative but the chorus is strictly rhythmical. The allegro quarter notes, taken at M.M. = 132, are accompanied by clapping the hands and stamping.

Although the statement that every song is composed for the dance is no longer strictly true of the later cultures, dance and song nevertheless remain very close. They spring from the same force—the impulse to motion. One is tempted almost to call this a truism. But the idea contained in it becomes significant only when used as a basis for understanding the essential unity of dance and song. Whether we speak of individuals or of entire tribes, peoples, and races, their melodies and dances must always be closely related. For both are determined by the same impulse to motion.

Investigations in this direction might point out new paths for the history of music. Such investigations are difficult at the present time, because the accounts of primitive peoples are generally limited to describing the dances without reproducing the music. On the other hand, the musicologist records the notes without describing the dance forms which go with them. The only noteworthy exceptions are the contributions of Bartók, Densmore, and Fox Strangways. But in the last analysis it does not make much difference to us whether a certain dance has a certain melody, because we are concerned only with the general relationship between the dance movements and the music of a people.

Von Hornbostel has already noted this general relationship. "The style of Indian music," he writes, "is peculiar neither to the stage of development nor to the culture, but rather to the race. It is very characteristic for the reason that it is only one expression of a trait (almost ignored by the anthropologists, with the exception of Boas) which distinguishes the race most sharply—its way of movement. This is so deeply rooted in the physiological that it persists for thousands of years and withstands the influences of natural and cultural environment and even of miscegenation. It determines equally the body movement of the dancer, the arm movement of the drummer, and the throat and mouth movements of the singer and speaker."

Herbert Baldus was the first to apply this knowledge. He compares the temperaments of the northeastern Chaco tribes—"the wild dance leaps, the vigorous rattle swinging, and the loud, violent singing" of one tribe with the corresponding characteristics of the other. The

Marquesas, MEN'S CHORAL CHANT — Handy & Winne

Zuñi, MEN'S CHANT — Stumpf

Wanyamwezi, DANCE SONG — von Hornbostel

Wasukuma, CHANT OF THE CARRIERS — von Hornbostel

Pueblo Indians, FROM A FUNERAL CHANT — Stumpf

Austria, LÄNDLER — Hamza

Mongolia, CHANT — van Oost

186

dances of the latter tribe are "a hesitant, indolent moving to and fro, and their musical instruments sound weak and timid, their drum as though muffled, their flutes never shrill, and even their war horn makes less noise than a toy trumpet. . . . No effervescent enthusiasm appears in their melodies. Their singing is soft and listless."

The close relationship of ordinary carriage, of temperament, of time, and of tone force is properly recognized here. Yet this is not enough. Even the melodic structure seems to be inseparably bound up with the way of movement of a people. Let us compare two characteristic melodies: one of the common songs of the Marquesa Islands in East Polynesia sung by a chorus of men accompanied by drums and the clapping of hands (Music example 1), and a song of the North American Zuñi (Music example 2).

One cannot help but feel that here one is dealing with two worlds. On the one hand the tranquillity of the quietly sustained single note, on the other the unbridled frenzy of the leap across two octaves, from mysterious negation to the most violent release of power, like the death-dealing leap of the beast of prey from the ambush where it has been crouching motionless—two poles of human classification, movement, and artistic attitude. "Tranquillity" and "leap" are the words which inevitably come to mind when two contrasting types of melody are to be distinguished. Tranquillity and leap are also, however, the two poles of all dancing: the most restricted sitting dance and the wild, unrestricted leap dance. And it is the Marquesans who are the sitting dancers and the Zuñi Indians who are the leap dancers.

Is this "chance"? Or will actual comparison of the expanded and close movement of the dance show a co-ordination with the expanded and close movement of the melody?

COMPASS AND STEPS. The chief region of the leap dance in Africa is the central eastern part. The Wanyamwezi dancers make "wild leaps," and in describing their music E. M. von Hornbostel emphasizes the fact "that intervals of a fourth and a fifth are comparatively frequent in the songs of the Wanyamwezi, and especially in the middle of the melody, the only place where they have the effect of leaps." Between the various parts of the melody, however, leaps of a sixth, a seventh, and a ninth frequently occur (Music example 3), and in two measures the melody abruptly drops down a tenth. The long melody of the neighboring and related tribe, the Wasukuma, also transcribed by von Hornbostel, consisting of two octaves less one note, contains many intervals of sixths and sevenths within and between the motifs (Music example 4).

Let us compare with them a well-known West African people such as the Pangwe of the Cameroons: even their most expanded songs seldom exceed the compass of a seventh, and their succession of steps is measured and almost entirely lacking in leaps.

In North America the Mexicans use an extreme form of expanded movement; their *peyote* dancers compare with the most daring leapers of East Africa, and a beautiful old Hopi clay vessel in the Ethnological Museum in Berlin shows an ithyphallic circular dance with violent leg thrusts (Plate 6). Their melodies are equally expanded: a very pathetic and moving funeral song of the Hopi, published for the first time by Carl Stumpf, brings within the compass of an octave plus a fifth the same intervals as the above-mentioned piece of the neighboring Zuñi (Music example 5).

In central Asia we come upon the expanded melodic structure of the central Ordos Mongolians, which has not been transmitted to us phonographically, but can scarcely have been misrepresented in its larger features, which alone concern us here (Music example 7). A single beat, for example, rises to the twelfth, and the diatonic gradations are left far behind by the enormous leaps.

Europe supplies us with an additional instance. The Austrian *Ländler* of the old style—before 1800, that is—had large leaps often covering as much as two octaves (Music example 6). The struggle between expanded and close movement, which was particularly violent in the Alpine regions, was finally decided in favor of close movement as well as of close melody. We find further evidence to confirm this view in Catalonia: the melody of the rapid, vigorous leap dance *contrapas* has a wide compass and also the other characteristics of the expanded movement group—free form and irregular rhythm.

The expanded melodic line forms an impressive contrast with the close melodic line of the group of peoples who dance with close movement. The genuinely monotonous chant of the Marquesa in their sitting dances was mentioned at the beginning of this section. The two and three toned melodies of the Vedda, the Andamanese, the Semang, and the Australians give a clear idea of the close dance world of the Asiatic pygmies and pygmoids and of the Korrobori (Music examples 8, 9, 10, and 11). We should not say that the dull narrowness of these structures is as primitive as the people themselves. For the no less primitive Veddoid Kubu of Sumatra sing melodies which in certain cases drop suddenly as much as thirteen tones (Music example 12). Thus, the Kubu have one dance and only one in which the movements, especially the steps and leaps, "become ever wider and more violent."

The Malaccan Semang are sharply differentiated from the other examples. None of the others has the curve, the "melodic line." There is something soft, yielding, swinging about the Semang melody—just as the dance of the Semang is soft and swinging. Again in Samoa we find a like parallel between dance and melody; Mieczyzlaw Kolinski has pointed out the relationship in music and dance between the primitive tribes of Malacca and Samoa.

Within the field of close movement this soft, animated melodic structure offers the strongest contrast to the recitative, intoning type which is represented in two of our music examples, the song of the Vedda and that of the Marquesa. The former consists of three not very strictly measured levels of pitch, one or two of which are held for a rather long time. Its "lesson tone" is a contrast to the "litany" of the Polynesian choirs: a single tone in endless repetition. The slow, close, ecstatic dances in the Celebes are also accompanied by singing "in a horizontal tone." The nerve-racking monotony of such music causes ecstasy. "Even I myself," writes Koch-Grünberg, a cool observer, in describing the chants of the Roroima-Orinoco district, "become so excited by the first part, the recitative spoken in a hurried, monotonous voice, that the sweat breaks out from all my pores."

After this section had been written, E. M. von Hornbostel, quite independently of this, attempted to systematize briefly the melodies of primitive peoples. One can find this system in a very obscure place as an appendix to a critical review of an inadequate book. His authoritative statement must be considered here.

He distinguishes between close melody, graduated melody, fanfare melody, and canonical imitation. "Close melody" has short motifs of two or three tones, small steps up to a whole tone, and narrow compass not exceeding a fourth. Close melody alone is found among the Vedda who have not been subject to outside influence, the Andamanese, and the Yamana and Alakaluf of Tierra del Fuego. It is found with other types of melody among the Kenta-Semang, the Papua of East New Guinea, and the Uitoto. He thinks it probable "that this type belongs to the culture which is represented by the southeastern Australians (Kurnai)—of whose songs unfortunately we know nothing—and which has left traces also in southern Asia (the Andamanese), Tierra del Fuego, and central California.

"Graduated melody drops gradually in a series of steps; the compass is very large (an octave or more); the intervals are fourths and fifths; there are pulsations on a single tone." This form has been diffused throughout Australia, and Torres Strait, among the Indians, and among the ancient Asiatics from the Chukchee to the Jenissej-Ostyak.

"Fanfare melody" has the so-called "broken triad." It is found among the pygmies of central New Guinea, the Karesau Papua, the mountain tribes of the Solomon Islands, and the Bushmen.

"Canonical imitation" occurs among the Sakai and Semang of Malacca, in Flores, Kiwai (southern New Guinea), and Bougainville (Solomon Islands).

If we now combine our own types with those of Hornbostel, the duality emerges clearly:

CLOSE MOVEMENT:	EXPANDED MOVEMENT:
Close melody	Graduated melody
Canonical imitation	Fanfare melody

And fanfare melody stands nearer to close movement than graduated melody. The Vedda, Andamanese, and Kenta-Semang, mentioned by von Hornbostel as examples of close melody, all dance exclusively with close movement. The same seems to be true of his other examples: the Papua of eastern New Guinea, the Tierra del Fuegans, the Uitoto, and the central Californias. The Sakai and Semang, who come under canonical imitation, also dance with close movement, and of Flores, Kiwai, and Bougainville we at least know nothing to the contrary.

Of the people whose song is classified as graduated melody, we know the ancient Asiatics and some of the Indian tribes to have expanded dances. And likewise in the fanfare melody group, the Bushmen dance partly with a modified form of expanded movement. For his remaining examples of graduated and fanfare melody, the dances are not adequately described in our sources.

Thus the conclusions of the leading authority in this field confirm our own.

EXECUTION. Wherever expanded dance dominates, the music also is dynamic and is based on dramatic alternation of strong and weak. Expanded dance peoples sing with great forcefulness, the introductory phrases decidedly *sforzato*, the high notes *fortissimo*, the descending scale *diminuendo*, with the low notes almost inaudible. Sometimes the voice leaves the realm of song and bursts forth in wild shrieking: with expanded movement in the dance and in music, the experience is momentarily intense and unbroken. Or the song becomes emphatic in the full meaning of the term as among the Indians, whose songs may be differentiated without difficulty from those of other races: before each attack the excited taking in of breath is clearly audible, the notes are blurred in *portamento,* and the longer notes pulsate. We find this type of *vibrato* also in the singing of the Wanyamwezi and other East African tribes which dance with expanded movement.

The close movement style has none of this dynamic quality. The contrast between loud and soft is less pronounced, and the emphatic *sforzati* are almost entirely lacking.

What is true of peoples is also true of the sexes—as in the dance. Observers have frequently stressed the fact that in contrast to men, women often sing with their mouths almost closed and their lips hardly moving.

RHYTHM. The intense excitement and passion of the expanded style are expressed not only in the compass and leap of the melody but also very strikingly in its rhythmic freedom. Wherever songs in this style have had to be transcribed into our notation, the musicologist has had great difficulty in putting in the bar lines to make a pattern intelligible to the modern student. The same is true of the dances. For sixteen measures of an expanded Mongolian song with a compass of twelve notes, J. van Oost uses eight different time signatures (Music example 13). In recording an expanded tobacco-begging song of the northern Ute in eight measures, Densmore employs seven different time signatures. In six measures of a Pueblo death song, Stumpf has 5/4, 3/4, 2/4, and 4/4; and Schünemann rightly dispenses with time signatures altogether in the expanded songs of the Kazan Tartars. Yet with all these efforts justice is not done the mysterious accentual character of these songs. They simply do not fit into any time scheme, they are rhythmically irrational.

In the province of close movement, on the contrary, the rhythm is strict and regular. A measure of a certain count, once established, is generally retained. And strangely enough, this measure is nearly always even. Of twenty-one Semang melodies, seventeen have even measures. And the greatest single territory of the close dance, eastern and southeastern Asia, is at the same time the center of quadratic rhythm. On the other hand, among nine melodies of the North American Bellakula published by Stumpf, six are uneven and only three even. This fusion of movement forms and rhythm explains why in modern Europe, almost without exception, the quiet introductory dance is in 4/4, the leap- or after-dance in 3/4 time.

In this connection it is noteworthy that also in the cosmological concepts of these peoples the contrast between even numbers and odd numbers is prominent. Among the matriarchal, agricultural, moon-worshiping cultures the even numbers are regarded as sacred, while among the patriarchal, hunter, sun-worshiping cultures the uneven numbers are favored—as with rhythm.

FORM. With expanded movement we find in almost all cases an open, flowing rhapsodic form. The open melody of the Indians lacks breadth and roundness. Its thematic material is a tiny metrical structure, often of only two tones, choppy and angular. It is strung together in a falling sequence like a stone rolling downstairs step by step. The motif always starts on a high note, and one sequence after another is added to form the whole. The Melanesian and often, too, the Asiatic melody, does not, however, grow out of a small motif; it swings forth in a daring curve, often with magnificent breadth and roundness—rich and multiform, like the dance of the Asiatic and Melanesian peoples in contrast to the step patterns, generally so uniform and bare, of the Indians (Music examples 7 and 15).

A mature "close movement" people would never construct its pieces in this fashion. We have already pointed to the Pangwe of the Cameroons as a contrast; we must look once again at a fragment of one of their songs (Music example 17); here the melody consists of six tones. Often it has even fewer; rarely does it reach the compass of an octave.

The steps seldom exceed the whole tone; the progression is diatonic.

But this is not what makes these few tones seem so familiar, so close to us, what reminds us "frequently of European folk melodies," as von Hornbostel points out. It is rather the clearly symmetrical pattern

6 eighths + 1 quarter / 4 eighths + 1 half
6 eighths + 1 quarter / 4 eighths + 1 half

and with this the introductory phrase of two measures ending with a semi-cadence on the dominant and the answering, concluding phrase ending with a full cadence on the tonic, just as our textbooks prescribe. This is a genuine "midget period" in the style of our folk songs within the modest compass of a sixth.

European influence? Nothing of the sort. On the contrary, it is found in all parts of the world. The Macuxi women of the Orinoco district sing the measures contained in Music example 18, and the children of Malabar lilt the tones of our Music example 19.

All doubts are silenced when we learn that a people so untouched by the civilization of the white man as the Semang of the Malaccan jungle not only have the same period formation, but show also in their less finished pieces the gradual development of this form which the European likes to claim as genuinely Western. Their motif almost always consists of two measures in duple or quadruple time (Music example 20). The most primitive tribe of the Semang, the Kenta, from whom this example is taken, are content with the repetition of the motif in the manner of an ornamental frieze. We find something similar as a substratum in much higher cultures. I give two examples which I took down by ear in Egypt in March, 1930. The first was sung in endless repetition by three street singers in Cairo to their own accompaniment on the frame drum (*tar*) and beaker drum (*darbuka*), the second with slight variations, but otherwise without alteration, on an improvised text, by a chorus of fourteen Nubian Barabra with song leader and *darbuka* on a Nile faluka at Assuan (without themselves rowing) (Music examples 22 and 23).

But even the Semang of a higher level answer such a motif with a symmetrically constructed response of two measures, thus creating the more advanced four-measure form (Music example 20). And even in so low a pygmy culture as Semang we may find a rise at the conclusion of the first and a fall at the conclusion of the second two-measure phrase (Music example 24).

If we were to designate this song form as antiphonal symmetry, it would have to be taken quite literally in the case of the dance song. For a large part of the close choral dances were sung fundamentally in antiphonal form by the men and women, or responsorially by a song leader and chorus; besides, this musical form was limited to the close choral. Responsive singing of this type can be variously conducted: the song leader and the chorus may sing for the same length of time, as among the Semang, or the song leader may be permitted a certain freedom of form, as among the Andamanese. The chorus is traditionally restricted to a brief and strictly regulated form. We have this structure in its most extreme aspect when the song leader and the chorus sing the same motif alternately, as in the boat song of Assuan on the Nile (Music example 23). On Madoera near Java four lines are repeated—here again the quadratic form! An unbroken chain leads from these examples to the alternating song of the European folk dances and to the "periods" of the medieval instrumental dances. Let us add here that in the large majority of cases leaders of these responsive songs are women.

It is very significant that the dance world of the South African Herero, which is an extreme sample of expanded movement, has the song leader but not the answering chorus. "Some thirty or forty men, all dripping with grease and red ocher, form a circle; two dancers and a song leader take their places in the center. The song leader sings the virtues of all the chiefs, and perhaps also those of the favorite oxen, and claps his hands in time while the other two dance with great leaps in the air. The men in the circle stamp the ground with their feet till it trembles."

More than a hundred years ago a Frenchman, Villoteau, recorded significant choral dances with their music of the same Nubian culture from which our Nile boat song comes. They had two rows of dances and also two choruses; the one row moved towards the other clapping, stamping, and singing; then as it was retreating, the other moved forward singing (Music examples 25 and 26).

The quite general fusion of the close song form and the return dance, of the up and down and forward and backward in music and in dance steps, can almost be taken for granted. For this rhythmical swing which is almost like breathing corresponds to the same course of tension and release in the one as in the other. The backward and forward movement of the body is the same course of tension and release that is reflected in the musical structure with its introductory and concluding phrases ending on semi and full cadences. It is one of those fundamental identities which evade intellectual explanation but are recognized *a priori* by people with alert minds.

Usually the change of direction forwards and backwards has a musical basis. Of the Marind-anim in the interior of Dutch New Guinea, Wirz remarks: "Singing the Gad-zi and accompanied by the beating of drums, the dancers take a few steps forward, stand still for a while, and then while singing the next motif, run back to place." Here the functional relationship is still quite crude, but in Hindustan it stands forth clear and fully developed.

When we declaim an amphibrachic foot in verse, we emphasize the middle syllable slightly and make a pause after the third: $- \acute{-} -$'. The Hindu applies this to music. He does not exactly make a pause in the melody to correspond with this pause in the verse, but renders it rather by a kind of break in the movement which has its own time value.

The technical name for this silent quarter is *khāli*. The singer, who sits and beats time, strikes the 1 2 3 with his hand on his thigh, but indicates the o by raising his hand with the palm upwards in the air. The same holds true for verse meters consisting of short and long quantities: on the second half of the long quantity there is a silent beat:

$$\text{4/4} \qquad \begin{array}{cccccccc} \text{I} & \text{2} & \text{3} & \text{0} & \text{I} & \text{2} & \text{3} & \text{0} \end{array}$$

When a meter of this type is danced, the dancer feels this silent beat as a restriction of movement: he puts his foot back. This three-syllable foot, or as we interpret it, four-beat measure, becomes in the dance: right forward, left forward, right backward, and so on. Other types of measure are treated accordingly:

3/4

rf lf   lf rf
   rb   lb

4/4

rf lf lf rf lf lf
   rb   rb

5/4

rf lf lf   lf rf rf
   rb rb   lb lb

6/4

rf   rf rf lf   rf   rf   rf lf
  lb lb   lb lb

7/4

rf lf lf   lf   lf rf rf rf
   rb rb rb   lb lb lb

This shows an impressive intimacy between word and dance and offers immediate proof of the functional connection between the step backward and the musical value. Consequently the dance song of the royal serving maids of Bhavnagar, in which the silent beats, Strangways assures us, were executed with backward step, must correspond to the indications in example No. 27.

It would be a mistake to assume that we are dealing here with a phenomenon of the high cultures. The same principle dominates also the native circular dance of the primitive Gond of Hindustan, and the rounds of four dancers among the Ghurka and the Garhwali:

First Quarter: All clap.
Second Quarter: Dancers B and D put their right palms against the left palms of A and C.
Third Quarter: All clap.
Fourth Quarter: B and D put their left palms against the right palms of A and C.

On each of the first three counts the dancers take one step forward, on the fourth, the silent beat, one step backward (Music example 28). Or a hundred Panjabi dance in a double circle around a fire, moving forward and backward. Fox Strangways does not say how the forward and backward movement corresponds to the oboe accompaniment, whether there are two or four measures for each movement. But this does not really matter. The melody (Music example 29), exactly like a European "small period," made up of an introductory phrase of four measures and a concluding phrase of four measures, indicates forward and backward movement just as much as each phrase does in itself.

Often we do not know to which dances a certain melody belongs; but we learn that any tribe has return dances as well as symmetrical melodies. If we add these cases, the material piles up. Of these we shall mention only two examples here: a Singhalese song consisting of solo, chorus, and drum accompaniment (Music example 30), and a song belonging to the peoples between Roroima and Orinoco. Unfortunately Koch-Grünberg, generally so splendid an observer, leaves us in the lurch here. From the little that he gives us we learn only that among many continuous dances there are also a few which are danced "now forwards, now backwards." Similarly, among the dance songs from this expedition noted down by von Hornbostel there are some with a strikingly finished song form.

This comparison, however, must not be taken to mean that the return dance grew out of the song form or vice versa. It merely confirms the fact that both have originated in the same motor impulse and that this motor impulse coincides with close movement.

We understand now why all over the world it is the women who prefer this form. It is the women who have sung for us our South American, Malaccan, and African examples, and it would be easy to add to them. More significant, however, is the fact that among peoples where the men have invented expanded melodies, the melodies of the women do not conform to the tribal pattern but are of the close variety and even in strict song form—just as we have seen in the dance. We obtain a very impressive picture by looking through von Hornbostel's musical appendix to Koch-Grünberg's Roroima work: of twenty-one chants of the Macuxi and Vapixana, eleven are, from the point of view of the European song, formless, nine are in strict song form, and one is doubtful. Of the last ten, however, seven are women's songs and another is given the neutral title of "chorus."

We find a parallel to this on the other side of the world: among the eight dance types of the Rumanians of Maramureş, whose music Béla Bartók has edited in hundreds of pieces, the two women's dances are the only ones in which the melody is constructed exclusively in the close song form.

This fact suggests the idea that the early history of music can no longer be regarded, as it so often has been, as a direct development from the primitive to the mature, from the simple to the complex and elaborate. This interpretation is outmoded in any case since for scientific method it substitutes "plausibility," the unfortunate habit of judging by ourselves completely different mentalities many epochs removed from us. "Primitive" and "simple," these are indeed concepts which we apply much too casually. What seems natural to us may not have been so to those ancient cultures; what appears involved and affected to us may have been the most natural thing in the world to the primitive because he did not share our impulses and our inhibitions.

The conclusions which have forced themselves upon us in the course of the last few paragraphs make it imperative for us to apply our knowledge of dance history to the history of music, and to understand the development of music among the various races from the same basic elements which also determine their dances.

Our investigation of dance movements was based on the strong contrasts between two basic cultures, that of the Vedda and that of the Andamanese. The Vedda, we found, are not fond of dancing. Their dances are convulsive and out of harmony with the body. The Andamanese are fond of dancing. Their dances are free and in harmony with the body. This contrast could be further expanded into a greater contrast between real dance peoples and peoples less gifted and less enthusiastic for the dance. This distinction based on the dance seems to correspond exactly to the musical distinction. What an impressive antithesis! On the one hand we see the Vedda with their restricted, almost tortured *parlando,* and on the other hand we find the Andamanese melody also, only in three compressed tones, but free, flowing, and made up of solo and answering chorus.

Intellectually this distinction goes through the entire world. This great duality of dances out of harmony with the body and dances in harmony with the body corresponds to a duality of recitative singing and melodic singing. The Vedda recitatives and the related airs of the Kubu and the Patagonians are not "primitive," but they are limited to quite definite groups of primitive peoples. Moreover—and this is the deciding factor—this spoken song penetrates into the more developed cultures which otherwise have incomparably richer tonal structures. Its chief province is shamanism. Where the medicine man performs religious ceremonies, the music approaches the liturgical intonation. And from the chants of the witch doctor it has descended by a long chain of heredity to the liturgy of the higher religions: it lives on in the *Saman* of the Hindu as in the *Leinen* of the Jews and the *Lectio* of the Christian churches. A by-way leads the chant with "spiritual possession" into the world of the Micronesian and Polynesian dancers. Whether the syllabic psalmody of the Hawaiian and Marquesan Islands is differentiated from that of the Vedda by spiritualization, it would be difficult for us to ascertain; we can perceive, however, their greater artistry.

Even among the Kubu the recitative seldom stands alone. Usually the voice begins on a high pitch in extreme tension and drops suddenly to intone listlessly in a very low pitch. Psalmody causes ecstasy. The unrestrained outcry, from which the voice abruptly falls, without any architectonic progression, without any of the gradations between tension and release—that is ecstasy.

Where shamanism reigns supreme, we find both these elements of style side by side. A third element is the extremely excited, emphatic, pathetic utterance, and a fourth, the lack of any clear and symmetrical song form. This is most obvious in North America.

In many cases the shamanistic Veddoid style—as in the convulsive dance—is crossed with an expanded style. This we know to be true both from our North American and our East African examples. The wide compass and the broad leaps are combined among the Indians with a convulsive introductory shriek and a melodic-dynamic dropping of the voice; among the Negroes, with a monotonous declamation.

Wherever the dance in harmony with the body is performed without restraint, two musical styles are clearly discernible. On the one hand we find a melodic line which liberally spans a wide tonal space, does not fear huge steps and even leaps, and seems, with its freedom in rhythm and form, to shun all restraint and prefers measures with three, five, or seven beats to duple and quadruple time. On the other hand we have a melody frequently carried alternately by the song leader and the chorus, a melody forcing its little motifs into strict antiphonal symmetry, into a song form constructed in the familiar way with an introductory phrase ending on a semi-cadence and a concluding phrase ending on a full cadence. This song form remains firm and steady in rhythm, prefers simple time, and in general calls for a quiet, passionless performance.

This fundamental duality clarifies the functional unity not only of the dance but also of music with the spiritual, social, and economic make-up of mankind. The same contemplative, patient, imperturbable, introvert disposition which through the ascendancy of female characteristics creates a predominantly feminine culture and leads from the food-gatherer to the planter level, makes itself felt in dance and music through close movement and through an urge towards the static and the symmetrical. The alert, impatient, vivid, and impulsive extravert disposition which leads to the dominance of the masculine qualities in a culture and to hunting and cattle-breeding, is reflected in dance and music through expanded movement and through the urge towards the dynamic and the asymmetrical.

Thus the predominance of the close song form in Europe would seem to be a heritage from agricultural ancestors. It is significant that open, free rhapsodic folk music appears among us only in the great cattle-raising regions.

Part Two

DANCE THROUGHOUT THE AGES

5. The Stone Age

THE PROTOLITHIC PERIOD

Lower Paleolithic Culture

THE only direct information we have about the early history of the dance comes to us from the rock paintings created by primitive man tens of thousands of years ago in what is now France. This information is meager, to be sure—especially since we must be on our guard against reading into the often very tangled maze of these rock paintings the things that we should like to see there. Only a very few drawings admit of definite interpretation. In most of them the conscientious scholar would rather forego positive explanation than run the risk of interpreting a battle scene as a war dance or a man with his arms raised as a shaman in an ecstatic dance. Pictures of the dance are probably rather rare in any case. For since the Paleolithic painter usually makes wish pictures in order to obtain by this means certain effects of sympathetic magic, he will have little reason to reproduce dances which serve the same purpose by other means.

We must be careful to avoid here the controversial problems of prehistory. We may very well make use of the broader conceptions of Paleolithic and Neolithic, but the finer subdivisions such as Aurignacian, Solutrean, Magdalenian, and Capsian, we shall do better to avoid than to investigate.

We should have to be satisfied with a very hazy picture of the early dance if we had not the abundant, in fact almost too abundant, supplementary material from the dances of the nature peoples of today. For the various cultures of the European past have their exact counterparts among primitive races at the present time. The prehistorian digs out of

Spanish or French soil the dwellings, shrines, and sepulchers of Paleo-lithic hunters with their utensils, tools, weapons, and skeletons, and determines from these material possessions the cultural level and trend. Excavations in many other places confirm and round out the picture of a certain civilization, and the ethnologist discovers, quite independently of prehistory, exactly the same picture among the southeastern Australians and other primitive peoples of a low level: they are in the same stage of culture, they have the same type of dwelling, of burial, of weapons, tools, and utensils, and they are lacking in the same skills and crafts. Or the spade of the prehistorian may uncover a later Neo-lithic culture which shows clearly the features of contemporary planter peoples with their rectangular huts, their pottery, and the peculiar characteristics of their weapons, tools, utensils, and cults. Whether pre-history speaks of the earlier and later Stone Age, of the Bronze Age and the Iron Age, or whether it defines the lesser cultural groups such as the Magdalenian, the Aurignacian, or the Solutrean, we almost always find their reflection in the culture of some primitive race of today. The ethnologist is almost always able to place an "is" beside the "was" of the prehistorian. What in Europe has died and sunk down layer by layer into the soil, lives on, regardless of time, in other parts of the world. Thus from the coexistence of races emerges a progression, and ethnology becomes history.

In a work dealing with the development of the dance, therefore, primitive peoples must not be omitted when we speak of Europe. The evolution of their dance is at the same time the early history of the dance in Western civilization.

The origins of human dancing, however, are not revealed to us either in ethnology or prehistory. We must rather infer them from the dance of the apes: the gay, lively circle dance about some tall, firmly fixed object must have come down to man from his animal ancestors. We may therefore assume that the circle dance was already a permanent possession of the Paleolithic culture, the first perceptible stage of human civilization.

THE STONE AGE

Middle Paleolithic Culture (Pygmies)

Our system of prehistoric ethnographical cycles and layers of culture as defined above is based on Oswald Menghin's comprehensive *Weltgeschichte der Eiszeit* (*World History of the Glacial Era*), published in Vienna in 1931. According to the Viennese scholar, the Middle Paleolithic culture, which is the earliest prehistoric period having counterparts in the present, is reflected in the cultures of diminutive races such as still exist in several parts of the world, in central Africa, in Asia on the Andaman Islands and in Malacca, and in central New Guinea. The chief characteristics of this group are acquisitive economy—food gathering, fishing, hunting—windbreaks instead of houses, earth burial, monogamy, private property, and monotheism. The formative arts, tattooing, and mutilation are still absent.

The dance of the pygmies we have already described in detail in several places. We discovered, especially among the African pygmies, a particular delight in and talent for dancing with a strong emphasis on lifelike imitation in war dances and animal dances, in which they have probably never been surpassed. The form of their choral dance is everywhere the loose circle in which the dancers do not touch.

One motif in particular, the encircling of a man by dancing women or of a girl by dancing men, can be traced both in the Europe of the old Stone Age and among primitive peoples today. From the European evidence, namely the rock paintings at Cogul in the province of Lérida in eastern Spain, which have been discussed in detail elsewhere, we should, of course, have to assume a later stage, the so-called Neolithic blade culture. But here ethnography must intervene to amplify and to correct. The recurrence of this theme, not merely in a single or in neighboring groups, but among pygmy peoples so widely separated by the great oceans of the world as the Bushmen of South Africa and the Negritos of the Philippine Islands, compels us to ascribe this dance form to an older, Protolithic period (Plate 1).

The mere encircling of a person or thing in the dance, as we have it here, and the imitative animal dance have already been distinguished in the systematic part of this book as the manifestation of two opposed tendencies and mentalities, which may be called introvert and extravert, imaginative and sensory, speculative and intuitive. There is no race, there is not even an individual who has not something of both mentalities, but in some the one and in some the other is dominant. At the same time we have discovered a number of dance qualities which, like all things human, do not allow of neat classification, but which nevertheless follow fairly obviously one type or the other. In general the division appears to be:

Extravert	Introvert
Cultivation of animal dances	Lack of animal dances
Outstanding dance talent	Moderate dance talent
Body-conscious loose dancing	Spasmodic dancing
Choral dance predominant	Solo dance predominant

Both types are completely developed and sharply differentiated at the level of the Middle Paleolithic culture. In the first group are the real pygmies, and in the second, pygmoids like the Vedda.

Late Basic Culture

TASMANOID BLADE CULTURE is Menghin's name for a culture characterized by acquisitive economy, windbreaks and round huts, spears and clubs as weapons, stone blades, earth burial, both monogamy and polygamy, body painting, tattooing, and nose piercing. This is the forerunner of the patriarchal, totemistic culture. In Tasmania itself, where the original inhabitants have died out, we learn but little about the dance. The initiation ceremonies of the Kurnai of southeastern Australia best illustrate Tasmanoid dancing. Their choral form is the circle —almost exclusively without touching; sometimes they follow a winding course to the dancing place. Men and women may dance together;

in Tasmania they remained separated. A noteworthy motif is the lifting up of the boys, which has parallels later in the agricultural rites. Animal dances are very frequent. Here, too, belongs that dance of western Australia in which the men plunge the spear into a large hole in the ground symbolizing the vulva. The Watchandi, who perform it, show themselves by the use of spears as weapons, initiation by scarification, and earth burial to be Tasmanoid.

AUSTRALOID COUP-DE-POING CULTURE. The main features of this culture are acquisitive economy, the boomerang, the axe, round huts, monotheism, and the knocking out of teeth. "On the whole it must be said that this cultural unit is extremely uncertain and may perhaps have to be radically revised."

The Colombian Uitoto, the chief American representatives of this culture, perform dances of a conceptional character: they beat on the ground with thick staves and the women answer each blow with a scream.

ESKIMOID BONE CULTURE. This culture is characterized by hunting and fishing, round huts, spears and bows as weapons, bone utensils, patriarchy, exposure of the dead in a circle of stones, monotheism, and skulls as trophies.

The Caribou Eskimo are the chief representatives of this level, and the only dance peculiar to them is the solo dance of both sexes with a light swinging of the pelvis backwards and forwards, and occasional dipping of the hips. As a rule they dance in one place. Only one or two take a few steps to the side, to and fro.

The Protolithic basic cultures, then, are familiar with the solo dance and with the choral dance in circular formation—almost entirely without bodily contact between the participants. The two great worlds of the dance are already clearly recognizable: the one imageless, with the characteristic encircling of a human being or an object, and the other imitative, with the animal dance. Clearly defined also are the sharp contrasts between dances in harmony with the body and dances out of harmony with the body, close dances and expanded dances.

The Neolithic Period and the Early Tribal Cultures

TOTEMISTIC BLADE CULTURE. The main features of this culture are acquisitive economy, round huts, clustered villages, daggers and spears, patriarchy, circumcision, sun mythology, witchcraft, and the use of red ocher. A peculiar delight in handicrafts is characteristic of the peoples of this cultural level. Their representations are close replicas of nature, especially in the case of animals. What ornamentation they have is for the most part rectilinear.

The intellectual trend manifest in these features also marks the dance. Pure totemists like the Arunta of Central Australia are, as dancers, out-and-out imitators. The themes are taken almost without exception from animals and are copied with naturalistic fidelity. The form of the dance here as before is the simple circle. In conformity with the masculine emphasis of these patriarchal cultures, often only men dance, and frequently women are excluded even as spectators.

The mask, too, has its main root in the totemistic blade culture. Dozens of figures which are part man and part beast are to be seen in rock paintings. Often only the head is animal, while sometimes the human being is recognizable only by the feet. In their anxiety lest it be possible to throw bridges across from their "field" to an alien one, some prehistorians have raised many, and in part extremely foolish, objections to the interpretation of these figures as "masks." They have suggested, for example, that the Paleolithic artist had become so accustomed to depicting animals that he inadvertently put animal heads on human beings! In the knock-kneed masks of the cave at Le Mas d'Azil from the Neolithic Period they have pretended to see "embryo children"!

Today there is no longer any possibility of doubt that in these cases we have masked dancers. Not even the assumption that they represent a kind of hunting camouflage for stalking game will suffice: pictures in which the penis is erect and in which the pursuit of the female animal is realistically presented preclude this interpretation. Here, as later in the mature mask dance, the purpose is a fertility charm. It would be vain, however, to seek in these mask dancers for the fantastic refinements of the Papua. They are probably in all cases genuine animal skins, which conceal the head or a large part of the body. The ancestor worship of the planter peoples and the fruitful combination of introversion and extraversion first give to the mask dance its full breadth and depth and to the mask itself its curious abstractness and grotesqueness (Plate 1).

EARLY PLANTER COUP-DE-POING CULTURE. Here the characteristic features are plant cultivation, rectangular huts, linear villages, axes and clubs, matriarchy, moon mythology, ancestor worship, shamanism, and burial in two stages. The art of the early planters is directed primarily towards ornamentation. Naturalistic representations are entirely lacking and the ornamentation itself is abstract and geometrical, with a peculiar tendency towards scrolls and curves, especially concentric circles.

With plant cultivation and matriarchy comes also an unparalleled transformation in the dance. The change in the ground plan of the hut from a circle to a rectangle, and in the form of the settlement from a casual cluster to a definite village scheme, is the result of an exceptional intellectual tendency which has had a corresponding influence on the dance. Besides the circle we now meet for the first time the form in which the dancers are drawn up in a line or even in two lines facing each other. The liking for concentric circles as a decorative motif is reflected in the dance with two and three circles. The delight in sinuous lines and winding curves in ornamentation finds expression in the serpentine movements of the dance chorus. On this point, however, and on the corresponding point in the section, "Late Planter Polished Axe

Culture," it would be well for the reader to consult the systematic consideration of the relation between the dance and ornamentation on page 165.

Not only the motor impulse has changed. In contrast to the dance of the pygmies and the totemists—in contrast, that is, to the dance of the real hunters—the dance of the planter culture is born out of an entirely un-naturalistic spirit. Not observation but meditation sets its goals. Not reality but dream and rapture give it its form. The planter dance is non-pictorial and introvert. The motifs and types, however, are determined chiefly by concern for fertility, especially for rain, by initiation ideas, shamanism, moon mythology, and ancestor worship. Out of shamanism comes the deeply ecstatic dance "out of harmony with the body," as we have called it, the convulsive dance with the healing of the sick as its chief aim. The dance through fire seems also to be shamanistic. Moon mythology introduces into the choral dance the motifs of rising and setting, of wandering, of waxing and waning, and of the struggle between light and darkness. Ancestor worship brings in the funeral dance and gives maturity and significance to the mask.

EARLY HERDER BONE CULTURE. Characteristics: herding, conical tents, bows and spears as weapons, monogamy, patriarchy, monotheism, earth burial, naturalistic tendency in art. "In spite of the splendid work of the Finnish scholars on the cultural history of their people," says Menghin, "we have as yet no clear picture of the early herder culture in its unmixed state." We shall therefore not attempt to fill in the history of the dance under this heading.

The Protoneolithic Period and the Middle Tribal Cultures

LATE PLANTER POLISHED AXE CULTURE. The successor of the early planter coup-de-poing culture, this culture is characterized by cultivation of the soil with picks, rectangular houses, polished axes, bows as weapons, matriarchy, skull cults, head hunting, cannibalism, fetishism, and magic. As with the early planters, the tendency in art is towards the geometric and ornamental; curves, spirals, and double spirals are preferred.

To the old legacy of dance is added the new motif of the head-hunter and scalp dance, and as a new form the expansion of the double to a triple and quadruple circle and still further. Another addition is the arrangement of a line of men and a line of women opposite each other. The high leaping dances, which were supposed to help the growth of the seed, seem also to belong here. The late planter culture, like all the other Middle Tribal cultures, did but little to expand and enrich the dance.

HORNED ANIMAL CULTURE. The special features of this culture are the domestication of horned animals, mostly round houses, lances, daggers, and clubs as weapons, patriarchy, circumcision, witchcraft, imageless cults, and little artistic inclination or achievement.

The dances of this culture, best known from their diffusion among the Dinka, Shilluk, and Herero tribes of northeastern and southern Africa, have as choral form the circle. Solo dances do not seem to occur; instead, we find dances in pairs without touching and with "choosing of lady." For the most part, however, the men dance alone. Animal and weapon dances are known.

RIDING ANIMAL CULTURE. Characteristics: horse breeding, conical tents, bows as weapons, patriarchy, aristocracy and plutocracy, declining monotheism. The dances of this cycle seem to appear at their purest among the Altai Tartars. They are phallic dances of an extremely erotic character performed by men. The facial mask behind which the dancers hide is obviously, together with shamanism, an importation from a matriarchal culture.

The Neolithic Period Proper, the Metal Age, and the Late Tribal Cultures

The Late Tribal cultures, the bridge to the higher cultures, are of two distinct types, which supplement and qualify each other: peasant culture and seignorial culture. The characteristics and boundaries of the peasant culture have not yet been sufficiently well worked out to be reduced to a brief formula. The dances of this culture stand out, to be sure, by reason of their strong accent on the sexual—not in the sense of undue phallic emphasis, but in that of mimetic representation of courtship and the near approach to the sexual act, which often took place immediately at the conclusion of the dance. In the choral round dance a line of men is often drawn up opposite a line of women, and sometimes the dance is divided into figures which wind and unwind in an intricate maze. In mixed couples the dance displays for the first time the motif of the wooing of a coy maiden and the embracing of a willing one. Female solo dances, which now play a much more important role, frequently employ the motif of libido and exhibition.

Nevertheless the libido dances, and especially the *danse du ventre* (belly dance), are no longer purely peasant dances. They belong at least in part to the domain of seignorial culture, in which Menghin includes, besides the European, the Sudanese, Malayan, Polynesian, Peruvian, and Mexican cultures. For in their transition from the purely devotional and social to the professional and theatrical, these dances take for granted the division of labor and the class distinctions of an aristocratic and urban culture, which demands and supports the formation of a paid dancing profession for entertainment and public performances.

If this path of seignorial culture leads to the spectacular dance of the Oriental peoples, with the pure peasant dances we are already in the midst of the folk dance of the Occident. For what survives today as the peculiar possession of the European "folk" is for the most part merely the common property of that great peasant culture which since the high Stone Age has been held by all the planter peoples of Europe, Asia, and northern Africa.

Omitting the third group, the table of this development would look something like this:

THE PROTOLITHIC PERIOD / BASIC CULTURES	
EARLY BASIC CULTURES	
Circular Dance without Touching	
MIDDLE BASIC CULTURES	
PYGMIES	PYGMOIDS
Circular Dance without Touching	
Animal Dances	Convulsive Dances
LATE BASIC CULTURES	
TASMANOIDS	AUSTRALOIDS
Circular Dance without Touching	
Animal Dances Serpentine Dances Sexual-lunar Dances	

THE NEOLITHIC PERIOD / TRIBAL CULTURES	
EARLY TRIBAL CULTURES	
TOTEMISTS	EARLY PLANTERS
Circular Dances Animal Dances Phallic Dances	Circular and Choral Dances Double Circles Moon Dances Funeral Dances
Mask Dances	

THE PROTONEOLITHIC PERIOD / MIDDLE TRIBAL CULTURES	
HORNED ANIMAL CULTURE	LATE PLANTER CULTURE
Circular Dances Animal Dances Couple Dances	Dances of Several Circles Men and Women in Opposite Lines

THE NEOLITHIC PERIOD PROPER THE METAL AGE / LATE TRIBAL CULTURES	
SEIGNORIAL	PEASANT
Dances with Mixed Couples Embracing Dance Wooing Dance *Danse du Ventre*	

6. The Evolution to the Spectacular Dance and the Oriental Civilizations

THE DANCERS

A Chinaman years ago went to France,
And attended at court a magnificent dance.
They asked if he knew this sport lively and gay,
And what was the name for it back in Cathay.
He laughed and replied: It's dancing there too,
But we leave it for others to do.

FONTANE

WHATEVER the nature of the dance, whether it is a rhythmic release of excess energy or a deliberate religious act, it needs no onlooker, not even a single witness. Nevertheless, in spite of its ecstatic and liturgical character, there early appears the germ of that great process of change which has gradually transformed the dance from an involuntary motor discharge, from a state of frenzied movement and a ceremonial rite, into a work of art conscious of and intended for observation.

The change was inevitable. As a purely emotional phenomenon the human dance might have remained as unfettered as that of the chimpanzee. But not as a religious rite. For if in addition to the creative impulse the essential attributes of a work of art are command of form, carefully balanced organization, and intelligent construction, the devotional role must needs already have made a work of art out of the dance. Its unique importance for the life and welfare of the tribe debarred

218

random improvisation; it called for planning and precise formulation and demanded of succeeding generations the most faithful adherence to tradition. For every error rendered the power and efficacy of the charm problematical. And both dancers and spectators kept watch over the accuracy. On the island of Gaua in the New Hebrides it is said that formerly the old men used to stand by with bows and arrows and shoot at every dancer who made a mistake. Consequently it was imperative to have as many members of the tribe as possible instructed in the perfect mastery of the dance form.

In primitive peoples such instruction was generally given in the bosom of the family or within the narrow divisions of the tribe. In the basic cultures, as among the Australians or the pygmies of central Africa, the mothers teach the little children to dance; in the tribal cultures the learning of the dances of the tribe is one of the most important parts of the initiation rites of the maturing youth. But this is not always sufficient: in certain tribes of New Guinea the sons are sent to places renowned for the dance so that they may perfect themselves and act as dance leaders and teachers in their own village. They prepare for dance festivals weeks, months, and even years in advance, until every movement and position is mastered. Dances of this kind inevitably become, without detriment to their religious function, conscious and acknowledged personal achievements. Even in the lower cultures we find here and there evidence of a spiritual copyright on the dance. On the Gazelle Peninsula in New Britain the right to every newly invented dance is protected not only for the inventor, but also for his heirs, and nobody would dare to perform without permission a dance which is not his own. When we hear, then, that in northwest Melanesia, in New Britain, on the island of Yap in the Carolines, and in the Fiji Islands, the handing over and rehearsing of a new dance was and is paid for, the change is very obvious. We must not assume, however, that such a dance, having become, as it were, an article of commerce, is thereby divested of its religious value. It is bought because the buyers hope to secure through their purchase powerful magic effects. But this magic is, of course, dependent upon their own performing power, and what could that be but art?

The individual participant in a ceremony of this kind which becomes a work of art cannot repudiate for himself the corresponding evolution into an artist. The mask dance has in a certain sense hastened this development. The tribe as a whole can no longer take part. The dance is limited almost exclusively to the male sex—but not even among the men is everyone suitable and competent for every dance. As long as the demonology is taken seriously, one person is closer to a certain spirit than the rest and is specially qualified to represent him and to become one with him. In this sequestration lies the germ of the spectacular dance: every dance divides the tribe into active members and passive, into performers and spectators. It is only a logical step further, then, when in even so early a culture as that of New Guinea special benches were built for the spectators at the big dances and when the Micronesian dances took place on stages and on bridges in tiers.

It is only an apparent contradiction that in the mask dance the performers accentuate their own individuality as they strive for the negation of self and the surrender of personality. Contrariwise, races among whom the maskless dance flourishes frequently travel the road towards self-conscious and audience-conscious egocentricity, towards virtuosity.

In the line dance especially, the spectators who are sitting in front, and towards whom the dancers are looking, inevitably become little by little the aim and object of the dance. On the island of Yap, the dance leader stands opposite the spectator of highest rank. This generally acts as a spur to the dancer, who feels himself the center of admiring glances —especially from the other sex—and stimulates the performance independently of its magical significance. The stimulus is in the main purely physical. The corporal achievement denotes strength, endurance, and skill. Strength and endurance have frequently been mentioned in the course of this discussion—they are still a part of the dance ideal of the European peasant lads today, and may even make their appearance in the ballroom in the form of the *volta* and the *nizzarda*. Although the muscular dances may be largely subordinated to the aims of the cult, they must nevertheless become for the youthful stalwart reveling in his strength an opportunity for the display of athletic prowess.

Closely akin to the muscular dance is the dance of skill. Here, too, there is a religious-ecstatic stage to be noted. In California and in Sierra Leone the dance sometimes degenerates into acrobatic climbing feats; and in Sierra Leone—in a pure early planter, head-hunter culture—the ecstatic character of these acrobatics is explicitly attested. This combination is rare, however, while the incorporation of sleight of hand, balancing tricks, and target shooting in the dance is common. It is significant that in the Old Egyptian the same word *ḥbj* is used to designate the ordinary dance and also the gymnastic exercise known as "the bridge," which is frequently depicted on the monuments of the Middle and New Kingdom (Plate 8). Many other instances may be cited: the Mexican girl, who while dancing the *rebozo* unties the knot in a sash on the ground with her feet; the maiden of Sumatra, who dances balancing three trays with lighted candles on head and hands; the rope dance of the Tibetan spirit dancers; the balancing tricks in ancient Greece; the juggling exhibitions in Cyprus; the dance leader of the *Glasltanz* with the full beaker on his head—in the Middle Ages and in the contemporary *Ländler*—and his African counterpart, the maiden of Loango who dances with a bottle on her head; the Swabian peasant, who wins the rooster if he knocks a glass of water off the pole in the dance; and in all parts of the world the sword dance, in which the lightning-swift yet quiet combat without wounding the opponent, the supple gliding and frisking of the dangerous weapon in a very narrow space without clashing or confusion, and the changing play of the sparkling blades unite in a superb masculine art, almost an artistic transposition and purification of the brutal business of battle.

Skill, physical build, suppleness, strength, and endurance are displayed—the good dancer is a coveted lover and spouse, and bad dancing is an obstacle to matrimony. But eroticism and aestheticism flourish in the same ground. The dancer who ceases to exercise magical charms and begins to exert personal charm instead is on the way to becoming a dance artist. Even in Australia the good dancer accepts congratulations from his friends, adoration from women, and remuneration from strangers. In Melanesia he is rated above a good singer, and in New Ireland the virtuoso dancer is "the finest thing in the world."

But this virtuoso is not a professional artist—he occupies about the same position as the celebrated amateur sportsman does with us. It was impossible for a professional spectacular dance in the narrower sense to develop in the middle cultures. It cannot exist without that social division into masters and servants which was brought to mankind by the Late Tribal cultures, the seignorial cultures. They were the first to cause the momentous split of the artistic form into two elements: the commissioned work of the artist and the enjoyment of the paying or ruling spectator. With this the art is placed fundamentally on the basis of performance for material rewards.

For the dance the next step was the formation of a dancing profession. The transition to the professional spectacular dance, however, is not and cannot be sharply defined. Both the Indian female dancers, whom we are in the habit of calling by the Portuguese name *bailadeiras* or bayaderes, and their counterparts among the Haussa tribes, the young Koka women, who are dedicated to the fetish and its priests and yet "entertain the intoxicated crowd at festivals with obscene dances to the accompaniment of singing and the beating of drums," are still more or less bound to the cult and go back to the maiden dance of primitive peoples.

The root of this apparent contradiction is the idea that the young chaste person possesses a particular magic power—many virgins included in the group increase the effect. We understand, therefore, why in the case of death on the island of Yap a number of young maidens are engaged at a high fee to perform a dance for the revival of the dead.

In regions verging on the higher cultures the isolation of such dance maidens is inevitable. For the destruction of the social unity of the people and the segregation of the various human activities into professional classes, ranks, and castes are essential characteristics of the higher cultures. The female dancers of the cult are withdrawn from the family and from the work of house and field, dedicated in early youth to the temple, drilled exclusively in their art, and maintained for the execution of the dance ritual. Here a curious change takes place, the particulars of which lie outside the realm of our interest. In the temple the dancer is *devadasi,* the slave of God, consecrated to God like the nun in the Christian cloister. But the surrender is by no means consummated by the mystical reception of the wedding ring; when the maiden is sufficiently mature, the stone phallus of the God Siva takes her virginity, and with this act she enters into the possession of the priests who are the representatives of the god.

By an odd exchange of symbols the vestal virgin becomes, in the temple of many religions, the sacred harlot—apparently in places where two contrasting worlds of ideas clash: fertility magic through untouched maidens and fertility magic through the stimulation of sexual intercourse. We have examples of this combination of consecrated temple dancers and paid prostitutes in the Near East of early times and also, it seems, in the related cults of ancient Mexico. In the narrower sphere of Hindu culture a royal court ballet develops out of the chorus of the temple dancers. Once the beloved of God, the dancer now becomes the concubine of the prince. But even with this decadence of the cult the magic and religious ideas still sound forth: if virginity be no longer demanded, nevertheless conception excludes the dancer from any further dancing. The indispensability of the invocation to the deity also bears witness to the original devotional significance: as the American Indians pray four times before the dance, so in India the dance is preceded by solemn prayer repeated four times, even if it is a public performance by an independent troupe. According to the strict Hindu view, dance without prayer is considered vulgar; he who witnesses it will be childless and will be reincarnated in the body of an animal.

It is thus chiefly ancient religious reasons which accord the greatest, and often indeed the only, share in the spectacular dance to the girl and not to the man. That woman has maintained, in spite of all the fading of the original religious significance, the position conceded to her is not surprising in a seignorial culture where the joys and pleasures are determined by man.

Every imitative dance bears within it the germ of the pantomime. Every dancer who, with acute powers of observation, feels himself into the living, and even into the lifeless, objects of nature, and re-creates with his own body their appearance, their actions, and their essence is an actor, a mime.

But his miming keeps mostly to the future and the present. The psychologist Jung once remarked: "Freud's word that the unconscious can 'only wish,' applies mainly to the unconscious of the extravert type." As a matter of fact, most imitative dances are wish dances. They represent what man needs and hopes to obtain through dancing: the fertility of the tribe and of the earth, growth, the favor of the stars, health, life, strength, luck in the chase, and victory. But there are exceptions. The propensity to apprehend every idea concretely in visible and active form is very deeply rooted in a certain temperament, in a desire for sensory perceptions, formation, and reproduction. Races and cultures of this type are irresistibly impelled, without any devotional aim whatever, to re-create all kinds of occurrences from life in rhythmic action. So that together with the future they dance a pure, wishless present. Like children they are able simply to regard the object and record it, to recount the characteristics of the animals in song and imitate their movements in dance.

This mimicry of the present takes the form, in the earlier cultures, of the portrait dances in which acquaintances are portrayed or caricatured, or friendship, love, jealousy, and hatred are depicted. In other places it becomes the imitation of passive movement as represented in inanimate objects. Melanesia in particular is inexhaustible in this respect. Every New Caledonian village has, as the conclusion to the commemorative feast of the dead, its own mimic dance with motifs from animate and inanimate nature, events from animal life, the rising, breaking, and subsiding of the waves of the sea, and the storm which tears off branches and uproots trees. A New Guinea dance of this kind has been described by R. Neuhauss: "Two rows of dancers represent the boat, three dance leaders armed with oars, the crew; the vessel runs into an adverse wind and is forced to tack about and this idea is splendidly expressed by the rows of dancers; the sea becomes more and more agitated, the swaying, leaping, and jumping of the dancers more and more rapid; the dance leaders, who have hitherto attempted to defy the elements by powerful strokes of the oars, run up and down, for the disaster is unavoidable. The waves tear the outrigger loose (the men representing the outrigger are separate from the others); with this the boat is entirely out of control and is driven hither and thither; the leaps of the men become wilder and wilder, and the crew rush from right to left to prevent capsizing. Then the dance ends."

The Ostyak of western Siberia dance a tree-felling pantomime: one is the woodsman, the other, standing motionless, represents the tree trunk; the latter, however, shows himself to be alive, throws off the covering cloth, and dances together with the woodsman. On the Aleutian Islands in the Arctic, two men dance a bird hunt; the bird falls, is caught—and turns into a beautiful woman, who sinks exhausted into the arms of the hunter. Here the transformation motif is so obviously formed out of the spirit of the disguise dance that one is forced to ask oneself if the prolific transformation theme of the myths and fairy tales is not largely derived from the dance.

What takes place here is a work of art, just as are those festive dances of New Guinea which are prepared for weeks, months, and years in advance until every movement and position is mastered. For it is just this mastery, this conscious and calculated elaboration and formulation which divides art from play and improvisation.

But this work of art is not yet a drama. It presents a section of everyday life—without beginning or end. It remains in the present. The threshold to the dance drama proper is only crossed when the past begins consciously and intentionally to enter into the dance theme.

The retrospective element in the dance theme originates in the martial sphere. Here it is a matter of life and death; no wonder, then, that events imprint themselves on the memory and press constantly for renewed expression. With us the simple man never tires of relating his war experiences—I except that overwhelming impact of the Great War which has oftener sealed men's lips than opened them. And similarly the primitive likes to tell his story in his own way in an impassioned chant as accompaniment to the dance. Catlin witnessed a "dog dance" among the Sioux, "in which each man lauded his own deeds in song, until it was enough to deafen one."

It is scarcely possible to speak of historicity, even in the most modest autobiographical sense, in connection with the self-laudation of the Indians. This portion of the past becomes to the unsophisticated completely the present. One sees the dancers "swinging their weapons as fiercely as though they were going to hack each other to pieces on the spot; at the same time they distort their faces in the most hideous manner and grind their teeth . . . they behave as if they were in the midst of battle. . . ."

But in the same realm of culture this retrospection finally rises above childish self-praise to become epilogue and history. When one of their number has been killed in battle, the Sauk and Fox Indians have the beautiful custom of dancing an hour a day for fifteen days before his wigwam and his mourning widow, presenting gifts for those left behind and praising in song the heroic deeds of their fallen comrade in arms. And when the Toba of the Gran Chaco go forth into battle, they perform a solemn dance during which they sing the praises of the military exploits of their ancestors. The dances themselves, however, remain imageless. No attempt is made to represent the narrative realistically, and even the weapon swinging of the Indians is emotional and not imitative.

This makes the situation clear. Memory is introversive. It is necessarily the function of the imaginative side of man, not the perceptive. Hence

226

the thematic retrospection will reveal itself first in imageless dances. This will be so even when the memory no longer clings to the immediate past—almost to the present—but seizes upon things which lie far back, when the remembrance of ancient migrations and natural phenomena is preserved, and when the consciousness of historical progression takes shape in the awed veneration of ancestors. To be sure, the severance of past and present may take place only very slowly. In his naïveté primitive man feels as reality what for us has become a pale semblance—the living existence of the past. And it is this very presentness of what has been that makes possible and imperative its constant representation.

Representation, however, calls for the perceptive faculty: the imaginative man is forced to ask aid of the sensory man, when he wishes to give concrete form to memory, and the sensory man is rewarded by the idea of the drama nurtured on the consciousness of the past.

Thus we note here and there in the narrow sphere of the commemoration of war, encroachments on the field of pictorial description—in the dance of the women on the island of Palau in the Carolines described on page 32, for instance, the motif of which was said to have been taken from the last war. But even in such cases as this, there is, with all the naïveté, less emphasis on the immediate thrill of sense perception than on the esoteric meaning, the challenge to the intellect. In Palau, indeed, the men were forced to confess their ignorance: "That is a dance of the women which only they can explain. When we men perform a dance, the women do not understand it either."

We have seen already in the mask dance the potent and fruitful union of the two basic forces: the imaginative, introvert, imageless and the sensory, extravert, imitative power. The great development which now sets in receives its impetus from the same combination of the imaginative faculty in ancestor worship with the sensory in the objectifying, imitative dance. The ancestor becomes the bearer of all the forces of nature; he is the demon of fertility or the spirit of victory, the moon god or the sun god. The dancer, however, possessed by his etherealized and deified ancestor and compelled to move as though he had been transformed into this spirit, is now drawn into the circle of those pantomimes which make manifest the operation of fertility, victory, the course of the stars. The dancer's function in this combination necessarily develops into drama. The venerable No play of Japan arises out of the temple dance of the virginal Shinto priestesses, in whom the spirit of the dead walks, and the Hindu actor acknowledges himself to be a dancer by his title *Nata* in Prakrit, which is the equivalent of the Sanskrit *nâtya* from *nrta,* "to dance." Meaningful movement, then, must proceed gradually to portray the heroic deeds and fateful sufferings of human beings. The fertility demon must submit to the law governing the rhythmical change of the seasons: he must bring blessing in spring and summer, but must sink down before the destroyer of all life in the fall to rise again victorious in the spring. The bright moon must fight against his dark brother until he is finally swallowed up by him at the close of the cycle. The sun struggles against the powers of darkness, and all these spirits and gods and their adversaries plunge into the motley world of animal forms and fates, upon which lively observation and fantastic imagination have been at work. But they disappear at the same time into the world of ancestors, whose memory is reverently cherished as a precious treasure, particularly by the matriarchal-agricultural cultures. Animals, ancestors, and nature spirits merge, and natural laws, sense perception, dream experience, and tribal tradition combine in a magnificent drama, which in the same breath expands human fate to cosmic proportions and interprets cosmic phenomena in human terms. At this level of development the dramatic dithyrambs of the Grecian Dionysus dancers approach the Egyptian festival plays at Abydos, in which priests and people together portrayed the death and resurrection of Osiris.

The Abydos festivals are for *Egypt* the culmination of a development which we are able to survey, although often with but sparse evidence, over a period of almost three thousand years—three thousand years which compress into a restricted area a clear picture of what this chapter describes: how in the union of introvert and extravert tendencies in the high cultures the spectacular dance originates which ultimately evolves into the mythological drama. For the Egyptians as for the Greeks, the dance is "joy"—the names themselves indicate this, and when in the middle of the second millennium King Thutmosis I has his daughter Hatchepsowet recognized as his successor, the nobles go forth rejoicing, dance and make merry, and all his subjects dance and leap. Almost at the same time a similar unorganized dance of joy is figured in Amarna.

But none of the vast number of dance pictures and none of the literary sources reveals a real social dance. At least the aristocratic Egyptian, whose life the monuments record, knew no choral dance in which he joined with others, no dance of couples, and no solo dance. That the peasants, on the other hand—as is to be expected—celebrated their old fertility rites in the dance is proved by the advanced harvest choral depicted in a relief on a tomb from the fifth dynasty at Giza about 2700 B.C. And this may have been handed down unchanged to later times: some of the dances can be interpreted without difficulty as rain charms. But already at that time the upper classes had long since relinquished the dance to others. When on the tomb of Ti, which also belongs to the fifth dynasty, the usual dance escort of the burial is depicted, the hieroglyphic annotation explains it as "the dance on the part of the harem." Indeed, a vase from the pre-dynastic period (the fourth millennium) shows a woman in the artificial pose of a professional dancer. The temples maintained dancers of both sexes as a special class. We find them over and over again in cult pictures, either in the quiet dance, as our illustration shows, with gentle steps and with arms outstretched in rhomboid form, or in the most daring acrobatic positions, in the bridge, the hand stand, or the candle (Plate 8). Here the acrobatic dance, the ecstatic origin of which we have indicated, still survives in its initial religious function—already detached, to be sure, from the purely ecstatic and transmuted into artistic skill, but still as a magic activity and not as a mere gymnastic exercise. Several times the round dances themselves are delineated in their various phases of movement, as though in a frozen motion picture: they are figure dances. It is not too farfetched, therefore, to interpret in the same fashion the fact that the name for the dance, *iba,* means also the men in the game of draughts.

Even at that time Egypt, as a true seignorial culture, imported solo dancers from countries famed for the dance, even for religious services. The monuments prove this, but the best evidence is that fascinating, almost passionate letter in which King Neferkere writes to his field marshal about an Ethiopian dwarf dancer:

"Thou hast said in this thy letter that thou hast brought a *Dng* [pygmy] of the dances of the god from the Land of the Spirits, who is like unto the pygmy which the divine chancellor Ba-ur-tet brought in the time of Asesa. Thou hast said to my Majesty that the like of him has never been brought back by any other. . . . Come at once to the Court by boat; . . . bring with thee this pygmy, which thou hast brought living, whole and sound from the Land of the Spirits for the dances of the god and that he may gladden and make happy the heart of the King Neferkere (who lives eternally). When he goes aboard the boat with thee, have trustworthy people stand behind him on both sides of the boat and keep watch lest he fall into the water. When he is asleep at night, have trustworthy people to sleep behind him in his . . . and look into it ten times during the night. My Majesty wisheth to see this pygmy more than all the gifts from Bia-ta and Puoni. And if thou comest to the Court having with thee this pygmy, alive, whole and sound, my Majesty will do more for thee than was done for the divine chancellor Ba-ur-tet in the time of Asesa, for it is the most cherished wish of my Majesty to see this pygmy."

This letter is nonetheless significant even if the writer was, as seems probable, still only a boy. It proves that the third millennium was already reaching back for the art of those Nilotic dwarf peoples who are renowned in East Africa for their dancing to this day.

If it is possible in these dances, especially in the chorals and in the acrobatic scenes, to discern clearly the continuation of the introvert, non-imitative side of the dance, there is nevertheless no lack of the extravert, imitative admixture so indispensable to high culture. Sometimes dancing maidens show how the king fells a vanquished enemy, or how the wind caresses the trees and bends the reeds, and again they portray "the abduction of a beauty" or "the secret of birth." We observe here that the old weather charms and birth magic have lost their devotional significance and become artistic dance pantomimes.

In the Middle Kingdom in the nineteenth century B. C. the myth of the vegetation god who dies and rises up again has entered into these pantomimes: the Osiris festivals at Abydos are known to have existed since the time of Sesostris III. What took place there is shown on a relief in the Louvre. And here at last we find what must not be wanting if the road towards the drama is to be traveled—mask dancers. Men with fantastic head adornments dance at the resurrection of the god, and falcon-headed souls welcome with shouts of joy the risen deity. It may perhaps be objected that there is no proof that the steles reproduce the play and that consequently the interpretation of the figures as "mask dancers" is ill-founded; perhaps the mythical event itself was imagined to be like this. But would the dancing actor have a different conception of it from the sculptor? Are not the reproductions of sacred scenes on church walls and in paintings in medieval Europe at the same time reproductions of the representation of these scenes in the mystery plays? Moreover, the picture on the Paris stele is directly connected with a text which tells not of the myth but of the festivals at Abydos.

With this the development of the strictly Egyptian dance is concluded. It is characterized throughout by a marked austerity and by expanded movement even in the dances of the female sex. About 1500 B. C. there comes a change in this. Just as the conquest of the Near East at this time robbed the music of its national character and gave it a feminine, Asiatic stamp, so the immigrant bayaderes from the conquered countries took their place beside the native dancers. This new dance, which is illustrated in the pictures of funeral ceremonies (Plates 8, 9) and festive banquets, has no longer anything of the masculine, unrestricted movement, the great strides, and the stiff, angular posture.

The lines flow softly and pleasantly; nowhere do they bend sharply and break; and even where the mood is impetuous and impassioned the movement remains close. This is the contribution of the Asiatic girls who brought to the Egyptian dance a true feminine style.

And now we turn to the dances of *Asia*.

Drama and play, myth and fairy tale need extraversion, which is strong in sense perception and true to reality. However, they need also an introvert admixture, not only for contemplation and recollection, but because the introversion of the predominantly feminine planter cultures lends to every art the power to fuse various elements together and to stylize them.

The simpler imitative dance reproduces the appearance, character, and movement of objects, but it is only a slice of life, a bit of nature acutely observed, a series of connected and repeated motifs like naturalistic ornamentation on a flat surface. Composition, structure, and climax can be contributed only by cultures which in the pictorial arts also understand not only how to arrange motifs in series but also how to interweave them, to relate them one to another, to bring unity out of multiplicity.

However—and this is the catch—with this power to fuse comes also the power to stylize: all introvert cultures tend to forsake reality, to proceed towards abstraction. In these cultures what is true of the ornamentation is often true also of the dances: it is necessary to be familiar with the motif in order to understand the meaning; it cannot be apprehended purely by the senses. This road next leads to the conventionalizing of the attribute. Sword and lance are replaced by sticks, and the painting of the body to suit the occasion is discontinued. Finally the attribute disappears altogether; the waving branch in the hand, the sacrificial blossom between the fingers, is dispensed with, and gesture alone suffices.

The superb art of the gesture dance originated in *India* thousands of years ago and from there penetrated to the East in the eighth century A. D. at the latest—it already appears in the reliefs of the Hindu-Javanese temple at Borobudur from about 800 A. D. India has in its own way forced this art into a rigid system of set rules: the *Nātya Sāstra* of Bhárata—written about the fifth century A. D., but based on traditions considerably older—and, somewhat more briefly, the *Abhinaya Darpaṇa,* the "mirror of gestures" of Nandikéśvara, are its great manuals. These works establish a language of gestures in which the entire representational field of the dramatic dance, according to the theme and emotion expressed, is assigned, down to the last detail, to the various parts of the body. The shaking of the head, for example, signifies negation; looking repeatedly in a certain direction expresses pity, surprise, fear, indifference, coldness, fire, the first moment of drinking, preparation for battle, repulsion, impatience, contemplation of one's own limbs, and a challenge to both sides. Twenty-four such movements of the head are distinguished. But these are only movements of the whole head; four more are allotted expressly to the neck, six to the eyebrows, and twenty-four to the eyes! That no more than fifty-seven positions should be assigned to the hands seems, accordingly, almost too few. But to this number must be added the endless symbols, the formation of which cannot be left to any other part of the body. The hands portray not only emotions and dramatic motifs: the position known as *pataka*—to mention only one—in which the thumb is bent across the outstretched fingers, expresses the beginning of the dance, clouds, woods, forbidden things, the bosom, night, the river, the world of the gods, horses, cutting, the wind, leaning backwards, wandering, bravery, clemency, moonlight, strong sunlight, knocking, waves, walking on the street, equality, the application of salve to the sandals, the dancer himself, swearing, silence, blessing, a good king, the leaf of the palmyra palm, beating, touching, the indication of a certain person, the ocean, the path of good deeds, reference to a remote person, moving along, the form of the sword, month, year, rainy season, day, and sparkling water. And besides this the hand also gives symbols for the higher world and the underworld, for the various gods, emperors, castes, rivers, trees, and animals.

For the European it is far from easy to attain an intimate understanding of this doctrine. We cannot help but see in it an abstractness, a hardening into convention, which is hopelessly removed from our ideals of free and personal art. But we must remember that in the West too there is no lack of sterile theories of art, and that living art transcends these theories. All theory analyzes and isolates the elements—all art unites them in an indivisible whole. A single gesture, which taken from the textbook and torn out of the sequence in which it belongs appears empty, bloodless, fettered, even absurd, may become in the flow of the artistic creation and in the organic succession of positions and movements, logical, clear, and compelling. This is the experience today, in this period of severe decline, of everyone who sees a good Hindu dancer. His dancing produces a strong and lasting aesthetic effect—such an effect as can be produced only by a great artistic performance in which the weight of personal creative power and the sureness of a fixed, impersonal style unite.

In all our enjoyment of the Indian dance, in all our joyous and intense experience of it, there remains something alien. We are sensible of the aesthetic effect, but feel at the same time that this is not sufficient, that it does not begin to exhaust the potentialities of the Hindu dance. The barrier which separates us from complete comprehension should not, however, be insurmountable. For the art of Europe, too, has not always desired to operate solely upon and through the senses. The works of the Middle Ages are laden with symbols and may not be called "intellectual" merely because they do not rely upon the knowledge and understanding of those to whom they give pleasure, but derive their devotional value, their religious and magical quality from the power of their very presence. It was the Italian Renaissance which first cut us off from that world; it destroyed the medieval unity of recognition and perception, of knowledge and feeling, and led us to an art which, freed of all symbolism, appeals only to the senses, only to sensation and apprehension.

In the struggle of these two great intellectual trends the sensory has prevailed over the imaginative in Europe; Asia continues along the imaginative road of progressive abstraction. The mask is a good example. It is losing importance in Asia; but its withdrawal has meant no gain for facial mimicry. Though in Bali the mask is still the central point of the dance, the deteriorated Hindu-Javanese art is already pushing it into the background, and the Cambodian resorts to it only when the dancing girls take the roles of demons and animals and the demands upon the imagination would be too great without it. The maskless dance of the southeastern Asiatic continent requires of the dancers complete immobility of face, and indeed of the whole head; for this abstract art the face does not sufficiently transcend the personal.

Of this final stage, in which the higher culture subjects the imitative dance to the inexorable law of a symbolic, conventional style, *Japan* presents the most comprehensive picture. Here we find what was once created in the austerity of the temple and the imperial court diffused through a thousand channels into the world of the teahouses. Even in the smallest village, the geisha dances the fairy tale of the fisher boy and the sea god's daughter, of the three ill-treated devils, or of the little spruce tree, which suddenly spreads out so that it is able to give shade to the emperor. Action, situation, persons, and accessories are merely indicated or suggested. Battle is implied by a light stamping of the foot; the splendor of the bottom of the sea, by the childishly gleeful chasing of a butterfly; rippling water, by a green veil at the end of the fan; the devil, by the two index fingers held over the nose. As the Japanese painter is able with a light stroke of the brush to bring the beholder under the spell of any situation or any mood, so the dancer can conjure up with his fan alone all that is necessary. It takes the place of sword and lance, it serves him as pilgrim's staff, which he seems to thump vigorously on the ground or to bend with his weary weight. The dancer swings it, lets it glide cautiously, lifts it up with an intent expression, and we have before us the angler. He carries it gently in his arms and we see the tender father with his babe. He thrusts it aside—and a man has opened the door of the house and is gazing rapturously into the blossoming garden. He opens the fan and seems to be reading in a book. The fan whirls in the air and falls to the ground—a leaf has fluttered down from the tree; it puffs out and passes over his shoulder—a sail on the river; it appears above his sleeve—the moon has risen.

It is impossible to express the restrained tenderness and simple grandeur of these gesture dances; they must be experienced, they cannot be described. We shall merely observe that a dance art of this superb character is bound up with cultures which possess also in painting and the plastic arts an incomparable ability to reveal with the vital flash of a single stroke the ultimate significance of a natural phenomenon. With the fleeting touch of a paint brush, with the angular twist of a carving tool, they divest gods, men, and nature of their chance reality and transport them into that land of dreams where the deepest essence of things, instead of being blurred in twilight, flashes forth in vivid clarity. That is the art of gesture. It is given to cultures of this type to lead the imitative dance to a climax. But in Europe, the world of perspective, of three-dimensional drawing of space, of photographic fidelity to everyday things, we have followed other paths.

7. Europe Since Antiquity

Greece

THE scattered elements which must be gathered from all places and periods and laboriously formed into a coherent picture are found united in European antiquity in one magnificent organism. The dance customs of remote ancestors, commonly relegated by mature cultures to a dark hinterland, are here preserved in pristine strength with the same love and protective zeal as among primitive peoples, and all those which later millenniums have begotten and brought forth flourish freely side by side with them. The progression of dance forms has crystallized into a coexistence. We find the same people circling round the sacred objects in meditation as did their earliest ancestors, imitating the ways and actions of animals, losing themselves and becoming possessed in the mask, and obtaining the power of spirits and the attributes of gods through the frenzied ecstasy of the dance. The same people re-experience in dream transports the fate of their ancestors and expand it into popular drama, into world drama—with the recognition of its relation to society in the round dance and with the stamp of individualism in the solo dance, with meek submission and with genial wisdom, solemn and grotesque, in earnest and in jest, in a boundless survey of everything human and superhuman.

The choral dance takes first place. Homer's accounts of the heroic age describe the merry choral dance of the young men, alone or together with the maidens, at marriages, at vintage, or simply to give vent to their youthful exuberance—*choreia,* the Greeks think, must come from *chara,* "joy."

"Also did the glorious lame god devise a dancing-place like unto that which once in wide Knossos Daidalos wrought for Ariadne of the lovely tresses. There were youths dancing, and maidens of costly wooing, their hands upon one another's wrists. Fine linen the maidens had on, and the youths well-woven doublets faintly glistening with oil. Fair wreaths had the maidens, and the youths daggers of gold hanging from silver baldrics. And now would they run round with deft feet exceeding lightly, as when a potter sitting by his wheel that fitteth between his hands maketh trial of it whether it run. And now anon they would run in lines to meet each other. And a great company stood round the lovely dance in joy; and among them a divine minstrel was making music on his lyre, and through the midst of them, leading the measure, two tumblers whirled."

Iliad, XVIII, 590–606.

Thus does Hephaistos picture it on the bronze shield destined for Achilles: Homer's Hellenes dance the ancient round dance out of which develop lines which run to meet each other; those in the middle turn somersaults—that is the meaning of the Greek word *kybistétéres*—and the dance leader leads with song and lyre.

The Greeks must have brought round dances of this type with them from their original home. But for the particular stamp of the dance the immigrants are obligated to the Cretan and Mycenaean culture, which they found in the new country and overran. Cretan sculptures illustrate for us dances in a circle around the lyre player, couple dances connected with cults, and the close swaying dance performed by large choruses of women before all the people.

The Cretans were always extolled by the Greeks as exceptional artists and acknowledged as their masters in the dance, and the best Greek dancers in modern times still come from among the descendants of these people. The story that Theseus, on his return from Crete to Athens with the youths and maidens he had set free, danced a round dance in crane step on the island of Delos and that this dance was long preserved on the island points clearly to Crete.

It also seems to point to China. In ancient China human sacrifices were made to dead princes. When about 500 B. C. a daughter of Ho-lu, King of Wu, took her own life, her father buried her with great splendor and constructed an underground passage to the sepulcher. Then he ordered the dance of the white cranes to be performed and enticed boys and girls together with the dancers into the underground passage. The door closed behind them. Sacrifice to the dead, boys and girls, underground passage, and crane dance—what a strange parallel! The Chinese crane dance was, like the Hellenic, a round dance, and it belonged to the cycle of vegetation rites designed to obtain rain, fertility, and regeneration. Can we doubt a very ancient connection here?

Let us turn again to the Cretan dances among the Greeks. The Dorians were the first to come into the territory of the Cretans and they remained there longest. Mere juxtaposition would not have been enough, however, if there had not been an additional deciding factor: the Dorians, who placed more emphasis upon social order and organization than upon individual freedom, were necessarily more inclined towards the choral dance than towards the solo dance.

The Spartans cultivated with particular zeal the Cretan form of weapon dance which in Greece was called the *pyrrhichē*, "[dressed in] red"; they practiced it from the age of five on. All the various meanings expressed in the art appear together in this dance. Outwardly it belongs to the category of the strictly imitative dances: a genuine guarding and fighting distinguished from gymnastic exercise only by artistic movement, rhythm, and musical accompaniment (short, equal, metrical units). It was justly regarded as a real preparation for serious warfare. The complimentary observation was occasionally made that such and such a man owed his military successes to his skill in the weapon dance, and Socrates's famous dictum that the best dancer is also the best warrior is understandable in this connection. The placing of fighting and dancing on the same level, which is characteristic of primitive peoples, prevails absolutely. And the tripping march to battle, which we have frequently noted among the natives, had an exact counterpart in the *embateria,* the anapaestic dance march with which the Spartans entered into an engagement. The leader of the fight was the dance leader, and was known by that name. The *pyrrhichē* did later, of course, become a pantomime and degenerated into a spectacular dance, and the old name lost its meaning.

But this gymnastic stage is not the original one. Close beside it and clearly recognizable is the magic stage. A Cretan-Greek story relates that the Zeus child would have been captured by Kronos had not armed men danced around the infant striking the shield with their swords. The frightening away of spirits, a motif which is still incorporated in the late European sword dance, is unmistakable here. This is obvious not only from the fighting but also from the apotropaic noise created by beating bronze on bronze. And the clash of the weapon dance sounds over dead bodies; we are familiar with this magic custom from primitive peoples too. In later antiquity the *pyrrhichē*—especially in Sparta— was also performed by women and, as spectacular dance, by professional dancers. The magic, the gymnastic, and the imitative—all these entities are closely related.

With the *pyrrhichē* three other choral dances entered—they are said to have been brought in by Thaletas of Crete—the *paians* to Apollo, the god of healing, which were originally magic dances against sickness and death; the *hyporchémata,* also dedicated to Apollo, in which the gestures and rhythm rendered the mythical action of the text; and the *gymnopaidiai* performed by naked boys in which the dance form was based on the motions of wrestling.

All these dances encroach on the field of the *emméleia,* the round dances of devout and solemn character sedately performed in honor of the gods, which Plato contrasts sharply with those of a stirring, warlike nature. No wonder, then, that the *emméleia* devolved mainly upon the women—it is the old distinction of close and expanded movement. Festive processions to the shrine and fluctuating circles around the altar are the forms these dances take. They have come down to us most beautifully in the marvelously preserved partheniads, in which the virgins, hand in hand like Graces, worship the goddess to the sound of hymnlike songs. Here we have magic elevated completely to worship, to devout celebration.

From divine worship in the narrower sense, from the mutual, popular veneration of the supermundane, the choral dance enters into the domain of family life: in the female rites on the tenth night after the birth of a child, in the ceremonies attending puberty, in the merry, mocking chorus of maidens at the door of the bridal chamber, and in the wailing procession to the grave.

If we wish to form a clear conception of these old Hellenic choral dances, we must take note of the dances which are still to be seen on Easter Monday in Megara near Athens. Not only does the devout earnestness with which they are performed, or rather celebrated, point to very old tradition, but certain peculiarities of form and position are depicted on a whole series of antique reliefs. In these *tratta* the women walk close together and take hold of each other crosswise: the first one grasps the hand of the third over the breast of the second; the second grasps the hand of the fourth over the breast of the third, and so on. And in this firmly linked chain they move, under the direction of a male or female dance leader, slowly and sedately, without rocking to and fro and without distorting a feature. The left foot crosses the right, the right steps aside towards the right, and the left is brought up with it. Then the right steps back obliquely to the right, the left crosses behind it, and the right again moves forwards obliquely to the right. Four women form the end of the chain without dancing: they sing in unison or two at a time in strophe and antistrophe.

If we seek the sharpest contrast to the *kalokagathia* (harmony) and *sophrosyne* of the *emméleia,* we shall find it in the cult of Dionysus and the other deities who for the Greeks personified the earth and vegetation. Ecstatic liberation from the self is as strong here as ever in any primitive people. The sacred madness lays hold upon the Greek women. Called by the voices of spirits, they leave their homes, ascend without stopping into the wilderness of snow-covered mountains, and rave for many days and nights in wild intoxication. They are maenads—"mad women." On hundreds of vases and reliefs we see the frantic stamping, whirling, and flying of the afflicted of God, and the spectator experiences the whole gamut of dance ecstasy from the blood madness of the human being become animal, who hurls the dismembered kid through the air like a discus, to the rapture of the transfigured saint who in the blessed choral dance has lost the earth and found her God (Plate 12).

From this wild activity artistic form slowly evolved, and finally drama. The writers reveal that Attic maenads conducted dance exercises according to the rules of Athens and Delphi in preparation for the Bacchanalia, and the vase painters were fond of showing how women with the distinguishing mark of the cult of Dionysus received instruction in the dance. The Dionysian cult itself conformed to the vintage festivals and permitted the men to take part. Disguised as satyrs and sileni with long beards, tails, and phalli, and accompanied by shrill oboes and inciting rattles, they appear in the vase pictures, completely abandoned to the god in drunken dance ecstasy, or tripping lasciviously around the resisting maenads. Here we stand midway between the mask dances of the Stone Age cultures and the unbridled Bacchanalia of imperial Rome, from which, by way of the infamous Lupercalia, the road leads down to the modern carnival. The name still indicates its venerable ancestry. For a *carrus navalis,* a ship on wheels, used to carry the chorus and dance leader of the dithyrambs in Greece, when he recreated the life, death, and return of Dionysus; and it was a *carrus navalis* on which in the year 534 B. c. the dancer and singer Thespis, with his chorus, answered the call of Peisistratus to Athens and in the singing dance of the goat's mask created the "goat song," the *tragodia.*

These things are not quite clear. It is certain that the choral dance with which we are dealing here, the dithyramb, is referred to from the first half of the sixth century on. Originally it was a circular dance of fifty garlanded dancers in the service of Dionysus, but also in the train of other gods. It was obviously a more lively dance than the *emméleia,* for its special name *tyrbasia* means violent movement. From the very first these dances seem to have been dramatic: the dance leader in the center is the god Dionysus, who with the vegetation of the earth lives, suffers, sickens, and dies and at a given moment awakens anew, like Osiris in Egypt and Attis-Adonis in Asia Minor; and in the circle surrounding him the fifty choral dancers share his fate, interpreting, suffering, and rejoicing with him. A relic of this dithyramb has been preserved in Sardinia.

The choral dance of the drama, to be sure, was not circular but linear in form: the chorus of the tragedy and of the satyric drama appeared as a rule in three rows of five singer-dancers, the chorus of the comedy in four rows of six. It seems clear, therefore, that the transition to the spectacular dance necessarily disrupted the vague circular formation. The chorus, upon which more than half of the drama frequently devolved, was stationed in the semicircle in front of the stage. Singing and dancing, it was the absolute monarch of the lyric interludes between the dramatic episodes, and now and then took part in the action.

So large a share in the drama could be possible only if the dance itself were possessed of dramatic potentialities. And this we know to be true from all that the Greeks have written about their dance. How could it have been otherwise in a people so exceptionally endowed with the visual faculty! Even the earliest forms of the imitative dance managed to survive into the classical period, animal dances in which the movements of bears, lions, foxes, and birds were imitated. If these were dances apart, dances of every type were subject to the domination of the *phorai* and the *schemata:* the *phorai* were gestures for the expression of emotions and actions; the *schemata* were gestures which expressed the essential character of a person. Many of these gestures, the *cheironomia* or "measured motion of the hands," are recorded for us: the hand on the head expressing grief and suffering; the stretching forth heavenwards of the hands to signify worship; the thrusting forward of the swordsman, and

243

a hundred others. Such gestures must make their appearance wherever by virtue of a visual and muscular predisposition the imitative dance is cultivated. But when the espying motif is expressed by putting the hand above the eyes, we are reminded of exactly the same movement in the Hindu and the Japanese dance. Our glance wanders involuntarily over these three high cultures and will not come to rest. They seem to have more and more in common. Not imitativeness as a whole, to be sure— that, of course, depends upon race and culture. The strong preference for the play of hands, however, is not matter-of-course, and the reduction of it to a system is still less so. Are there connections from people to people here? The connections between India and Japan are proved and acknowledged. But they seem to have spun their web across to Greece too. In India the ritual language of the hands is an ancient possession; the Veda requires it. One would certainly not wish to deny the old Greeks the gift of gesture—they belong to a Mediterranean race and to a race of peculiar histrionic ability. Nevertheless, the classical period became notoriously sparing in the use of gesture; decorum demanded that the hand should not be drawn out from under the upper garment on the street. Not until the Alexandrian period does gesture seem to have become freer and more significant, and then the door had opened wide to Oriental influences.

The stream of Asiatic dance which burst in at this time must have colored the whole domain which we include under the term *komos*: the entertainment of guests, when the food is cleared away, the wine poured, and paid singers, jugglers, and dancers, mainly female, enter the room. Countless vase pictures illustrate these dances: girls in all the positions and poses of the old fertility rites, well-known dances which, divested of their religious significance, have degenerated into the exhibition of bodily charms and the calculated provocation of male desire. This one theme glimmers through all kinds of performances from the distorted love antics of lascivious dwarfs to the judgment of Paris on the naked beauty of the young dancers. And if the statue of the Venus Callipygus is really a bayadere, as she is described for us in a similar pose in Alciphron's hetaeric letters, the divinity of the dancer unintentionally sounds forth once more in the midst of all this debasement.

The history of the dance in Greece, then, has as little to record of actual invention as that of any other culture. All that it offers in theme, type, movement, and form has been anticipated by primitive peoples and by the advanced Asiatic cultures. We find here the same groups of ideas—initiation, fertility, marriage, war, and death—and by the same association of ideas, war dances at funeral ceremonies and in later times at fertility festivals. There are the same types: abstract and non-imitative on the one hand, and concrete and imitative on the other, animal dances, masquerades, and pantomimes. There are the same movements: expanded movement with leaps and throws and close movement with wrenching and whirling. There are the same forms: circular dances with either or both sexes and line dances in which a row of men is drawn up opposite a row of women, labyrinths, processions, solo dances, and at a late period couple dances.

One would naturally expect that with so individual a culture and so pronounced a talent for dancing the Greeks must reveal their distinctive qualities in this field also. Nowhere is their distinctive character more completely expressed than in the choral dance. When the Oriental peoples arrive at an art form of the choral dance, they extract the ultimate from its ecstatic nature: the individual mind and will of the dancer are extinguished, everything personal is wiped out, and he moves in strict conformity like a puppet controlled by the strings of an invisible master. But when the Greek sculptors have carved in marble the lineaments of a choral dance, the observer admires the joyous rhythm which binds together, into a harmony more than personal, movements that arise from an inner compulsion and accord with the law of the dancer's own body.

Rome

Nemo fere saltat sobrius.

"No sober person dances"—Cicero's remark illustrates the absolute contempt of the rationalist with no capacity for the ecstatic for an art which flourishes better in that soil than in the dry region of the mere intellect. The history of the Roman dance is indeed more than barren. It falls easily into three sections.

In the first, the Old Roman period, we have the choral dances of the men of certain corporations: the spring processions of the sowing priests for the purification of the fields, and the weapon dances of the warriors and the priests of Mars, who were grouped together under the name of *Salii,* which is equivalent to *saltantes* or dancers. Actually these chorals had very little of the dance about them, even if Plutarch does praise the grace and suppleness of their movements. The *Salii* stamped "like fullers" in repetends of three beats, which may be assumed to have been anapaestic. From this tripedal character their dance takes the name of *tripudium.* As a choral dance proper it had a dance leader whose movements were answered by the two choruses of older and younger men as they walked around in a circle to the rhythmical beating of the shields. Obviously we must suppose a deliberate pace; otherwise Lucian could not have called the *tripudium* the most majestic of dances.

About the year 200 b. c. begins a second section of Roman dance history: Etruscan and Greek choreography enter in, the dance plays a greater role than heretofore in public life, and it becomes the fashion in private life—even the patricians send their sons and daughters to dancing school. Perhaps for the first time the dance has become a "social" accomplishment. In vain do the conservatives warn and declaim against it; in vain does Scipio Aemilianus Africanus about 150 b. c. close the dancing schools. Rome has been captivated by an art which is and remains alien to its inner nature (Plate 13).

The third section covers the Empire. It is marked by the recognized domination of the Etruscan, Greek, and Oriental dance, and especially of the mature Greek pantomime, dramatic action without words.

This dance is the exact counterpart of the imitative dance of the Orient. Here as there, the myth is conceived and rendered as dance. "The dancer's principal task," says Lucian, "is to draw continually, as I have said, upon his unfailing memory of ancient story; the memory must be backed by taste and judgment. He must know the history of the world, from the time when it first emerged from Chaos down to the days of Egyptian Cleopatra. These limitations we will concede to the pantomime's wide field of knowledge; but within them he must be familiar with every detail. . . . Since it is his profession to imitate, and to show forth his subject by means of gesticulation, he, like the orators, must acquire lucidity; every scene must be intelligible without the aid of an interpreter; to borrow the expression of the Pythian oracle

> Dumb though he be, and speechless, he is heard

by the spectator." Once in the time of Nero a pantomime was danced before the Cynic Demetrius: "The time-beaters, the flutes, even the chorus, were ordered to preserve a strict silence; and the pantomime, left to his own resources, represented the loves of Ares and Aphrodite, the tell-tale Sun, the craft of Hephaestus, his capture of the two lovers in the net, the surrounding Gods, each in his turn, the blushes of Aphrodite, the embarrassment of Ares, his entreaties,—in fact the whole story. Demetrius was ravished at the spectacle; nor could there be higher praise than that with which he rewarded the performer. 'Man,' he shrieked at the top of his voice, 'this is not seeing, but hearing and seeing, both: 'tis as if your hands were tongues!' "

Lucian tells further "of the high tribute paid to the art by a foreigner of the royal family of Pontus, who was visiting the Emperor on business, and had been among the spectators of this same pantomime. So convincing were the artist's gestures, as to render the subject intelligible even to one who (being half Greek) could not follow the vocal accompaniment. When he was about to return to his country, Nero, in taking leave of him, bade him choose what present he would have, assuring him that his request should not be refused. 'Give me,' said the Pontian, 'your great pantomime; no gift could delight me more.' 'And of what use can he be to you in Pontus?' asked the Emperor. 'I have foreign neighbors, who do not speak our language; and it is not easy to procure interpreters. Your pantomime could discharge that office perfectly, as often as required, by means of his gesticulations.' So profoundly had he been impressed with the extraordinary clearness of pantomimic representation."

The triumphal march of this pantomimic art is very significant. The Romans, who had little inclination or aptitude for dancing, give themselves up to the enjoyment of the imitative dances with enthusiasm, though without participation. The dance as ecstasy, as an artistically restrained enhancement of life, must remain alien to the sober, realistically minded Roman; he is held only by the dance which gives food for thought.

NORTHERN ANTIQUITY AND THE EARLY MIDDLE AGES

Of the dances of non-classical antiquity we have extremely little direct information. But proof that the ancestors and predecessors of the modern peoples of Europe knew, loved, and cultivated the dance is superfluous. We need neither to point to the dance motifs in northern mythology nor to the many dance prohibitions in the early Christian Church. That the old Europeans danced, and in the main how they danced, is shown from the same cultural levels of the prehistoric period all over the world. The survey which introduces the historical part of this book reveals also the dance treasures of European prehistory, and since we might refer again and again in the course of our presentation to the continuity of themes, motifs, movements, and forms of primitive dances in the European dance, a sufficiently clear picture is given. The dance treasures of the non-classical Middle Ages correspond for the most part to those of modern primitive peoples, assorted and distributed according to the peculiarities of movement and the forms of occupation of the various races.

Even with Christianity the theme and content scarcely change their outer garb. The charms for fertility still occupy the central position; with undiminished power they dominate at Shrovetide, the first of May, and at weddings, at midsummer, and at funeral ceremonies. The whirling dance as a charm for rain, the circling of the maypole and the fire, the mask dance, the exchange of sex, and the sword dance remain unaltered, and with them the entire group of old ideas: the promotion of fertility through erotic dancing and nakedness on the one hand, and through virginal dancers on the other. Two examples must suffice here. The erotic dancing of the Goths is attested by Caesarius of Arles about 500 A. D.: after the sacrificial banquet the revelers rise and dance according to a demoniacal rite to the accompaniment of sexually obscene songs. How strongly the belief in the fertility power of the pure continued to operate, however, is almost grotesquely illustrated by an old account from Anglo-Saxon England: in Easter week a Christian priest had the little girls perform a dance in which a priapic symbol was carried in front!

The nude dance of the cult easily slips over into the lubricious exhibition dance of professional women dancers. Thus Theodora, the notorious wife of the Byzantine Emperor Justinian I in the sixth century, had before her marriage appeared naked in the circus.

Animal dances are comparatively rare. Not often do we meet with indications such as the anger of Bishop Caesarius of Arles (about 500) that at the New Year even baptized women disguised themselves as deer or bitches, covered themselves with the skins of animals, or put on animal heads.

Even in the later folk dances we find surprisingly few remains of animal motifs. To be sure, the Bavarian and Bohemian dance has preserved certain of these. The horn adornment of the September *horn dance* at Abbots Bromley, which has an exact counterpart in southern India, recalls the old animal-mask dances. And quite by way of exception, we hear that "in olden times" on the peninsula of Mönchgut on the island of Rügen, the fishermen used to dance on the shore before setting out to hunt seals. We are not certain even here, however, that it was an out-and-out animal dance. Even our children's games, the guardians of the oldest customs, do not provide much evidence—except the Slavic—of an old dance heritage in which there was a tendency towards dances imitating animals.

We see clearly from these facts that as far as the dance is concerned the peasant cultures have covered up the older hunter cultures to an astonishing degree. And with this we have perhaps succeeded in making a small contribution from the field of dance history to the ethnology of Europe.

The old store of dance is stimulated, fertilized, and expanded by the addition of the stock in trade of the traveling "joculator," who was a combination of dancer, juggler, singer, poet, musician, and actor. *"Spielmann"* he was called in Germany—and "to dance" is the oldest meaning of the word *spielen*. This *Spielmann* or minstrel brought to the non-classical countries of Europe the motifs of the antique art dance, which seem more remote to the northern peoples. The chief of these, I should consider, was the hand dance. The Greeks were the great pantomimists of antiquity; the hand gesture was one of the main constituents of their art, and even today we are familiar with the wealth and expressive power of the gesture in the domain of Hellenism and perhaps in southern Italy. This mode of speech is foreign to the north, and yet we find here also the hand dance so strongly developed that considering the unfavorableness of the surroundings it is natural to infer influence. When in the *Lay of Rudlieb* in the eleventh century the varied gestures of the hands are expressly extolled—*neumas manibus variasse*—when the miniatures of the Heidelberg Manesse manuscript depict the most expressive hand dances, we recall the offices of the joculators. Can we find confirmation in the words of a German prince of a later period, Prince Ludwig of Anhalt-Köthen, who in the year 1598 speaks of the German dance *with juggler's hands?*

The attempt to infer the movements from the oldest names of the dances can have no appreciable result. For all dance words seem to have suffered the fate of expansion of meaning. The Old French word *tresche* from the Old High German *dreskan,* in modern German *dreschen* and in English *thresh*, denotes the presence of stamping dances. A second Old High German word, *salzón*, which with its Anglo-Saxon cognate *sealtjan* comes from the Latin *saltare*, may not, however, be translated offhand as *springen*, "to leap." In classical Latin it is used to designate the stamping dance of the priests of Mars, which was far from a leaping dance, and in medieval Latin it was constantly contrasted with the *ballare* as a choral dance. In modern German usage *springen* is still frequently used in the sense of *laufen*, "to run." The Gothic *laik* gives the Swedish *lek*, "circular dance," and, in spite of some phonetic difficulties, the Old French *lai* and the Middle High German *leich*. The Gothic *plinsjan* comes from the Old Slavonic *plęsjati*, for which the meanings "to dance," "to leap," and "to dance in a circle" are specified. It is obvious that there is practically no conclusion to be drawn from these words.

THE LATE MIDDLE AGES

The Great Outburst of Dance Ecstasy

At the beginning of this book it was necessary to state repeatedly that ecstasy in the broader sense is preserved in all dancing, even in the most conventional social dance—ecstasy as an irresistible urge to the dance and as a sloughing off of the world and the self in and through the dance. This we shall not discuss again here; it fits into normal life and may be reckoned as a healthy phenomenon. On the other hand we have had, in the earlier part of the book, countless examples of compulsion and abandonment so strong and so perverse that they must be regarded from our point of view as abnormal and diseased. We shall deal here only with these pathogenic excesses in the West and their gradual decline.

In the eleventh and twelfth centuries there are increasingly numerous reports that on days when somebody dies or at Christian festivals men and women begin suddenly and irresistibly to sing and dance in the churchyard, disturb divine service, refuse to stop at the priest's bidding, and as a result are finally cursed to dance the whole year through until a sympathetic archbishop removes the ban. This is the gruesome motif of the dance curse which Hans Christian Andersen in his popular fairy tale has fashioned into the story of the little Karen, who cannot find rest until the executioner has cut off her feet.

The Bohemian Leo von Rožmital found a strange example when he came to Brescia in the year 1466. He saw a gigantic crowd of people who had flocked together from the surrounding country, as was their annual custom on this day, to dance on a mountain from sunrise to sunset, so that they had to be brought back in a wagon completely exhausted. They were forced to do this as a punishment from God because once on this mountain the dancers had failed to salute the Corpus Dominicum as it was carried by.

Generally, however, these frenzied dances took place in the churchyards. Here, in accordance with an ancient belief, the dancers sought communion with their dead. It was literally a *danse macabre*. For in the Arabic *ḳabr* means "grave," *mákbara*, "churchyard," and *maḳábr*, "churchyards." There can no longer be any doubt that the name has come from the Arabic, since we know that one of the roots of the dance of death goes back to the Arabs.

For a thousand years the ecclesiastical councils opposed these *obscoeni motus, saltationes seu choreae* (obscene dances) in church and churchyard—each time the evil was to be rooted out, and each time the attempt failed.

What these festival dances were and how they were performed is scarcely ever told. Only one writer of the twelfth century, Giraldus Cambrensis, has left us in his *Itinerarium Cambriae* an exact description: "You may see men or girls, now in the churchyard, now in the dance, which is led round the churchyard with a song, on a sudden falling on the ground as in a trance, then jumping up as in a frenzy, and representing with their hands and feet, before the people, whatever work they have unlawfully done on feast days; you may see one man put his hand to the plough, and another, as it were, goad on the oxen, mitigating their sense of labor, by the usual rude song: one man imitating the profession of a shoemaker; another, that of a tanner. Now you may see a girl with a distaff, drawing out the thread, and winding it again on the spindle; another walking, and arranging the threads for the web; another, as it were, throwing the shuttle, and seeming to weave. On being brought into the church, and led up to the altar with their oblations, you will be astonished to see them suddenly awakened and coming to themselves."

What is revealed in these dances is not a "relic" of "paganism," but a piece of ecstatic inner life, which since the Stone Age has been disguised and concealed through innumerable racial influxes but never extinguished, and which must break out through all restraints at the favorable moment. When volcanoes which have long been extinct become active again, there are first a few small partial eruptions and then one day enormous masses are flung out and rush along burning, destroying, and burying everything that is living. Similarly, about the middle of the fourteenth century that uncontrollable dance madness, born perhaps out of the dances to avert the plague, which is known to physicians as *chorea major* and to laymen as St. Vitus's dance, broke out in the valley of the Rhine:

> Amidst our people here is come,
> The madness of the dance.
> In every town there now are some
> Who fall upon a trance.
> It drives them ever night and day,
> They scarcely stop for breath,
> Till some have dropped along the way
> And some are met by death.

Harried by plague, long wars, and endless misfortunes, and stirred to the depths of their being, hosts of distracted people roll westwards from place to place. Singly or hand in hand they circle and jump in hideously distorted choral dances—for hours at a time, until they collapse foaming at the mouth. And wherever they rave, the hysterical psychosis lays hold on the spectators, so that, quivering and grimacing, they enter the circle and under a fearful compulsion join in the dance. The evil lasted for months; physicians and priests were powerless. And it continually flares up anew. In the fifteenth and sixteenth centuries new eruptions occur, and there are recurrences far into the seventeenth century.

In Italy there raged at the same time and on into the eighteenth century another form of dance mania—tarantism. This malady was thought to be caused by the bite of the Apulian spider *Lycosa tarentula.* From the melancholia which followed the bite, only the wild jumping dance of southern Italy, the *tarantella,* which like the spider takes its name from the city of Tarentum, brought temporary release. In contrast to the German St. Vitus's dance, the movement here is, like fever, rather a kind of assistance from the sick person himself in the curing of the disease. But as in Germany it infected the spectators and induced in them the same manic depression.

What sort of dance was the *tarantella?* In Naples, Goethe tells us, it is "common among the girls of the lower and middle classes. At least three of them take part in it. One of them beats on the tambourine and shakes the bells on it from time to time without beating on it, the other two, with castanets in their hands, execute the steps of the dance. As in all cruder dances, the steps are not distinctive or graceful in themselves. Rather the girls keep time with their feet while they trip round for a while in one place, then turn, change places, and so on. Then one of the dancers will exchange her castanets for the tambourine and stand still while the third begins to dance. And thus they may go on amusing themselves by the hour, without being conscious of the spectators. This dance is only an amusement for girls; no boy would touch a tambourine."

What Goethe describes is a faded, metropolitan survival. The *tarantella* of the dance mania did not look like that. A good description of its modern but true traditional form brings it close to the Roman *saltarello* and the Tuscan *tresca*. This description tells how the dancer, kneeling, adores his female partner and then, as though sated, speedily forsakes her again; how with a thousand turns and tricks he now holds aloof and now rushes upon her. His gambols and capers are grotesque and yet charmingly light and tender. His bearing is now proud and resolute, now querulous and elaborate. Legs and arms, even the fingers, strumming on the tambourine, and above all the glance, ardent, languishing, suddenly bold and shameless, reinforce the expression of the posture. The girl comes out of her corner, now wayward, now willing. Her smile is eloquent, her eyes are drunken. She swings her skirt; she picks up the corner of it as if she were going to gather things in it; or she raises her arm so that the hand hangs down loosely over her head as though from a hook, while the other hand presses against her heart. Now she is the axis around which the male dancer rotates. "What a dance," exclaimed Rilke once, "as though invented by nymphs and satyrs, old and as though rediscovered and rising up anew, wrapped in primeval memories—cunning and wildness and wine, men with goat's hooves again and girls from the train of Artemis."

We are more likely to find an approach to the phenomenon of tarantism through this demoniacal, primitive *tarantella* than through Goethe's insipid city dance in which the girls "dance away the happiest hours of their youth." Johann Hermann von Riedesel, who shortly before Goethe's journey investigated the enigmatical connections between these dances very thoroughly, saw in Otranto a girl of twenty-two dance uninterruptedly for ten hours and reported that thirty-six-hour dances without eating or drinking occurred. He ascribes it less to the sting of the tarantula than to the general lushness of the south Italian midsummer and assumes the cure to be the result of the increased circulation of the blood through the dance. But the dancers are mainly peasant girls. Would they be likely to need exercise for the circulation of the blood? How poverty-stricken the rationalistic interpretations of the eighteenth century appear! How they pale before the fearful, divinely mad ecstasy of the dance!

These things can be understood only in the light of the extreme excitability that characterized the people of the Middle Ages, when none, from the youngest to the oldest, was immune to this infection of the mind. The history of dance manias in the north as in the south records striking examples. In what is known as the "Great Hallelujah" of the year 1233, all the people of Italy, in the grip of an ecstatic urge, followed round after the penitential preachers and carried with them branches and burning candles. And from Germany four years later, in 1237, it is reported that more than a hundred children of Erfurt were suddenly and irresistibly impelled by some morbid hallucination to set out on foot for Arnstadt. Many of them died of exhaustion; others were afflicted with palsy for the rest of their lives. From this it is but a step to the story of the Pied Piper of Hamelin, who lured the children into the mountains with the music of his pipes:

> However proud each boy in heart,
> However much the maidens start,
> I bid the chords sweet music make,
> And all must follow in my wake.
>
> GOETHE

If for the children we substitute pope, emperor, journeyman, soldier, beggar, and noblewoman, and for the Pied Piper the Grim Reaper, we find ourselves in the midst of the pallid world of the dance of death.

From the ranks of the living the Inexorable One summons dancer after dancer. None is spared, neither woman nor child, neither emperor nor peasant:

> His cruell daunce no man mortall can stent
> Nor lede his cruell cours after his intent
> The pope nor Emperour, if they be in his hande
> Hath no maner myght his sore cours withstande.

.   .   .   .

> The bysshop, lorde, the Pore man, lyke a state
> Death in his daunce ledyth by the sleue.

Since the close of the fourteenth century, poets and painters have described how the skeleton figure of death steals up on mortals unawares and carries them off from their joy and splendor, their hope and despair, sometimes linked in a long chain, hand in hand, sometimes two by two.

> Once we were men as you are now;
> But one day you shall be like us.

Thus wrote a King of Mecca at the beginning of the third century, and this prophecy of death has never since been silent. From the Arab world it has found its way into the Occident, and in all languages churchyard portals warn:

> As you are, so were we;
> As we are, you shall be.

Since the twelfth century this idea has taken literary form in the dramatic legend of the three dead men, once great lords, who preach to three living men of high rank about the vanity of all earthly glories in the face of death. Finally the painters seized upon this grateful material; the first fresco to fix the legend in form and color was the world-famous "Triumph of Death" from the fourteenth century in the Campo Santo at Pisa. How could the vanity of rank and riches in the great reckoning have been more vividly impressed upon the mind of the faithful than by the overwhelming power of such a picture? (Plates 18, 19.)

Why did the Middle Ages seek to pour into the mold of the choral dance ideas of death and equality before death? Obviously there are three different underlying concepts:

1. The relationship between the living and the dead in the dance;
2. The dance as the form of movement peculiar to the dead;
3. The dance of the dead with the living as a warning of death and departure from life.

The first two concepts reach far back into primitive folklore. The consummation of the union between the living and the dead in the dance is an idea characteristic of all civilizations in which the religion has arisen from ancestor worship. Every dance has this power. California Indians, circling around a woman, begin to dream of the dead. Moreover, in dances using impersonation, the union reaches the point of an incarnation of the deceased in the form of a doll or a masked dancer. The Batak of Sumatra introduce into their dance a puppet in effigy of their departed chieftain. And before the burial of a Yoruba of West Africa, a man draped in the shroud of the deceased and wearing a portrait mask over his face begins to dance. In the first case death is practically denied, but in the second the dead man is unmistakably marked as dead by the shroud. He is no longer represented as belonging to the living. A custom of certain Tibetan monasteries carries us a step further: besides two buffoons, there appear in the choral dance of the living two other figures with skulls and wearing tight-fitting white costumes on which skeletons have been painted. It is no longer a question of one dead person but of death as a concept, as the last stage of everything living.

The second idea—the dance as the form of movement peculiar to the dead—originates in the more universal conception that all supermundane, otherworldly motion is dance. Stars, gods, and spirits all dance. Even among the people of the Stone Age, this conception was given concrete form in gruesome pictures of the dance of death. The most striking one is the vision of a Chavantean Indian of East Brazil: a host of skeletons whirled about in a dance, in chaotic confusion. The putrified flesh hung from their bones and their eyes were withered and sere in the sunken sockets. The air was heavy with the foul stench. . . . Thus did the Indians learn that no heaven of bliss awaits them up yonder, however the stars may gleam and charm. This is almost the same medieval vision that Goethe saw:

> They crooked their thigh bones, and they shook their long shanks,
> And wild was their reeling and limber;
> And each bone as it crosses, it clinks and it clanks,
> Like the clapping of timber on timber.

The mystical dance of death has become a horrid apparition. This conception, and also the *memento mori,* is more crudely expressed in a volume of woodcuts assembled in Mainz about 1491:

> Come along, come along, ye masters and men,
> Haste ye hither whate'er ye ben,
> Or young or old, or high or low,
> Ye all must to the dance house go.

And between the Stone Age and the Middle Ages stands classical antiquity with the same vision. A relief on a tomb in Cumae, an early Greek colony on the west coast of Campania in Italy, depicts three shriveled corpses dancing, and similar dancing skeletons are represented on Roman vases. This symbolism entered into the very midst of their joys and festivities: Roman hosts used to have little silver skeletons dance on the dinner table. To the ancients this symbol always meant *carpe diem.* At the feasts of the wealthy in Egypt, Herodotus tells us, a man used to go around, when the meal was over, with a wooden image of death in a coffin. . . . He would show it in turn to each guest and say: "Behold this image, then drink and be merry; for this is what you too will be, when you are dead."

But not until the Middle Ages was the last of these three ideas developed: the dance of the dead with the living as a warning of death and departure from life. There is a legend that at a ball of Alexander III of Scotland a ghost appeared and took part in the dance; shortly after that the King died.

This is a different kind of *memento mori*. No longer is it "One day death will come—enjoy your life," but "Death will come soon—make use of your life." Death has come horribly close, stands ominously near, and already the menacing hand is raised. Powerless, mankind obeys the inevitable summons.

The man of the Middle Ages was more accustomed to receiving new and strange ideas through the medium of the choral dance than through any other. Only in the form of that dance, which he had seen since a child and in which he had himself taken part, did the picture resolve itself immediately into a clear experience for him. The choral dance robs the participants of their own wills—as though in a trance they follow the leader, who seeks out the path for them, closes and opens the chain, ties and looses the knot. How could poets and painters have presented to the mind the idea that all, all must go the same road towards the same goal with the same trials and tribulations, more forcibly than in the dance of death which brought them all into the round dance?

They could do this the more readily because the people of the fourteenth century had not found in the choral dance merely the ecstasy of happiness. The man of the Middle Ages had learned in his dances, too, the ecstasy of mortal terror and of despair. He had seen those hideously distorted dances which people performed against their wills and the curse of which only the grace of God could remove. And he had recently experienced how mortal terror and despair raged in frenzied dances and how the Great Destroyer snatched his victims from among the dancers. The dance had changed for him from healthy enjoyment into painful suffering, from festive pleasure into fatal pestilence and consuming madness. The leader guiding at will the exuberant youths on flowery spring meadows into ever new convolutions of the dance, and Death drawing after him everything living, great and small, rich and poor, in irresistible rhythms—the dance as a symbol of living and of dying—in no comparison can the terrific tenseness of the Gothic soul be more clearly comprehended.

The painted dances of death do not always reflect the features of the real dances of the time. The movements of the dead person are often absurdly and grotesquely distorted. This lies partly in the nature of things. Everything incongruous has a comic effect—the giant who walks trippingly like a dwarf, the child who puts on his father's hat, the man in woman's clothes. The skeleton which, instead of moldering in the grave, stands upright, walks and acts like a living person, belongs among these incongruities. And what could be more anomalous than the convulsive rhythms of the most youthful and most lively movement of man in the fleshless, clattering bones of the dead? Can it be that he is really dancing, actively and consciously? Is he really moving those arms and legs and feet, which do not seem to have grown thus organically at all? Are they not tied onto him like the limbs of a puppet which are made to leap and dance by invisible strings in the hand of the master?

We look at the pictures of the death dance and suddenly the stark skeletons begin to move, and the way in which they move is curiously familiar to us. This posture, this placing of the feet, these gestures, do we not know them from the temple friezes of ancient southeastern Asia, from Angkor Vat and Borobudur, and from the modern dancers of the Indian world who, in accordance with a tradition thousands of years old, like the marionettes of the shadow play, dance so remotely, so impersonally, and yet more than personally? And the absurd behavior of the whole mummery of distortion and perversion is already familiar to us. With horror we beheld it when in demoniacal primitive folk masks the dead were revived in strange dances. And now we realize that it could not be a brilliant invention of the mind that formed the dance of death, but that like all other concepts of ultimate things, it is a conglomeration of fantastic images born of grandiose dreams.

The Pre-Minnesinger Period

We have no direct evidence about the dance of the pre-minnesinger period, except perhaps in the Bavarian wooing dance of the eleventh century, which will be discussed in the next chapter. As indirect evidence, today's dance of the ancient northern islands, Iceland and the Faeroes, fills the gap. Their music has also preserved many features of the turn of the second millennium. The dances of this northern world have very unjustly been regarded as relics and reflections of the minnesinger period on the Continent. If this were so, certain essential parts of the courtly dance would not be lacking, particularly those parts which can be explained only from the peculiar nature of the courtly ideal.

The Faeroes are familiar only with the chain dance without arrangement according to sex, hand in hand, in a circle, or, in a narrow room, in an oval—the Norwegian *Innbrot* and the *Rimpfenreie* of Middle High German poetry. As was still done in the *branle* of the sixteenth century, the left foot is put forward twice and the right is drawn up to it; then the right foot steps back or sideward, and the left follows in such a way that the movement is a turn toward the left. There are occasional leaps. In serious songs the hands are held at the level of the hips, in gay and lively songs at the level of the shoulders. These songs—ballads in the double sense of dance song and heroic story—are always sung. No instruments are used. One person sings the verse, the others join in the refrain. Often while the leader is singing the verse, they dance in one place, and only during the refrain do they stir from that spot. Here, of course, the whole attention is fixed not upon the dance but upon the content of the song, and the feet and arms follow its mood closely. As with primitive peoples, dances of one sex, men alone or women alone, seem to predominate.

The same is true of Iceland. We shall note merely as a special peculiarity the swinging forwards and backwards of the trunk with only the right foot on the ground. In both regions the choral dance is familiar, but not the dance of separate couples, which arose out of the *cortezia* of the minnesinger period. Their dance is pre-courtly.

The dance of the northern Middle Ages, in the light of the Danish ballads from about 1200, is no monument of minnesinger culture, but rather of the transition to the real courtly form of life of the minnesinger period. It is not significant that the setting and the participants in the dance were courtly: the ballads, of course, always deal with well-known, brilliant personalities upon whom the full light of tradition falls, not with nameless peasants and tradesmen. But for the very reason that the circumstances and participants are the same as those of the minnesinger dance, the disparity is the more obvious. The distinctive motif, the subordination of sex to idea, symbol, play, and etiquette—this motif is almost entirely lacking. The entire dance is continuous and un-circumscribed, as with primitive peoples. The knight does not grasp the maiden tenderly by the hand nor yet by a kerchief that she holds out to him, but takes her possessively under his fur mantle. And often enough it does go as far as actual possession; as with so many primitive peoples, the couples withdraw from the dance into a quiet corner. Consequently the king was forced to acquiesce when a knight refused to allow his sister to accept the king's invitation, because it was not fitting for her to go to a dance where she would find herself in ribald company. It is mainly servant maids we hear of as dance partners rather than ladies of courtly rank. Nothing could be less in the spirit of the minne-singers.

The form corresponds exactly to that of the Faeroes. It seems to have consisted altogether of open or close chain dances; there is no suggestion of a dance of separate couples. Side by side with the dances in which both men and women take part are those for men alone and for women alone, which, however, may be led by a dance leader of the other sex. Walking, stepping, and jumping are the movements. The accompaniment is always sung, never fiddled. Here, too, we have a contrast to the custom of the minnesinger period. In the Danish ballad dance (*Folkevisedans*), this pre-minnesinger choral has persisted to the present time.

The solo dance of the juggler of the guild is sharply distinguished from this popular and social dance. It represents an elaboration and at the same time a profanation of old religious dances. Even as early as the transition from antiquity to the Middle Ages, we found the devotional nude dances of the women perverted into lewd exhibitions. In the eleventh century the chronicler Adam von Bremen complains of the dissolute women dancers who amuse the people with indecent movements. The sacred fertility charms have lost their significance.

In the ninth century the professional spectacular dance was illustrated in the pictures of Asaph, the musician of David, which appear in the miniatures of the psalmbooks—notably in the psaltery of Charles the Bald in Paris and in the *Psalterium Aureum* in the Saint-Gall monastery. The whirling dance which is clearly indicated here was often shown later with greater clarity in illustrations of the story of John the Baptist and Salome.

The most beautiful Salome dance appears in a capital sculpture of the twelfth century from Saint-Étienne in Toulouse, now in the museum of that city. The left leg crosses the right, both feet are turned inwards with the tips touching, the trunk takes up the turn to the right and the head carries it further, so that the sagittal surfaces of the right leg and of the head are placed at an angle of more than ninety degrees to each other. This unmistakable circular movement is emphasized by the billowing veil.

Other sculptures show—often likewise in the John the Baptist story— that there was no dividing line between the professional dance and pure acrobatics. The Salome of the bronze door of San Zeno at Verona and that of a thirteenth-century cathedral sculpture in Brunswick form the "bridge" to the sound of the fiddle. The acrobat on a cloister capital from the twelfth century in Toulouse does the same. On a capital in the Church of Saint-Georges-de-Boscherville in Normandy, also from the twelfth century, the instruments accompany a headstand, and occasionally we see the preparation for that perilous dance between the swords of which we have already spoken. These are motifs with which we are familiar from antiquity, from Egypt and Greece. But the genealogical tree of the medieval juggler-dancer goes further back—to those nature peoples who have carried the development through from almost somnambulant, religious-ecstatic dance acrobatics to a deliberate exhibition of breakneck feats.

Other pictures, the clearest being those in the famous Manesse minnesinger manuscript, show that lively play of hands and fingers, the *neumas manibus,* of which the *Rudlieb* poet speaks several times, and which has become a German peculiarity. Even three or four hundred years later, in 1598, Prince Ludwig of Anhalt-Köthen is surprised that they do not dance in Florence as they do in Germany *with jugglers' hands.* It is the northwestern branch of those expressive hand dances of which we have made the acquaintance in the Indian and Polynesian world, and a direct heritage of the pantomime of antiquity.

Together with all these things which have been handed down, however, we have also the immediate influence of Oriental professional dancing girls, such as those which the Emperor Frederick II brought with him from the East in order to entertain his guests with acrobatic tricks and wrench dances. The precious ivory carvings of the twelfth century in the Florentine National Museum convey a vivid impression of this art.

It is always but a fleeting glimpse into the world of these jugglers that the sculptures afford us, and we should have to be satisfied with this partial knowledge had not an Old French legend of the Virgin Mary from about 1200, *Del Tumbleor Nostre Dame* (The Tumbler of Our Lady) preserved for us the beautiful story of an old minstrel who, unable to sing and read, renders his ecstatic homage to the statue of the Mother of God in the dance, until he falls down exhausted. In the hundred and twenty verses devoted to his dance, however, the word *dancier* does not appear. At that time, apparently, it had only the meaning of a dance of couples or a society dance. *Tumer, treper, sauter* are the words used for what he does. *Treper,* from the Old Norse *trippa,* means "skip" —*al fuer de cavreçon Qui trepe et saut devant sa mere,* "as a kid skips and leaps in front of its mother." *Tumer* is more difficult to interpret. Boehme, who had met with the word in other sources, translates it as "to move in a circle" and identifies somewhat hastily the early dance type with the later courtly *umgênden tanz* (revolving dance). This is out of the question; *tumer* stands at the opposite extreme from that courtly dance. True, the Old High German stem *tûmôn* means "to turn," not "in a circle," however, but rather "to turn around." The related *tumba* means in Old Norse "to fall down" and in Rumanian "somersault," and close to it is the Italian *tombolare*, "to turn a somersault." We may also remember in this connection that the Germans call the dolphin, which jumps swiftly out of the water, a *Tümmler*. The Virgin legend proves that our interpretation is correct. For the juggler clearly turns upside down: *Lors tume les piés contremont Et va sor ses .IJ. mains*—he raises his feet and walks on his two hands, as is sometimes shown in the miniatures. At intervals he dances around the statue. These dances around the statue, *tors*, have their provincial nicknames as the *branles* have later: *de Mes* (Metz), *de Chanpenois, d'Espaigne, de Bretaigne, de Loheraine, romain*. As a matter of fact the *branles* circle too. Is it the distinctive steps of this popular choral dance that the juggler executes? *Et les tors c'on fait en Bretaigne*, the poem calls them. Were they, perhaps, a kind of *triori* or *passepied*? And after the manner of the *branles* he becomes quite tame, dances *mignotement*, and puts his hand over his forehead—*Et met devant sen front sa main*. Only here does the poet use a real dance word, *baler*.

We note that the dance of the juggler is, in contrast to the European popular and social dance, for the most part expanded. It doubtless springs from the early period of the spectacular dance when physical build, strength, suppleness, and dexterity were the aim and content of the dance. Is it not delightful to see how the line of this dance of skill, which had once lost the seriousness and devotion of the religious dance, here turns back to its old stem with the devout worshiper of the Virgin?

The Minnesinger Period

Language furnishes the first key to the tightly locked door which shuts off our view of the dance of the minnesinger period; the second is supplied by the literary works of the time. Several dozen dance names appear. Most of them testify by their relationship to that universality of the dance which breaks through all boundaries of language and nationality. Strangely enough, together with the heritage of antiquity, the South German dialect is strongly represented outside Germany also: among many other names we have *espringale*, upon which the French form does not sit very convincingly; *ridda*, that derivation from the Old High German *ridan*, "to turn," hallowed by Dante's use of it, and its expansion *riddon*; *tresca-tresche*, the old form of *Dresche*, "threshing," which from the evidence of the *Gieus de Robin et de Marion* of Adam de la Hale (about 1285) meant at that time a chain dance and still survives in the Italian folk dance as *trescone* or *ntrezzata*; and above all *danse-danza*, which all the European languages have made their own.

The name *Tanz*, which first returns to Germany about the end of the eleventh century, has long been disputed. An attempt has been made recently to derive it from the Frankish *danea*, "threshing-floor," and a hypothetical word *danetsare*, meaning "to tread as on the threshing-floor, to stamp gently," has been constructed. But the *Tanz* was not stamped. Another correspondence on the basis of sound has been pointed out also from the Romance side and a hypothetical Frankish word *dintjan* suggested, although only by inference, to be sure. The meaning attributed to this word, "to tremble lightly," certainly comes closer to the pattern of the Icelandic word *dynta*, "to move the body to and fro." It would allow of an exact correspondence to the Middle High German *swanzen* and further to the French *bercer* and the Italian *dindolarsi*.

This typical movement to and fro of the dancers at the height of the medieval period is most beautifully illustrated for us in the miniatures of the Manesse minnesinger manuscript in Heidelberg. The swing of the hips, the rectangular position of the elbows, the turning inwards of the feet—this is exactly the ideal of movement of all those primitive peoples who lie in the line of development of cultivators of the soil from the food-gathering pygmies through the early and late planters and down to the peasants, in whose culture that of modern central Europe also has its roots.

Frankish influence in France, as reflected in the dance words, needs no explanation. The German influences in Italy are not recognized to the same degree, but the history of culture tells of the settlement of many South Germans at the turn of the second millennium as far down as the province of Modena. Already at that time the dance was fertilized by the same Alpine countries, which later, in the eighteenth century, brought about a revolution in the ballroom with the introduction of the waltz, and whose passion for the dance a traveler in Bavaria in the same eighteenth century cannot emphasize enough:

"The people here are excessively fond of the pleasure of dancing; they need only hear the music of a waltz to begin to caper, no matter where they are. The public dance floors are visited by all classes; these are the places where ancestors and rank seem to be forgotten and aristocratic pride laid aside. Here we see artisans, artists, merchants, councillors, barons, counts, and excellencies dancing together with waitresses, women of the middle class, and ladies. Every stranger who stays here for a while is infected by this dance malady."

Indeed, the first dance description of modern Europe comes from Bavaria, just at the turn to the second millennium, when we hear for the first time of Bavarian colonies in northern Italy. It occurs in the Latin courtly poem of *Rudlieb*:

> The youth springs boldly up, against him is his maiden.
> He is the falcon like; she glides like the swallow;
> No sooner are they near than they shoot past each other;
> He seizes her with ardor, but she flees his grasp.
> And no one who beholds them both could ever hope
> To equal them in dance, in leap or gesture.

It is not a question here, as has been said, of an animal dance—falcon over against swallow—but of that dance of courting and coyness, which has already been discussed in detail and which still persists down to our own day in Bavaria itself as the *Schuhplattler*.

But a kind fate has preserved in still another place this dance so vividly described in the *Rudlieb*—and that just where, on account of the German names, we should expect to find traces of the old German dance —in Italy. Here the classical dance of the country people is performed by two men and two women. They enter the circle and walk around it stamping their feet, the men backwards and the women forwards, and then the opposite. Next the women, holding the hems of their skirts gracefully, turn towards their partners, while the men, as in the Bavarian *Schuhplattler,* dance swiftly towards them. This is the same basic motif as in the dance of the *Rudlieb:* the wooing, fleeing, and seeking each other out of the couples. Then, too, there is the "stamping," which has been preserved in Germany as the name of a Neidhart dance song from the thirteenth century. And this dance also, which so clearly shows the features of a German couple dance, still bears a name of German origin—*trescone.*

In the literary references these names from German and Latin are paired in a strange way:

Middle High German	*reigen*	*tanz*
Medieval Latin	*chorea*	*ballatio*
Italian	*carola*	*danza*
Provençal	*corola*	*dansa*
Old French	*carole*	*danse*

There is no doubt that we have here two separate, indeed opposed, concepts, which supplement each other. About the year 600 Isidore of Seville speaks of *choreis et ballationibus.* About 1150 Erec sings: *Puceles carolent et dancent* (The maidens carol and dance). ("Carol"—to dance in a ring to the accompaniment of song. NED.) At the beginning of the thirteenth century we hear in the *Stamheimer* of *tanzen unde reien* (dance and carol). These are not synonyms heaped up here through the poet's joy in words; for numerous places call special attention to the contrast:

> *Rayen und tantzen*
> *Springen und schwantzen.*

> (Carol and dance,
> Leap and prance.)

HEINRICH VON NEUSTADT,
Apollonius von Tyrland, 1057/8.

More clearly:

> *Cil et celes qui s'esbatoient*
> *Au danser sans gueres atendre*
> *Comencierent leurs mains a tendre*
> *Pour caroler.*

> (Youths and maidens who disport
> Themselves in dancing now begin
> With scarce a wait to join hands in
> The choral.)

FROISSART (1337 to c. 1410),
Poésies.

Most clearly:

> *Li uns danse, l'autre querole.*

> (Some dance, others carol.)

Herbert, *Dolopathos* (beginning of the thirteenth century).

In the face of such evidence there can be no doubt of the contrast. But the hope of making out immediately from the written sources, from descriptions, or at least from qualifying adjectives the nature of this contrast is doomed to disappointment. The dance leader conducts the *Reigen;* he also leads the *Tanz.* The *Tanz* is glided, and the *Reigen* too; jumping, stepping, moving to and fro—all these movements are to be found in both *Reigen* and *Tanz.* If we wish to emerge from this confusion, we must proceed from the known fact that in the course of time the German word *Tanz* with its Romance derivatives *danza* and *danse* has become dominant. It covers today the various forms of rhythmic movement with the exception of the march, and includes also, therefore, what was originally distinguished from it as *Reigen, chorea,* or *carole.* When this expansion began can scarcely be determined. It is certain that the fourteenth century no longer distinguished sharply among them. Boccaccio, for example, in his *Decameron* has the seven ladies and three gentlemen of his court of love dance at the end of the day: Dioneo and Fiametta strike up a *danza* and the others then begin to *carolare;* the evening of the seventh day, however, sees them "now dancing to the music of the hornpipe of Tindaro, and now caroling to other sounds" (*danzare, quando al suono della cornamusa di Tindaro, e quando d'altri suoni carolando*).

The *Reigen* as a form is quite definite: a chain of dancers, who move hand in hand, either in an open or closed circle, or in an extended line. The circle is indicated in literature by the *ronde carole* of the *Printems d'Yver,* or by the occasional comparison of the stone circles of the British Bronze Age—as at Stonehenge—to a gigantic *carole,* and above all by the name *carola,* Provençal *corola.* The meanings which are given to this word in the etymological dictionaries of the Romance languages are all untenable and are rejected by other scholars. The only possible derivation—which, although the most obvious, has yet never come into consideration—seems to me to be the Latin *corolla,* "a little garland, a little crown." As a matter of fact we find the name *Kronentanz* or *crown dance* for the circular dance in German popular speech.

In contrast to the circle, the choral dance in extended line formation is most clearly described in a French fairy tale romance of the twelve seventies, *La Manekine* by Phelipe de Remi:

> *Tel carole ne fu pas veue*
> *Pres d'une quart dure d'une lieue.*

> (Such a choral ne'er was seen
> A quarter league in length, I ween.)

We are familiar today with these very long lines from the French-Provençal *farandoule*, the German *Kehraus*, and the Swedish *Langdans*. The *Reigen* or choral dance often formed figures. It was *krumb* (crooked), and *manicvalt* (manifold); as *Rimpfenreie*, it might be "puckered, pressed together"—especially when the space in the room was too narrow and the dancers

> *wunden sich dan unde dar*
> *und brâchen sich her unde hin.*

> (Within a ring the dancers wound
> About, without the ring a few.)
> *Trojanischer Krieg.*

A fresco from about 1340, "The Good Regiment" by Ambrogio Lorenzetti in the Town Hall at Siena, gives us the most beautiful picture of a choral dance of this type: nine aristocratic ladies take each other by the hand and leave the circle to perform the arch dance, as we have already seen it among primitive peoples; a tenth with the tambourine leads the singing. Figure chorals with a limited number of participants must also have been danced; the *Treialtrei* was performed *selbe zwelfte* (twelve together), and it may perhaps have survived into the nineteenth century in the *Zwölfertanz* (twelve dance) of southern Bavaria. For the medieval *Reigen* dance has been preserved in more or less all countries of Europe, most clearly perhaps in northern Spain and in the Balkans. The Balkan *kolo* means "wheel," and similarly the Salzburger calls the choral dance a *Rädel* (little wheel), the Spaniard a *rueda* (wheel), and Dante in the *Paradiso*, XIV, 20, has the dancers execute a *rota*.

But there is also a real wheel with felly and spokes. In the Moravian Kuhländchen, eight peasant lads form a narrow circle; four throw themselves backwards so that their feet meet in the center, the other four begin to move in a circle, turning with them the ones that are half lying down. This dance is called the *Mühlrad* or mill wheel. In the Ötztal is called the *Stern* (star) and is a miller's dance. For the dance which corresponds most closely to it, however, we must look not in the medieval choral dance but four thousand years earlier. It was described in the Old Egyptian Kingdom and designated as the choral of the wine press.

The later medieval descriptions, which go under the name of *Tanz* (dance), make use also of the name *Reigen* (choral dance) up to a certain point, but "walking" in separate couples or in groups of three is never referred to as a *Reigen*. This must determine the character of the *Tanz* in the narrower sense. The *Reigen* is a choral dance, the *Tanz* a couple dance.

> *Geuden giengen si gelich*
> *Hiwer an einem Tanze.*

> (They moved about as if they were
> Wife and husband in a dance.)
>
> NEIDHART

Gelich hiwer—like married couples. And again it is a *Tanz* when

> *Och mohte man dâ schouwen*
> *Ie zwischen zwein frouwen*
> *Einen clâren rîter gên.*

> (And one saw also there
> Between two ladies fair
> A knight unblemished dance.)
> *Parzival.*

> *Ie zwischen zwein frouwen stuont,*
> *als sie noch bî tanze tuont,*
> *ein ritter an ir hende:*
> *dort an enem ende*
> *ie zwischen zwein meiden gie*
> *ein knabe, der ir hende vie;*
> *dâ stuonden videlaere bî.*

(On this side find we ladies two
Who many kinds of dances do—
A knight holds each by hand.
And yonder takes his stand
Between two younger maidens fair
A boy, who dances with them there.
The fiddlers play the melody.)

MEIER HELMBRECHT (thirteenth century).

This is the old trio form with which we are already familiar from primitive peoples. A fourth example:

Diu edel küniginne guot
Den ritter bî der hende vienc:
Mit im sî ze tanze gienc.

(Now the noble queens and good
Link by hand the stately knight,
Dance with him from left to right.)

MELER

The Burgundian painting of a courtly revel from about 1430 in the museum at Versailles, as well as the fresco of the Church Triumphant in the Spanish chapel of the Church of Santa Maria Novella in Florence from the second half of the previous century, brings us both forms, the circular choral and the dancing group of three, side by side.

If the *Reigen* is a child of the ancient choral, which was generally ring-shaped, then the *Tanz* in the narrower sense is the child of that comparatively early couple dance of the Neolithic culture, in which the union of the sexes was to bring about the fertility of the fields and of the tribe. The motif of this dance, which has passed over into the medieval form, consists in wooing with provocation, coy withdrawal, arch threats, and ultimate yielding or, less dramatically, in the immediate union in kiss and embrace. If the *Reigen* is only merry active play, the symbolic-expressive is preserved in the couple *Tanz;* the *Reigen* simply *is;* the *Tanz,* on the contrary, *represents.* The *Reigen* comes from the non-imitative side of the dance world, the *Tanz* from the imitative; the former from introvert, the latter from extravert, culture.

But by the Middle Ages these two forms of culture had already met and mingled for thousands of years—and the dances belonging to them could hardly have been kept entirely pure. The choral took on dramatic ingredients and the couple dance incorporated more and more interludes in the style of the choral dance.

The dramatization of the choral has its modest beginnings among primitive peoples. The Ao Naga in Burma move slowly in a circle and from time to time one of their number breaks away and launches forth in leaps and fight exercises. In the Melanesian and Upper Burmese weapon dance, the warriors first walk around slowly in two circles and then set upon each other howling. The trend becomes very plain when in the European folk choral dance of our day, in the Balkan *kolo,* for example, we find, as a survival from an earlier period, that two or three dancers separate from the chain and execute a little pantomime in the center of the singing group. That the medieval period at its height was quite similar has been convincingly demonstrated by Joseph Bédier. Here the imitative dance unites with that old Mesolithic idea of possessing an object, person, or event by rhythmic encirclement, of incorporating it, enhancing it to the point of greatness and universality. The activity within the circle, Bédier has concluded from French literature of the thirteenth century, is a simple, charming distribution of flowers and branches, or, in the old analogy of the spring as a season and as an age of mankind, a love play: abduction, jealousy, wooing with flight, persecution, affectation, and final union in the kiss. And what the kiss suggests, conceals, and promises is consummated in the woods. Maternal and marital rights are suspended on the night of the *kalenda maya;* precepts are silent when in the sacred hour the unity of nature and mankind is established.

A very fresh picture of such a choral dance in the first half of the thirteenth century is given in the *Romance of the Rose:*

> E'en as I came within the close,
> A glorious burst of song uprose;
> For one, whose name was gladness, loud
> And clear-voiced sang amid the crowd
> Foregathered there; full well she knew
> To modulate her tones with due
> And gentle cadence, now to fall
> And now to rise high over all.
> Her note was clear as silver bell,
> And, gently swaying, rose and fell
> Her supple form, the while her feet
> Kept measured time with perfect beat:
> 'Mid her companions ever first
> Her voice was into song to burst,
> For in that art divine did she
> Exceed all rivals facilely.
> Then through my frame I felt a throe
> Of joy to see them dancing go,
> As man and maid in measure trod
> With twinkling feet the springing sod.
> While minstrels sang, the tambourine
> Kept with the flute due time I ween,
> And rondelettes burst forth amain
> To merry tunes of old Lorraine
> So sweetly, that I doubt if e'er
> Was heard such music otherwhere,
> For that fair province doth excel
> In heaven-born music's tuneful spell.
> Then saw I cunning jugglers play,
> And girls cast tambourines away

Aloft in air, then gaily trip
Beneath them, and on finger-tip
Catch them again, with skill so rare,
That all men stood a-wondering there.
Then came two damsels 'tired with taste
That Venus' self had not disgraced,
And suited well their dainty dresses
The wondrous plaits that bound their tresses:
Their kirtles thin but reached the knee,
Through which their forms showed pleasantly.
I saw the twain toward Mirth advance
With agile leap and darting glance,
Then both flew forward with a bound,
Just missed a kiss, then flung them round
As though they feared some wrong they'd done,
Then lovingly embraced anon,
And then once more did they retreat,
A-playing with their winsome feet
A thousand antic turns; so quaint
And strange they were, that I should paint
Their wonders feebly did I try
To show the supple subtlety
With which their lithe light bodies swayed;
Such tumult in my breast it made
As never dance and song I deem
Had done before in sooth or dream.

Tr. F. S. Ellis.

Unlike the choral dance, which tends towards dramatic representation, the couple dance has from early times had tendencies away from imitation: we have seen examples from the northeastern African Galla and from the Old Mexican Nahua of non-pantomimic stepping in couples. The union of non-imitative stepping and imitative action in the couple dance is natural enough. For the longer duration of such a social pastime and the succession of one couple after another would almost of necessity turn the couples not dancing for the time being from simple spectators into participants, and thus at the same time separate the individual pantomimic episodes from each other.

The popular couple dances of almost all European countries have this constant alternation—a proof of its great age. In the German *Deutschen*, procession and slow waltz succeed each other; in the Bohemian *husička*, sixteen polka beats alternate with a pantomime of threatening; the Hungarian dancer leads his partner in a slow introductory dance, releases her when the lively wooing leap dance begins, and then with the resumption of the slow introductory melody takes her hand again. The Italian folk dances correspond closely to this. In the *trescone* the men and women begin with a stamping procession—only after this is over do the women turn to their partners, and while they move, holding the hems of their skirts gracefully, the men with raised arms dance the pantomime, the *ballo*. Most of the Italian folk dances are on this order. In the *bergamasco*, for example, there is a procession in a circle, then as the music changes (*al variare del suono*) a waltz in couples, then a procession again. In the *giga* there is first the procession, then the whirling of the woman on the hand of the man, and then another procession. The *girometta*, the *lombardina*, the *monferrina*, and many others are similar.

We understand now why in the Middle Ages the terms "carol" and "dance" must have been confused. The dramatized choral dance and the couple dance with the procession characteristic of the choral dance are finally to be distinguished almost only by the choral form of the procession: the former with the unbroken chain, the linking of hands to the right and left, the latter with the march-like parade of couples and groups of three, one after the other.

The high society of the Middle Ages, however, must have attached a particular value to the procession. Joy, love, courtliness, *joi, amor, cortezia*—the three essentials of the service of love (*Minnedienst*)—

278

which for centuries impressed themselves on the courtly manner, had also, or indeed especially, to determine the dance. In the dance the veneration of women and the play of love expressed themselves artistically in the most immediate way, because here man took himself as the formative theme. *Joi* found expression in the choral dance, *amor* in the couple dance; *cortezia,* however, made use of a particular form of the couple dance in which the desire for love, divested of the rough attack and the violent, animal-like wooing, is subdued to shy veneration and in which the union is expressed in tender, respectful handclasps and in rhythmical gliding steps. Love in all its nuances, from violent passion to playful frolic, love denied fulfillment by rigid custom—how could it have found a more striking and beautiful symbol than in this airy proximity, inflamed by music in the symmetry of movement, in which the contact, subdued and dissimulated, scarcely dares to suggest itself?

It is the force of *cortezia* which has changed the original relationship of procession and pantomime. From a simple framework the procession becomes more and more the main part of the dance; the pantomimic content steps into the background. We see this very clearly in the period after the culmination of the Middle Ages, in the fifteenth and sixteenth centuries. In the fifteenth century the pantomime still plays an important role, but it has already departed from tradition, lost its fresh independence, and been conventionalized by dance teachers into rigid figures. There are already dances which are practically imageless, and which almost completely discard the pantomimic. In the beginning, the sixteenth century too presents the same picture: couple dances which consist simply of a continuous movement of both couples together, and those in which the couples separate to dance a pantomime. The *pavane* is non-pantomimic; the *galliard, courante, canaries,* and *bouffons* are pantomimic. The *galliard,* after a general promenade through the hall, calls for separation and a parade dance of the man in front of his partner. In the *courante* and *canaries,* a strongly marked scene of wooing and coyness is performed after the promenade by couples. In the *bouffons,* procession and battle play alternate. But this combination of procession and pantomime is on the decline. In the second half of the century the whole pantomimic part is dropped from both the *galliard* and the *courante;* and shortly after that the *canaries* and *bouffons* disappear from the court dance. Not until after 1550 does the procession also break away from the pantomime; and it is only after 1550 that the courtly dance is in a position to dispense with its pantomime.

It is hardly necessary to state that the pantomimic part was more strongly emphasized among the peasants than among the knights. For the pantomimic is a heritage from a period which greatly antedates the formation of the courtly ideal. Consequently we should not, as is often done, distinguish socially between courtly "dance" and rustic "choral round," even if the villager occasionally imitated a *hovetänzel* (court dance) and the knights were fond of joining in the choral round. This distinction is out of the question. The difference lies rather in the manner in which the dances are executed. It is natural, of course, that the peasants, creating directly from the source of all dance, should give themselves up to its motor and sensory enjoyment with unrestrained exuberance and passion. Their dance was the ultimate intensification of the feeling of life. The very names reflect this: the "skip" dance, *Gimpelgampel,* the French *virelai,* which had to suffer a metamorphosis into the "rapid" *firlefei,* and the *Hoppaldei* or *Hoppelrei,* which the painters and engravers of Dürer's, and indeed of Ostade's, time were still so fond of portraying (Plates 22–24).

In the *Hoppaldei* the peasants rushed around "like wild bears" and moved in couples "as though they wanted to fly." All parts of the body had to assist; the arms waved, the head shook, the shoulders heaved and rolled: a true heritage from the shaman period, like the dances of the present-day Siberians. The *Houbetschotten* (head shaking) referred to by the minnesinger Göli, about 1230, may have been the same as the *tour dou chief* in Adam de la Hale's *Gieus de Robin et de Marion* (about 1285), and his *Ahselrotten* (shoulder rolling) simply the South Italian *spallata* and the Neapolitan *repoluna.* As late as the year 1598, Prince Ludwig of Anhalt-Köthen on a visit to Florence expressed surprise that the dancers there did not "roll their shoulders this way and that" as in Germany. There was striding with the feet wide apart, and, as so often outside Europe, also limping, and especially, by the girls too, leaping. These leaps were a fathom long, and *hôher danne ein hinde* (higher than a hind)—higher, too, than the mothers and the moralists liked. In this final exaggeration of every movement, in the increasing of the step to the leap and swing, in the literal interpretation and complete realization of all the erotic symbolism, they restored to the dance its original power and significance. Grasped boldly, the girls flew high into the air, and with them their billowing skirts, to the delight of the spectators; and when the music stopped, thrown by an ingenious trick, they lay exposed on the ground. The boy, however, kept on leaping until he could leap no longer—until the blood streamed from his nose, ears, and mouth. This is pure primitivism.

It is obvious that the refined circles of the court and the nobility with their minnesinger ideals would polish and restrain such dances as these, the more so, since the knight in the service of arms, in hunting, and in tournaments had other opportunities for the sportive display of strength. *Joi* and *amor* had come under the yoke of *cortezia;* no better proof could be desired than that Middle High German *gofenanz,* the name for the courtly dance, is from the Old French *convenance* (seemliness), even if not quite in the modern sense. With his helmet, shield, and sword, the man put away crude strength and brought charm, grace, and tenderness to the love play in the dance. What the dance lost in immediate symbolism and in vital, full-blooded color, it gained in artistic formulation, in delicate shading and suppleness. Henceforth we have in Europe two poles: the peasant, embodying the original power, significance, and earthiness, and the aristocratic, in which the precious stuff of earth is polished to sparkling crystal.

These two dance worlds, however, are not separated by any hard and fast line. In unappeased and unappeasable longing, they reach out their hands from either side to snatch what is denied their own world. The courtly manner of life climbs over all the so carefully protected class walls to the people. Stunted, coarsened, distorted though it might be when it got there, it nonetheless surely reached the bottom and clung on there long after it had been abandoned by the upper classes. Neidhart, speaking of the peasants, says

> *si solten hoppaldei pflegen,*
> *wer gap in die wirdikeit,*
> *daz si in der spilstuben hovetanzen künnen?*

> (They ought to do the *hoppaldei*.
> Why should such as they presume
> To do the *hovetanz* in villages?)

But the courtly dance (*hovetanz*) itself is only something that has arisen out of the great storehouse of the folk dances, whether choral dance or couple dance; the Stone Age, the old hunter and tiller cultures have created them, and the hunters and peasants of the Middle Ages, as of modern times, have preserved them in their truest and purest form. From the people, the upper level of society has taken what it has used in every age, now the choral dance, now the wooing dance, and now the *Ländler*, ultimately to return it purified and ennobled in its meaning. In ceaseless exchange primitive peoples give power and receive in return art and manners.

Thus two forms of the same dance frequently exist side by side: Pastor Neocorus relates that about the year 1590, the Dithmarschers had two long dances (*lange dantz*), the "graceful" *trymmeken-dantz* and another which is performed "almost altogether in leaps and skips." Characteristically enough, the "graceful" one had already gone out of use. Among the country people the "wild" form always wins out in the long run, and the "tame" one, as we have seen, always wins out among the upper classes.

Clearly, however, this "taming" must have affected especially the pantomimic. Taming in this connection really means nothing but the concealment of the openly erotic, of the sexual. The love scene which interrupts or accompanies the choral dance, the naturalistic play which is confined within the framework of the dance procession, becomes more and more lifeless and is smoothed out into an episode in which restrained marching and gliding give place to a free, spirited skipping and leaping.

Regarded from this point of view, the medieval evidence assumes a new aspect. An example from the thirteenth century leaves scarcely a doubt that within the same "choral dance" a gliding part was followed immediately by a leap dance:

> *Ez wart nie schöner reige*
> *gemachet von deheiner schar,*
> *sie wunden sich dan unde dar*
> *und brâchen sich her unde hin.*
> *man hôrte lûten under in*
> *tambûren, schellen, pfîfen.*
> *lis ûf den füezen slîfen*
> *und dar nâch balde springen. . . .*

> (No fairer choral dance
> Was seen, afar or nigh around.
> Within a ring the dancers wound
> About, without the ring a few.
> The drummers beat, the pipers blew,
> Their music did direct the stride.
> Lightly the dancers did the glide
> And afterwards the leap. . . .)
> *Trojanischer Krieg.*

Here we have the model for the classical pairs—introductory dance and after-dance, *basse danse* and *tourdion*, *pavane* and *galliard*.

A passage from Froissart is still more explicit:

> *La estoient li menestrel*
> *Qui s'acquittoient bien et bel*

A piper et tout de novel
Unes danses teles qu'il sorent,
Et si trestot que cessé orent
Les estampies qu'il batoient,
Cil et celes qui s'esbatoient
Au danser sans gueres atendre
Commencierent leurs mains a tendre
Pour caroler.

(Here are all the minstrels rare
Who now acquit themselves so fair
In playing on their pipes whate'er
The dances be that one may do.
So soon as they have glided through
The estampiës of this sort
Youths and maidens who disport
Themselves in dancing now begin
With scarce a wait to join hands in
The choral.)

The musicians fiddle an *estampie,* and the dancers give themselves up to it. No sooner is it over than the dancers, even before another piece is begun, join hands for the choral.

This change has long been brewing inwardly. The alternation of procession and pantomime within the same dance, which comes right down from the Stone Age to modern times, has more than one motive, more than one significance. When in the weapon dance the Melanesians and the Naga now simply circle and now attack each other, this change is determined by a basic rhythmic law: the periodic oscillation between repose and movement, between tension and release. This law is deeper and stronger than the alternation of procession and pantomime. When the pantomime fades away, the rhythmic swing from slow to fast, from gliding to leaping, remains. The majority of all true European folk dances are built in this way, and, moreover, the unanimity shows the great age of this contrast. The sacred *romaiika* of the Greeks, the death dance of the last heroic Suliote women, who in 1803 threw themselves singing and dancing into an abyss before the eyes of the Turks, consisted of the slow "prelude," *zyganos,* and the rapid *chorós.* The Hungarian *lassú* is followed by the stormy *friss.* Whether we think of German dances or of the Catalan *sardana,* we always find the same thing.

At the same time, however, another common characteristic becomes clear: in most cases the time changes, and usually the slow phrase is in quadruple and the quick phrase in triple time. The Austrian *Schwabentanz* calls for four-four time in the procession and three-four time in the turning dance, and the Polish *mazurek* is followed by an *obertas* in three-four time. Apparently a very ancient impulse is represented here. For even in discussing the dance music of primitive peoples, we were compelled to recognize a parallel relationship between expanded movement, imitativeness, and uneven time on the one hand, and close movement, non-imitativeness, and even time on the other.

This alternation of phrase and time, which the folk dances have preserved from ancient periods up to the present, is now also being substantiated by the historical sources as one of the most important phenomena of the dance for many centuries. It determines the classical association of introductory dance and after-dance, of *bassadanza* and *saltarello,* of *pavane* and *galliard;* it is the vital nerve of the fourteenth-century *balletto* of the dancing master; it gives us the key to the interpretation of the fourteenth-century *rotta,* and also of the dance possibilities of many songs of this period.

Let us now turn to the music of the medieval dance.

In the older literature we sometimes find the dance leader as soloist with the chorus of dancers singing the responses, and sometimes the minstrel with his fiddle carrying the dance melody. The choral dances of the northern Middle Ages, as well as of the present in the Faeroes, were never accompanied by instruments, only by song. In the Old Norse *Bósa Saga* and in the *Rudlieb,* however, the harpist occasionally appears. This apparent contradiction is explained by the natural contrast between the choral dance and the pantomimic couple dance. In the chain dance the communal spirit peculiar to it is expressed in choral singing. It is possible for all the participants to sing together, since they are all making the same simple, strictly regulated movements. In the couple dance, so long as it is truly pantomimic, however, this communal feeling and also the uniformity of movement are lacking. Here only the spectators can sing: the dancers must devote their attention exclusively to step, gesture, and pantomime. Instrumental accompaniment is proper to the couple dance.

It is hardly necessary to emphasize by examples the fact that in courtly literature the choral dance was almost always sung. In the following pages we shall hear of maidens who *caroled* and sang (*qui queroloient et chantoient*); of maidens (*virgines*) who led chorals (*coreas ducunt*) and at the same time sang *cantilenas;* of a maiden (*maget*) who led the song while all the others followed.

In the *Tanz,* on the contrary, there was a surprising amount of instrumental accompaniment, especially of rebecs and "fiddles." As in the Meier Helmbrecht reference above,

> *ie zwischen zwein meiden gie*
> *ein knabe, der ir hende vie;*
> *dâ stuonden videlaere bî.*

(Between two younger maidens fair
A boy, who dances with them there.
The fiddlers play the melody.)

And when, as in the above quotation from Neidhart, *si gelich Hiwer an einem Tanze* (they moved about as if they were wife and husband in a dance), *muosten drîe vor ihm gigen und der vierde pheif* (three must fiddle in front and the fourth one pipe). In the dance of three, which we have mentioned in the same connection, Gawain calls for a fiddler.

Thus we note that one or more fiddlers have been the usual accompaniment of the dance. But such thin music by no means always sufficed. In a beautiful passage in the didactic poem *Echecs amoureux* from about 1375, we have evidence that the loud instruments, on account of the noise they made, were preferred for dancing:

> *Et quant il vouloient danser*
> *Et faire grans esbattemens,*
> *On sonnoit les haulz instrumens,*
> *Qui mieulx aux dansez plaisoient*
> *Pour la grant noise qu'ilz faisoient*
> *La peuist on oir briefmant*
> *Sonner moult de renuoisement*
> *Trompez, tabours, tymbrez, naquaires,*
> *Cymballes (dont il n'est mes guaires),*
> *Cornemusez et chalemelles*
> *Et cornes de fachon moult belles.*

> (Whene'er that they were fain to dance
> And frolic, gathered in a crowd,
> The dancers called for music loud—
> 'Twas this that always pleased them best,
> And ever added to their zest.
> One could hear each instrument
> That sounded forth its merriment.
> Trumpet, tabor, drum and bell
> Cymbals (which they played so well)
> Cornemuse and chalumeau
> And horns that they did loudly blow.)

This preference is really much earlier. But the ladies do not seem to have shared it:

> *Da huop sich michel reie*
> *von maniger hande gaudine,*

Von tantze grozz geschreie,
  weder mit tambur noch mit busine
Wolten sich die frowen lan betoren:
Videln, herpfen, rotten und ander
  suzze doene sie wolten horen.

(There were dances round about
  And joy was in the air
While many a cry rang out.
  Nor tabor's beat nor trumpet's blare
The ladies fair could captivate;
The tones of fiddles, harps and zithers
  They did most appreciate.)
                              Titurel.

The music of the medieval dance is almost a chant, a *cantilena.*

> I hear the maidens modest
> Strumming *cantilenas* new
> As they lead the evening chorals.

The word *cantilena* is not to be understood as *cantio lenis* in the mistaken modern sense of a soft, flowing melody, but on the contrary quite in the true, original meaning of a monotonous singsong. The *cantilenas* were short, catchy dance songs repeated over and over again.

Every *cantilena* consisted of

> Refrain = *responsorium, refractorium, ripresa, volta* and
> Verse   = *versus* or *pes.*

It is worth noting that the names for the parts of the song are words connected with movement: *volta* means "turn" and *pes versus* means "turned foot." Here the technical language of poets and musicians has faithfully preserved the concept of the return dance, which lies at the bottom of all song forms. Wieland unconsciously followed this tradition when in 1793 he translated the French word *refrain* into German as *Kehrreim.* The refrain was sung by the dance chorus, the *pedes* by the song leader, who was also the dance leader:

> *Ein maget in süezer wise . . .*
> *Diu sanc vor, die andern sungen alle nach.*
>
> (A maiden sweet of manner . . .
> Led the song, the rest sang after her.)

The simplest form of such a *cantilena* was the *rotundellus,* the *rondo,* with two melodic parts, one of which remains constant for the verse, the other for the refrain. "A *cantilena* of this type is sung in the West, in Normandy, by girls and boys at festivals and banquets as entertainment." In the form *a b b a* the *cantilenas* were called *ballate* or *cantiones, chansons.* That these songs were danced is attested in the year 1332 by Antonio da Tempo: *ballatae cantantur et coreizantur* (the ballads are sung and danced). The *rotundelli* are described as chorals or dances sung in rondo fashion, especially by the French. Thus we have in the *Lancelot:*

> *Si trova VI puceles qui queroloient*
> *et chantoient une novele chançon.*
>
> (Six maidens there were caroling
> The while they sang a ballad new.)

If in the beginning song and dance were one, this is no longer true with the growing expansion, enrichment, and elaboration of the form. For *cantilenas,* which retained, to be sure, the same melody in the refrain, but had different melodies for the various verses and even added supplementary verses or *additamenta,* the special designations *ductia* and *stantipes* were introduced. The *ductia* were distinguished from the *stantipes* by a lightly flowing melody.

The word *stantipes,* about which there has been so much unnecessary debate, is easily explained according to the prosody of Antonio da Tempo (1332). The *ballata* consisted regularly of four parts. The two middle parts or *mutationes* were popularly known as *pedes.* Occasional supplementary parts *eiusdem qualitatis et quantitatis* (of the same quality and quantity) were commonly known as *stantiae*. The Vulgar Latin *stantia*, which is sufficiently familiar from Italian literature of the sixteenth century, really means "delay." *Stantipes* is thus a pleonastic formation: a *pes* which, because it was irregular, bore the name *stantia*.

Stantipes and *ductia* were considered difficult. Consequently they "absorbed the minds of the youths and maidens" and kept them from thinking evil thoughts. The *ductia* in particular was supposed "to have power over the passion called love."

But this difficulty seems to explain why apparently none of these songs was danced any longer. The union of words, music, and dance demands simplicity and clearness. The dancers, however, preserved the more mature song forms by giving up singing and entrusting the complicated melody to the musician. As instrumental pieces also they were called *stantipes* and *ductia*. Their subdivisions, however, were no longer called *versus* and *responsoria*, but *puncti* (periods). By "period" we understand a melodic section which rises to a semi-cadence and then repeats to end with a full cadence. This is the same principle which we have already discussed in connection with the return dance. The *stantipes* had six or seven such periods; the *ductia,* three, or at most, four. A third instrumental form, the *nota,* which has not hitherto been described, also had four periods. All these forms were *illiterati,* or without text, even when executed *voce humana,* when the dancer hums the tune, as Neidhart von Reuental writes:

> *Wol sing ich des reien wíse*
> *Nâch der ahselnoten líse.*

> (Well I sing the choral air
> On the "shoulder-nota" fair.)

These verses also establish the *nota* as a dance piece. Wolf cites more examples. Further, the instrumental *ductia* is said with its *recta percussio* "to excite the mind of man to graceful movement, according to the rules of dance art and to control his movements in the *ductia* and choral dances." We have no information of this kind about the *stantipes*. This may be no indication, however, since Grocheo says nothing either of the *nota* or *rotundellus* as dances. He seems to dismiss the *stantipes* as a dance, however, when he denies to it the *recta percussio* which the *ductia* possesses. This passage is not clear. Grocheo's sentence in which he states that the *stantipes* "is determined by the periods, because it lacks the rhythm which we find in the *ductia* and can be recognized only by the difference in periods," does not seem to make sense. It cannot possibly mean that the *stantipes* has no rhythm—to be without rhythm, according to Grocheo, does not mean *percussione carere* (without time), but *non ita praecise mensuratum esse* (not in exact measure). All that he says is that it lacks the rhythm which we find in the *ductia*. The rhythm of the *ductia,* however, is *percussio recta,* and the passage immediately becomes clear if we translate this expression not as "correct rhythm," but as "even rhythm," in the sense of the later mensural theory, as expounded by Grocheo himself, according to the concept *minima recta* = two semi-breves. And indeed, those sustained melodies, which according to Grocheo's definition must be and have been called *stantipedes,* make it obvious that we are dealing with dance pieces, which are, moreover, in *percussio non recta,* in triple time.

A whole series of dance melodies from the thirteenth and fourteenth centuries has been published by Johannes Wolf and by Pierre Aubry, and recorded by myself in *L'Anthologie Sonore,* 16. Wolf's collection contains five complete dances and four fragments from the thirteenth century. We must agree with Wolf that at least one of these dances is a *stantipes;* it has the six "periods" which Grocheo allots to this category. There is another one which might also be called a *stantipes* in spite of its five periods. Each period has the same number of bars and is repeated twice, the first time with an open, the second time with a closed, cadence. The rhythm becomes clear only when we group the three-four beats of the Wolf script in fours and halve the value. We then get twelve eighths which must be read partly as beginning on an unaccented, partly on an accented, beat.

The dance music of the following century, the fourteenth, is illustrated mainly in two manuscripts: one in the Bibliothèque Nationale in Paris, from before 1325, containing eight *estampies* and two *danses royales*, which have been published in Aubry's collection, and the other in the British Museum containing eight *istampite*, four *saltarelli*, one *trotto*, and two pieces entitled *Lamento di Tristano* and *La Manfredina*, which have appeared in the Wolf collection.

The *estampie*, which we shall consider first, was not a new form. A song by the troubadour Raimbaut de Vaqueiras (1180–1207), the famous *Kalenda Maya*, of which both words and music have come down to us, is according to historical evidence the melody of an *estampie* which was played by two French fiddlers at the court of the Marquis of Montferrat. The piece begins on the upbeat and has three periods like the *ductia*.

It has been mistakenly objected that the *estampie* was not a dance. Passages in two French poems leave no doubt that it was:

> *Je ferai une estampie si jolie,*
> *Balle un petit, je t'an proi.*

> (I shall do an *estampie*,
> Come dance a bit, I beg of thee.)

The second one, *"La estoient li menestrel,"* has been quoted on page 283.

The names, Italian *istampita*, Provençal *estampida*, and French *estampie*, have now been traced back to the Frankish *stampôn*. One of its ancestors must therefore have been a stamping dance. For philological reasons there can be no question of derivation from *stantipes*.

If the *estampie*, like the other dance melodies, also has periods, with a semi-cadence the first time and a full cadence in the repetition, these are enormously long drawn out, often fifteen times the usual length. The *estampie*, however, never had as many as six periods, but only four or five. We may perhaps conclude from this fact that the *estampie* developed from a fusion of the *ductia, nota,* and *stantipes.* Rhythmically the *estampie* corresponds exactly to the *stantipes* of the preceding century. The sixteen *estampies* of the Paris and London manuscripts have been correctly transcribed into three-eight, six-eight, and three-four time. A living music and dance picture, however, appears only when the values of the mensural signs are still further abbreviated and the obviously larger rhythmical units are grouped together into measures. This gives us again the same forms beginning on accented and unaccented beats in four-four and twelve-eight time.

The *estampie* must have been a quiet gliding dance, since in the same London manuscript it is contrasted with the *saltarelli* as the *pavane* is with the *galliard* in later collections. It must have been a forerunner of the gliding dances of the fifteenth century, the *allemande* and the *basse danse.* The music confirms this. For the time signatures correspond with those of the fifteenth and sixteenth centuries: four-four and twelve-eight time beginning on the upbeat are the rhythms of the *basse danse;* and the German forerunner of the *Tanz* of the fifteenth century, which has been preserved by the French in the sixteenth century as the *allemande,* is in quadruple time beginning on the downbeat. If the presence of the initial upbeat brings the *estampie* into the immediate neighborhood of the *basse danse,* its absence does not at all remove it from this class. For at the beginning of the fifteenth century there was a rule which in the *basse danse* allowed the upbeat in the treble to precede the original tenor which began on an accented beat.

The four *saltarelli* of the fourteenth-century manuscript in the British Museum have been notated by Johannes Wolf partly in six-eight and partly in four-eight time. This again is correct as far as the notation is concerned, but it obscures the distinctive character of the rhythm. From an analysis of the form, it would be necessary to group two, three, or four of these *battutae* together in one measure. We would then have:

Saltarello no. 9, triple time beginning on the upbeat (9/8);
Saltarello no. 11, triple time beginning on the upbeat (3/4);
Saltarello no. 12, duple time beginning on the downbeat (12/8);
Saltarello no. 15, duple time beginning on the upbeat (4/4).

Those in triple time are genuine Italian *saltarelli,* as Cornazano describes them later in the fifteenth century, and the one in duple time beginning on the downbeat is, according to the same authority, a German *saltarello* (*quaternaria*). The one in duple time beginning on the upbeat, which so strikingly resembles in theme *La Manfredina,* referred to above, appears to be a kind of second *rotta* in comparison, rather than a true *saltarello.* The term *rotta* will be explained below.

In the midst of the group of *saltarelli* in the London manuscript are two pieces with song titles without any indication of the dance categories to which they belong, the *Lamento di Tristano* and *La Manfredina.* Considering the strict arrangement of the manuscript, we might assume from their inclusion here that both these compositions were *saltarelli.* Upon closer examination, indeed, it appears that these beautiful minor melodies are in triple time beginning on the upbeat, as was the rule for the Italian *saltarello* of the fifteenth century. It need not be emphasized that in reviving this *Lamento* in dance form it should be taken as a gay *saltarello* and not as a sentimental plaint.

In the *Lamento* and in the *Manfredina* the three parts of the main dance are followed by three parts of an appurtenant *rotta* with the same motif and in duple time. The Italian word *rotta,* from *rompere* = Latin *frangere,* "to break," is simply the *refractorium,* the refrain of the *cantilena.* The name appears much later also: in Caroso's dance manual from the end of the sixteenth century the *rotta* comes after the *galliarda,* and Johannes Wolf is even able to produce two examples from the seventeenth century. Obviously the *rotta* is the same as the *ripresa,* which in the sixteenth and seventeenth centuries likewise follows the *saltarello* and the *galliard.*

The parts of the *rotta* were probably not played in succession after the *saltarello* proper, but alternated with it. It is apparently just a remnant of the old "procession" which came between the pantomimic episodes of the original *saltarello*. In the contrast of the duple time of the *rotta* with the triple time of the *saltarello*, we undoubtedly have that *al variare del suono*, which in the Italian folk dance today still indicates the alternation of procession and pantomime. About 1600, on the contrary, the *sciolta* of the Italian dance melodies "resolves" the rigidity of the customary even time into the freer three-four time. We have here perhaps a root of the later *trio*, which at least has variation of tempo and preserves in its *cantabile* the suggestion of a *refractorium*, a refrain. It is noteworthy that in the German *Ländler*, which is closely related to the *saltarello*, the *trio* disappeared, as did the processional dances between the various parts of the *Ländler*.

The *trotto* is also included with the *saltarelli* in the London manuscript. From a single reference we learn that this name was used to designate a *ballada* in *tempus imperfectum*. Nothing is said of the manner of this dance. Nor do we know how the *trotera*, mentioned by a contemporary Spaniard, Juan de Hita, in the *Libro de buen amor*, v. 1513, and the Scottish *schaik a trot*, referred to in the *Complaynt of Scotland* of 1548–49, were performed.

Trotto is derived from the Old High German *trottôn*, which later becomes the Middle High German *treten*, meaning "to step." The poets often state that a dance was *getreten* or stepped. Of seventeen references where *treten* occurs in connection with dancing, six definitely speak of the *Tanz* or couple dance, two more of instrumental accompaniment (which is, of course, characteristic of the couple dance), and two of the choral. In four cases another type of movement, the leap, is found in this connection, but the word *treten* is never used where there is any mention of gliding. Thus it appears that the leaping dance—whether a choral or a *Tanz* in the narrower sense—used "steps," not "glides," between the leaps, which could not, of course, follow immediately one upon another. Since wherever the word *treten* is used without any reference to dancing, it always indicates a vigorous setting down of the lifted leg, we must generally assume a similar significance when it is used to describe the dance.

The mere fact that the London manuscript expressly includes a *trotto* among the *saltarelli,* which were of course "stepped," would seem to indicate that in certain dances "trotting" was implied. There are several facts to support this conclusion. About 1480 the people of Erfurt danced a *Trottartt* which "had never been seen before and is still danced to this day." It would have been impossible to say, however, of the ordinary stepping or leaping dance that it had never been seen in central Germany at the end of the fifteenth century. A few years later Sebastian Brant sings of the *Drotter* in his *Ship of Fools.* The context is noteworthy: Death bears the people off in the dance, and many a man who *noch nit hat gedacht, das man den vordantz jm hatt bracht* had now to dance the *Drotter*—many a man who has not been aware that the introductory dance was over, finds that it is his turn to dance the last dance of all. This establishes the order.

Whether the *Trappeltanz* of Vogtland in Saxony is a descendant of the *trotto* is an open question.

There is another piece of significant evidence. In 1560 we find in a poem by the court trumpeter of Königsberg, Paul Kugelmann, the two verses:

> da muss denn einher draben
> der firlefanz von schwaben.

> (Then one must trot
> The *firlefanz* of Swabia.)

This points to the trotting movement in the literal sense of the Italian, but at the same time describes more accurately a peasant dance often referred to in the Middle Ages—the *Firlefei, Firlefanz,* or *Fulafranz.* This was a Swabian trotting dance with leaps, of which we read in Neidhart: *Gar weidenlich trat se den fulafranzen* (Quite boldly then they step the *Fulafranzen*). The German *weidenlich* has the same significance as the name *galliard*, which we meet in the sixteenth century. The *galliard*, indeed, throws light on the *trotto*: the dancers were incited by shouts to *bei trotti* and *salti leggiadri*, to "fine steps" and "light-footed leaps," intermingled with stamping. The *trotto* mentioned in connection with the leap was a violent, springing step.

However, I should like to warn against overestimating the documentary value of the music manuscripts which have been preserved. Such manuscripts are not, as we are too ready to suppose, like contemporary music designed for the use of any casual purchaser and consequently as intelligibly written as possible. The old dance music is much more reliably preserved by the heirs and successors of the minstrel world, the peasant musicians. I quote here a few sentences from a description of the *Landla* by Commenda, one of the best authorities on the Austrian folk dance:

"Almost every minstrel had his own copy of the *Landla* tunes familiar to him. He guarded them jealously, as they had often been handed down from generation to generation. These notes could be correctly deciphered only by the expert, however. The music for dancing was never played from notes but always from memory. . . . The various *Landla* transcriptions hitherto known and all the published *Ländler* which adhere faithfully to the originals are in 3/4 time. . . . The musicians, however, play these pieces sometimes in 3/4 and sometimes in 2/4 time, according to how the dancers divide their steps. . . . The question of time is not the only difficulty that the transcriptions of the old *Ländler* present. Almost always it is only the essential parts of the melody which are fixed and from which the whole *Landla* is built up in the playing. . . . The old *Ländler* musicians, who were accustomed from their youth to this way of playing, have abbreviated their notation as much as possible. They did not consider the prelude, interlude, and postlude very important. They usually knew only one of each which could be transposed into all keys. Such obvious things they either did not write down at all or put in only once at the beginning, or at most, at the beginning of eight measures in a new key. . . . The most important parts of all the *Landla* transcriptions are the series of eight-measure groups carefully arranged according to key, which contain the melody. . . . Each of these eight-measure *Landla* must be regarded as the nucleus from which, in the course of the performance, the accompaniment of eighty or more measures for the procession has to grow. . . ."

This is by way of warning to those who are inclined to put too much faith in music manuscripts.

THE FIFTEENTH CENTURY

General Characteristics

In the fifteenth century Italy broke away from Gothic domination; the north, where this style continues to hold unlimited sway, at least softens its rigid austerity and secularizes its transcendental leaning. Early Renaissance and Late Gothic meet in their strong emotional quality, in their love of scintillating multiplicity, and in their mingling of melancholy and gaiety, anxiously avoiding everything heavy, serious, or ceremonial. The love of multiplicity and the aversion to magnitude together often result in the exaggeration of the importance of small individual features and the inability to fuse them into an artistic whole.

The dance is at once a product and a symbol of this period. There is no attempt to clarify outlines. The main dance of the time, the *basse danse,* does not even prescribe a fixed order of steps. As variegated as the colors in the kaleidoscope or in those magnificent Burgundian tapestries of the period, the movements are constantly being combined in new ways, so that *memoria,* the power to learn by heart all these combinations, is spoken of as the chief requisite of the art of the dance. In contrast to the *saltarello,* the *basse danse* is the ceremonial gliding dance of the court. But it would be a great mistake to think of it as a solemn procession of the nature of the later *pavane.* How often the lively rhythms of the *saltarello* break in! It is impossible to be serious for long. And how often the vigorous *saltarello* adopts the even more rapid steps of the *piva!* Everything is pell-mell. Each dance can, in the main, be performed like any other dance, the *piva* executed *in passo di saltarello;* the *saltarello, in bassadança;* the *quaternaria, in saltarello;* the *bassa danza, in piua,* or any way one wishes to do it. Eighteen different versions were known. Nowhere is the emphasis placed on the larger features; the details are all-important.

To what extent this attitude is a heritage from the Middle Ages, it is difficult to say. That much of it may be so seems probable from the fact that it is the same both in the north and in the south, in the two countries which in the fifteenth century were models of courtly culture. France and Italy are scarcely differentiated; they have the same vocabulary of steps, and the *saltarello* is known in Italy also as the *passo brabante.*

If we are able to speak here for the first time of a vocabulary of steps, it means that we have arrived at an important point in the history of the dance. An independent profession of dance teaching has arisen, especially in northern Italy.

Hitherto the professional dancers have been wandering mimes and despised jugglers; the northern Italian dancing master had a respected position. He was the companion of princes and might be their confidant; indeed, at Venetian weddings, where it was the custom to present the bride first in a silent dance, he might appear in place of the father.

There were a surprising number of Jews among these teachers. About the middle of the fifteenth century we find, at the court of Urbino, Guglielmo Ebreo of Pesaro, who "excelled all men in the dance," and Ambrosio, also from Pesaro. A generation later we have Guglielmo's pupil, Giuseppe. There must be an old tradition here. For the only dance master of whom we hear in the Middle Ages was also a Jew, Rabbi Hacén ben Salomo, who in the year 1313 in the Church of St. Bartholomew at Tauste in the Spanish province of Zaragoza had to teach the Christians to perform a choral dance around the altar.

Later masters are the two Jews from Ancona, Grescion Azziz and Emanuel de Rabbi Jalomacis, to whom the Pope in 1775 granted the privilege of teaching dancing and singing, and that Sieur Isaac d'Orléans (Plate 26), who about 1700 played a role at the French court and of whom the English poet Jenyns wrote:

> And Isaac's Rigadoon shall live as long
> As Raphael's painting, or as Virgil's song.

With the establishment of dance teaching as a profession in the fifteenth century comes the beginning of dance theory. It started with Domenico, or Domenichino, of Piacenza at the beginning of the fifteenth century. Students of world renown followed him with deep devotion and spread his teaching in oral and written instructions. A Parisian manuscript, the Domenichino treatise, gives a late, anonymous summary of his teaching. But considerably before this two famous disciples had continued his work independently. About the middle of the fifteenth century Guglielmo Ebreo of Pesaro wrote *De praticha seu arte tripudii vulghare opusculum,* and Antonio Cornazano published his *Libro dell'arte del danzare,* the dedication of which is dated 1455. A fourth work, signed by Giovanni Ambrosio of Pesaro, corresponds in title and content to that of Guglielmo. Together with these Italian treatises, we have about the same time from France and the Netherlands the precious manuscript of *basses danses* in the Royal Library in Brussels, in which the music is preceded by a detailed guide to dancing, and in 1521 from England the brief *basse danse* manual of Robert Coplande.

Dance teacher, dancing master—this is a new picture. No medieval author had anything to say about this. The time is past when everybody could dance from natural inclination and learned the unwritten rules from observation and participation. The spontaneity is gone. Courtly dance and folk dance are separated once and for all. They will continue to influence each other, but they have fundamentally different aims and different styles.

The contemporary engravers occasionally give us a glimpse into this world of the "untamed" dance. Israel van Meckenem depicts the dance "for the ring": four men move to the sound of the one-hand flute and the tabor in the most grotesque manner; arms and legs seem to be thrown out of joint; the trunk is bent back almost horizontally; and the head is flung backwards. The judges give the ring to the one who can dance most wildly. A similar dance is depicted on a page of *Das Mittelalterliche Hausbuch*. To the same kind of music two young fellows dance opposite one another, the trunk inclined, one knee bent, and the other leg thrown forward as in the Ukrainian *prisjadka*. These are real bravura and skill dances on the border line between dance and sport, as they are still to be found among peoples with a special aptitude for the dance, like the Alpine peoples, the Hungarians, the Slavs, and the Norwegians. The carved figures with which Erasmus Grasser decorated the Ratssaal in Munich in 1480 are the finest examples of this art from the point of view both of the dance and of sculpture. These so-called *maruschka* or *moriska* dancers are among the most beautiful illustrations of all times and all countries; and so are the sculptures on the *Goldene Dachl* at Innsbruck (Plate 20). They show an extremely fine understanding of bodily movement and at the same time the admirable dance knowledge of southern Germany at that period.

The courtly dance, however, has turned away from all that sort of thing. Its movements have become very much more restrained. The lively *piva* is no longer considered decent, and even in the *saltarello* there is only occasional leaping.

A particular circumstance, which like the change in the dance is a result of the increasing gap between the upper and lower classes, contributes to this end; namely, the change in dress. Since the last third of the fourteenth century, the gentlemen had been wearing a very short doublet and tight-fitting hose. At first glance this costume seems to facilitate free movement. But the contrary is the case. The man who cannot move because of his skin-tight clothing becomes a favorite butt of the poets. In addition there are the extreme shoes, the points of which project as much as two feet beyond the toes. In a dance of several persons these shoes must have created a problem of peculiar difficulty; at least—as contemporary pictures show—they prevented the dancers from turning their feet out naturally. For the ladies the close of the Middle Ages is the heyday of the train. Noblewomen trailed as much as five yards of the heaviest material behind them, and the burghers' wives permitted no official decree to interfere with their doing the same. A glance at Dürer's wash drawing of a Nürnberg woman in dance costume shows better than any description that expanded dancing must have been impossible in this garb.

But it is not a question only of expanded movement. In "society" all originality, all spontaneity, all improvisation are extinguished. The pantomime, at one time free to express emotion unconventionally, has crystallized into fixed forms given to it not by the dancers but by the dance teachers. The dance, which hitherto had been the child of passion and irresistible impulse, is now the product at once artistic and artificial of the masters. It is a work of art the correct figures, positions, and steps of which must be learned according to rule.

The textbooks serve this purpose in the most complete detail. They expound dozens of dance compositions step by step and attempt to systematize movements. But like all similar treatises they do not explain things which were self-evident to the author and his circle of readers and needed no exposition. Nevertheless, we are able to acquaint ourselves with most of the movements and the technical names for them. In the following section the most important of these will be discussed.

The Movements

THE KEY LETTERS. In the fifteenth and sixteenth centuries Italian and French authors all make use of the same letters for the designation of the main movements:

b = *branle*	c = *continenza* or *congé*
d = double step	r = *ripresa* or *démarche*
R = *reverenz* (bow)	ʃ = single step

This system of letters is obviously not the oldest dance script: in the municipal archives at Cervera a page with Spanish dance notation from the second half of the fifteenth century has been preserved. Five symbols are used:

$$\text{+} = R \qquad\qquad \text{=̄} = d$$
$$\text{=} = \int\!\int \qquad\qquad \| = b$$
$$\text{3} = r$$

The interpretation of these five symbols is not difficult. The horizontal cross can be explained from its position at the opening, *d* from the expressive juxtaposition of the symbols—one long step between two short ones—and the z-like symbol by its striking similarity to the *r* of the Brussels manuscript. The two vertical strokes might easily have been confused with the ∫∫. Their position in the context must have indicated to the expert that they stood for *b*. Similarly, the two horizontal lines indicated single steps ∫∫.

We notice that the symbols give a pictorial representation of the steps. The horizontal lines naturally tell the direction of the movement. Thus the single and double steps run horizontally, and the *branle,* as a side step, vertically. The 3 also reproduces the form of the movement and helps to clarify for us the obscure idea of the *démarche.* And this symbol is particularly important because it illustrates the connection between the picture script and the letter system. In this relationship the letter system can only be the derivative member.

THE TIME VALUE OF THE MOVEMENTS. The single movements were allotted a definite time value both by the Italians and by the French. In Burgundy the unit was the *note,* in Italy the *tempo.* We have evidence of this from two theoreticians, one from the fifteenth and one from the sixteenth century:

> *Ogni tempo si diuide in quatro parti* (Cornazano).
>
> *Quaelibet longa fit ex quatuor semibreuibus* (Arena).

Both these references are substantiated and supplemented from the *basse danse* in the *Orchésographie* of Thoinot Arbeau: the step unit equals one longa or four semi-breves. Thus we have:

Tempus or *Note* = ◗ = ◇ ◇ ◇ ◇
or, modern 𝅝 = ♩ ♩ ♩ ♩ or ♩. ♩. ♩. ♩.

FRENCH DANCE TERMS. *Branle. Le branle se doibt commencher du pie senestre / et se doibt finer du pie dextre et sapelle branle pour ce que on le fait en branle dun pie sur lautre.* (The *branle* should begin with the left foot and should end with the right foot and is called *branle* because one does it by shifting from one foot to the other.) Thus, according to this excerpt from the Brussels manuscript, the *branle* is a side step with a swaying shift of balance. In Arbeau's time, therefore, it is considered unorthodox to perform the *branle* by swaying the body to and fro twice on closed feet.

Congé. This word appears first in 1445 in the Nancy suite of dances printed below. Here it indicates the concluding movement of the individual dances. Since in the Brussels manuscript every *bassedanse se finne par branle* (ends with a *branle*), and since the word *branle* does not appear at all in the Nancy suite, *congé* must be equivalent to it. This becomes certain from the fact that Arena in 1536 writes *congedium* instead of *branle*. But even before this, in 1521, Coplande notes that in some French cities they call the *branle, congé,* "in englysshe leue" (leave). Arbeau uses *congé* to mean "farewell." It indicates *le congé qu'il fault prendre de la Damoiselle, en la salluant, la tenant tousiours par la main pour retourner ou l'ō a commencé* (the leave one takes of the lady, bowing to her, and keeping hold of her hand while returning to the place from which one has started).

Démarche—the same as the Italian *ripresa* ("in some places of fraunce they call the repryses desmarches," writes Coplande in 1521) —is not explained in the Italian sources, but it is described in the Brussels manuscript and in Coplande:

Vne desmarche seule se doibt faire du pie dextre en reculant et sapelle desmarche pour ce que on recule/ et se doibt faire en esleuant son corps/ et reculer le pie dextre pres de lautre pie.

A repryse alone ought to be made with the ryght fote in drawynge the ryght fote bakwarde a lytyll to the other fote.

La seconde desmarche se doibt faire du pie sinistre en esleuant son corps et se tourner vng petit deuers la femme et puis amener le pie dextre aupres du senestre en esleuant son corps pareillement.

The seconde repryse ought to be made (whan ye make .iii. at ones) with the lyft fote in reysynge the body in lyke wyse.

Le tierce se doibt faire en pie dextre comme la premiere et se doibt faire au dit lieu la ou se fait la premiere.

The thyrde repryse is made in place and as the fyrst also.

The two formulas are almost identical; on some points, however, they supplement each other. Apparently there is no actual walking backwards, but just a swaying back. While the body leans back, the right foot is drawn back close to the left—evidently from the first position to the third. The second *démarche* is a quarter turn to the right towards the lady; the left foot is certainly not drawn backwards, but to the side, and the right foot follows. The dancer is then in his original position and can execute the third *démarche* like the first one. All the foot movements are accompanied by the straightening of the body and were certainly performed on the toes.

The musical value of the *démarche* in the *basse danse* is the longa.

Double, pas double, double step: the left foot starts—the right is drawn past it, and the left follows. The first, third, and fifth double steps begin with the left, the second and fourth with the right foot. The time value of the *double* is the longa.

Reprise means the same as *démarche* in the fifteenth century. What Arbeau understands by it later is simply the *movimento* of the Italians.

Révérence is a bow to the lady at the beginning of the *basse danse.*
It is done with the left foot.

Simple, pas simple, simple step: one foot moves forward slightly and
the other is drawn after it. The time value is one breve. The first of
two *simples* begins with the left foot, and only after a double step with
the right. Here as with the double steps, the movement is accompanied
by a straightening of the body.

The pictures of the time show, in contrast to the later dance, a fundamental difference in the placing of the feet. There is almost no trace
of the spreading of the feet at right angles, as prescribed in the "positions" of the seventeenth century; they are almost always in a straight
line, as we have already seen.

ITALIAN DANCE TERMS. *Aere,* also written *aiere,* is in general "behavior, bearing, gesture," corresponding to the expression "to give
oneself airs." In particular, however, it means the straightening and
drawing up of the body.

The bearing of the woman is still determined by the ideals of the
minnesinger period. Her walk must be measured, dignified, and light,
her manner modest and gentle, but at the same time grave and stately.
Her eyes must not gaze haughtily and wander around, but must be
demurely lowered—a rule familiar also to the dance of Java and northern Spain. In a beautiful simile, Dante has described how a woman
should move in the dance:

> *Come si volge, con le piante strette*
> *A terra ed intra sè, donna che balli,*
> *E piede innanzi piede appena mette.*

> And as a lady turns her when she dances,
> With feet close to the ground and to each other,
> And one before the other scarce advances.
>   *Purgatorio,* xxviii, 52.

306

Campeggiato = movimento. See the discussion on page 322.

Continenza corresponds to the French *branle*. From Cornazano's definition, however, we learn nothing except that it has the time value of half a *tempus* (breve), half the value, that is, of a *branle*. Since Guglielmo Ebreo always states precisely on which foot the *continenza* is to be performed, *in sul pie manco* or *ritto,* on the left foot or on the right, we must conclude that the feet were placed slightly apart, not in close position.

Contrapasso is the alternating step. Three of these have the time value of two breves ⊏⊐ = 𝄽𝄽. Guglielmo Ebreo's Siena manuscript mentions *uno contradoppio* in two *bassedanze*. In both cases a backward movement is indicated, but nothing more definite can be determined.

The *contrapasso,* or "counter step," like other types of step such as the *branle,* the *ripresa,* and the *volta,* has given its name to an entire dance: the Catalan introduces his national dance, the *sardana,* with a *contrapás,* a quick, vigorous round dance in which there is much leaping and crossing of the feet. The Italian *contrapasso* of the end of the sixteenth and the beginning of the seventeenth century, mentioned by Caroso in his dance manual *Nobiltà di Dame* and by Giambattista Marino in his great epic *L'Adone,* has scarcely any relation to this Catalonian dance. It may, however, be related to the Spanish *contrapás,* which from allusions to it in Spanish literature seems to have been danced there in the seventeenth century. This foreign round— *baile extranjero*—was danced by two couples with figures, *vueltas* and *meneos,* "movements." We do not know, however, whether they were the same as the Italian *movimenti*.

Galoppo is prescribed in the Siena manuscript of Guglielmo Ebreo for the *mignota,* a *bassadanza* for three.

Mezzavolta (meçavolta) = half turn in one breve (⊓ = o). In the Domenico manuscript the *mezzavolta* is given only a semi-breve, but this is obviously a misprint.

Movimento means in general any movement, but in particular the rhythmical bending of hips, knees, or ankles. The time value is a semi-breve (□ — ♩). Compare the *scossetto*.

Ondeggiato, "wave movement," is a slow rising on the toes with a sudden dropping back. See the discussion on page 322.

Passo doppio = double step, like the *double*.

Passo sempio = single step, like the *simple*.

Posata, "halt," appears in the *bassadanza*, *Ays*, of the Siena manuscript of Guglielmo Ebreo. To this we can add a remark of Cornazano's: "To stop for the length of a breve now and then and stand as though dead is not ugly"—as in the *tango*.

Ripresa is often mentioned but never explained. There can be no doubt, however, that it was a backward movement corresponding to the *démarche*. Its initial letter *r* denotes in the French system of lettering the *démarche*, which is also called *reprise* in the Nancy suite. There is no other Italian term for a backward step. The time value of the *ripresa* is, like that of the *démarche*, one breve. And in one place Guglielmo Ebreo says expressly: "The men move backwards with two *riprese*." These *riprese* he calls *in portogallese larghe;* the ordinary *ripresa* must therefore have been brief. It could not have been standardized, however, for Cornazano considers it foolish to distinguish between long and short *riprese* and *continenze*. After a long *ripresa* comes a short one, he says, and vice versa. That the *ripresa* was occasionally a movement of the hips seems to be indicated by the phrase *sul galone*, or in Guglielmo Ebreo, *in galone*.

Riverenza = bow. Duration ♩ — ○.

Salto = leap. Duration □ = ♩.

Scambio, in Cornazano *cambiamento*, may be what Caroso in the next century calls *scambiata:* one foot is put forward, the other crosses it and touches the heel of the first from the outside, and the first steps back again.

Scossetto means "a slight trembling." In some dances, in the *Lioncello* mentioned by Domenico da Pesaro and included by Guglielmo Ebreo, for example, the man performs a *scossetto, e la donna gli ri-*

sponde. This fixed formula is also met with several times in Cornazano but under the name of *movimento;* he does not know the *scossetto* at all. From this it appears that the *scossetto* is a *movimento.* The movement is nowhere explained. It may perhaps correspond to the *Houbetschoten* (head shaking) and *Ahselroten* (shoulder shrugging) mentioned by the German minnesingers.

Sopra and *sotto* are terms which require explanation. Kinkeldey mistakenly assumes, from the fact that they occasionally appear with the phrase *dalla mano* (*di sopra*), that they mean right and left. This is out of the question, however, since the hands are always distinguished as *ritta* and *manca. Dalla mano* is the literal counterpart of the later German dance expression *"von der Hand, losgelassen,"* meaning "having let go of hands." This is quite obvious from Guglielmo Ebreo's description of the *Prigionera* of Domenico in which *dalla mano* is always followed by *e poi si piglino per mano* (and then they take each other by the hand). It is clear from many contexts, however, that *sopra* and *sotto* mean "forwards" and "backwards" and refer to the direction of the dance. It will be sufficient here to cite one example, the *bassadanza* of Domenico known as the *Dampnes;* here the first gentleman goes *ch'è dinanze,* in front of the lady—*dinanzi alla donna;* the second, however—*quello che è di sotto,* behind her—*dirieto alla donna.*

The English dance vocabulary has corresponding terms to describe the direction of the country dance: "top" is the end at which the musicians and spectators stand, "bottom" the opposite end. We have the same thing in the Spanish *arriba y bajo.*

Squassecto in the *Ballo rotibolo* of Guglielmo's Siena manuscript is probably the same as the *scossetto.*

Stracorsa, in the *fodra,* a *bassadanza* in Guglielmo's Siena manuscript, is not clear. The verb from which it is derived, *stracorrere,* may mean "to run beyond the goal" and also "to run to and fro." *Stracorsa* is undoubtedly identical with

Trascorsa, which Cornazano calls a *movimento accidentale,* an incidental movement, of which the time value is *ad beneplacitum.*

Volta tonda = a complete turn. Time value ⊓ = ♪ . The *volta* was usually taken with two single steps and a double step.

SPANISH DANCE TERMS:

Aire = *aere.*
Contenencia = *continenza.*
Contrapás = *contrapasso.*
Meneo = *movimento?*
Paso doble = *passo doppio.*
Paso sencillo = *passo sempio.*
Quebradito = *movimento.*
Represa = *ripresa.*
Reverencia = *riverenza.*
Saltillo, "skip."
Salto, "leap."
Vuelta = *volta.*

Much of what the theoreticians say becomes clear when we read the poem *Adone,* in which the Italian poet Marino has given a detailed description of a dance.* Terpsichore's testing and feeling out of the dance space before she begins is the *compartimento di terreno* of Cornazano and the *partire del terreno* of Guglielmo Ebreo. The hundred ways of swinging the hips and "playing" the thighs give a picture of the *movimenti corporei;* the correct beating or stamping of the tempo, "not too much nor yet too little," is nothing other than the obscure *partire delle botte* of the Italian dancing masters. Both forms of the *battuta* in the leap, the crossing and the striking, and the intricate, rapid movements of the legs, the *entrechat,* the *capriola intrecciata,* also stand forth clearly and alive. And three-dimensional space, of which the moderns are so fond of talking, is, we note with amazement, already a familiar

* The author has printed and translated this poem in the German edition of this book.

concept to the ancients. To be sure, his *Adone* was not written until the beginning of the seventeenth century and was printed in 1623. But Terpsichore's solo dance, of which Marino sings, is bound to no age. Going beyond the baroque and beyond Italy, he creates in the artistic wisdom of his plan the immutable ideal of all dance.

The Dances

The BASSE DANSE, though not of Spanish origin, is mentioned for the first time in the Spanish poem *La Danza de la Muerte*. The King declines Death's invitation to dance: *Yo non querría ir á tan baxa danza.* Unfortunately the date of the poem is not certain; some scholars attribute it to the fourteenth century and others to the beginning of the fifteenth. In any case the *basse danse* has been known since about 1400.

The *bassadanza,* as the Italians call it, is according to Cornazano the queen of dances: a slow and stately, but at the same time light, courtly dance with small gliding steps and a rising on the toes. Both as music and as dance, it probably derives from the *estampie*. But in the fifteenth century, according to a verse in the *Nef de Santé,* it was considered novel—a *façon De danser sur le nouvel art*. It continues into the sixteenth century, steps into the background about 1550, and gradually disappears. Only in Italy and in Spain do we still come across the name in the beginning of the seventeenth century; but the dance which bears it now, a mixture of *galliard* movements and *galliard* rhythms, variegated, tattered, has but little to do with the old *basse danse*.

The *basse danse* has one characteristic which for a long time it shared with no other dance: in the fifteenth century it lacked any regular arrangement of steps, any repeating phrase of movement. The *piva* and the *saltarello* have in the main only double steps. The *quaternaria* strings together periods of two simple steps and one *ripresetta*. The movements peculiar to the *basse danse* consist of bows, simple and double steps, and oscillations sidewise and backwards in endlessly varied succession, according to space and the ingenuity of the dance instructor and the master of ceremonies. The only plan that we can discover is in the distinguishing of definite groups of steps. The Brussels manuscript recognizes seven of these *mesures*. It points out in the very first sentence that there are three *mesures: la basse danse tout premier est en trois parties deuisees.* The interpretation that the dance is divided into three parts is false, linguistically as well as technically; *partie* should be translated as "heading," *deviser* (not *diviser!*) as "arrange." These three headings are *grande, moyenne,* and *petite mesure.* The *grande mesure* comes only at the beginning of the dance, *pour entrée de basse danse;* it comprises one *démarche,* one *branle,* two *simples,* five *doubles,* two *simples,* three *démarches,* one *branle.* The *moyenne mesure* has only two *simples,* three *doubles,* two *simples,* three *dé-marches,* one *branle.* The *petite mesure* consists of two *simples,* one *double,* two *simples,* three *démarches,* one *branle.* At the end of the introduction four further headings appear: *mesure très-parfaite, plus que parfaite, parfaite,* and *imparfaite.* The *très-parfaite* has *simples* before and after the *doubles,* three *démarches,* and one *branle;* the *plus que parfaite* is the same but with only one *démarche;* the *imparfaite* has three *démarches,* but no *simples* after the *doubles.* Obviously the *parfaite* is missing, or more correctly the *imparfaite.* For the *parfaite* must surely be the form with three *démarches,* while the *imparfaite,* corresponding to the *plus que parfaite,* must have had only one *démarche.* This group actually appears; it is found, for example, at the end of the fourth dance in the Brussels manuscript. A plan of twelve groups of steps is presented there:

Mesures

		r	b	ʃʃ	d	d	d	d	d	ʃʃ	r	r	r	b	grande
très-parfaites	{			ʃʃ	d	d	d			ʃʃ	r	r	r	b	moyenne
				ʃʃ	d					ʃʃ	r	r	r	b	petite

		r	b	ʃʃ	d	d	d	d	d	ʃʃ	r		b	grande
plusqueparfaites	{			ʃʃ	d	d	d			ʃʃ	r		b	moyenne
				ʃʃ	d					ʃʃ	r		b	petite

parfaites	*r b ʃʃ d d d d d*	*r r r b*	*grande*
	ʃʃ d d d	*r r r b*	*moyenne*
	ʃʃ d	*r r r b*	*petite*
imparfaites	*r b ʃʃ d d d d d*	*r*	*b*	*grande*
	ʃʃ d d d	*r*	*b*	*moyenne*
	ʃʃ d	*r*	*b*	*petite*

Starting foot: *l r lr l r l r l*   *r l r (l)*

From the important description of the *basse danse* contained in a Spanish manuscript from the sixteenth century in the library of the Academia de la Historia at Madrid, it appears that the first of the three *r*'s was equivalent in time to a double step—*la primera que ha de durar tanto como un doble;* the other two were apparently only half as long.

This by no means exhausts the number of combinations. At a court festival at Nancy in 1445, the following dances were performed:

Basse danse de Bourgogne

3 *simples*—5 *doubles*—3 *simples* to the right—3 *reprises*—1 *congé*—3 *simples*—1 *double*—3 *simples* to the right—3 *reprises*—1 *congé*.

De la reyne de cessile

3 *simples*—4 *doubles*—1 leap forward—1 *double* to the left—3 *simples* to the right—3 *reprises*—3 *simples*—1 *double*—3 *simples* backward—3 *reprises*—1 *congé*.

De bourbon

3 *simples*—2 *doubles*—1 leap—1 *congé*—3 *simples* to the right—1 *levée*—3 *simples*—1 *double*—3 *simples* backward—3 *reprises*—2 *congés*.

De Madame de kalabre

4 *simples* and 3 leaps—4 *doubles*—2 *simples* backward—2 *reprises*—1 *congé*—3 *simples*—1 leap on the right foot—2 *congés*.

Madame la daufine

4 *doubles*—2 *doubles doubles*—3 *pas menus* backward—2 *levées*—4 *simples*—3 leaps—2 *congés*.

Madame de façon

3 *simples*—1 *double*—3 *pas menus*—1 *levée*—1 *congé*—4 *doubles*—3 leaps—1 *double* to the left—3 *simples* to the right—3 *reprises*—2 *congés*.

Falet

1 *congé*—3 *simples*—4 *doubles*—3 steps to the side—2 *reprises*—2 *simples*—2 *doubles*—3 *simples* backward—1 *congé*.

The succession of three single steps constantly prescribed here conflicts with the directions in the Brussels manuscript: *iamais nya que deux pas simples ensemble selon lart de bien danser*—according to the rules of good dancing there must never be more than two single steps together.

The theory of group steps is, however, apparently limited to the north. None of the Italian manuscripts so much as mentions it. It is supported, nevertheless, in Robert Coplande's English translation of an unknown French *basse danse* manual in 1521, although the system is not so thoroughly worked out. For example:

La *brette* / foure measures.
R. b. ʃʃ. d. ʃʃ. r. b.
ʃʃ. d. r. b.   *Half parfyte.*
ʃʃ. ddd. r. b.
ʃʃ. d. ʃʃ. r. b.

La *royne* / foure measures.
R. b. ʃʃ. ddd. r. b.
ʃʃ. d. r. b.   *Unparfyte.*
ʃʃ. ddd. r. b.
ʃʃ. d. ʃʃ. r. b.   *Parfyte.*

The principles of execution are just as inconsistent as the arrangement of steps in the *basse danse*. Sometimes two and sometimes three or four participants are called for; sometimes they proceed in couples, sometimes *alla fila,* "in a chain." The dancer is very gentle with his partner; there is none of the rough play of the peasant dance, the *volta,* or the German turning dance. That they did not take hold of each other's hands as we do today is most beautifully illustrated in the carvings on the chests in the Florentine Academy Instead, the gentleman closed his fingers loosely around the lady's carelessly extended fingertips, either from above or from below. Accordingly, we often find in dance descriptions the expression *gli toccha la mano*—he touches her hand. At least in Spain there must have been in the sixteenth century a *basse danse* without touching: the Spanish manuscript referred to above counsels the gentleman to hold the hilt of his dagger with his left hand, but to let the right arm hang *como muerto*—as though dead.

According to a description in the Brussels manuscript there is a large and a small *basse danse;* the one is performed at the beginning and starts off with the bow, the other starts with the *pas de breban,* the Brabant step or *saltarello,* and consequently needs no bow. It does not state, however, that the *saltarello* must follow the *majeur,* but without this assumption the sentence *Basse danse maieur se commence par basse danse* would have no meaning. This results in the two combinations

Basse danse majeur + Pas de breban
Basse danse majeur + Pas de breban + Basse danse mineur.

It might be objected that there is no indication that the *saltarello* is preceded by a *basse danse.* Not only would it be unheard of in any period to begin a suite with a leaping dance; but Cornazano writing at the same time particularly stresses the fact that the *saltarello* always follows the *bassadanza.*

The triple nature of the *basse danse* is further attested by certain circumstances in the sixteenth century. Arena speaks of the *basse danse mineur* as *moytia brevis*—just as in the Austrian *Landla* the second part is called *Halba* (half)—while Arbeau refers to the *retour de la basse danse*, the return of the *basse danse*. The bow is missing here also. There is one change, however: the shorter *basse danse* stands no longer in third but in second place; the *saltarello* has moved back to third place, and in France is now called the *tourdion*.

The movements have remained the same; their gay variety has not been lost, but lives on under the name of the "irregular" *basse danse*. This designation is new; it indicates the crystallization of the dance into a normal type—into a succession of steps which corresponds exactly to a formula written down by Arena in 1536 and by Arbeau half a century later:

I. *Basse danse. Révérence, Branle, 2 Simples, 1 Double, Reprise, 1 Double, Reprise, Branle, 2 Simples, 3 Doubles, Reprise, 1 Double, Reprise, Branle, 2 Simples, 1 Double, Reprise, Branle, Congé.*
II. *Retour de la Basse danse. Branle, 1 Double, Reprise, Branle, 2 Simples, 3 Doubles, Reprise, 1 Double, Reprise, Branle, Congé.*

In symbols:

I. *R b ʃʃ d r a r b ʃʃ d d d r d r b ʃʃ d r b c*
II. *b   d r b ʃʃ d d d r d r b   c*

Neither of these successions of steps fits the formula of twelve *mesures* given in the Brussels manuscript, while conservative Spain, according to the Madrid manuscript, has retained a succession of steps which corresponds to the *mesure grande très-parfaite*.

Consequently every *basse danse* is different choreographically from every other one; the number of movements changes. It is therefore impossible, before the crystallization of the plan in the sixteenth century, to compose *basses danses* in advance. As accompaniment the musician takes a melody, a "tenor," and expands and contracts it rhythmically until it fits. As a result the melodies in the Brussels manuscript are given only in choral notes, without the time value of the single notes. The rough number of these notes and of the groups of steps is placed above—*Beaulte a xxxix notes a iiij mesures*—and the step symbols are placed below—*R b ʃʃ d r,* and so on. The only value of this method is that it gives the musician an opportunity, before the dance begins, to decide quickly how he will have to play to bring melody and dance together. That there would be no attempt to preserve the original rhythm of a song used as a dance melody will not disturb anybody familiar with the suppleness of late medieval melodic form and with similar phenomena in modern jazz.

As a rule the music was performed by several musicians, except where the simple melody was carried by the lute with chords by the cross-flute without any other accompaniment but the drum. Trios of shawms and trumpets, or lute, harp, and drum were used to accompany the *basse danse.* But other instruments also appear: Giovanni Ambrosio da Pesaro mentions the organ, and the Netherlander Israel van Meckenem in his Herodias engraving depicts zink, trombone, and beaked flutes with small drums. Giovanni Ambrosio states very clearly that every instrument plays its own melody, even the drum. Apparently the song melody which formed the foundation was elaborated in three voices according to the laws and traditions of impromptu counterpoint, and the drum—the pictures of the time reveal also how it was beaten— seems still to have had something of the rhythmical independence of the Orient.

The direct evidence of the musicians and theoreticians, particularly the directions of the contemporary lute players, is not sufficient to determine even approximately the tempo. We learn something of the relationship of the various dance tempi from a diagram of Cornazano's and from his statement: *in piua dui in un di bassadança, et han tutti due suo ordine*—the steps and rhythms of the *bassadanza* are twice as slow as those of the *piva.* With this our objective knowledge of the tempo of the *basse danse* comes to an end. The absolute time values can only be approximated. But this evaluation is not entirely baseless, since the results of two different computations coincide strikingly. The *basse danse* is the slowest dance. If any natural progression of movements is to be possible at all, the outside limit for the double step in quadruple time is six seconds. This means that ♩ or ♪ = M.M. 10. This measurement can be confirmed by an unobjectionable piece like the *basse danse* melody *Iouyssance vous donneray* in Thoinot Arbeau. If this twelve-eight melody is played by any number of musicians, the majority will take it at ♦ = M.M. 40. According to this it would seem that the tempo of the *basse danse* must be set at ♦ or ♩ = M.M. 40.

The rhythm of the *basse danse* has been discussed in detail by the author in an article in *Acta Musicologica* for 1931. The essential points of this study will be reviewed briefly here.

The first clear account is given by Cornazano in 1455: *Di bassadança ogni tempo si diuide in quatro parti. El uodo è una, cioè el primo moto surgente, poi ciaschun de gli tre passi che si fanno ne consuma uno quarto, che uiene a compire quatro.* Each tempus of the *bassadanza* is divided into four parts: the upbeat is one, that is to say the first rising movement (lifting the foot and straightening the body); then each step that is made is allotted one quarter beat, which makes four altogether. Arena agrees with this when in 1536 he says that in the *bassadanza, quaelibet longa de illis fit ex quatuor semibreuibus.* Blume is mistaken, therefore, when he finds in Arena "a fundamental change in dance form, which deserves to be strongly emphasized." Kinkeldey, more recently, is also mistaken when he claims *mensura perfecta* for fifteenth-century Italy. He has doubtless been influenced by the trapeze scheme given by Cornazano for the comparison of the duration of the steps but not for the rhythm (!) of the four types of dance, and makes use of the same measuring rod, the *tempus perfectum,* for all four of them.

The Paris Domenico manuscript says practically the same thing—that the *bassadanza* is *di major imperfecto, se comenza al suo tempo in lo vuodo e compisse in lo pieno.* It is in *tempus imperfectum* and in *prolatio major,* begins with the upbeat and ends on the downbeat.

Thus it would be, according to our notation, a duple or quadruple time with triplets, which is equivalent, for example, to twelve-eight time (as in the *estampie!*):

The manuscript repeats this in several places; it cannot be an error.

The situation in the *basse danse* of France and the Netherlands is more difficult than in the Italian *bassadanza*. All our information must be gleaned from the music and theoretical introduction of the only document extant, the Brussels manuscript. The introduction is difficult to understand, because the same technical terms are used sometimes musically and sometimes choreographically. The music is for the most part written in choral notes: their pitch is indicated, but not their time value. The steps written in alongside, however, do not correspond at all to the number of notes. Several musicologists have tried to explain this. But E. Closson's attempts at interpretation are just as unsatisfactory as those of his opponent Hugo Riemann, and the more recent efforts of Friedrich Blume have still not brought certainty.

It seems to me that the great mistake of all these scholars has been their trying to determine the rhythm of the *basse danse* from the mensural pieces. But when among almost sixty numbers only two of them are written entirely, and three of them partly, in mensural notes, and all the others are in unmeasured choral notes, does it not prove rather that these mensural pieces are complete or partial exceptions for which the rhythm must be given because it deviates from the ordinary rhythm? Can we be sure, then, that the mensural pieces in the Brussels manuscript are "pure" *basse danses*?

Number 58 gives precise directions: *Lomme se part de la femme marchant deux ſſ auant apres une double desmarchat Et ce temps pendant la femme se tourne sur pie coy.* (The man leaves the woman, taking two single steps forward after a double *démarche*. And during this time the woman turns on the toes.) A little later: *Ichi fait la femme che que lomme a fait Et parellement lomme ce que la femme a fait.* (Now the woman does what the man did, and likewise the man does what the woman did.) Numbers 55 and 56 contain similar directions. In 55: *Lomme et la femme ensemble doibnent ce cy / deux fois / Et puis sensuit la basse danse.* (The woman and the man must do this twice. Then the *basse danse* follows.) Then: *Lomme et la demme ensāble unefois. Lomme ce cy tout seul et puis / la femme toute seule. Lomme et la femme ensemble deux fois.* (The man and the woman together once. The man alone and then the woman alone. The man and the woman together twice.) In 56: *Puis ycy laisse lomme sa feme / et le [!] feme aussy apres laisse son homme. Eux deux ensemble font ce cy / sensuit la basse danse.* (Now the man leaves the woman and then the woman also leaves the man. These two do this together. The *basse danse* follows.) None of the other pieces mentions anything like this, and no description of genuine *basses danses* tells of such figures. Number 25 adds: *se danse a III psoñes en la maniere qui sensieut* (is danced by three people in the following manner), which indicates that it is an unusual type, as does also the foreign *Honneur* below the *pas.* Finally, Numbers 30 and 58, in contrast to the *basses danses* in choral notes, are simply called *Danses: La Danse de Cleues* and *La Danse de Rauestain.* Upon closer observation we note that the step unit in these dances is ◇ ◇ ◇ · ◇ ◇ ◇. We have an example here of what Cornazano refers to in 13 r: *Bassadança . . . si può dançare in modi cinque. . . . Quinto, pur in saltarello, mettendo dui passi di saltarello per uno tempo di bassadança.* (The *bassadança* . . . may be danced in five ways. . . . The fifth, only in *saltarello*, substituting two *saltarello* steps for one *bassadança* tempus.) If we take into consideration also that numbers 55 and 56 are labeled simply *en pas de breban,* and are therefore danced in *saltarello* step, and if we recollect that in both numbers the final sentence is *sensuit la basse danse,* it immediately becomes clear to us that the mensural pieces in the Brussels manuscript are entirely unsuitable to illustrate the rhythm of the *basse danse*—because they are not *basses danses.* It will be shown later that these pieces are free dance compositions of an imitative character.

The only reliable theoretical source for French dance practice is Arbeau's *Orchésographie*. To be sure, this work did not appear until 1588. But at that time the *basse danse* "had been abandoned for forty or fifty years" and the author, who has a good memory, is referring not to the second, but to the first half of the sixteenth century. Thus the source is half a century closer to the Quattrocento than the date of his manuscript suggests.

The music of the *basse danse*, says Arbeau, is *en mesure ternaire;* this has been mistakenly translated as "triple time" and the music has been transcribed accordingly. Actually, it is duple *Tempus imperfectum in prolatione maiori,* or twelve-eight time, as we have been able to ascertain from some of the *estampies* and from the Paris Domenichino manuscript. Arbeau's notation leaves no doubt. Each *pas* consists of one *quaternion* or four *mesures* of three semi-breves—not four beats (what an enormous unit!), but

In other words, Arbeau's *mesure ternaire* is the same as Domenichino's *Tempus imperfectum majus* and, since the division of the semi-breve does not concern the dancers, practically the same as Arena's *Tempus imperfectum minus* and Cornazano's quadruple rhythm. The *basse danse* is at all times and in all countries in even time.

This knowledge will be useful in dealing with the transcriptions of the late *basses danses* printed in the sixteenth century. The quadruple rhythm beginning on an unaccented beat is considerably better adapted to the eighteen *basses danses* published by Attaingnant in Paris in

1529 than quadruple rhythm beginning on an accented beat or than triple rhythm. An example is included in this book.

The SALTARELLO, called by the Spaniards *alta danza* and by the French *pas de brabant* or *breban,* was gay, light, and expansive, but only rarely a leaping dance in the true sense. Only good dancers, and they only *rarissimo,* were permitted to leave the ground (*dispiccare el suo tempo da terra*). The *saltarello* consisted rather of *passi doppi* in rapid tempo. It was danced *ondeggiato, per releuamento del secondo passo curto che batte in meço de l'uno tempo e l'altro, e campeggiato per mouimento del primo passo che porta la persona.* The ladies must take two *passi sempi ondeggiati e campeggiati in un solo tempo* and occasionally insert three changing steps.

Ondeggiare is, according to Cornazano's explanation, *uno alçamento tardo di tutta la persona et l'abbassamento presto.* A slow lift and quick drop are only possible in rising on the toes, so this must be the meaning here. The lift comes on the second short step: in the double step, the beginning foot makes a short step and, after the other foot has been drawn past it, a second short step, to reach the same spot. The term *movimento* reappears later in the dance vocabulary of the seventeenth century and is easily explainable there: *mouvement* is a flexing of the joints of foot, knee, and hip. *Campeggiato* remains obscure. It cannot be explained from the Italian. E. Levy, however, compares it with the Provençal *campejar* and translates it by *"tourner, voltiger,"* "to turn." This would fit in quite well. But the meaning "leaping joint or knee joint" from the Greek *kampē,* which in the Romance languages became *gamba, jambe* (leg), is still better. *Campeggiare* would then be the verb corresponding to *movimento,* and Cornazano's *campeggiato per mouimento* would be perfectly intelligible.

Cornazano's cloudy description becomes clearer when we compare it with a Spanish manuscript from the following century in the library of the Academia de la Historia at Madrid, in which there is a good explanation of how the *alta* should be danced. First a procession: bow, simple step, and five double steps, and at the end of each a *quebradito*. This *quebradito*, literally "a curtsey"—*quebrar en medio* means "to bend"—confirms our interpretation of the expression *campeggiare per movimento*. After the procession comes the dance figure proper:

1. Single step with the left foot forward; single step with the right foot backward.

2. *dar un saltillo sobre el pie derecho juntamente echando el izquierdo adelante en alto.* Hop on the right foot and thrust the left foot forward. This is what the French called *grue*.

3. *Luego ir á dar con el izquierdo en el derecho y juntamente levantarse atrás en el alto.* The left strikes against the right and at the same time is flung backward. This movement is not mentioned in the description of the Italian *saltarello*. It appears, however, in the description of the German *quaternaria*. It is simply the *ripresetta battuta detro el sicondo passo*, of which we shall speak later.

4. *Luego ir á dar con el derecho en el izquierdo y hacer sobre él dos quebraditos:* the same as Number 3, with *movimento*.

5. *Luego dar un saltillo sobre el pie izquierdo y tornar á hacer otro tanto hacia el otro lado.* Two hops in different directions on the left foot.

The whole thing is repeated. *Danzando sólo,* it continues, *en lugar de la mudanza que hace la dama, porque se cumpla el tañido, dan dos saltillos adelante y otros dos atrás.* The person dancing alone performs, instead of the figure, two hop steps forward and two backward in front of the lady, to fill out the music. We must conclude from this that the figure was usually danced by the gentleman alone and then, once more, by the lady alone.

According to Cornazano, the time of the *saltarello* is to the time of the *bassadanza* about as five is to eight; therefore ◊ =♩ = M.M. 64. Again according to Cornazano the *saltarello* is in triple rhythm beginning with an upbeat; the fourteenth century has already provided us with several examples of this. On the other hand, the fourth book of the *Intabolatura de Lauto,* printed by Petrucci in 1508, contains *saltarelli* beginning on the downbeat as well as on the upbeat: here the old name is used for a new dance—the *galliard.* In his *Lautenbüchlein* of 1540, Hans Newsidler gives the *Hupff auff* (introductory skip) of an Italian dance the parenthetical subtitle *saltarella;* and in Octavianus S. Fugger's lute book of 1562, we meet as a late example a *saltarello de megio.* What was called *saltarello* about 1600—the third part of the *Laura suave* of Caroso, for instance—is placed after the *galliard* in the suite, and in contrast to it, is greatly abbreviated rhythmically.

After the rigid separation of the court dance and the country dance, the *saltarello* became the dance which always followed the *basse danse.* These two dances fused into an inseparable unit in which all the nuances in the human mind and in the spirit of a dignified festival found expression: ceremonial grandeur and impish exuberance, restraint and wantonness, gravity and license. Even in the Middle Ages we have this contrast of the two forms: dances which were stepped (*geschritten* or *getreten*) and dances which were leaped (*gesprungen*). The *istampita* and the *saltarello* have become one.

This unity was so strongly felt that as a rule the second dance had no melody of its own, but only a rhythmic abbreviation of the melody of the first dance. In Number 55 of the Brussels manuscript, *Roti Boully,* we already have an example of this custom. The second dance was not usually written down: the musician had to read it from the music of the first dance, transposing it into another rhythm *cum proportione,* as it was called in the mensural theory of the time. Consequently the after-dance was often known in Germany as the *Proporz.*

The QUATERNARIA or *quadernaria,* according to Cornazano's important testimony, was popular in Germany; indeed, the *quaternaria* became so completely identified with the German after-dance that the Italians called it the *saltarello tedesco.* It had a very simple arrangement of steps: *dui passi sempi et una ripresetta battuta detro el sicondo passo in trauerso.* This probably means that there were two simple steps each of which received two quarter beats, and that on the fourth count the last foot performed a *battuta,* moving backward at the same time. What still remains obscure is cleared up by the Spanish description of the *alta,* which has already been referred to in the previous section: *Luego ir á dar con el izquierdo en el derecho y juntamente levantarse atrás en alto.* That is, just after the left leg has been thrown forward, it swings back against the right, and apparently as the foot is set back, the body is lifted. From the combination of *quaternaria* and *saltarello* movements in this Spanish description, we may perhaps conclude that there was a fusion of these two dance types in the sixteenth century.

The *quaternaria* is in quadruple rhythm beginning on a downbeat, and from this it gets its name: in the mensural theory *divisio quaternaria* is the division of the breve into two semi-breves of two minims each. We have already seen forerunners of this type of *saltarello* in the melodies of the fourteenth century in the last chapter. We can again determine the tempo by a comparison with the *bassadanza:* since Cornazano teaches that the time values of the *quaternaria* and the *bassadanza* are as five to six, we may assume the approximate value of the quarter notes to be M.M. 48.

The idea of an after-dance in quadruple rhythm sounds rather strange and suspicious. Perhaps the only discrepancy here is that we moderns are speaking of compound rhythm and the older writers of primary rhythm. If we write a *Ländler,* the real German after-dance of our time, as

instead of

the result is in one case quadruple time and in the other case triple time, without any change in rhythm at all. Up to the year 1900 the metronome mark for the *Ländler* was M.M. = 48. In the modern transcription this mark would change to ♩ ▬ ◊ . But in other places we have found this same M.M. 48 for the ◊ of the *quaternaria*. Thus the time value of each of the four semi-breves of the *quaternaria* corresponds exactly to that in the *Ländler,* bringing these two dances close together; only in the open after-dance there was a single step to each group of three notes, whereas in the *Ländler* there are three steps to each group. We have also musical proofs of the close relationship that was felt between these two dances: the after-dance which follows *ein seer guter welscher tantz* (a very good Italian dance) in Hans Newsidler's *Lautenbüchlein* of 1540 is, in spite of its ostensible Italian character, a pure *Ländler:*

The PIVA. To connect this word with the French *pivot,* "angle, pivot," as Diez does, seems to me the wrong approach. It appears with the same spelling as the name of a bagpipe; "dance to the bagpipe" would make good sense, and would bring the *piva,* through its name, close to the English hornpipe and the French *musette.* Boccaccio speaks of a dance of this kind to the bagpipe at an aristocratic manor on the evening of the seventh day in the *Decameron.*

The *piva* was another peasant dance which the gentry had taken up, but had already abandoned by about 1450. If it was still danced then, however, the lady must have been restricted to natural steps; the gentleman was permitted as many turns and leaps to all sides as he wished. The basic movement of the dance was the vigorous double step.

The *piva* could also be danced *a spinapescie*—"in herring-bone pattern." In the *Ballo Giove* of the Domenico, which Guglielmo Ebreo also mentions, the three participants dance *tre tempi di piva a spinapescie, tramèzandosi l'uno l'altro tanto, che ogni uno torni al luogo suo*—apparently a zigzag movement, in which the person in the middle must dance through those on the outside in the opposite direction. This is perhaps a forerunner of the zigzag movement of the later *courante*.

According to Cornazano the music of the *piva* was also called *cacciata*. There is the possibility here of a significant association. In all the Slavic languages the idea of leaping or skipping is expressed by a very similar word: Polish *skakać*, Czech and Serbo-Croatian *skákati*, Ukrainian *skakáti*, Russian *skakátj*, Low Wendish *skócyś*, and so on, which are related in turn to the Lithuanian *śókti*. This resemblance can be offered merely as a suggestion. If it could be proved, it would show conclusively connections with the Slavic countries.

According to Cornazano, this music was in quadruple time beginning on the downbeat and twice as quick as that of the *basse danse*. Its $\circ = \downarrow$ may therefore be estimated at about M.M. 80.

The *pive* published by Petrucci in 1508 for Giovanni Ambrosio Dalza, in the fourth book of the *Intabolatura de Lauto,* do not contradict this. It is confusing to ascribe to them three-eight time. The mensural signs ⌐ ⌐, which are placed above the fingering in the lute manuals, do not stand for one measure each, but for one beat—just like Arbeau's *mesure ternaire* in the *basse danse*.

The CALATA. A poem by Simone di Golino Prudenziani from the second quarter of the fifteenth century enumerates—apparently as dance pieces—*calate de maritima et campagnia*. In 1508 the Milanese lutist, Giovanni Ambrosio Dalza, published among other dance airs in the printer Petrucci's fourth book of the *Intabolatura de Lauto* two kinds of *calate, a la spagnola* and *a la taliana;* and as late as 1615, *calate* were danced at the court of the Medici in Florence.

Dalza's *calate* are not, as has been said, "very different in time and rhythm." Here, too, we must guard against confusing *mensura* with measure: just as in the *basse danse, quaternaria,* and *piva,* the division in the *calata* may be now two and now three eighths; the rhythm, however, is always quadruple—four-four or twelve-eight. There is no difference here between the Spanish and the Italian *calata*. The speed, to judge from the tempo marks, is comparatively lively.

Of the dance itself we can discover nothing. The name, however, still appears in the Spanish church dance of today: the third to the sixth figures of this *Sakral-Contre* are called *calado,* and the movement which gives them this name, *calarse*—literally "to make way through" —is the interweaving, the intersecting, of one row of dancers by the other.

The BALLO. Of these standard dances the Italian masters say only what is absolutely necessary, whereas for the irregular dances, intended exclusively for the higher circles of society, they give the most detailed instructions, *che son fora del uulgo, fabricati per sale signorile, e da esser sol dançati per dignissime madonne et non plebeie.* This is quite understandable, since it could be taken for granted that the former were familiar and the latter not, because they were frequently composed by the teachers themselves and apparently for definite occasions. Later authorities like Caroso and Negri ignore the permanent dances entirely and limit themselves to their own inventions. These irregular dances or *balli* bear special names and have distinct subjects. The commonest of these is again the courtship motif in its various forms: *La Mercantia,* the woman who confers her favors upon all, represented by a lady with three gentlemen, one beside her and two behind—eleven measures of *saltarello,* then a halt; the gentlemen in the rear take six *riprese* to the side; the lady turns; one of the two gentlemen takes three steps forward, turns the lady around him, and returns to his former position in three steps; now the other gentleman does the same; the original cavalier turns and approaches the lady again, and in this manner the pantomime continues. Or *La Sobria,* the woman who gives her favors to only one. Here we have the old group of three, one woman between two men (*gioue, bereguardo, leoncello*), which seems to live on in the Argentinian *palito.* Or perhaps the intertwining of two men and three women (*verçeppe*): all

328

form a chain, the ladies in the center; the *saltarello* commences, then a halt, and now begins a play with alternating turns, circling, and changing of places. Such a *ballo* may have as many as ten participants.

We must understand clearly that these pantomimes are purely choreographic. They have lost all traces of acting—glance, play of feature, gesture—and with them all realistic representation. What remains is only a succession of figures which do not actually depict the scene, do not make it obvious, but suggest it schematically to the initiate. The painting has become ornament, the pantomime of gesture has become a pantomime of figures.

This development must not be regarded simply as a decline of acting ability. It is rather a necessary outcome of the separation between the two great worlds of the dance. Together with the increasing limitation of movement in the courtly dance, the trend is away from the mimetic, and again imitativeness and expanded movement, non-imitativeness and close movement show themselves to be of like origin and spirit.

An unmistakable sign of the denaturalization and stylization of these pantomimes is their compression into the rigid frame of a procession: we do not find the name *saltarello* at all among Guglielmo Ebreo's titles. He knows only two kinds: *bassadanza* and *ballo*. Upon closer inspection we notice among his *ballo* descriptions certain recurring directions: *poi faccino sedici tempi de salterello—in prima quindici tempi di salterello—in prima sedici tempi di piva—in prima faccian tre tempi de salterello tedesco*. His *balli* are dance pantomimes for which the *saltarello, quaternaria,* and *piva* provide the frame. Much the same is true of Cornazano, and as we have shown above, exactly the same thing happened in Burgundy.

Thus the most distinctive mark of the *ballo* musically is the free change of time within the same piece: frame and picture must be clearly distinguished by the rhythm. This is why the *balletto* in the later musical dance suites has change of time as its peculiar characteristic.

The *bassadanza* is much more rarely brought within the frame of the *ballo*—and even then often in company with the *saltarello*. This is easily explained. For in the second half of the sixteenth century we see the disappearance, or at least the decline, of dances combining procession and episode. Others, like the *galliard* and the *courante*, eschew the pantomime. All these are after-dances, or at least lively dances. The introductory dances, the *allemande* and the *pavane*, indeed even the *basse danse* itself, are in the sixteenth century pure processions without pantomime. In the fifteenth century, however, we have pantomime as the chief element of the *saltarello* and only a little pantomime in the *bassadanza*. Furthermore, Guglielmo Ebreo, who expressly states that part of his *balli* had already been composed by his teacher Domenico, makes no mention whatever of a non-pantomimic *saltarello*. The further back we go in the Middle Ages the more conclusive it becomes that the after-dance was a pantomime. The Italian folk dance of which we have spoken before has maintained this medieval position in its regular division into procession and episodic-pantomimic *ballo*. Now the development becomes clear:

slow procession + lively pantomime

episodic "farcical" *bassadanza*

slow procession + (lively procession + pantomime)
slow procession + lively procession

The CHAIN ROUND, which was again to play a decisive role from the second half of the sixteenth century on, was completely ignored by the dance theory of the fifteenth century. That it was nevertheless danced is obvious. The historians, painters, and etchers show, moreover, that it was danced even in courtly circles. But at that time it was not considered quite proper—it is indicative that Count Baldassare Castiglione's *Cortegiano* of 1514, the book of etiquette of Italian Renaissance society, permits the *brando* and *moresca* to be danced only in *camera privatamente, ma in publico no così, fuorchè travestito*—only in private, but not in public, unless disguised. In Petrarch's opinion there was nothing more absurd than to see silly girls and soft, effeminate men running round in a circle, turning about and acting foolishly—*stultas muliercu-las, & viros, mulierculis molliores . . . circumferri, redire, ineptire.* This dictum may really not have been taken so seriously until two hundred years later, in a more formal period.

The figures of such a *brando* were probably the same as those of the chain dance in all times and all countries. A lively, rustling, fluttering round of angels in Antonio Rossellino's altar relief of the birth of Christ in the Montoliveto church at Naples from about 1475 illustrates the familiar motif: one after another through the whole circle the dancers whirl under the raised hands of their partners.

GERMAN DANCES. Of the dance in Germany in the fifteenth century we have scarcely any direct evidence and in particular no theoretical sources. For the German dance occupies an exceptional position. Undisturbed by all the changes and fashions of the international world launched now in Italy, now in Spain, and now in France, it goes its own way. Whether it is owing to the lack of really dominant courts or to the proximity of the small courts and patrician circles to the common people, whether it is owing to the superb and still unspent strength of the German folk dance, or to all these things together, the aristocratic and bourgeois society of Germany shows no disposition to abandon the native dances in favor of foreign ones. Hence dance masters and dance manuals are lacking, and any century of German dance can be determined from any other: its basic features have scarcely altered since the Middle Ages. Therefore, in order to make conditions in the fifteenth century clear, we need only refer to the section on the German dance in the next chapter. Just the open dances must be discussed here.

Like other peoples, the Germans combine a quiet introductory dance and a lively after-dance and call it simply *Tanz.* The quiet introductory dance seems to be explainable from the French *allemande* of the following (sixteenth) century: Thoinot Arbeau, of whom we shall speak in the next chapter, in 1588 calls this dance one of the oldest. It was an open couple dance of courtly nature like the *basse danse*, but sharply contrasted with it. Instead of the variety of movement characteristic of the Latin *basse danse*, the *allemande* had monotonous groups of steps—

> Step to the right
> Step to the left
> Step to the right
> Point foot to the left

forwards and backwards at will and with a certain stateliness—*plaine de mediocre grauité*. In Arbeau each (half) step gets one minim, and consequently each group of steps, one breve. Eight of these groups form the first part, their repetition the second part; the third part, apparently the old *quaternaria,* was danced in a lively skipping manner to another melody. Occasional contractions of the melody from eight to six groups of breves—the modern *Ländler* is similar in this—force the dancer to omit some of his steps; the reverse is true of the *basse danse.*

The couples proceed one behind the other through the hall, and turn at the end, without letting go of hands, unless the gentlemen choose to change partners. Here we encounter again, as in the popular *Greifpolka,* in the Austrian *Wechselbayrischen,* in the Bohemian *Strašák,* and in the earlier *polonaise,* the ancient motif of the exchange of ladies which marks the dance of the Nilotic Dinka and—with more serious implications—that of the southern Australian and New Mexican cultures. This motif has also passed over into an Italian *ballo:* in the dance of jealousy, *La Gielosia,* composed by Domenico da Pesaro, the foremost dancer goes backward from lady to lady; in the intervals all three couples together perform four *tempi di piva tedesca.*

In the seventeenth century, in 1636 to be exact, Father Mersenne reckons the *allemande* among the dances which have died out. People were content just to play the music of this dance.

The German after-dance, popularly called the *Hupfauf,* corresponded to the Italian *quaternaria,* which has already been discussed.

332

The close turning dance will be fully treated in the next chapter. As a heritage from the old peasant cultures of the Danube in the late Neolithic period, the turning dances have a place in every part of German, or at least of South German, history, in the fifteenth century as in the Middle Ages and in modern times, right up to the day of the *waltz*. If the period covered in this chapter has a special significance for their development, it appears to be this: they have won a place for themselves at the dances of good bourgeois society. According to a Nürnberg police order of the fifteenth century, both women and men were forbidden to do what must, from the description, have been the turning dance. Further proof of this is found in the poem by the Nürnberg meistersinger, Kunz Has, quoted in the next chapter, and also in many contemporary etchings and paintings.

The MORESQUE is the most frequently mentioned of all the dances of the fifteenth century. Whether balls, masquerades, or ballets are described, such names as *basse danse, saltarello,* and *piva* are seldom mentioned; it is almost always stated that the participants danced a *morisca*. Yet this dance is one of the most difficult to classify and characterize in all dance history. *Morisco* is the Spanish name for a Moor who after the country was reconquered remained there and became a Christian. The *moresque,* therefore, must be understood primarily as the shape which the romantic memories of the Moorish period in southern Europe took in the dance. It appears first in two forms: as a solo dance of approximately the type which might have been performed by dancers at the Moorish courts, and as a couple or group dance in which the motif was a sword combat between the Christians and the Mohammedans.

When the Bohemian, Leo von Rožmital, came to Burgos on his European tour in 1465–67, a great count invited for his entertainment beautiful maidens and women, "who were very richly dressed in the heathen or Turkish manner and almost everything, even the serving of the food and drink was done according to heathen customs. The women and maidens danced delightfully in the heathen manner. . . ." And at

Braga in Portugal he met another count "who had many heathens around him and many to serve. They had to teach my lord the heathen airs and sundry boys and other young fellows, who were pure heathens, performed strange and indeed charming heathen dances." Here we have the incursion of the genuine *moresque* dance into the Christian world of Europe.

Thoinot Arbeau tells of having seen, in the first half of the sixteenth century, after the serving of the evening meal in aristocratic houses, a young fellow—blackened to look like a Moor, with a white or yellow band around his forehead and bells on his legs—perform the *moresque* through the length of the hall and back again. He notates it in two-four time and gives the following order of steps:

Stamp	Stamp	Stamp	Stamp	Stamp
right	left	right	left	both heels

Since the stamping with the whole foot was too tiring, they limited themselves to the stamping of the heels. The few suggestions offered by Lope de Vega in his *Maestro de danzar* (1594) give quite a different idea: *floreta* (= *fleuret*), *atrás* (back), *contenencia, media vuelta, voladico* (leap?). And much later, in 1664, the Bolognese priest Sebastiano Locatelli observed a minstrel in Lyon dancing the *moresque* to the sound of the castanets.

Choral rounds on the theme of the sword combat between Christians and Mohammedans were performed in the ancient manner right up to the present time by the council and cathedral chapter at Toledo and by other Spanish corporations. In 1665 in Milan, Locatelli was very much surprised to see twelve Spaniards in the Corpus Christi procession dance a *moresque* with blows of the sword in front of the monstrance. In Guatemala they seem still to persist as *bailes de los moros*—four white men and four Moors portray with sword and bells the legendary war between Charlemagne and Tamerlane. A *moresque* on a large scale was

334

performed in Corsica up to the nineteenth century: a dance battle-pantomime with a hundred and sixty participants in two groups was waged for three or four hours to the sound of a single violin.

In Europe, however, the name *morisca* covers many choral dances in double file formation into which the particular motif of religious strife does not enter. Chorals of this kind, widespread among primitive peoples of a certain cultural level, are also very frequent in Arabian countries today, nor are they lacking in Moorish Spain. This is seen clearly from the highly prized *zambra,* which used to be danced to the sound of flutes and oboes—Arabic *zamr* means "oboe." This dance was, as the poets depict it, a *danza morisca,* executed by *moros* and *moras* hand in hand. In the Portuguese town of Pedrogam Pequeno this dance lives on as the *St. John's round* and in Toledo as the *cathedral dance:* the dancers, arranged in two files, move towards each other with swaying movements to the sound of castanets and return to their places in a curved line.

Considering the diffusion of double file choral dances through all parts of the world, it would not do to regard the *contre* dances of Spain simply as Moorish importations. But the preference of the Spaniards for these varied double chorals, as reflected in the dance poems of the sixteenth and seventeenth centuries, is largely owing to Arabic influence. This influence only becomes really effective when with the passing of political danger the internal resistance to the alien culture disappears. The choral dances of the Toledo choir boys, which originated in the West Gothic-Mozarabic liturgy and did not change over from the circle to the double front form until much later, are very indicative.

By a strange irony of fate the *moresque,* the most exotic element in the medieval dance, has in Europe given, if not its theme, at least its name to the national dance of a very un-Moorish and un-Spanish people. The English *Morris Dance,* to which we refer, is perhaps the dance most closely bound up with the life of the British people. It was therefore very properly revived in 1899.

Its characteristic form since the fifteenth century has been a group usually of six men with a fool, a boy dressed as a woman—Mayde Maryan—and another man carrying around his hips the cardboard figure of a horse. All of them wear fantastic costumes hung with many bells. Blacking of the face is also common. The musician has a flute and a small drum or a bagpipe, today often a violin or an accordion.

The *Morris Dance* is definitely expansive and is based on manly strength. It has neither turns nor dancing on the toe, neither gliding nor swaying; its step is a vigorous thrusting forward of the one leg, while the other skips lightly. This thrust may resemble an ordinary marching step, but may also be intensified so that the foot flies up as high as the knee of the other leg—like the Prussian goose step. Besides this step the *Morris Dance* also has leaps a foot high. The loud ringing of the bells must accentuate the energy of the thrust and fall. The arms are swung vigorously at the same time, and in some instances we also have at the conclusion the shouting so characteristic of dances of strength.

The classical form is still two rows of three dancers each. With innumerable variations these rows move to and fro, or they combine in a chain, or perform opposite each other. In certain figures the sticks are struck together rhythmically when the partners meet, as among primitive peoples. The circle is rarely used. Yet it is undoubtedly the older form, not only because line dances in themselves are later, but especially because it still bears obvious traces of the old fertility ritual. One of the ring dances is called *bean setting* and requires rhythmical stamping and raising of the dance stick: the dibber or planting stick makes the holes in the ground to receive the seed. Here the *Morris Dance* is close to the Malayan sowing round.

Is this *Morris Dance* really related to the *danza morisca,* or are they connected only in name? That both may have the double file choral form would scarcely prove a connection. Nevertheless, all doubt of their relationship is silenced when we hear that the same melody which Arbeau gives for the genuine *moresque* in France was printed as a *Morris Dance* in England in 1550 and is still played by English fiddlers today.

The relationship between the *moresque* and the *Morris Dance* explains why many features of the latter recur in the modern church dances of Toledo and Seville. As in the *Morris Dance,* the choir boys of these two cathedrals stand in two rows opposite each other and execute a succession of figures: to and fro, forward and backward, in a circle, in a large chain and in a small (heys, *cadenas*), five different figures of meeting and interweaving (cross over, *calados*), two crosses, the large S, and the simple "alas" figure. If these are all figures common to the *contre,* nevertheless the relationship between the *Morris* and the church dance appears very close when we note also that the boys have bells attached to their clothes and that the Toledans occasionally introduce the stick-dance figures and female disguise. It becomes still closer when we hear that up to the Elizabethan period in England the *Morris* was also danced in the church at Whitsuntide. And the fact that the classical number of participants in the *Morris Dance,* six, was once the same for the Spanish cathedral dance makes it almost irrefutable—and even today, although there are ten performers, they are still known as *los seises,* "the sixes."

But are not several of the special motifs of the English *Morris Dance* lacking in Spain? Have not the Britons, besides the six main dancers, the man disguised as Mayde Maryan and the other man with the hobbyhorse around his hips, and was not the music provided by a single musician with a one-hand flute and a tabor?

In the Balearic Islands, where there is an ancient tradition of Moorish dancing, the Spanish church dance, it seems, can be traced much further back than in Seville and Toledo. Its classical forms are *cossiés* and *cavallets.* In the first of these *bailes,* just as in England, six men, a man dressed as a woman (*dama*), and a *diablo* dance; all are ornamented with bells. The *ball de cavallets* is a *contre* of many figures. In the form of this dance found in the city of Felanitx there are six dancers richly hung with bells and with hobby-horses around their hips, and one man dressed as a woman; the musical accompaniment is furnished by a pipe and a small tabor in one hand!

Northwards, in the valley of the Rhone, we find reminders of the hobby-horse dance. The engraver Bernard Picart (1673–1733) has caught in one of his plates *Leis Chivaou frus,* the dance of the merry horses: a double file of dancers with large cardboard horses around their hips dancing to the sound of the drum and the one-hand flute.

And now there is no end to it. We are drawn from dance to dance, from country to country, from the Basque *zamalzain* and the German *Schimmelreitermaske* (masque of the man on the white horse) to the ecstatic hobby-horse dance of the Javanese—which, thanks to the kindness of Dr. Kunst of Bandoeng, I am able to illustrate with two excellent photographs (Plate 3). From ancient China in the north comes another horse dance, the characteristics of which are not known. And to the west, in central Asia, the Tadjik dancers of Pamir tie a stick with the mask of a horse's head in front of their bodies and, after much whipping, "die." Here close to the source we find the motif divested of its religious and spiritual significance. A Greek dance is shown in Plate 11.

Between Asia and western Europe we must pause once again. Is not the dance of Mallorca that same hobby-horse dance which is performed to the point of extreme ecstasy by the Rumanians and Bulgarians at Whitsuntide and other annual festivals? In the Balkans only men are present, in uneven number; a kind of brotherhood unites them. One is the dance leader, another the fool, with saber or whip, masked and sometimes carrying a phallus and making indecent gestures, and another bears a horse head on a pole. All have bells on their legs; some, the *Arapi,* "Moors," blacken their faces; occasionally some of the young men disguise themselves as women, veil their heads, and speak in a falsetto voice. The dance itself is executed with vigorous movements and leaps in a circle around the fool. As a rule a kind of fencing game seems to be connected with this dance; formerly swords were used, today they use only wooden sabers. When two such groups meet, they engage in bloody combat—if somebody is killed he is buried on the spot without a priest, and the murderer goes unpunished.

The meaning of this dance is unmistakable. The annual festivals as special occasions, the fool, the phallus, the whip, the fertility demon in the shape of a horse, the leaps, the bells, the feminine disguise, the sword game—these are all well-known defense and fertility motifs. The *joc de călușari,* the "hobby-horse dance," is a pure life and vegetation choral. The sick were led to it and mothers laid their babies in the arms of the dancers.

How does this dance compare with those of England, Spain, and the Balearic Islands? In order to find our way here, we must apply the statistical method: the less mutilated and corrupt are dances in which form and purpose point so clearly to great antiquity, the older they must be; that is to say, of several variants the oldest must be those which most closely agree. If we compare them with this in mind, we obtain the following result:

> England—Rumania
> England—Mallorca
> England—Mallorca and Spain—Rumania
> Spain—Mallorca
> Spain—Rumania.

Thus the *Morris Dance* and the *joc de călușari* have the most characteristics in common, the Rumanian dance and the Spanish cathedral dance the fewest. The *Morris* and the *călușari* represent the oldest type. There is still another proof which supports this. Their essential divergence appears in the double file arrangement and in the formation of figures—both of which are characteristic of the peasant and seignorial culture, the highest level, that is, of the Tribal culture. The *Morris* has the double file and the figures, the *călușari* does not know them at all. This makes the succession still clearer:

> Rumania—England—Mallorca—Spain.

The order is attested by the extremely ancient features of the *joc de călușari.* The seriousness of the battle is not the decisive factor. It is the accompanying circumstances which are significant: the denial of Christianity in the omission of the priest and the denial of the State in the freeing of the wrongdoer. And there is above all a custom to which we have not yet referred: after the dance the attributes of the fool are destroyed and buried. We are familiar with this anxious destroying and relegation of objects used in the cult, especially the masks, from many cultures in which totemists and old planters unite. The performance of the dance exclusively by men also belongs to this level. Indicative of a masculine culture, too, is the fact that the Rumanians regard their dance as a sun ritual. Furthermore, the uneven number prescribed for the participants and for the years they pledge themselves to dance also points to masculine culture.

All these parallels might seem to make it doubtful that the *Morris Dance* originated in the Moorish dance. But what about the blacking of the face in England and in Rumania, where in addition the blackened fool is called the *Arap*? There is no contradiction here. For the blacking of the face to designate the earthly or subterranean opponents of the ethereal forces is an ancient religious heritage. Since, as we shall demonstrate later, this original significance is intimately and inextricably linked up with the whole dance, we have no occasion, indeed we have no right, to bring in the struggle between the Moors and the Christians as an interpretation of the blackening. But what about the name *Arap*? This is easily explained. The original religious meaning had disappeared in the late Middle Ages, and it was almost inevitable that the contemporary use of "black" and "Moor" as synonyms should take its place.

But we must look once more from the *căluşari* to the *moresque:* the wild, bloody, indeed fatal combat between the two groups has no counterpart in England, or in the Spanish church dance, or in Mallorca. We noticed, however, that one form of the *moresque* depicts a battle between two sides. Now the connection of all these dances becomes clear. The dances described belong in the broad group of the fertility rites and transgress on the domain of the sword dance. Their essential features were already developed in the Early Tribal cultures of the Miolithic period. The contact of the Middle Ages, in action and reaction, with

Oriental ideas, led almost inevitably to a re-interpretation of two motifs which had become unintelligible: the blacking of the face and the combat between two sides—the former in all European countries, and the latter characteristically only in the western Mediterranean district, for which every struggle between two sides had to take on the special significance of the war with the Moors for over seven hundred years. Thus the concept of the *moresque* is for the most part nothing but a late revaluation of ancient fertility ceremonies.

The COURT BALLET. The choral dance, especially the *moresque,* when performed as a court entertainment, becomes a ballet. The spectacle which Charles V of France presented before the German Emperor Charles IV in 1377 was of this type. Two heavily armed wagons drove up to the festive board; one represented the city of Jerusalem with the Saracens, the other a galley with the soldiers of Godfrey of Bouillon; after a long, stylized combat the crusaders stormed the city. Even in the fifteenth century the *entrée de morisque* at the court is almost synonymous with *ballett;* and in the Italian ballet also, the Moorish combat and the bell-bedecked fencers long occupied a special position. Under the name and in the form of the Moorish dance the ancient mysteries of growth and life from the masques and mummeries penetrated the entertainments of the court.

This tradition was brought to an end in Italy. The Renaissance and humanism imposed a stricter dramatic unity upon the ballet and substituted themes from classical mythology for those of medieval romance. To get some idea of these mythological, allegorical spectacles, we should look at the well-described ballet which was performed in 1489 at the marriage of Galeazzo Visconti, Duke of Milan.

The guests were led into the banquet hall, where the table was bare. At the same moment disguised figures entered the room through another door: Jason and the Argonauts appeared in war attire, did homage to the newlyweds, and spread the Golden Fleece as a covering over the table. Then Mercury appeared: he had stolen a fatted calf from Apollo and everybody danced around three times, like the Jews around the golden calf. To the sound of horns Diana and her nymphs brought in Actaeon, transformed into a stag, and congratulated him on his good fortune in being eaten by Isabella, the ducal bride. Orpheus carried in the birds which he had caught when, charmed by his song, they had come too near. Theseus and Atalanta hunted the Calydonian boar in a wild dance and proffered their captive in a triumphant round. Iris in her chariot brought the peacocks, Tritons served the fish, and Hebe and the Arcadian shepherds, Vertumna and Pomona, nectar and dessert. . . . After the meal Orpheus appeared with Hymen and the gods of love. Connubial Faith, brought in by the Graces, presented herself to the Duchess, but was interrupted by Semiramis, Helen, Phaedra, Medea, and Cleopatra singing the charms of unfaithfulness. Connubial Faith ordered them out and the goddesses of love threw themselves with torches upon the queens. Whereupon Lucretia, Penelope, Thomyris, Judith, Portia, and Sulpicia laid at the feet of the Duchess the palms which they had earned by a life of chastity, and, rather unexpectedly, Bacchus, Silenus, and the satyrs appeared to conclude the ballet with a lively dance. . . .

In all the high cultures, in ancient Egypt as in India, eastern Asia, and classical antiquity, the mimetic powers crystallize in the dance into a work of art intended for exhibition—the ballet. The pantomimic dance leaves the realm of society and falls into the hands of professional dancers, who perform it more and more as a spectacle for the people. But the situation within and outside Europe is not the same. In the Orient the transition takes place almost imperceptibly. Natural phenomena, hunting and agriculture, combat and love, myth and tribal history—all these themes glide smoothly from the old, purely religious dance, which desires only to be itself and to work magic, into the new form which desires to make believe and produce aesthetic effects. In Asia and in Greece and Rome the spectacular dance is nurtured by the religious faith and mythology of the nation; its themes are the gods and the forces of nature and the popular heroic myths, which touch upon the world of the gods.

To the rapt spectator they remain as serious, as much a part of his life and the life of his race, as they once were to the worshiping temple-goer. Consequently the ballet of the Orient is in the deepest sense true and inspired.

The European ballet has also grown organically. But the line of ancestors is too long, this late descendant is too far removed from the creative dawn, and its blood is thin and vitiated. The European ballet also plunges into a world of gods and heroes, but this world is not its own—it is far distant from the living piety and tradition of the people. The European ballet also depicts natural phenomena and human activity, combat and love. But already, hundreds of years before its establishment, these motives have lost their magic and religious significance and have become merely spectacular. The European ballet is no longer in the service of God and Nature, but in that of the ruling princes. Its beginning and end are cringing flattery, not God-fearing piety and devout prayer—and what goes between is empty play.

Its use of fencing has no longer anything to do with the primitive struggle against spirits; its love scenes have left the broad world of the all-fertilizing Eros; its masks, spirits, and gods are degenerate remnants of May festivals, carnival mummeries, and the compositions of dancing masters, without any connection either with the lineal past or with the living present. Magnificent images have become petty caricatures, spiritual symbols have become empty allegories.

At this stage the ballet has but slight interest for us. It belongs essentially to the history of festivals and the theater. To be sure, the dance plays an important role along with poetry, music, costume and decoration, but it meets scarcely any new problems in the ballet. At best it finds there only a new field of activity, a new application, and a new outlet for its mimetic powers. And only at this point does it demand our attention. For it becomes plain here that the tendency at the close of the fifteenth and in the sixteenth century to remove pantomime from the social dance, of which we have spoken above, does not denote any simultaneous decline in the popularity of the pantomime or the ability to perform it. Rather the social dance discards the pantomime because the latter is flourishing more vigorously outside the purely social realm. The ballet has taken its name from the free, mimetic dance creations of the fifteenth century: it has become their successor and has robbed the social dance more and more of its imitative powers and forced it into the imageless category.

1500–1650

THE AGE OF THE GALLIARD

General Characteristics

The period from 1500 to 1650 has left us four great monuments of the dance, two Italian and two French. The two French works cover half a century. In 1536 Antonius de Arena, *Provençalis de bragardissima de Soleriis,* published a remarkable little book entitled *Ad compagnones qui sunt de persona friantes, bassas dansas et branlos practicantes* in macaronic Latin verse with scraps of Provençal, Italian, and French, which treats among other things the contemporary dance. Incomparably more thorough and more serious is the *Orchésographie* brought out by Thoinot Arbeau in 1588. His real name was Jehan Tabourot—he has transposed the letters to make his pseudonym—and he was a cathedral canon. This is fortunate in a way. For this book is free of the annoying qualities of the professional manuals. The professional dancer is a poor expounder. He devotes himself rather to his own inventions than to general principles and expects his readers to be familiar with the basic concepts and to have practical instruction: "If my honored reader," writes a dance teacher of this sort in the eighteenth century, "should not be satisfied with this description of *cotillions,* he may give me the honor of a visit and I will make these dances clear to him both in theory and practice." Arbeau, on the other hand, writes his thick book in the lively form of a dialogue between the expert and the eager student. "Capriol" leaves no question unasked, and "Arbeau" does his best to give him a clear and exhaustive answer. He describes every dance with all its deviations, he deals with the most minute partial movements, and illustrates them; indeed, he is the only one who gives sample melodies on which the corresponding dance movement is indicated note by note.

Anyone who opens up, after Arbeau, the *Ballarino di M. Fabritio Caroso da Sermoneta,* which has appeared in so many editions, must be very much disappointed. Caroso does not know how to explain, and the dances which he describes are *diuerse sorti di Balli & Balletti,* but not the most popular. Even less satisfactory is the second dance author of the time, Cesare Negri, *Milanese detto il Trombone, famoso, & eccellente Professore di Ballare,* as he proudly styles himself on the title page of his *Nuove Inventioni di Balli, Opera vaghissima,* published in Milan in 1604. The pompous use of his own portrait as frontispiece suggests that we may expect more self-complacency than information from this author. As a matter of fact, his description of the *passi* is derived from Caroso, and aside from his own dance compositions, which are elaborately described in a special chapter, he has little of his own to offer the student except the *Luoghi è gran personaggi doue, & alla presenza de quali ha l'Auttore ballato,* and again in a special chapter the *Nomi de i Prencipi all presenza de quali ha l'Autore ballato.* The study of the literary products of dancers is not always a pleasure.

The virtuosity complacently reflected in these Italian writings is, however, in the last analysis merely a sign that the social culture of Italy in the sixteenth century is on the decline. In the chaos caused by the conflict of beliefs and the friction between the Latin and the Gallic spirit, France prepares to take over the leadership in the world of court and social life and at the same time the cultivation of the higher forms of the dance. For the time being, to be sure, the two styles are sharply differentiated from each other. When Ercole d'Este is wooing Renée of Lorraine in 1528, he himself dances *a la Italiana* at the Court of Saint-Germain, while the natives dance *a la Francese.* And for a long time the music books retain this distinction: "in Italian style" and "in French style." But the transition is shown clearly when about 1520 Federigo Gonzaga in Rome takes dancing lessons *alla francesca.*

But this change affects only social dancing. For the professional dance during the second half of the century, the most celebrated dancers of Milan and other northern Italian cities were called to the royal court in Paris and kept there on the most handsome terms. And for the ballet the Italian ladies among the Queen's maids of honor were especially preferred. Milan and Lombardy were still the chief centers of the art of dance.

Arena in 1536 mentions only two society dances, the *bassadanza* and the *brando:* the old distinction of couple dance and choral dance still holds. But soon the *basse danse* disappears, and this can be explained only in relation to the general change in the position of the arts. The various styles are classified to a degree hitherto unknown, and that clean-cut division of types which still persists makes its appearance. The desire for separation, classification, and purification goes through all forms of intellectual life: in religion it brings about the reformation and the counter-reformation; in scholarship, the humanistic severance of worldly knowledge from ecclesiastical dogma and the demarcation of the various disciplines. What happens here is reflected also in the arts. The ingenuous mingling of sacred and mundane themes ceases: heaven and earth are carefully kept apart. Serious subjects may no longer be brightened up with *divertissements;* everyday life and the description of manners receive in their proper place the treatment due them. In music the fatal separation of vocal and instrumental forms begins, and within these forms religious and worldly needs, restrained and abandoned moods, serious and gay feelings create their own particular fields.

In the dance we note the same tendency toward the rejection of all mixed forms. The *basse danse* is the first victim. The unhesitating interpolation of *saltarello* measures in the midst of the stately procession was as shocking to the Renaissance as the playful fluttering of little cupids on the tombstones of the past century. The struggle proceeds further against the intermingling of gliding or leaping dances with pantomimic scenes. The *galliard* and the *courante,* in which the chief emphasis is on the non-pantomimic, must forego the pantomime. The various *branles,*

346

on the other hand, in which the choral movements merely furnish the frame for the completely or partly pantomimic couple dance, gradually discard the choral round and retain only the dramatic episodes.

At the same time the different categories are more sharply distinguished: the "stepped" couple dance becomes simpler, graver, and more stately—a ceremonial procession devoid of levity in which at court and state functions kings comport themselves like bishops and cardinals.

The real dance needs of the young people, however, are now freed from the tyranny of courtly solemnity and seek satisfaction in more lively dances. How this takes place is extremely indicative of what happened in France between 1550 and 1650. Heinrich Morf once remarked of the French language around 1550: "Word coining is the order of the day and foreign and native, classical and dialectical are combined with uncontrollable zest. Wealth of vocabulary is the motto." If we substitute "wealth of dance forms" for "wealth of vocabulary," Morf's sentence expresses precisely what takes place at the same time in the field of the dance. The dance of "uncontrollable zest" is the *galliard*. The picture has changed considerably. The preceding period assigns the role of after-dance to the quick stepping and leaping dances; the ceremonial *bassadanza* is the main dance in every respect. The *galliard* is also an after-dance; but its introductory dance, the *pavane*, is of relatively slight importance and soon leaves the field. The *galliard* absorbs the entire gamut of the dancer's movements. Arbeau takes fifty pages to cover all its varieties and deviations. We shall seek in vain a ceremonial dance to put beside it. Even at the beginning of the seventeenth century, in the reign of James I, an English court ball consisted of *galliard, branle, branle, galliard, branle, courante. Galliards, branles, courantes*—even at the court the ceremonial dance could be dispensed with.

The number of gay dances, on the other hand, increased tremendously. Never were so many lively, excited dances performed. And the dancer of the French Renaissance does the same thing as the word coiner of the period: what is lacking in the written language, the provincial dialects must supply; what is missing in the courtly dances, the peasant dance of the country districts must provide. The popular chain choral plays, together with the *galliard*, the leading role. It is now called the *branle* instead of the *carole*, and the name is qualified in various ways: *branle des lavandières* (the washerwomen's dance), *des pois* (the pea dance), *des sabots* (the clog dance), and especially by local designations—*branle de Bourgogne, du Haut Barrois, du Poitou*. The Gapençais district must furnish the *gavotte*, Brittany the *triori;* the *bourrée* is taken from Auvergne. Never has so much folklore been danced. Movement does not stop at international boundaries; there is a *branle d'Ecosse* and a *branle de Malte*. Spain contributes the *pavane*, Italy the *galliard*, Germany the *allemande*, and the Canary Islands the *danse des Canaries*.

At a great feast which Catherine de Medici as Queen gave at Bayonne in 1565, groups of dancers from the French provinces performed during the meal, each *à la façon de son pays:* the girls of Poitou accompanied by the bagpipe, the girls of Burgundy and Champagne by the drum, fiddle, and shawm; the Breton girls danced *passepieds* and *branles gais,* and the girls from Provence danced *voltas* to the sound of cymbals. All the other provinces were similarly represented—native folklore illustrated in the dance.

We see dance and literature continue further along the same road. At the close of the century both turn towards Spain. The novel is constructed on Spanish models, and the motley tragicomedy of Alexandre Hardy draws consistently upon the matter of the Spanish stories. Cervantes and Alarcón are imitated, and Corneille writes a *Cid*. At the same time the Spanish dance is introduced; *zarabanda, chacona, pasacalle, folía* become familiar dances north of the Pyrenees. But we must draw a distinction here: the introduction of the Spanish *pavane* at the beginning of this period grew out of the Hispaniolization of social fashions, which was most clearly expressed in the changes of dress. What happens at the end of the century, however, is a Hispaniolization of art which is no longer the result of political and dynastic or courtly and social currents, but of that romanticism which turns away from the formality and flatness of civilization to the ebullience of the provincial and towards the mysterious aroma of the exotic—that romanticism which was able to combine the apparent antitheses of ultra-realistic painters of peasants, soldiers, and rogues, and those fugitives from reality, the explorers, the gold-seekers, and the visionaries.

We shall quote here what an outstanding authority on modern Spain has to say of this semi-exotic Spanish dance in the passionate, panto-mimic form in which it began to have an influence in France at the turn of the century.

"We are accustomed to think of dancing as a movement of the feet, but the Spanish dance is more than that. In Spain they dance with movements of the hands as in India, Java, and Japan, they dance with the hips, with movements of the body as in Africa and Arabia, and the feet serve less for the locomotion of the dancer than as the physical expression of his emotions. The charm of the European dance lies in the contact of man and woman, in the common rhythm and harmony of movement. The European dance is a physical duet, the captivating charm of which lies in the unison of motion. One dances for oneself, not for others. The poetry of proximity is given perceptible form in the dance. The Spanish dance is fundamentally different. Its charm lies in the spectacle, not in the contact. It is the physical expression of an emotion. It symbolizes sensual receptivity and sensual power. Indeed, the most remarkable thing about it is the strongly marked symbolism of rejection. It is much oftener a dance of coldness than of ardor. In love as in the dance resistance and coldness are the best means of enticing men and driving them to madness. But aside from its aim of exciting the onlooker, the Spanish dance has still another goal—and that is self-excitation. The dancer fascinates the spectators and dances herself into a state of ecstasy. The motion of the hips, the *zarandeo,* with which it is possible to express every degree and shade of sensuality from lasciviousness to the magic flame of ecstasy, is of incredible suggestive power. One might say that in this movement lies the magic of sex. And to this swaying and twitching of the body, the mysterious art of which Eve learned from the serpent in Paradise, the Spanish dancer subordinates the turning and twisting of the hands, the skipping and gliding of the feet, and last but not least the play of the eyes. The symbolism of the dance would far overstep all boundaries of moral censorship, were it not that the natural decency of the Spaniard interposes to redeem it. This sense of decency has not only freed these dances of all unpleasant and repulsive qualities, but has even adapted them to the conventions of the bourgeois home. Nowhere does one see the *sevillana* danced more beautifully and more purely than in the *patio* of a bourgeois house in Seville."

We called these dances semi-exotic. This was rather for the sake of comparison: the *sarabande* and the *chaconne* are truly exotic dances. They originated in the melting-pot of Central America, were brought home to Andalusia by the colonists, stripped of their cruder suggestions on Spanish soil, polished, painfully adapted to European non-imitativeness and close movement, and in this transformation introduced into the courtly dance north of the Pyrenees.

In the adoption of the exotic and Spanish dances as well as of the peasant chorals we have for the first time since classical antiquity an impressive illustration of the law of regeneration in the dance. When the dance in a too highly refined society becomes anemic, it absorbs the elemental strength necessary for its existence from dance regions which lie closer to the roots, closer to natural locomotion and its spirit. As long as it finds this strength in its immediate environment, as long as the peasantry of its own country has preserved to some extent the native dance heritage, it finds nourishment there. But where the driving force and momentum are broken, where the people bring to the old dances the fine manners of the upper classes in a cruder form, or even adorn their own festivals only with pale reflections or caricatures of the courtly dance, fresh blood must be taken from the dance of foreign peoples, who are more primitive in their way of life and superior in physical mobility and expressiveness.

But in the very midst of such a process of absorption the true features of a period stand forth with special clarity. For the process is never a mere borrowing of the foreign property. And it is the change which the folk dances and foreign dances have to go through before they are accepted in the new environment that is significant and instructive.

The general polishing and "taming" of which we have spoken before may be taken for granted here. But we can observe also a very impressive alteration in details. We turn over the pages of Arbeau and find still the forward thrust of the leg as *grue,* the backward thrust of the leg as *ruade,* the sideward thrust of the leg as *ru de vache.* There is also much said of the *saut majeur* and the *saut mineur,* of *cadence* and *capriole.* Such movements are hardly met with at all in the seventeenth century. Instead, every dance is fitted into the step pattern—bending step plus gliding step. The best illustration of this is the development of the *courante* which was danced in the sixteenth century with single and double straight steps, in the seventeenth with the *coupé* and the gliding step. The description of the *bourrée* is similar—in Auvergne it was stamped. Of the *sarabande* we know at least that it was danced with gliding steps. And finally from a peasant round of Poitou comes the apotheosis of the bending step, the *minuet.*

We are faced here with an entirely new sense of movement. Leap and leg thrust have ceased. All violence, exertion, and angularity are banished. The glide and bend has about it something of the ideal of the perfect courtier, as Count Baldassare Castiglione described it in his *Cortegiano* in 1514: *una certa dignità, temperata però con leggiadra ed aerosa dolcezza di movimenti.* A certain dignity: on the first count the dancer rises on his toes—the preceding bend is nothing but the upbeat or the impetus to the lift. The entire movement has grandeur, repose, and fullness, without the haste of angular movement, without the impact of the tensed outline of the body. Expanded dances like the *volta* and the *canarie* have lost ground, and by the end of this period we have arrived at pure close movement, which after 1650 becomes, as *douce manier,* the guiding principle of all dance.

Together with the transformation of the dance comes a subtle change of rhythm. In the sixteenth century four-four time predominates: *basse danse* and *pavane, passamezzo, canarie, courante, bouffons,* and most of the *branles* are in quadruple time; only the *tourdion, galliard, volta,* and a few of the *branles* are in triple time. At the end of the century the situation is altered. The *courante* changes over to six-four time, the *passepied* to three-eight; *padovane, menuet,* and *sarabande* are written in triple time; the *intrada* and *polonaise* in spite of their simple march character follow the general tendency towards triple time. Only the *bourrée, gigue, rigaudon,* and a few *branles* retain two-four or four-four time.

The relationship between the change in rhythm and the change in dance need scarcely be pointed out: the succession of steps—bend, lift, glide—takes three counts. But the determining force behind these changes is the great inclination of the baroque to seek expression rather in breadth than in height. A visit to any picture gallery will show that in the seventeenth-century rooms the broad form appears more frequently than the high form, and that the fashions of this period are wide, full skirts, millstone ruffs, and broad-brimmed Rembrandt hats. The new rhythm is essentially a manifestation of the same tendency. The duple time has a conciseness and tenuity which do not accord well with the tendency towards breadth in the contemporary taste.

The observation of the increasing use of triple time does not dispose of the question of rhythm. The significant point artistically is rather the combination in the dance of each two measures into a group of six quarters. Here we have again the old Oriental and medieval ambiguity as *divisio senaria imperfecta* and *divisio senaria perfecta,* as $2 \times 3/4$ or $3 \times 2/4$. This ambiguity already appears in some of the sixteenth-century dances in triple time and is quite common in those of the seventeenth century. It is most clearly seen later in the *minuet* and in the *passepied,* where the bar line cuts through the middle of one of the bending steps, so that the masters had to recommend that the first count in the second measure of the group should not be accented, so as not to confuse the dancers. The situation is scarcely less clear a hundred years earlier in the *galliard:* here too the concluding fourth step of the preceding group comes on the first beat of the second measure:

Music:	3/4	♪	♪		♪	| ♪		♪	♪
Galliard:	2/4	l.f.	r.f.	|	l.f.		r.f.	| leap	
Minuet:	2/4	bend		|	bend			| r.	l.

This fundamental rhythmic intersection of dance steps and dance melody produces that vague, shimmering quality of which baroque art is so fond and which is one of its most distinctive characteristics.

The Movements

FRENCH DANCE TERMS:

Assiette, posture.

Branle as in the fifteenth century.

Cadence, high leap with final position.

Capriole, high leap from the bend (*plié*) with a movement in the air indicating the next position.

Congé = branle.

Conversion, reversal at the end of the hall, in which the lady moves forward and the gentleman backward until the turn has been completed.

Découpement, diminution of the double step.

Démarche as in the fifteenth century.

Entretaille, a lifting of the foot, *pied en l'air,* during which the weight-bearing leg moves or skips sidewise to the place of the lifted leg.

Fleuret: deux minimes noires & vne blanche, sur lesquelles le danceur fait deux pieds en l'air & vne greue sans petit sault s'appellēt fleuret.
Fleuret, according to the French practice of the sixteenth century, is therefore a brief lifting of each foot on the upbeat with a forward thrust of the first on the downbeat:

        r. l. r.

Grue, in the old spelling *greue,* meaning "crane," is a simple thrust forward of the foot—apparently a courtly-bourgeois modification of the old leg thrust mentioned on page 29. The Greeks, indeed even the Schilluk of northeastern Africa and the Russians (*žuravlj*) of today, derive dance steps from the walk of the crane.

Hachure = *découpement*.

Marque pied, drawing up of the toes of the free foot to the standing foot.

Marque talon, drawing up of the heel of the free foot to the standing foot.

Pas double as in the fifteenth century.

Pas simple as in the fifteenth century.

Pied croisé, the lifted leg crosses the calf of the standing leg almost as in the Hungarian folk dance.

Pieds joints, the feet at right angles with equal division of weight (first position). *P. j. oblique*, the same with unequal division of weight.

Pieds largis, legs spread with equal division of weight (second position). *P. l. oblique*, the same with unequal division of weight.

Position, posture, position with one leg placed forward (later the fourth position).

Reprise, in contrast to the *reprise* of the fifteenth century = *movimento*.

Révérence, the free leg is moved from the fourth position behind the standing leg; the lady curtsies slightly with both knees. *R. passagère* = *riverenza minima*.

Ruade, thrust of the leg to the rear. A beautiful illustration is shown in Théodore de Bry's etching (Plate 24).

Ru de vache, thrust of the leg to the side.

Saut majeur, high leap for which time is allowed.

Saut mineur, skip for which no time is allowed.

ITALIAN DANCE TERMS:

Cambio or *scambiata*, one foot forward (fourth position), the other crosses touching from the outside the heel of the first; the first foot moves back.

Continenza as in the fifteenth century.

Fioretto = *fleuret*.

Passo doppio as in the fifteenth century.

Passo is the simple step which in the fifteenth century was called *sempio*.

Passo puntato or

Puntata = grue.

Ripresa = balancé, side step with *continenza.*

Riverenza = révérence.

Scambiata = cambio.

Seguito means "swing of the leg." There are several distinctions: *seguito grave,* the forward swing of each leg followed by a half step; *seguito grave a tordiglione,* the forward, sideward, and backward swing of the leg, that is, the combination of the *grue,* the *ru de vache,* and the *ruade;* each leg takes one quarter beat; *seguito spezzato,* forward swing followed by a lift of the heel; half beat; *seguito ordinario,* forward swing followed by *seguito spezzato;* whole beat.

Trabocchetto, the one foot is placed to the side and the other follows with a swing. On a half note it is called *trabocchetto grave,* on a quarter note, *trabocchetto minimo.*

SPANISH DANCE TERMS:

Cabriola = capriole.

Cruzado = pied croisé.

Floreta = fleuret.

Puente = arch, bridge.

Puntapié = grue.

Rompido = pas double.

Sustenido = standing on the toe.

Vacío = pas simple.

Open Couple Dances

The PAVANE. By the middle of the sixteenth century the *basse danse* had practically died out in Italy and France; only in some of the "inventions" of the Italian dance masters did it lead a precarious existence. In its place appeared for several decades as a festive introductory dance *Ain Spanyelischer hoff Dantz,* as the German lutist Hans Judenkünig called it, the *pavana* or "peacock dance."

The first occurrence of this word illustrates the strange confusion with the similar-sounding name of the city of Padua, which resulted later in the denial of the Spanish origin of the *pavane* and its ascription to Italy. Petrucci's fourth book of the *Intabolatura de Lauto* (Venice, 1508) contained the first *pavanes.* The headings are correct, but on the title page they are called *Padoane diverse.* The French, further removed from the influence of the name Padua, have always written *pauanes;* even Attaingnant's first dance book of 1529 uses this title. But later there was really a *padovana* in Italy; it appears first in Antonio Rotta's lute collection of 1546. This dance has nothing to do with the *pavane*—it is in six-eight time and occurs in the same suite with the ordinary *pavane* of the period in Italy, the *passamezzo.*

A "peacock dance"—it was danced proudly, showily. The performer strutted about, suggesting with mantle and dagger the spread of a peacock's tail. It was intended to express not charm and lightness, but ceremonial dignity. In its step and rhythm princes walked. The piper played a *pavane* when a bride of good family proceeded to the church, or when priests, or masters and members of important corporations, were to be escorted in dignified procession. So solemn was the *pavane* that the Spaniards, Salvá and Juan Timoneda, each dedicated one to the Mother of God, though, to be sure, Timoneda's was put on the Index. On the other hand, descriptions of bourgeois and folk life never touch on the *pavane* at all.

In comparison with the *basse danse,* it represented a considerable simplification. Instead of the many movements in ever-changing succession, the dancers had only one group of steps: two single steps and one double step forward or, if desired, also backward. The melody was in four-four time:

First measure	Second measure
◇ ◇ ◇ ◇	♩
♩ ♩ ♩ ♩	o
l r r l	Double step

♫ ♫ ♫ ♫   as drum accompaniment

The PAVANE D'ESPAGNE. Towards the end of the century all dancing became less strict. The gravity and rigidity of the *pavane* could not remain unaffected. Hence about 1600 there came from Spain a diminished form in which the music was more ornate and in which occasional skips (*fleurets*) were added to the movement:

◇   ◇   ◇   ◇
♩   ♩   ♩   ♩

1st measure:	l. forward	r. drawn up	r. forward	l. drawn up
2nd measure:	l. forward	r. drawn up	*fleuret*	*fleuret*
3rd measure:	*fleuret*	*fleuret*	*fleuret*	*fleuret*
4th measure:	*fleuret*	feet together	foot thrust r. and l.	feet together

The *spagnoletta* in three-four time, which occasionally appears in the music books and which in Spain itself was called the *españoleta*, has nothing to do with the *pavane d'espagne*. The *spagnoletta*, Michael Praetorius assures us, was "invented in the Netherlands and rarely danced in France." There is also an old Catalan dance called the *espunyolet* after the village of Espunyola. Just as little related apparently is the *pavaniglia* included by the Italian dancing masters Caroso and Negri. In Spain this dance was expressly designated as the *pavanilla italiana* and was danced at the Spanish court in 1608 by three princely couples.

PASSAMEZZO, or more properly *passo e mezzo*, "a step and a half," was the name of a lighter and somewhat more lively *pavane* of Italian origin.

As early as 1536 we find in Hans Newsidler's *Newgeordent künstlich Lautenbuch* a *welscher tantz Wascha mesa,* the baffling name of which is explained in the *Newes Lautenbüchlein* (1540) by the same master as *Passa mesa, Ein welscher tantz* (*passa mesa,* an Italian dance). In France it was danced along with the *pavane* in single couples by young people. In Italy, however, the name and idea of the *pavane* disappear at the moment when, in 1546, the *passamezzo* appears in Antonio Rotta's *Intabulatura del Lauto.* In 1603 J.-B. Besard is able to say definitely in his *Thesaurus harmonicus* that a *passamezzo* is the same dance that the French call the *pavane.* By 1636 it was no longer danced.

The GALLIARD, called by the Italians *gagliarda,* by the English *gaillard,* by the French *gaillarde,* and by the Spaniards *gallarda,* appeared at the end of the fifteenth century in Lombardy:

> Sopra quegli a ballare incominciorno
> Ed a saltare *all'usanza lombarda,*
> Che, chi piace, è un moto molto adorno,
> E chiamasi ballare *alla gagliarda.*
>
>   BOJARDO, *Orlando innamorato,*
>   3, 2, 36.

These verses must have been written in the fourteen eighties. Attaingnant prints *galliards* in Paris in 1529; they are found in England about 1541; in Antonio Rotta's *Intabulatura del Lauto* of 1546 they replace the *saltarello.* In Germany they were not yet known at that time.

The Spanish claim to the *galliard,* which is frequently advanced, cannot be upheld. One must guard against drawing conclusions about a whole category from the origin of one dance, when only a variation or perhaps merely a certain melody is mentioned. The few places which refer to a *gallarda española* are countered by others which—like the passage in Calderón's *Jardin de Falerina*—designate the *galliard* simply as *francesca.*

The *galliard* is, as long as the *pavane* lives, its regular after-dance—

bold, wanton, as the name implies, without gliding steps, composed entirely of leg thrusts and leaps. It was the only dance of the time which was performed bareheaded, with the hat in the hand. The measure consists as a rule of twice three minims, which is equivalent to six eighths. From this dance come the five thrusting steps which were known in dance language for two hundred years briefly as *les cinq pas*—"sinka-pas," Shakespeare calls them. On the fifth eighth, however, there was a leap:

grue   grue   grue   grue   sault   grue

Jules Ecorcheville has written in detail about the ambiguity of six-eight time. In Spain the *galliard* seems to have appeared exceptionally in duple time also; Caroso gives, too, a *Gagliarda di Spagna* in 2 × 2 rhythm. In a poem of John Davies's from 1596, sun and earth dance a *galliard:* they move "both back, and forth, and sidewaies." Similarly, Mersenne assigns to the same dance free movement *de biais, de trauers, & de long par tous les endroits de la sale.* Thus the *galliard* was danced forward, backward, sideways, and diagonally.

To begin with, the *galliard* had also a tendency toward the pantomimic. The dancer traversed the hall once or twice with his partner, released her, and danced in front of her; she retreated dancing to the opposite end of the hall; the dancer here surpassed his previous performance, and so it went on with increasing intensity, until the musicians laid down their instruments—as we see, the old familiar play of courtship and coyness. Today, Arbeau complains, people dance it tumultuously and are satisfied to execute the *cinq pas* and *quelques passages sans aulcune disposition.* The rejection of the pantomimic is absolute. The *galliard* was certainly stormy in the first half of the century, and it seems questionable whether it was ever sedate. Zuccolo describes how the spectators egged the girls on with shouts and cries until they executed *bei trotti,* light-footed leaps, clever *fioretti,* lightning-swift turns, and many *rimesse* and *continenze,* stamping their feet from time to time. Arena is reminded of a cockfight. Anyone who limited himself to the *cinq pas* was considered a clod. Queen Elizabeth of England used it for her morning gymnastics: at the age of fifty-six she danced, upon arising, six or seven *galliards.*

Yet the tempo of the *galliard* could not have been rapid. The leaps themselves require a certain retardation of the speed. As a matter of fact the tempo of the *galliard* has been overestimated not only today but also in the seventeenth century. In 1641, J. Vierdanck finds it necessary to point out expressly in the preface to the first part of his *Paduanen, Gagliarden, Balletten und Correnten,* "because of the great abuse occasionally found in the tempo, that the *pavane* and especially the *galliard* require to be taken at a very slow tempo, quite different from that of the *courante,* as is well known to all experienced instrumentalists, for without this they cannot achieve their proper effect."

Romanesca is neither, as is often said, another name for the *galliard,* nor even for another dance; it is simply the title of a certain fashionable *galliard* melody of the sixteenth century. This is clearly seen from a passage in which Arbeau speaks of a *galliard* melody and then continues: *A Orléans quāt nous donnions des aulbades, nous auions tousiours sur nos Lutz & Guiternes la gaillarde appellée la Romanesque: Mais je la treuuois trop fréquentée & triviale. . . .* (At Orleans when we performed the aubades, we always played on our lutes and guitars the *galliard* called the *romanesque:* but I found it too hackneyed and trivial. . . .)

The *galliard,* like the *saltarello,* might also be followed by a *ripresa.* Its character is not quite clear. At the end of his *Terpsichore,* Praetorius gives *vier Reprinse, zum Beschluss der Galliarden, Wie dieselbe von den Frantzösischen Dantzmeistern diminuiret und coloriret werden* (four *ripresas,* for the conclusion of *galliards,* as they have been diminished and colored by the French dancing masters). They were probably musical codas in the form of variations.

The TOURDION, which is also written *tordion,* was performed by the French in the sixteenth century as an after-dance to the *basse danse.* It is merely a variation of the *galliard* with the same six-eight rhythm and the step pattern:

	I	II
1st eighth:	l. high	r. high
2nd eighth:	r. high	l. high
3rd eighth:	l. high	r. high
4th eighth:	r. high	l. high
5th eighth:	leap	leap
6th eighth:	position	position

The foot is only slightly raised, however, almost glided; the leap is moderate—the preceding *basse danse* has a restraining influence on the movements. This is the main difference between the *tourdion* and the gayer *galliard.* A turning movement which would justify the name *tordion* cannot be discovered.

With the *basse danse,* the *tourdion* also disappears. Only rarely, as for example in Caroso, do we meet at the turn of the seventeenth century a "balletto" *Tordiglione* in triple time. And from the court of Aranjuez in the year 1622 it is reported that the Queen with her ladies danced *el turdión.*

The COURANTE of the French, mentioned for the first time in 1515 by Clément Marot in his *Epître des Dames de Paris,* was originally a pantomimic wooing dance. Three young men invited three girls, led them one after another to the opposite side of the room, and left them standing there, while they themselves returned. Then one after another they went back and made themselves agreeable with amorous looks and gestures, dusting and pulling up their shoes, and arranging their shirts. The ladies, however, refused their hands and turned their backs, and the dancers had to go back again to their places without having achieved their purpose, and in great despair. At the end all three came forward and, on bended knees and wringing their hands, begged for mercy. Forgiven, they danced helter-skelter the *courante*. The typical coyness motif—an amorous wooing with strong *ritardando,* in no wise "fantastic, hot and quick," but already a game and a conscious caricature of the original form. This is an illustration of why the whole pantomime had to be rejected about the middle of the sixteenth century, because of its lack of sincerity. Only the procession remained.

Its rhythm is indefinite. The group of semi-breve-minim, or quarter-eighth, reigns almost supreme. Not only an organ version by Bernhard Schmid from the year 1577, but even the *bransles courans* of Claude Gervaise, published by Attaingnant in 1555 in his *Sixieme Livre de Danceries,* are in this form. Only Arbeau gives an out-and-out quadratic rhythm:

l	r	r	l	l	r	r	l		r	l	l	r	r	l	l	r

| ſ | ſ | | d | | ſ | ſ | | d |

| Movement to the left | Movement to the right |

We might even suspect an oversight in the conscientious Arbeau, if Mersenne had not in 1636 stated that one could choose any time desired. The time of a dance piece, however, could only be *ad libitum* insofar as it did not interfere with the form or pattern of the steps: the composer is free only to subdivide the beats for the various steps. Publishers of old music manuscripts who in their respect for the empty medieval notation transcribe ◊ ♪ with ○ ♩, or at least with ♩ ♩, would surely force upon the dancer the most peculiar limping movements, suitable to certain moon dances of primitive peoples. When the mistakes of bad transcription are corrected, however, we have the same simple set-up as in the *basse danse:* ◊ ♪ ＝ ◊ —the triple quality lies only in the mensural

music, not in the modern rhythm. Two-eighth groups on the one side
stand over against three-eighth groups on the other:

2/4

6/8

l   r   r   l

According to Mersenne, the execution is

bend lift draw up
plier lever poser

This did not make much difference, since the tempo remained rapid on
into the seventeenth century; "swift corantos" they are called about the
year 1600 in Shakespeare's *Henry V.*

Untouched by all the inter-rhythmic variations, the dance movement
remained a constant alternation of two simple steps and one double step
to the left and the same steps to the right—*une course sautelante d'allées
et venues,* a skipping to and fro, as Mersenne describes it. Two measures
to the left, two measures to the right: the couples had to cut through the
room in a zigzag, so that Thomas Platter of Basle could relate that in
1596 his boatman had had to cross the Rhone in a high wind from bank
to bank, *comme quand on danse la courante.* This zigzag movement
seems to have been anticipated already in the old *piva* of the fifteenth
century. It brings the *courante* into close relationship with the *branles,*
and we understand why in 1550 Claude Gervaise uses the name *branles
courans.*

Johann Kuhnau, cantor of the St. Thomas Church in Leipzig, recommends as late as 1689 that they be taken "rather quickly." But in the
meantime in France, about the middle of the seventeenth century, the
lively *courante* had become a *danse très-grave,* which had scarcely anything but the name in common with the old dance. Bassani in 1677
marks it *Largo.* The couples marched around the hall, linked or sep-

arate, with or without holding hands, in a fairly regular step pattern. They differentiated:

Courante simple consisting of forward steps;
Courante figurée consisting of forward, backward, and sideward steps.

They distinguished further the short and long *pas:*

Short *pas* = straight step + *temps de courante* or *pas grave* (bend, lift, forward glide),
Long *pas* = bending step + bending step with glide.

As a rule two short and two long *pas* followed each other periodically. Each of these *pas composés* took six quarter notes of the music, each single step three quarters, which meant that all the bending steps came on the upbeat.

The real period of this later *courante* is the second half of the seventeenth century. Louis XIV is said to have preferred this dance to any other and to have danced it better. As late as 1697 at the wedding of the Duke of Burgundy it was the *courante* which inaugurated the ball. The last example I know of is the account of a Jewish wedding at Frankfurt am Main in 1699. Soon after 1700 it was no longer danced in society— "unpractis'd long," Jenyns writes of it in 1728. But for decades it was considered by good masters the basis of dance art and was made the center of their teaching. In this capacity it received the nickname of the "doctor dance." Apropos of this choreographic doctorate we may quote a contemporary verse:

> I join the dancers hand in hand
> In minuet and saraband,
> And ask myself to what avail
> As sweat forms on my features pale.
> I am a doctor indiscreet,
> My brains are surely in my feet.
>
> ALBERTUS VON GOMINN

The DANSE DES CANARIES is, after the *courante,* the main courtship and coyness dance of the sixteenth century. One couple dances through the hall. At the end the gentleman leaves his lady and dances backwards. He goes forward once more and back again, and then the lady does the same.

The movements are bold (*gaillards*), bizarre, and exotic. The combination of skip and stamp, and the alternation of heel and sole in the stamping are characteristic. The *canario,* therefore, is closely related to the *Schuhplattler,* and still more closely to the wooing dances of eastern Europe, especially to the Bohemian *Proti-sobě.* Its rhythmical motif is predominantly a dotted three-eight figure; only Arbeau notates it with two eighths:

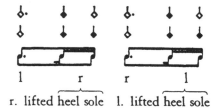

We find the same notation in Mersenne in 1636. Besides the *batteries de pieds,* to which Arbeau also draws attention, he adds semi-caprioles, pirouettes, and similar movements. In its day this dance was considered *grandement difficile* and only people with much practice and very agile feet attempted it.

Even the old dance literature leaves open the question whether the strange name and the somewhat uncourtly movements really go back to the Canary Islands or to some deliberately exotic court ballet. There can be no doubt, however, that the decision must be given in favor of the Canary Islands. For the earliest example of the *canario* comes from the country which would be the natural intermediary if it were an importation from the Canaries but not if it were merely a court ballet—from Spain. Diego Pisador first mentions it in 1552—not with the colorless appellation *danza* or *baile,* but as a funeral piece, as *endechas de Canario.*

The association of a wild sexual dance with funeral festivities will not surprise the readers of the first part of this book. It will rather serve to confirm the fact that the *danse des canaries* must have come from the Canary Islands through Spain to France. In Spain itself the *canario* is regarded as the father of the *jota*.

The CASCARDA was a couple dance *à tempo di quattro battute triple,* that is, in twelve-eight time. I am unable to interpret the name. Is it perhaps derived from *cascare,* which has supplied to several Romance languages the word for "yawning"? In Caroso's description it has six figures (*tempi*), in which sometimes both partners—preferably in a circle, *in ruota*—sometimes the lady and the gentleman separately, dance. The first figure, to which we shall limit ourselves, consists of

> *Riverenza breve*
> *Rota*
> 4 *spezzati ordinari*
> 2 *passi puntati minimi* (1 forward, 1 backward)
> 4 *seguiti battuti de Canario.*

In this pattern of figures lies, it seems to me, the historical significance of the *cascarda:* the multiplicity of the old pantomime has here crystallized into this fixed succession of figures, which later constitutes the structure of the *contra dances.*

The BERGAMASCA, a dance in even time, from Bergamo, has been known since 1569: the third book of the *Villotte* of Filippo Azzaiolo, published in that year by Gardano in Venice, contains two of them. Even before 1600 it was well known in England, for at the end of the *Midsummer Night's Dream* Shakespeare has Bottom dance a "bergomask." It would be wrong, however, to regard it on this account as a clumsy "clown dance." The *bergamasca* or *bergamasco* was a popular round dance of couples in which all the dancers executed a little *en-*

trechat every six or nine steps. The form described by Ungarelli is apparently degenerate.

To a lively two-four melody, man and woman move around in a circle, the man forwards (*in avanti*), the woman backwards (*all'indietro*). When the melody changes—*al variare del suono*—they embrace and perform a turning dance—*fanno alcune giravolte pure in tondo*—and then begin anew. Thus the *bergamasca* presents the characteristic alternation of fleeing and yielding, of denial and surrender, which forms the content of all wooing dances. The description given by Pratella stands about halfway between that of Ungarelli and that of Massaroli.

The SARABANDE came in from Spain. But did it originate in that country? Its still unexplained Spanish name, *zarabanda,* sounds so much like the Persian سربند , *sar-band,* meaning "wreath for fastening the feminine headdress," that the possibility of this etymology must be taken into consideration. But the time is too late for a Persian-Arabic origin: the *sarabande* was not known until the end of the sixteenth century. Cervantes emphasizes that at the beginning of the seventeenth century *el endemoniado son de la çarabanda* (the diabolical sound of the *sarabande*) was something new. And the Jesuit historian, Juan de Mariana (1536–1623), explicitly states: In these years appeared a dance and song, so indecent in its text, so repulsive in its movements, that even the most respectable people were inflamed by it. It was usually called the *zarabanda.* Small wonder that it became a favorite target of the moralists, and indeed even of legislation. In 1583—this is, as a matter of fact, the first dated mention of the dance—the singing and reciting of the *sarabande,* in whatsoever place, was punishable with two hundred lashes; in addition, men were given six years in the galleys, and girls were exiled from the kingdom.

On this point all the old sources agree: the *sarabande* was a sexual pantomime of unparalleled suggestiveness. But only rarely do we come upon anything more explicit. The earliest account is given in an obscure place at the end of the reminiscences of the Basle physician, Thomas Platter the younger. He saw the *sarabande* danced in Barcelona in 1599: there were always several couples together—once, in the street, some fifty—men and women opposite each other playing the castanets, mostly in backward motion with absurd twists of the body, hands, and feet.

A little later we meet the *sarabande* in Italy. "Woe to the dirty fellow who has brought this barbarism upon us," cries Giambattista Marino, the father of the ill-famed *"Marinismus,"* the turgid baroque poetry, in 1623. The girls with castanets, the men with tambourines, exhibit indecency in a thousand positions and gestures. They let the hips sway and the breasts knock together. They close their eyes and dance the kiss and the last fulfillment of love. Almost more important than this description is Marino's statement that the *sarabande* and the *chacona* are fundamentally the same:

> *Chiama questo suo gioco empio e profano*
> *Saravanda e Ciaccona il novo Ispano.*

Il novo Ispano—New Spain was the name of Yucatán, and that the *chacona* came from the American colonies we know from other sources. To be sure, the contemporary Mariana considers it a Spanish invention, and his opponent Ortiz, agreeing with him only in the absolute condemnation of the *sarabande*, tries to derive the name from a diabolical woman in Seville. Nevertheless he mentions also that others ascribe it to the (American) Indies. This contradiction hardly surprises us. For the dances of the colonies were first taken up by the dance-mad Andalusians and brought by them to their native province. Spreading thence over the peninsula, they might easily pass for Andalusian. Although it must appear fairly certain that the *sarabande* with its unimpaired primitivism was picked up not in Europe of the sixteenth century but in Central America, another small factor must be taken into consideration: namely, that a native beaked flute of Guatemala is called the *zarabanda*. Never has an instrument been named for a dance, but dances, on the other hand, have frequently been called after instruments. The *sarabande* may be added then to the well-known examples of the *piva, musette, gigue, tambourin,* and *hornpipe.*

Nowhere has a *sarabande* on American soil been explicitly described. But this does not make much difference. For we have seen that Lope de Vega explains the *sarabanda* and the *chacona* as one and the same dance, and Esquivel Navarro, the Italian dance writer of the seventeenth century, maintains that *sarabanda* and *jacara* (*xacara*), as well as *rastro* and *tarraga,* are simply different names for the same thing. Similarly *lundu* and *batuque* are not distinguished essentially, and a poetic eulogy of these dances in the Portuguese *Cartas Chilenas* from the eighteenth century uses the names indifferently for the various courtship dances of the mulattoes. Our translation attempts to render word for word everything of importance for the dance:

> The nimble mulatto girl dressed as a man
> Swings in the fiery *lundu* and *batuque,*
> Like the maiden who gracefully raises her skirt
> She flutters around on the tips of her toes,
> She opens her arms to the friend of her heart
> And presses herself against him: *embigada.*
> Her partner, winding and twisting his body,
> Now places one of his hands on his head,
> And the other he carelessly sets on his hip,
> Or snapping their fingers they follow the music.
> I'll pay you, I'll pay you, he cries, whereupon
> With a powerful leap he seizes the wench. . . .
> Oh happy dance, into the lowliest huts
> Didst thou enter. The wives of the negroes,
> And all the mulattoes did honor to thee,
> Their bellies grotesquely supported by girdles;
> Together with rascals and gutter-snipes tattered

Who shoeless would stamp in the dust of the street.
Yet today in the towns and the cities the portals
Of mansions and palaces open to thee.

As a matter of fact, by 1618 the much abused and despised *sarabande* could be danced together with the *tirdión* (*tourdion*) within the frame of a comedy before the Spanish court! Three years later, in Lope's comedy *La Villana de Jetafe,* it is rejected by a lady as too old, too much outmoded—*está muy vieja.* . . .

At this time it was introduced into France. In 1625 the "Spaniards" dance it in a Parisian court ballet, *La Douairière de Billebahaut.* But in its emigration it does not seem to have brought much with it across the Pyrenees but the three-four time, the castanets, and the leg bells. Again the sources are silent on the essential features: aside from Mersenne's brief remark that its *pas* were *composez de tirades, ou de glissades* (composed of gliding steps), we do not know how the *sarabande* was danced in France or in any other country which imported it, as long as it remained a society dance, that is to say, until 1700. For it seems to have come to the end of its career by 1697, when it was danced at the wedding of the Duke of Burgundy at Versailles. Shortly after this it was out of fashion in the ballroom.

It lives on in the theater, however, and we find occasional references to this ballet *sarabande.* But how much this theatrical dance of the eighteenth century has in common with the society dance of the seventeenth century, it is impossible to discover—probably very little. For whether French or Italian, whether Feuillet or Lambranzi, the accounts are contradictory. Indeed, we should be almost driven to despair by the uncertainty of the contemporary dance writers, if it were not obvious to us that the theatrical dance adopted little more than the names and musical forms of the old social dances and combined with these musical forms, rhythms, and tempi a random succession of movements from the perennial *pas coupés, chassés,* and *tombés* of the dance artist's store. Gregorio Lambranzi in his *Nuova e curiosa scuola de' balli theatrali* of 1716 says quite freely and undogmatically: "Concerning the manner of dancing, I shall endeavor to show as far as is necessary what steps must be used for each figure. But it is not my intention to bind anybody to my method; rather I shall leave each dancer the freedom to apply it at his own discretion." He starts the *sarabande* with a *coupé*, "whereupon the *pas, tombés, sison,* and *boure* follow; the rest of this *sarabande* each dancer may perform as he pleases."

We have contradictory information concerning the tempo: in 1677 G. B. Bassani requires *presto* and *prestissimo* for his *Balletti, Correnti, Gighe e Sarabande;* in 1689 Johann Kuhnau recommends that the *sarabande* be taken slowly; in 1756 J. J. Quantz allows each quarter only one count ($\downarrow$ = M.M. 80); and in 1787 the Frenchman Compan praises its *mouvement gai & amoureux.* In the *Zodiacus musicus* of 1698 Schmicerer does not indicate the tempo of any of the dances; only the *sarabande* is marked *Adagio è staccato*—even at that time the tempo must have been uncertain. The *sarabande* was no longer a living dance.

In the rhythm, we find to a still greater extent that ambiguity of the mensural system which applies to the three-four time of the other dances; it fluctuates between triple and quadruple with a strong preference for the quadruple.

The CHACONA is one of those dances about which many irrelevant things have been said. It does not come from Italy (*ciaccona*), nor yet from the Basques. Nor is it, as H. Riemann states in his music dictionary, doubtful whether it has ever been danced at all.

It is mentioned for the first time in the year 1599: the *entremés* of the *Platillo,* which Simon Agudo wrote for the wedding of Phillip III, introduces into its verses an invitation to go to Tampico in Mexico and there dance the *chacona.* Two or three years later it has become well known and even popular throughout Spain. The American origin, merely suggested by Agudo, is made very clear and unmistakable by other poets; according to Lope de Vega (1618) it came by mail from the West Indies to Seville:

> *De las Indias á Sevilla*
> *ha venido por la posta.*

Quevedo calls it the *chacona mulata* and Cervantes the *Indiana amulatada.* For the first time the dance of the mixed races of Central America invades Europe.

It was still preserved in Portugal in the nineteenth century: in the Corpus Christi procession at Lisbon the fishwives of the neighboring village of Friela danced *uma dansa mourisca*—an "exotic" dance, that is to say—which they called the *chacoina.*

In accordance with its origin the *chacona* was sensual and wild; *vierten azogue los pies,* says Cervantes—like quicksilver run the feet. Even more than the *sarabanda* it was regarded in the seventeenth century as the most passionate and unbridled of all dances.

Of the step pattern we learn nothing; only of the stage dance of the French ballet does Compan describe the changing steps. Later, in the nineteenth century, a four-beat step was known as the *pas de chacone:* fourth position with the left foot forward; on the first count the right foot swings into the fourth position in front of the left; on the second comes a quarter turn to the right and a skip on the right foot, while the left is flung sideways into the air, struck against the right, and again flung high; on the third count, the left foot goes into the fifth position behind the right, and on the fourth, the right is flung very high and with it the whole body turns a full circle. All the movements are large and high. They are excellently characterized by Cervantes' remark.

The music was a constant repetition of a four-beat *ostinato* at the same pitch, accompanied in variation fashion by a treble. This was regarded as the distinctive quality of *chaconne* music outside Spain. Whether it was also obligatory in Spain must remain doubtful: a *chacona* published in 1674 in Gaspar Sanz's *Instrucción de Música sobre la Guitarra española* is not worked out in strict *ostinato*.

The PASSACAGLIA as a musical form is most closely related to the *chaconne*. Musical history has tried to distinguish it from the *chaconne* by the transposability of the *ostinato*. The choreographic sources say nothing of this. They distinguish the *passacaglia* rather by its more deliberate movements and by the less emotional quality of the melody. Moreover, the true Spanish *passacaglia* is said to be in duple time. In the Spanish *La Escuela de Danzar*, an *entremés* written by Navarrete y Ribera in 1640, a new dance is demanded:

> *Quisiera un baile nuevo. . . . Un Pasacalle?*
> *Eso es de azotados.*
> *Dios me libre de bailes arriesgados.*

This passage can be translated literally, but is difficult to explain: I desire a new dance. . . . A *pasacalle?* That is one of the whipped (or "flogged" or "motley") (dances). God preserve me from dangerous dances.

The name is a corruption of the Spanish *pasacalle,* meaning "street song"; the real Italian cognate, likewise derived from the Spanish word, is *passagallo*.

The PIE DE JIBAO or *gibao* was a Spanish court dance in couples, which was first mentioned in 1560 and was considered old-fashioned by the beginning of the seventeenth century. We do not know much about it. *Jibado* means "humpy, hunchbacked," and the word *corcovado* used by Navarrete y Ribera to describe this dance in *La Escuela de Danzar* has the same meaning. Esquivel Navarro ascribes to it the *movimiento grave* of the *sustenido,* of the toe stand. Contemporary Portuguese literature calls it the *pé de chibáo*.

The DANSE DES BOUFFONS was a sword dance of four persons with the following step pattern:

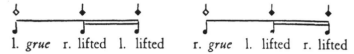

l. *grue*   r. lifted   l. lifted   r. *grue*   l. lifted   r. lifted

One of the dancers entered the hall and walked around it; the others joined in one by one, and finally the whole group made a round in the opposite direction. After each encounter, another round forwards and backwards was danced. The encounters themselves need not be dealt with here; they have been described in great detail by Arbeau.

Closed Couple Dances

The VOLTA occupies a unique position amongst all the court dances of the Romance world. Instead of dancing alongside or opposite each other, back and forth, to and fro, scarcely touching each other, with a mere suggestion of couple form, the *volta* dancers, in close embrace, turn constantly and without separating leap high into the air. This lively dance brings into the refined ballroom an unwonted influx of power and primitivism, of impetuous energy, meridional *gaillardise,* and self-confident vigor.

With the right foot raised high in the air, the dancers hopped on the left and turned at an angle of ninety degrees, took a long stride and again a quarter turn, then sprang high as they made a third quarter turn. Since each figure consisted of only three quarter turns, the dancers did not reach their original position until four figures had been performed.

The turning made it impossible for the partners to stand side by side. They had to move almost as one person, if the lady were not to dance backwards all the time. The lady therefore placed her right hand on the back or the collar of her partner and carried her skirt with her left. For the male dancer, however, the instructions were: left arm around the right hip of the lady; left thigh as a rudder

374

against her right thigh; right hand, in order to assist her in the leaps, underneath the busk, the flat front part of the corset. This is illustrated in the charming engraving by the contemporary artist Théodore de Bry, reproduced in Plate 24.

We cannot blame the German zealots of that time when they call the "shameful way" in which the lady is held "indecent" and the entire dance "filthy." "It should really be looked into by a well-ordered police force and most strictly forbidden," they said; the more so since this dance "was the bearer of misfortune and brought to pass many murders and miscarriages." This cry for the police, however, turns out to be plagiarism. The original is found in Guillaume Bouchet (1526–1605), where it sounds much more intelligent and more intelligible: *La volte, la courante, la fissaye, que les sorciers ont amenées d'Italie en France, outre les mouvements insolens et impudiques, ont cela de malheur qu'une infinité d'homicides et avortemens en adviennent, faisant mourir et tuant tous ceux qui ne sont point en vie.* (The *volta,* the *courante,* the *fissaye,* which the magicians have brought from Italy to France, besides their bold and indecent movements have this misfortune, that a great many murders and miscarriages result from them, causing to die and murdering all those yet unborn.) Arbeau is less exercised about it; he simply asks whether it is really proper for a young girl to take such big steps, but is more interested in the danger of the dancer's becoming dizzy from the constant turning. The "shameful" touching disturbs him as little as does that indiscreet flying of the skirts which so delighted Brantôme, the chronicler of the immoralities of the Paris court about 1570, because the *volta, en faisant volleter la robbe, monstroit tousjours quelque chose agréable à la veue, dont j'en ay veu plusieurs s'y perdre et s'en ravir entre eux-mêmes* (by causing the dresses to fly, always reveals something pleasing to the sight, and I have seen some led astray by it and delight in it among themselves). Besides, the more diffident ladies knew how to protect themselves by girdles and pantalets expressly designed for the purpose.

If I understand correctly the description given by the Basle medical student, Thomas Platter the younger, of the carnival in which he had participated at Montpellier in 1596, the couples danced only one figure of three quarter turns at a time, then remained standing together, while the others performed theirs, so as to be ready to dance again—the *volta* was too strenuous for continuous turning. According to Arbeau the step pattern was

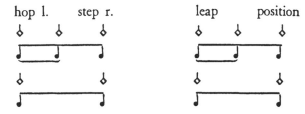

When Thomas Platter was studying at Montpellier, the *volta*, together with the *branle, galliard,* and *courante,* was the chief dance—Provence is its native place. It was first introduced to the Paris court, if Vieilleville's secretary Carloix is correctly informed, by the Count of Sault in 1556. It is all the more strange to note that even before 1600 it was firmly established in English dance instruction.

> They bid us to the English dancing schools
> And teach lavoltas high, and swift corantos.
> SHAKESPEARE, *Henry V,* III, 5.

But still stranger is its early appearance in Germany. When Thomas Platter's elder brother Felix was studying medicine in Montpellier in 1553, he told his people at home in Basle about the *volta* as something with which they were thoroughly familiar. Indeed, in 1538 the Westphalian engraver Heinrich Aldegrever portrays quite unmistakably in his series of wedding dances at least the characteristic grasping under the busk (Plate 23). Again and again the French writers claim French origin for the *waltz;* the *volta* is said to be its mother. The lifting high of the lady, however, can be traced several centuries earlier in Germany; the turning in close embrace, as we shall see in the next section, struck the French essayist Montaigne, when he saw it in Germany, as something out of the ordinary; and the grasping under the busk, which is not a part of either the *waltz* or the *Ländler,* was depicted in Westphalia decades before the *volta* found its way from Provence to Paris, and nobody could ascribe to Westphalia any particular inclination towards Provençal customs. What then remains? We shall not for our part blow Germany's trumpet in reply: the roots of all turning dances are lost in the twilight of Neolithic vegetation cults.

The *volta* itself did not live to see the descendant credited to it: Mersenne mentions it for the last time among the living dances in 1636. It must have died out shortly after that.

> I know a French *nizzarda* and a nice *galliard.*
> Nizzarda? What dance is that?
>
> LOPE DE VEGA, *El Maestro de Danzar* (1594)

The NIZZARDA. Lope de Vega does not answer this question very satisfactorily:

> Capriole, embrace, and leap,
> —How embrace?—In the French way. . . .

The answer which Lope's comedy fails to provide is given in great detail about 1600 by the Italian Federigo Zuccaro, who being a painter is a good and reliable observer. The gentleman invites the lady; in *courante* step they hasten three or four times hand in hand through the hall and embrace; the gentleman puts his left hand behind the lady and grasps her arm in front with his right; then, always dancing forward, he makes her leap three times in the air; in the end, with his knee as support, he lifts her up high and lets her down again, and a kiss is the reward for his strength and agility. Anyone who does not know how to dance the *nizzarda* is not a courtier, not a gentleman, and not a Piedmontese. Let us not forget that Nice is in Provence—geographically also the *nizzarda* is close to the *volta*.

How long the *nizzarda* was danced, I cannot say with certainty. Bartolommeo Corsini, who died in 1675, mentions it in his mock-heroic poem *Torracchione Desolato*.

> Out of the dance much mischief grows.
> SEBASTIAN BRANT, *The Ship of Fools*.

GERMAN TURNING DANCE or DREHTANZ. In the sixteenth century, Germany, like England, lies outside the great world of the dance; Caroso's book *Il Ballarino* speaks only of the dances *sì all'vso d'Italia, come à quello di Francia, & Spagna*. Germany is so far removed that, as it has been reported, Bartholomäus Sastrow first saw the *galliard* danced by Spaniards in 1548 and did not even hear correctly the unfamiliar name of this strange dance; it is so far removed that the Basle physician, Felix Platter, has to emphasize in his memoirs the fact that in 1554 as a student in Montpellier he was able, to the surprise of the other Germans, to pass his first test in Italian dancing after having been there a little more than a year. Even to his considerably younger stepbrother, Thomas Platter, the *volta, courante,* and *galliard* are in 1595 *danses étrangères*. When Prince Ludwig of Anhalt-Köthen came to Florence in 1598, he noticed to his astonishment that they did not dance here as in Germany "with jugglers' hands" or "roll their shoulders now here, now there."

On the other hand, the close turning dances of Germany for a long time seem strange to the Latins. When the Bolognese priest Sebastiano Locatelli came to Sitten in the Canton of Wallis in 1665, he had to participate in a turning dance, although he was not familiar with this type of dance and soon became dizzy. Montaigne had seen the turning dance in 1580 in the house of the Fuggers in Augsburg, when he was traveling to Italy, and described it in his diary: with both hands on the back of his partner, he holds her in such a close embrace that—as we see in the engravings of Aldegrever and of his German contemporaries (Plate 23)—their faces touched. As an afterword we might add Simon Dach's verses:

> Whoso the dance did first discover
> Had in his mind each maid and lover
> With all their burning ardor.
>
> *Braut-Tantz.*

These etchings are very instructive. The dancers they show us place both hands firmly on one another's backs in performing the turn. Here and there they pass each other back to back, and they skip with hands raised high. All these are well-known features of the Bavarian and Austrian *Ländler* in its present form. From it, therefore, we may reconstruct the old German *Drehtanz.*

The *Ländler,* which got its name from "Landl," the mountain region of Austria (sometimes called the *Steirer,* after Steiermark), is a glided turning dance at a moderate tempo—even in 1900 the older musicians played it 3/4 = M.M. 48—in separate figures. Among these figures are: the spinning of the girl on the upraised hand of her stamping partner; the simultaneous spinning of both partners in opposite directions with hands clasped high above their heads—according to a fresco by Benozzo Gozzoli in the Campo Santo at Pisa (before 1485), this was also the custom in ancient Italy; the "gliding through" beneath the arm; the change of sides in dancing past each other back to back; the turn in close embrace. "The faces are pressed together, even if the sweat is running down both of them." This figure dancing, called by the peasants *Schaim* in contrast to the simple waltz or turning dance, is very much weakened today.

At the conclusion of his work on the *Ländler,* E. Hamza writes: "In dancing the *Ländler,* the man frequently lets go of his partner (purposely!) and claps his hands in time to the music. The other men react to this, begin likewise to clap, and all stand together, in a circle with their faces touching. The girls walk round the outside. This is kept up as long as it amuses the boys—*die Buam gfreut.* Then each one takes his partner again and the dance goes on as before." This little known passage is of the greatest significance to us. For it is obviously a relic of the old procession which alternated with the figure pantomime.

Lenau's verses give a more vivid picture of the *Ländler* than any other description:

> High o'er the maiden's head
> Then raises he his arm;
> His finger as a pivot,
> She circles round about
> Like strength to beauty joined.
> How straight ahead he dances
> In noble attitude,
> And causes then the maid
> Light whirling from the right
> To glide beneath the left.
> His nimble partner now
> Must circle at his back,
> Dance round and round about him
> As if he wished to be
> Encircled by his love,
> As if he wished to say,
> "Describe for me the circle
> Of all my hopes and joys."
> And now the blissful couple
> Take hold each other's hands
> And with a supple movement
> Slip through each other's arms.
> His eyes are fixed on her
> And hers see only him.
> Perhaps they mean to say,
> Why can't we two, united

In one another's arms
Spend all our life together
In such a dance as this?
NICOLAUS LENAU, *Der Steyrertanz.*

That it was not always light and charming, however, we learn from the experience of the immortal Simplicius Simplicissimus at that aristocratic ball which ended so ignominiously for him in the goose-pen: the dancers "made such a stamping and howling that I thought they had all gone mad; for I could not imagine the purpose of all this wildness and fury." And he learns "as a matter of plain truth, that those present had agreed to break down the floor of the hall by force."

Even before this the cities had accepted this altogether too obvious love pantomime of the peasants with mixed feelings. In 1551 the Council of Greifswald decreed that the dances at weddings with the shameless bussing of women and maidens was too uncouth, and whoever should dare to do this after it was forbidden would be ordered before the *Lubisch* tree and punished without respect of person. At South German weddings, however, the turning dance became more important than ever. The Nürnberg meistersinger Kunz Has complains about 1525:

When they have weddings nowadays,
They dance no more as years ago
When dancing was discreet and slow.

. . . .

Now they dance the wild *weller,*
The spinner or what they may call it.

J. Bolte's conjecture that the *Weller* is not a German dance is surely a step in the dark. Here it is a question only of the meaning *"Dreher, Wälzer"*; the *Weller* is a turning dance and its name is the first mention of the word *Walzer*. That it also means "spinner" is clear from the last line of our quotation; the rapid turning movement is equally characteristic of the *"Wälzer"* and of the process of spinning.

Even the "mad *Weller"* might be peaceful; indeed, it might be adapted to the court. The Emperor Ferdinand III (1637–57) preferred the German to the French manner of dancing, and the Emperor Leopold I (1658–1705) flatly forbade the French dance. During the reign of Charles VI (1711–40), the duchesses were allowed to participate in German dances, although the Emperor and Empress merely looked on.

The adaptation of the turning dance to the court, however, did not result in any fundamental transformation. No dance has ever resisted taming so stubbornly. Ever since the fifteenth century, municipal decrees and church sermons have fulminated in vain against the impropriety of the turning dance with its bussing and embracing. While the symbolism of all other dances has faded out, the turning dance alone has preserved in its movements the uncompromising expressiveness of the love pantomime, even at the court. As late as 1759 Casanova dances at the court of the Elector of Cologne an *allemande,* in which apparently there was turning and in which one had to kiss the lady. In a later section we shall see that the German turning dance evades propriety right down to the day of the *waltz.*

This rather ill-behaved *Dreher,* occupying a central position in the German dance, must bear the blame for Germany's having become the classic country of antagonists and prohibitions of the dance. An English traveler recounts in 1740 how in Bremen his suggestion to dance a mere *contra* after dinner was received with profound silence; the company acted as if they had been struck by lightning at this shocking proposal.

The original wooing dance of single couples played a role beside the *Dreher,* at least in southern Germany. Phases of this dance are illustrated in Jost Amman's woodcut of the Bridge of Adultery and especially in the charming etchings of Virgil Solis.

In the extreme north of Germany the turning dance and indeed the couple dance were unknown. About 1590 the *Dithmarsch Chronicle* of Pastor Neocorus assures us that couple dances penetrated that region from the south only after the last feud in 1559.

The ENGLISH DANCE. Embracing and kissing were not limited to the German dance. Other countries too enjoyed this liberty. To taste the beautiful lips of maidens was for Arena of Provence one of the essential delights of the dance, and in Italy there were frequent occasions to reprimand the abuse of this old privilege. In England, however, kissing and dancing were inseparably linked. A polemic of 1583, *The Anatomie of the Abuses in Ailgna* by Phillip Stubbes, censures among other abuses—as do its many counterparts in Germany, France, Italy, and Spain—particularly the dance: "For what clipping," it says, "what culling, what kissing and bussing, what smouching and slabbering one of another, what filthie groping and uncleane handling is not practised in those dancings?" For kissing is good manners and the lady has a right to expect it:

> I were unmannerly to take you out,
> And not to kiss you.
> SHAKESPEARE, *King Henry VIII*, I, 4.

Whoever omits it "shalt be taken for a rusticall." Stubbes informs us that in England they danced "cheek by cheek": this position is familiar to us from the German dance; only in the closed couple dance is it possible.

Choral Rounds

The BRANLE, which the Italians called *brando* and the English *brawl* or *round,* has taken its name from the old balancing movement. Its essential characteristics were chain-like joining of hands and the sideward movement of the dancing couples in an open file or closed circle. In many cases, however, the simple choral included a pantomime: in the *branle du Poitou* and in the *gavotte* a wooing dance was performed by the leading couple, after which they went to the rear of the line, and all the other couples repeated this procedure in turn; in the *branle de Malte* the dancers rushed in to the center of the circle and then spread out again; in the *branle des lavandières,* the men and women shook their fingers at each other threateningly and clapped their hands as if they were doing a washing; in the *branle des pois* now the men and now the women stood still; in the *branle des hermites* the dancers crossed their arms and bowed as hermits do. The variations seem inexhaustible.

The themes and steps of the different *branles* are greatly mixed, and yet the choral dance of the Middle Ages in all its types and forms is best preserved in it. Indeed, it goes even farther back than the Middle Ages, retaining much of the primitive choral dance. But of course different periods bring different features to the fore. If Italian society of the first half of the sixteenth century scorns the *brando* as a public dance, the French court from Henry III down to Louis XIV, on the contrary, not only permits it but gives it the most prominent place at balls. Different themes must have been emphasized. Since we know that in the French court dance that form of the *branle* predominated in which after one or two rounds one couple left the chain, danced briefly together, and took up their position in the rear, we must suppose that the form regarded by the Italian nobles as beneath their dignity was much more a simple round dance.

The significance of the *branle* for French society is seen clearly from the fact that it was danced in groups. At the beginning of a ball there was always a series of at least three *branles* in definite order: the sedate *branle double* for the older people, the more lively *branle simple* for the younger married couples, and the rapid *branle gay* for the young people. Gliding, skipping, running—this series of three prescribed by Arbeau, Mersenne replaces in 1636 with a suite of six:

1. *Branle simple*
2. *Branle gay*

3. *Branle à mener ou de Poitou*
4. *Branle double de Poitou*
5. *Branle de Montirandé*
6. *Gavote*

The suite increases in liveliness and any solemnity that may be left, remarks Michel de Pures, is dispelled by the *gavotte*.

Even this succession of *branles* may well be a remainder from the Middle Ages. For something similar has been preserved in the folk dance outside of France. It is reported of the Hungarian choral dances in 1660 that they began with solemn steps, became gayer (*plus gai*) and ended *par une espece de gavotte*, in which men and women turned in couple dances without leaving the semicircle of the chain. Besides these basic *branles* and the succession of airs adapted to them, the French were also familiar with a number of deviations and combinations, under the name of *branles coupés*, which were played and danced in succession, something like the German *Ländler*, which is really a series of different melodies with similar construction to which the dance figures may or may not be alternated.

Finally, at the court balls of Louis XIV and Louis XV only the *branle à mener* and the *gavotte* remain. They were given first and second place and followed by the *courante* and later the *minuet*.

The *branle double* was the most sedate of the *branles*. It is described by Arena of Provence in 1536 as a return dance: three steps forward and two back, five steps altogether. In 1588 Arbeau gives it a little differently: after the bow, a double step to the left and another to the right. Hence the name *branle double*. Double step here means that one foot is placed twice to the side and the other twice drawn up to it. The double to the right was made a little shorter, so that the dancer gradually moved toward the left. That the one authority speaks of forward and backward, the other of left and right, is no contradiction. For as long as the chain dance does not form a circle, the dancer moves diagonally, whether forward and backward or left and right.

The melody began on the downbeat and was in quadruple time. Each measure consisted of one double step, and on each quarter—equivalent to a semi-breve—there was one foot movement. Only on the last quarter of the second measure could both feet be lifted high successively.

The difference between the *branle simple* and the *branle double* was that in the former a simple instead of a double step to the right was made. Hence two quarters had to be dropped and the time changed from twice four-four to six-four:

◇ l. placed
◇ r. drawn up
◇ l. placed
◇ r. drawn up
◇ r. placed
◇ l. drawn up

In the second measure the last two quarters were taken differently: instead of a simple step to the right there were three foot thrusts. The whole system is as follows:

Here also Arena differs: according to his rule, three foot movements were made forward (to the left) and one back (to the right). Mersenne's *branle simple* is in quadruple time and is expanded to twelve movements in ten *pas*. It seems to have fused into the *branle double*, which is no longer mentioned.

The *branle gay* is in sextuple rhythm (6 minims). The movement to the left was performed thus: starting with the feet wide apart, the right foot was raised high and set down beside the left foot; on the second minim, the left foot was raised high and set down to the side; on the third and fourth this was repeated, but the left foot remained in the air during the fifth minim. On the sixth there was a pause.

r. high   l. high   r. high   l. high   Pause

The rhythm of the *branle gay,* the law of which has always proved a pitfall to modern editors of old dances, becomes very clear. In modern editions we find four-four and three-two time naïvely and casually mixed. How could this possibly have been danced? We must not be led astray by the mensural system of the old writers: it has nothing to do with our time system and must be ignored when we add bar lines to modernize the reading. The step and tone periods of the *branle gay* consist of six minims, which could not possibly be crossed by a counter-rhythm. Anyone who refuses to use a sextuple rhythm as the basis here, even if he considers any concern with the dance superfluous in the treatment of dance music, must be warned from the purely musical point of view that in forcing quadruple time upon the composition, he will continually throw corresponding parts of the theme into different positions in the rhythm.

An expanded—not as Ecorcheville will have it, an abbreviated—form is likewise described by Mersenne as in nine-eight time; it has eleven *pas* with twenty-four movements and eight-count sections. The musical structure is confirmed by the suites.

The *branle du Hault Barrois*—named after the district of Bar in France and introduced to the court by de Duilly in 1556—was similar to the *branle simple.* Every new position was arrived at by a jump with both feet, and arms and shoulders were in constant motion. One is reminded of the shoulder rolling in the medieval peasant dance. As a matter of fact, it was the ordinary amusement of lackeys and chambermaids. Young people of rank danced only in the shepherd plays. Arbeau says, "It should be good to dance in winter to make oneself warm." The melody upon which he bases the step pattern is the *branle de Monstierandel,* which is apparently the same as the *branle de Montirandé.*

The *branle de Montirandé:* Whence the name comes, we do not know. Mersenne mentions it as the fifth of his *branle* suite and gives it a very rapid tempo, eight-count divisions, and sixteen movements. A first part has eleven, a second twelve, and a third ten *pas.* The *Terpsichore* of Praetorius includes a very regularly constructed *bransle de Montirande* in five voices.

The *branle de Bourgoigne* was light and quick:

♩	♩.	♩	♩
l. out	r. drawn up	l. out	r. drawn up

Exactly the same choral step still occurs today as the *Tospring* at weddings in the Danish town of Ringköbing—a remarkable proof of the folk origin of the *branle.*

The *gavotte* takes its name from the *Gavots,* the inhabitants of Gapençais in upper Dauphiné. It was a succession of *branles* intermingled with *galliard* movements. After dancing for a while one couple stepped into the center, and the gentleman kissed all the ladies, and the lady, all the gentlemen. Either that was the end of it, or couple after couple followed the first with the same kissing procedure. At the conclusion the host's partner handed a bouquet to the person who was to arrange the next ball.

Arbeau gives the following step pattern to a quadruple melody:

◇	◇	◇	◇
♩	♩	♩	♩
l. spread out	r. drawn up	r. strikes and crosses	r. *grue,* crosses
skip	skip	skip	skip

◇	♩	♩	◇	◇
position	r. strikes	l. strikes	r. *grue*, crosses	position with capriole
skip			skip	skip

Arbeau's explanation agrees in the main with Zedler's: "a certain kind of dance which takes place in a circle. The ancients have put it together from various ring dances, and at the same time have introduced many leaps or other movements. Nowadays, however, since the art of the dance has achieved greater perfection, the *gavotte* is danced in a more decorous and much better manner than formerly." Unfortunately this writer also assumes the younger, "more decorous" *gavotte*, as it was danced at the court of Louis XIV, to be familiar. We learn only that it was a gay four-step dance *alla breve* beginning on the upbeat. We may take it for granted, however, that it coincided with the dance described by Father Mersenne in 1636: one or two rounds; then the first leader of the *branle à mener* bows before his lady, dances eight *pas* in front of her, bows again, and returns to his place with her; all the couples repeat this in succession; then there is a general bowing and the ladies are led back to their seats.

The column *gavotte* of the nineteenth century has nothing in common with the old one.

From these basic forms innumerable hybrids have arisen. The musicians included them all in one suite under the collective name of *branles de Champagne coupés* (mixed), *de Camp, de Henault, d'Avignon*.

We shall give a few examples. The *branle Cassandre* differs from the *branle double* only in having, after the four double steps to left and right, one simple and one double step to the left. In the *branle Pinagay*, after the first double step, the left foot is lifted high, and after the second double step, the left, right, and left are raised in turn; after the third and fourth double steps, however, there is no lifting of the feet.

The *branle Charlotte* has a double step to the left followed by two foot thrusts, a double step to the right without thrust, a simple step to the right with three thrusts, a simple step to the left with three thrusts, and a double step to the right without thrusts. The *branle de la guerre* consists of double steps. While the first four receive the usual time value of one longa, however, each of the next four gets only one breve: the steps are taken twice as fast. Three *grues* and a leap with *capriole* form the conclusion.

The BRANDO, the direct Italian counterpart of the *branle,* has lost a little of the stamp of the choral dance by the end of the sixteenth century. The circling and the linking of hands have not been entirely given up, but have become much less important. Two gentlemen and two ladies form a square—not side by side in couples, but diagonally opposite each other, so that the two gentlemen and the two ladies form opposite corners. From this position they go through fourteen figures with steps and skips, forward and backward, right and left, changing places and partners—in short, they dance a regular *quadrille.* The music has six parts; these parts differ in rhythm, and the rhythm even changes within the individual parts. Another type arranged by Negri, the *brando di Cales,* was danced by six persons in three couples.

TRIORI. The *passepied* belongs to northern Brittany, the *triori* to southern Brittany, writes Noël du Fail in his *Baliverneries* in 1549. The *triori* is danced *à trois pas vn saut,* in three steps and one leap, and it is three times as *magistrale & gaillarde* as any other dance. Noël du Fail has scarcely claimed too much. Eight years later Panurge describes the Breton dance as a kind of *cancan:* the women alone danced, lifting their dresses in front and kicking their legs up to the ceiling—obviously a fertility dance. Arbeau gives the following step patterns to two four-four measures:

l. foot placed
r. foot drawn up
l. foot placed
r. foot lifted
leap to the left in final position
l. foot lifted (heel to the right)
r. foot lifted (heel to the left)
l. foot lifted (heel to the right)

In conclusion, instead of the three foot thrusts, there might be side-ward movements with the heels raised high and kept close together; on the last note there was also a foot thrust.

Even in Arbeau's time this choral was almost unknown outside Brittany.

MEASURE was the English name in the sixteenth and seventeenth centuries for a dance of indefinite construction. All that we know is that it was slow and ceremonious and full of changes—"mannerly modest, full of state and ancientry," Shakespeare calls it. We may safely assume that it was close to the choral dance. For in 1595 Davies, in his poem *Orchestra*, compares the thirteen annual revolutions of the moon with *measures*, and in the same poem he states that the peasant rounds have had to give place to the more polite *measure*. There is no music by this name; apparently it could be danced to any stately dance melody. It disappeared in the time of Charles I.

1650–1750

THE AGE OF THE MINUET

General Characteristics

The seventeenth century belongs in the broad concept of the baroque in spite of its strong tendency to play back and forth between the classical and the non-classical poles. What the author has written, in connection with the history of music, of the arts in the baroque period is also true of the dance: "All their peculiar manifestations arise from the great fact that in the seventeenth century we have perhaps for the first time in world history a clear and strong division between the active and the passive in human culture, between creators and spectators, between artist and audience."

In the dance this means the growing importance of the ballet. We have not spoken of the ballet at the French court in the sixteenth century and during the reign of Louis XIII—not even of the founding of the so-called *ballet de cour* by Baldassarino Belgiojoso, whom the French called Balthasard de Beaujoyeulx. Indeed, we confessed in the section on the fifteenth century that within the history of the dance the beginnings of the ballet do not much concern us. If there is anything which interests us in the French court ballet of this age, it is its stamp of aristocratic dilettantism: together with a few professional dancers, high society itself supplies the participants, and the ballet is primarily designed for courtly society, even if the broader public is not excluded. Under the great successor of Louis XIII this state of affairs does not immediately change.

When we learn that Louis XIV in his own person dances the roles of the gods in court ballets, we are reminded of the ecstatic dances of the kings possessed by gods in the Sudan and in Polynesia, or of ancient Mexico with the princely choral of Motecuhçoma: "he [the god] comes in dancing followed by the two great Kings, Naçaualpilli, King of Tetzcoco, and Totoquiuaztli, King of Tepaneca, who dance on either side of him. Fear hovers over the assemblage while they dance." The dancing Louis is feared by none but admired by all. He is not possessed by the god, for he is not dancing the God in whom he believes. The dance of the Sun King is the futility of egomania.

But the violent revolution in the arts in the seventeenth century, referred to above, forced the ballet into a new course in the reign of Louis XIV. The same power which brought the nascent opera from the ballroom to the stage, from the seclusion of court festivities to the world of public theaters, has turned the *ballets de cour* and the *ballets du roi* into dance spectacles for a paying audience. In 1661 the art form of the ballet enters into the program of the newly established *Académie Royale de Musique et de Danse*. The gay pastime of carefree amateurs had become the serious work of professional dancers. Such metamorphoses are always contingent upon greatly enhanced artistic demands. They are both the cause of them and the result.

Thus the age of Louis XIV marks a peak in the artistic development of the dance, and contemporary writers are aware of this: *"La danse est parvenue au plus haut degré de sa perfection,"* exclaims Rameau proudly. Indeed, an English poet of the period demands for the dance equal rights with all the other arts:

> Hence, with her sister arts, shall dancing claim
> An equal right to universal fame;
> And Isaac's Rigadoon shall live as long
> As Raphael's painting, or as Virgil's song.
>
> JENYNS

When the English poet places the dancer Isaac (d'Orléans) beside Raphael and Virgil, he admits that France leads in the dance, and he says this still more clearly:

> None will sure presume to rival France,
> Whether she forms or executes the dance.

The artistic strength of the French dance of that time, however, lies mainly in its technical perfection. Here is no striving for expression, vitality, and naturalism, but for the classical ideals of clarity, regularity, and balance, even if bought at the price of rigidity. "They believe in the creative power of artistic prescriptions," Heinrich Morf once said of this period. In the domain of poetry this faith in rules led to the formation of a controlling and regulating body, the Academy; the painters followed with an *Académie de Peinture,* and the dancers were not left behind.

In 1661 thirteen dancing masters freed themselves from the fetters of the medieval guild, the *Communauté de Saint-Julien des Ménestriers,* which bound them to the musicians. In spite of the temperamental opposition of G. du Manoir in his capacity of *roi des joueurs d'instruments et des maîtres à dancer de France,* they formed an *Académie de la Danse* on the model of the *Académie de la Peinture et de la Sculpture* and the next year their statutes were approved by the King. The oldest and most experienced dancers were to belong to this body, and they wished to be able to teach without the master's certificate—as independent artists, that is, and not as artisans.

Nothing is heard of the accomplishments of this Academy, but that does not matter: it was the necessary expression of a period which laid the chief emphasis on pedagogy and principles in the arts. The systematic spirit of the dance instruction of the time can be traced in the foundation of the teaching method on a scheme of invariable basic positions of the head, the trunk, the arms, and the legs as the beginning and end of each movement.

Head:	seen from the front	Body:	in equilibrium (*d'aplomb*)
	inclined to the side		inclined to the side
	in three-quarter		diagonally (*épaulé*)
	inclined forward		inclined forward
	thrown back		flexed

To the feet, also, five basic positions are assigned and all the steps fall within them. They are called simply the five positions:

1. Heels together (final position)
2. Heels a foot apart (spread)
3. Left heel firmly at the ankle of the right foot (*emboiture*)
4. Left heel a foot in front of the right (step position)
5. One heel at a right angle to the point of the other foot (leg crossing)

394

In these positions lie all the possibilities of combining the steps, forward, backward, and sideward, without loss of balance. Charles L. Beauchamp (1636–1705), Louis XIV's dancing master for more than twenty years, is said to have been the first to outline these positions. In practice, of course, they had been known for thousands of years—we find most of them among the ancient Greeks, indeed among primitive peoples.

Raoul Auger Le Feuillet, a pupil of Beauchamp and likewise a member of the Academy, invented the first modern dance notation since the fifteenth century: he was the predecessor of Fischer-Klamt, Laban, and Neumann. The plates which he includes in his work *Chorégraphie, ou l'art de décrire la danse par caractères, figures et signes démonstratifs* (Paris, 1699) indicate the initial position of the feet, and their floor pattern, and he writes in with special signs the various steps and leaps. The system of the fifteenth century could only indicate the most important step pattern, but the new system gave also the direction and the succession of figures. The former was designed for the social dance, which could move freely about the room; the latter for the stage dance, the choreographic problems of which were complicated by the narrowness of the stage and the necessity of facing the audience. But in both cases only the feet were considered—trunk, head, and arms were completely ignored.

The English translator of the *Chorégraphie,* John Weaver, deserves our special attention, because his *Anatomical and Mechanical Lectures Upon Dancing* (London, 1721) are the first attempt to base dancing and dance instruction on the knowledge of the body. From this side, too, an attack was launched against the former indifference. Shortly after this the great Noverre was to require in the ballet master a knowledge of anatomy.

Processes of this kind—the intensification of the technical and artistic, systematization, notation, rationalization, and the organization of instruction—have the same drawbacks in all arts and in all cultures. They reveal a general decline of the instinctive, of the natural, and the unself-conscious in the performance; soon the joy in artistic achievement will consist less in taking part than in looking on. The fate of the Asiatic communal dance after the methodical ordering of all movements proves this no less than does the history of the European social dance between the reigns of Louis XIV and Louis XVI.

When Louis XIV came to the throne, a pronounced change had already taken place in the dances themselves. Their romantic and folkloristic features had faded just as much as those of the contemporary literature, and the gay variety of types, forms, and movements had been lost. The Spanish dances and the folk dances of the past generation now lived on only in the music of the composers; they no longer had anything to do with the living dance. To be sure, the new age reacted against the *préciosité* of the first half of the century and turned again to "nature"—not to *la grossière nature,* however, but to the sensible, simple, clear naturalness of classical antiquity.

As a matter of fact, the *minuet,* the new dance of the period, comes from the people, from nature. But now that the enthusiasm for the picturesque and primitive has vanished, it is no longer this origin which is praised but rather its magnificent courtly transformation. What a happy fate, exclaims Dufort in 1728, that the *minuet,* ugly, insignificant, and lowly as it was, could become so splendid (*pomposo*) in the course of time that one entirely forgot its humble birth!

The *branle, courante,* and *gavotte,* which with the *minuet* as conclusion formed the customary dance suite at the court of Versailles, had similarly forgotten their rustic origin and adapted themselves to the ceremonious formality of the *bal paré.* In all four dances the court society formed a column in couples; the King with his partner performed the first dance and went to the end of the line; the other couples did the same, until the King was leading again. Then his Majesty withdrew to the throne and left the others to continue dancing.

The popular chain dance in the form of the old *branle* has been done away with. When it comes in again by a back door, it appears in

English dress as the *country dance* or *contredanse*. The ancient basic forms of the choral dance, the circle and the double file, have here gone through the mill of aristocratic life in Britain and have been refined into figure dances of incredible variety. As early as 1717 Taubert writes that the *"Anglicae* and English dances, which were both a pleasure to dance and lovely to look at, were accepted almost everywhere at this time."

With these two types of dance the repertory of the time is exhausted: "everywhere we look now, whether in the distinguished courts, or in the towns at weddings, parties, and banquets absolutely nothing is danced but the minuet and some English dances, which certainly pleases many a miserable dancer and dancing master." Literary sources such as Casanova's memoirs confirm this. And it is said that in Paris gentlemen "had taken lessons for two and more years and still had never got beyond the minuet."

Although the traditional duality of choral dance and couple dance still exists, there is no longer the contrast of close and expanded dance. The "tread" and leap movements are practically abolished; the *saltarello, tourdion, canaries,* and *volta* have disappeared from the dance hall, and the five positions expressly state that the feet shall never be more than one foot apart. Close movement reigns supreme and persists to this day—the step becomes *menu* (small), indeed *menuet* (tiny), and the *pas de menuet* is introduced into all dances, even into the English chorals. This is in the main a conscious process; the "honest dancing master" finds "the *douce* manner of this period the most pleasing," finds "that the very best dancers forego the large variations which come from those famous dances and which could easily be employed in the *menuet,* because of the freedom of its form, and that they cultivate a very *douce* manner not only with the hands and feet but with the whole body."

The relationship between the two types of dance shifts rapidly. Taubert barely mentions the *contre* and does not devote even a single sentence to it in his bulky volume in 1717. Dufort in his *Ballo nobile* of 1728 at least appends a note about it to his very detailed exposition of the *minuet*. However, in 1767 the *minuet* appears for the last time in the index of a dance manual (Chavanne's). Meanwhile, in the short space of time between 1755 and 1783 seventeen special monographs are devoted to the *contre,* and what is almost more significant, it is lampooned in 1796 in the *Elementos de la Ciencia contradanzaria* of "Don Preciso." The *minuet* is out of favor; Moreau de Saint-Méry's elegant dance book of 1789 mentions the *sévérité, avec laquelle on s'est accoutumé à juger le menuet depuis quelques années.* Nevertheless, it was still taught in the nineteenth century.

The advance of the *contre* is analogous with the rise of bourgeois society and the decline of the aristocratic culture. To be sure, the *contredanse* borrows some of its steps from the *minuet, courante,* and *bourrée.* How could it be otherwise! But it is a choral dance, the basic forms of which are older than the single couple dance. We can scarcely attach too much importance to what is happening here: the resumption of the choral dance marks the end of that *cortezia,* which as the creation of the troubadour period had for more than five hundred years provided the social order with content and standards of behavior. People were even conscious of this up to a certain point. Formerly, as Moreau de Saint-Méry expresses it, the enjoyment of dancing suffered from a kind of vanity which had devised a ceremonial system for all private balls. It took method, even research, to determine who should open the ball and in what succession each guest should dance his first *minuet.* Finally, says Moreau, people began to feel that a party is not a course in etiquette, and for a long time society turned promptly to the *contre* as soon as the *grands parens* had begun a *minuet* and kissed each other for the sake of appearances.

What a contrast! What a significance even the bow has with which the dancers introduce the ceremonial rite of the *minuet!* Dufort devotes two whole chapters to it, Taubert sixty pages, and Chavanne almost his whole book. And after the bow comes the gallant play: the sexes meet and separate gracefully, glide past—the erotic is stylized to the last degree, everything is suggested, refined, and generalized to the point of formalism. Eros here is devotion, not love; discipline, not impulse. To dance the *minuet* is to pay homage to woman.

To dance the *minuet*, however, also means to create aesthetic values, and Goethe, the son of a people to whom the *minuet* was strange, records his astonishment at the Roman carnival: "Nobody ventures unconcernedly to dance unless he has been taught the art; the minuet in particular is regarded as a work of art and is performed, indeed, only by a few couples. Such a couple is surrounded by the rest of the company in a circle, admired, and applauded at the end." The *contre*, on the other hand, is merely a pastime and a social game. Not only the ceremony but also the spontaneity have gone out of the love play. Without the power of the folk choral and without the exaltation of the court dance, the *English dance* unites the guests of an evening by the spell of rhythmical movement into a chance casual community. At the German courts it might happen in the carnival that "society" danced the *minuet*, but "the *contre* dancers were made up of all kinds of people whose pleasure it was to join in." A chance community—without serious purpose, indeed without art. The *minuet* dancer takes lessons for years; the *contre* dancer remains for the most part a dilettante in the worst sense.

And the contrast between these dances and between the people who danced them is reflected in the contrast in the manuals. It is a strange experience to turn from the authors of the *Ballo nobile* to the writers of the directions for the *contre*. What the former say and leave unsaid is simply what Molière's immortal dancing master expresses:

Il n'y a rien qui soit si nécessaire aux hommes que la danse. . . .
Sans la danse, un homme ne saurait rien faire. . . . Tous les mal-
heurs des hommes, tous les revers funestes dont les histoires sont
remplies, les bévues des politiques, et les manquements des grands
capitaines, tout cela n'est venu que faute de savoir danser. . . .
Le Bourgeois Gentilhomme, I, 2.

There is nothing so necessary for men as dancing. . . . Without dancing a man can do nothing. . . . All the disasters of mankind, all the fatal misfortunes that histories are so full of, the blunders of politicians, the miscarriages of great commanders, all this comes from want of skill in dancing. . . .

This is not at all exaggerated: is there anything, asks the dance teacher J. M. de Chavanne in 1767, more useful for young people than to be able to enter a drawing room without self-consciousness, to address a person of rank with decorum, and to have an easy carriage, without the stiffness of marionettes, such as one sees every day? What are children until they have had instruction in the dance?

The teaching itself is almost a mystery; the books require sometimes more than twelve hundred pages in order to treat all the odds and ends and the gamut of movements and possibilities. Every detail seems to have tremendous importance and the student is expected to give his undivided attention.

No sooner does the *contre* appear than the emphasis changes. The *Dancing Master,* which in 1650–51 gives for the first time the "Directions for Country Dances," says briefly and simply in a few lines of the preface: "The Art of Dancing, called by the ancient Greeks Orchestice, and Orchestis, is a commendable and rare Quality fit for young Gentlemen and Ladies, if opportunely and civilly used." That is all. Then follow several hundred dances: the notes are in two lines; the basic position is indicated with a few suns, representing the gentlemen, and a few crescent moons for the ladies, and the sets and movements are described in telegram style—"Back all, meet again," or "Sides all, set and turn." The matter-of-factness of it can hardly be surpassed. Most of the later *contre* books do not approach it, but the pretentious tone has vanished. When in 1771 Gallini publishes his *Critical Observations on the Art of Dancing,* he begins with the painful admission that he is sensible of the ridiculousness or presumption of a teacher who attributes to his art more value and importance than are due it;

and when De la Cuisse in 1762 writes, under the title *Le Répertoire des Bals*, a *Théorie-Pratique des Contredanses*, they are *décrites d'une manière aisée . . . pour les pouvoir danser facilement* (!). The book is intended, like the *contre* itself, *pour tout le monde* and therefore written *à la portée de tout le monde*. For the dancers no longer know anything. Four dancing masters were engaged for the carnival in the amphitheater at Madrid; they "watch the *contre* dances constantly and direct those ignorant of the dance." Often there is only one person in the company who knows the dance and sometimes even he does not know the melody; or he knows the melody, but not the figures, and the dancers look at one another *et restent court*.

These things, however—the flight from the *minuet* into the *contre* and the growing indifference even to this dance—have a deeper cause in a certain repugnance for something which is a vital necessity of the dance, for lightness. The genius of high baroque art tends downward rather than upward, toward weight rather than elevation. The pompous architectural style of the period has nothing of the upward striving, of the earth-spurning quality of the Gothic cathedral. A Versailles palace lies broad and heavy and immovable on the ground, impressive in its mass. The people of 1700 have also a different feeling about their bodies and movement from their ancestors of the last five hundred years. Their *cortezia* has lost the gay, elastic, youthful quality and has exchanged it for a phlegmatic, periwigged dignity, which is quite out of keeping with the dance. Let us not be deceived by the fact that the external art of the dance was never greater than in the period of the *minuet*. Does not a pedantic art always step into the foreground when the inner urge, the driving necessity has slackened? Rameau expresses this very thing: *Il ne convient pas à de grandes personnes de sauter et de se tourmenter dans les danses figurées, où ce n'est que mouvements doux et gracieux qui ne dérangent pas le corps de ce bon air qui est si fort usité par notre nation.* (It is not seemly for great personages to leap and toss themselves about in figure dances, for it is only gentle and gracious movements which do not take from the body the dignified air so much cultivated in our country.) And in the biography of Louis XIV we read that in 1660 Racine's *Britannicus* was acted before him and he heard the lines:

> *Pour mérite premier, pour vertu singulière,*
> *Il excelle à conduire un char dans la carrière,*
> *A disputer des prix indignes de ses mains,*
> *A se donner lui-même en spectacle aux Romains.*

Louis XIV was unwilling to provide a "spectacle for the Romans," and henceforth danced no more in public.

Italy had led the way. In 1620 an Italian priest speaks of the *regolare maestà* (formal majesty), of the *portamento* (noble attitude), and of the *regi passi alteri* (regal, haughty steps) of the Venetian ladies. But it is mainly French observers who are struck in Venice by the *marcher grave et lent* (slow and solemn movement). *"Tout le plaisir ne consiste qu'a voir vingt ou trente personnes se promener de suite, comme on fait dans les allées des Tuileries et au Luxembourg."* (All the pleasure consists in seeing twenty or thirty persons walk in succession, as they do in the alleys of the Tuileries or in the Luxembourg.) He refers here to that ceremonious, un-dancelike striding that is continually being ascribed unjustly to the courtly dances of the Middle Ages, to the *pavane* and the *basse danse*. This danceless dance belongs exclusively to the high baroque period.

The Movements

Balancé, Italian *bilanciato*, Spanish *balanceado*, *Valanceado*, side step to and fro or forward and back with change of weight from the first to the second foot.

Ballonné, from Position I the one foot is raised high; as it is lowered, the other flies upward, so that both meet in the air.

Battement, *battuto*, *batido*, the lifted leg is struck against the standing leg or strikes it in crossing in front or behind; the latter movement corresponds to the *pied croisé*.

Bilanciato = *balancé*.

Cadente = *tombé*.

Caido = *tombé*.

Campanela was the Spanish term for a half circle of the free leg.

Chassé, scacciato, sacado, generally a side step with the other foot drawn up. The directions are rather contradictory.

Contretemps, contrattempo, contratiempo, in bending step (*demi-coupé*) a skip is taken on the standing leg, while the free leg is thrown rapidly backward and forward. The touching of the floor after the skip comes on the downbeat.

Cortado = *coupé*.

Coupé, tronco, cortado, a bending step followed by a straight step or a slide. The body straightens again on the downbeat.

Demi-coupé, mezzo-tronco, medio cortado, a bending step followed from the fourth position through the first and back to the fourth.

Echado (Spanish) = *jeté*.

Elevé, rialzato, is the knee stretching, probably the *ondeggiando* of the fifteenth century?

Entrechat (*capriola*), *intrecciata,* "interlaced" leap with several crossings of the legs in the air.

Fleuret, fioretto, floreo, a bending step followed by two steps on the toes (*fioretto semplice*), bending step and changing step (*fioretto iscacciato*), or bending step *mezzo gittato* with two single steps (*fioretto in gittato*). The movement may go forward, backward, and sideward.

Gittato = *jeté*.

Glissade, sdrucciolata, sideward glide.

Glissé, sdrucciolo, gliding step. *Se glisser signifie un pas très-lent* (Gliding means a very slow step).

Intrecciata = *entrechat*.

Iscacciato = *chassé*.

Jeté, gittato, echado, bending step with skip on the standing foot. Its duration is half a measure.

Mouvement, movimento, a flexing of the joints. *Mouvement du cou de pied* ("arch"—not *coup de pied!*), raising and lowering of the foot; *mouvement du genou,* flexing of the knee; *mouvement de la hanche,* flexing of the hip. Since Beauchamp, who was the first to concern himself with the position of the arms and prescribe rules for them, the *mouvements* of the arm have also been distinguished. Steps which are mainly a flexing of the ankle are accompanied by a flexing of the wrist; steps which are controlled mainly by the knee joint call for a movement of the elbows; the *pas tombés* demand an accompanying movement of the shoulders. In all cases the arms are stretched out freely so that the hands are held at the level of the diaphragm.

Pas composé, a group of steps composed of several *pas simples.*

Pas simple, no longer a sliding step, but each single step of a group.

Piegato = *plié,* bending step.

Pirouette, pirueta = spinning turn.

Relevé = *élevé.*

Sacado = *chassé.*

Saut, salto = leap. The rebound comes on the downbeat.

Scacciato = *chassé.*

Sdrucciolata = *glissade.*

Sdrucciolo = *glissé.*

Sfuggito, gliding of both feet.

Temps, tempo, tiempo = group of steps repeated periodically.

Tombé, cadente, caido, lowering of the foot from the toe position. If preceded by a bending step it is called *pas tombé, pas de gaillarde.*

Tricoté. On the first count the right foot moves out of the fifth position behind the heel of the left foot; on the second count the left heel is lifted and the foot glides into the first position beside the right foot; on the third count the right foot glides into the fifth position in front of the left foot; on the fourth count the left foot is lifted slightly off the floor. Both feet are always kept close together.

Tronco = *coupé.*

Valanceado = *balancé.*

Couple Dances

The MINUET, mentioned by Du Manoir as early as 1664, passes for a folk dance of Poitou, but as an art dance, it is a child of the *courante*. The name comes from *(pas) menu*, "small." We hear of *pas menus* as early as the fifteenth century. After the end of the seventeenth century the *minuet,* as successor to the *courante,* was the real, almost the only, court dance and the staple of dance instruction—*la porta della danza.* It remained unsurpassed in its blend of dignity and charm, restrained sprightliness and aloof gallantry, and perhaps the most beautiful example of that *stile simple* introduced at the accession of Louis XIV.

The *minuet* was performed in open couples; spectators and partners were saluted with ceremonial bows. With dainty little steps and glides, to the right and to the left, forward and backward, in quarter turns, approaching and retreating hand in hand, searching and evading, now side by side, now facing, now gliding past one another, the ancient dance play of courtship appears here in a last and almost unrecognizable stylization and refinement.

Refinement, but not artificiality. For everything remained simple and transparent. The dance followed along a clear line and its movements were plain and economical. There were no *pas d'invention,* no *menuet brodé;* the body was held *droit sans balancement, ni geste d'aucun membre.*

A certain limited uniformity prevails in the *pas* of the *minuet:* they consist of two bending steps and two straight steps; each of these groups of four steps takes two three-four measures; and they always begin with the right foot. The details and the sequence, however, are variously specified. The classical form, as prescribed by Rameau, Dufort, Chavanne, and Compan, for instance, is as follows:

1	2	3	1	2	3
♩	♩	♩	♩	♩	♩
r. bending step forward straightening		l. bending step gliding straightening	r. straight forward		l. straight forward

The *pas* extend over the bar line—a pitfall for uncertain dancers. Hence the careful Dufort advises striking the first beat of the first measure but not the first beat of the second. From this we understand, too, why the good *minuets* of the older style receive, through the concluding half note in a phrase of two measures, a strong accent on the fifth count and, almost imperceptibly, extend melodically over the bar line—a charming refinement of the rhythm, reminiscent of the ambiguity of the six-count measures of medieval and Oriental music. We frequently meet with suspended rhythm in the dance; the violin accompaniment of the Austrian *Ländler* offers attractive examples.

Taubert in his *Honest Dancing Master* recommends a simpler step pattern more in keeping with the music:

♩	♩	♩	♩
Bending step r.	straight l.	straight r.	bending step l.

The tempo has undergone a decided transformation. In Kuhnau's *Neue Klavierübung* (1689) it is "rather rapid," and in 1752 J. J. Quantz requires "two quarter notes to one pulse beat." Since he reckons the pulse beat at eighty to the minute, we can put the tempo at ♩ = M.M. 160. Three years later, in 1755, the dancing master Hänsel states that the tempo should be twice as fast as that of the *polonaise,* thereby agreeing with Quantz. Not until the nineteenth century is *adagio* used.

The "floor pattern" of the *minuet* was originally a figure 8, then an S, still later a 2, and after the reform of the Parisian dancing master Pécour, about 1700, it became a Z. This means that on a Z-shaped floor plan the gentleman and the lady performed the dance with and against one another. After the ceremonial bow they joined hands, danced one step (i. e., group of steps) forward, and turned with two further steps so that they were facing each other diagonally from the inner corners of the Z. Now they let go of hands and the figure proper began: two steps on the horizontal lines of the Z to the right and two steps back; then two further steps on the diagonal line past each other; with a turn the dancers have now reached the inner corner of the Z, where the partner had been previously; two steps to the right and two to the left on these horizontals complete the figure, and a counter-figure brings the dancers back to their original positions. The clearest directions are given by Rameau (Plate 25).

This static character is strangely alien to the dynamic concept of the middle of the century. Voltaire once compared the metaphysical philosophers to the *minuet* dancers, "who, most elegantly adorned, bow a few times, mince daintily across the room exhibiting all their charms, move without progressing a single step, and end up on the very spot whence they started." Something of this impatient spirit of the new age makes itself felt here and there towards the end of the century. At the Court of Cassel, for instance, the dancers no longer began the *minuet* one couple at a time, but danced all at once as in the *contre*—"which gave rise to a certain amount of confusion."

Finally the radical change in social conditions and ideals at the close of the eighteenth century took the ground away from under the feet of the *minuet*. It was deposed and condemned to death. In 1891, however, it was revived for about ten years. But this new *minuet* with its many figures has hardly anything but the name in common with the old form.

The PASSEPIED, in contrast to the *triori,* was the choral dance of northern Brittany, where no Breton is spoken. Praetorius in 1612 explains the name from the fact "that in this dance one foot must be struck against and crossed over the other." In 1597, half a century after Noël du Fail mentioned the *passepied* for the first time, King Henry IV of France decided to travel to Blois in order to learn the *passepied de Bretagne*. However, it is not recorded as a real court dance until 1665, and by 1767 it is no longer danced in the *salons*.

During its courtly period the *passepied* was regarded as a gay *minuet* in varied figures in three-eight time beginning on the upbeat, and as in the case of the *minuet* it often happened "that two measures were written as one." Its relationship is not clear, however; we can only guess at it. Perhaps the *passepied*, like so many *branles*, had adopted the courtship pantomime of lady and gentleman repeated couple by couple, and had gradually, in imitation of the courtly style, discarded the connecting chain processions as superfluous and distracting.

A letter of Madame de Sévigné's of July 24, 1689, confirms this dual character. Writing of the son of the seneschal of Rennes, she says: *"Il danse ces belles chaconnes, les folies d'Espagne, mais surtout passepieds avec sa femme, d'une perfection, d'un agrément qui ne se peut représenter; point de pas réglés, rien qu'une cadence juste, des fantaisies de figures, tantôt en branle comme les autres, et puis à deux seulement comme les menuets, tantôt se reposant, tantôt ne mettant pas les pieds à terre. . . ."* (He dances these beautiful *chaconnes*, the *folies d'Espagne*, and especially *passepieds* with his wife, with a perfection, with a harmony, impossible to describe; no set steps, nothing but a true cadence, with the most whimsical figures, now in the *branle* like the others, now alone in couples as in the *minuet*, now very serenely, now scarcely touching their feet to the ground. . . .)

The BOURRÉE did not take its name from the word *bourrée*, "a bundle of twigs," but from *bourrir*, "to flap the wings." This idea, however, is not borne out by either the folk dance or the society dance. In its native land, Auvergne, there are a double file choral dance and a couple dance by this name. This choral dance is performed by a file of men and a file of women facing each other. As the two lines dance repeatedly forward and back, the leader on the right and the dancer opposite him break from their lines and change places, and one after another their neighbors follow their example, until all have left their original places. As a couple dance it is performed in open style without touching, to the accompaniment of the bagpipes or a hurdy-gurdy. The men dance with arms raised high and the women with their skirts held gracefully. Apparently it is close to the Italian *trescone*. On the count of one in a three-eight rhythm beginning on the upbeat, the heels are struck together, and on the count of three, the left heel is stamped. This does not always hold, however. For in Languedoc every *bourrée* —like those in the suites of the seventeenth and eighteenth centuries— is in four-eight or *alla breve* time. In certain parts of this region all dances in four-eight time are called *bourrées,* and in other parts *rigaudons;* dances in triple time are called *montagnardes.*

The statement that Margaret, the sister of King Charles IX (1560– 74), introduced the Auvergne *bourrée* to the court is not quite accurate. It is true that in 1565 the *bourrée* was danced at a court festival in honor of Catherine de Medici, but it was danced by natives of Auvergne, and as a folk dance; as homage to a province, not as a society dance or even a ceremonial court dance. Arbeau, Mersenne, and especially Caroso and Negri leave us in the lurch—their silence proves that the *bourrée* remained a pure folk dance far into the seventeenth century, even though Praetorius occasionally mentions it. As late as 1676 Madame de Sévigné deplores the fact that this dance, the most beautiful in the world, is not known at Versailles. *"C'est la plus surprenante chose du monde; des paysans, des paysannes, une oreille aussi juste que vous, une légèreté, une disposition . . . enfin, j'en suis folle."* (It is the most surprising thing in the world; peasants, with an ear as fine as yours, a lightness, a skill . . . indeed, I am quite mad about it.) Thus she writes to her daughter from Vichy, and continues: *"Je voudrais bien vous envoyer pour la noce deux filles et deux garçons qui sont ici, avec le tambour de basque, pour vous faire voir cette bourrée. Enfin les Bohémiens sont fades en comparaison."* (I should like to send you for your wedding two girls and two boys who are here, with their tambourines, so that you could see this *bourrée*. Indeed, the gypsies are tame in comparison.)

When the *bourrée* finally arrives at the court, it is in alien dress, in the uniform of the ballet. Its step pattern resembles that of the other art dances of the time: the *pas de bourrée* is a *demi-coupé* + a *pas marché sur la pointe du pied* + *demi-jeté* (a bending step followed by a straight step on the toes and a jump on the standing leg). But since this jump may very easily occasion an undesired accent in the flow of movement, the *pas de bourrée* may be replaced by *fleurets*, executed by the ladies, that is, by a bending step with two concluding straight steps.

The SISSONNE, the name of which probably derives from a certain Count F. C. de Roussy of Sissonne, has not, so far as I can discover, been recorded as a dance in earlier times. The later dance step *temps de Sissonne* consists of a leap from the *plié*.

The GIGUE borrowed its much disputed name in the seventeenth century from the English *jig*, which in turn comes from the Old French *giguer*, "to dance." This verb can be traced through the hypothetical Frankish *gíga* to the Old Norse *gígja*.

The tradition is that the *jig* became a courtly dance in the time of Queen Elizabeth and was introduced to the continental courts in the reign of Louis XIV. The form of this society dance can be determined only from Feuillet's book (1699) on the dance. Since he designates it there as a *gigue à deux*, we may infer that the *gigue* was a couple dance, but also that it had not always been a couple dance. Moreover, we must remember that Feuillet is not recording society dances but ballets of the Paris opera, which were at best stylizations of the society forms.

Very different is the *giga* which has survived as a couple dance in Italy up to the present day. The two partners make three rounds and then perform *il suo balletto*—presumably a courting dance. Thereupon they join hands, take three steps forward and, changing hands, the same number back. In the fourth figure the woman raises her left arm, which the man seizes with his right, and gives her right hand under her arm into the left hand of her partner; with their arms thus interlaced, the man whirls his partner, until they separate to begin anew.

Nor does Danckert's historical study of the *gigue* provide any more precise information as to its execution. Though from enumerations such as Martin's "Irish Hayes, Jiggs and Roundelays" (1589) or Heywood's "Country measures, rounds, and jiggs" (1603), it might seem that *jigs* were "always chorals or round dances for several persons," nevertheless we are forced to conclude that *jigs* were not dances of this kind. The fact, too, that country dances are designated as *jigs* in Playford's *Dancing Master* proves merely that the very fashionable country dance figures were also set to *jig* melodies. As late as 1843, for instance, people danced hand in hand "round the table to the measure of an Irish Jig."

As a matter of fact the true *jig* of the Scots and Irish is not bound to any definite form. Danced by one or more persons, it is quick and fiery—"hot and hasty, like a Scotch jig, and full as fantastical" (Shakespeare, *Much Ado About Nothing,* II, 1). The Scot does not dance with the "insipid formal movements" of the French and English. Like the ancient *kordax,* the Ukrainian *hopák,* and the French *rigaudon,* the *jig* calls for a lively stamping of the heels and rapid foot work with a quiet torso—in which it resembles the other Scottish dances also:

> But hornpipes, jigs, strathspeys, and reels,
> Put life and mettle in their heels.
>
> BURNS, *Tam O'Shanter.*

Ecorcheville and Danckert have described in detail the many forms of their inciting, terse, and energetic duple rhythm.

The RIGAUDON presents the historian with a difficult problem. The uncertainty begins with the name: the most recent Romance philologists have been unable to suggest anything better than Rousseau's untenable derivation from the name of an "inventor," Rigaud. But surely the word must be related to the Italian *rigodone* = *rigolone* and the corresponding diminutive *rigoletto,* "circle dance."

The *rigaudon* is one of the liveliest dances—"the nimble, the sprightly rigadoon," Jenyns calls it in 1728. Descriptions of its courtly and artistic forms do not appear until the eighteenth century and then only sporadically and contradictorily. Dufort explains the *pas de rigaudon* as a changing step plus a leap. Compan disagrees. He regards the *rigaudon* as a Provençal dance. It is a light dance in duple time and is executed in one spot. Starting with the first position the dancer bends the knee, leaps up, and in so doing thrusts first the right and then the left leg out from the hip. Then comes another *plié,* a leap, and return to the first position. The nineteenth century supplies a more detailed description of the *pas de rigaudon:* on the first count the right foot is lifted about two inches and put down again; on the second, the left foot is thrown to the left side, while the right foot hops; on the third count, the left foot comes to rest in the first position; on the fourth, the right foot swings quickly forward and backward and the left foot springs back into the fifth position. The legs must be stretched (nineteenth century!). The sideward movement of the leg described here was attributed by Compan to Languedoc; in Provence the legs were thrust forward and slightly crossed. This may explain why for many dance teachers the *pas de rigaudon* was simply a crossed step.

A peculiar contrast to these stylized forms of the dancing masters is presented by that popular *rigaudon* which still lives in a few isolated districts of Dauphiné, the Cévennes, and the Massif Central. It is performed in couples and consists of a turning dance as the first part (*les danseurs tournent en rond*) and a double file dance as the second part. After the young man has danced opposite his own girl, he steps over in front of the girl of his left neighbor—the ancient motif of exchange of women. In the second part, the *rigaudon* proper, one of those innumerable courting dances takes place: the man moving vigorously, leaping, shouting, clapping his hands and snapping his fingers, and turning his partner by the hand, the girl more quietly, her arms hanging by her side and her eyes cast down, retreating and approaching—all to the accompaniment of singing.

412

The contradiction is probably explained by the fact that the term *rigaudon* is not exclusive. We learn, for example, that in Languedoc the names *rigaudon, bourrée,* and *montagnarde* are used interchangeably; what is called *rigaudon* in one place is known as *bourrée* in another. *Rigaudon,* then, is a collective name for the folk dances of southeastern France.

The FOLÍA, "madness," was originally a Portuguese carnival dance —that is, a fertility dance. Covarrubbias describes it in 1611 in his *Tesoro de la lengua castellana* as a noisy Portuguese dance of many step patterns to the accompaniment of castanets and other instruments. Some of the dancers carry masked figures on their shoulders; others, dressed as girls with pointed sleeves, turn, dance, and play the castanets. So great is the din, so fast the tempo, that it seems as though they had all gone out of their minds. Hence the dance was given the name *folía.*

The Spaniards adopted it and cultivated it with zeal, apparently in the form of a wooing dance: to a *sarabande*-like melody in three-four time, one or two persons danced vigorously and ardently with erotic gestures. North of the Pyrenees the repeatedly described *basso-ostinato* melody of the *folies d'Espagne,* as it was soon called, with its characteristic minor seventh, became more popular than the dance itself. However, we have evidence that in France at least the *folía* was also danced. A letter of the Marquise de Sévigné of July 24, 1689, proves that there was a society dance of this name, and Feuillet's *Chorégraphie* mentions it as a dance of the theater. Both sources state clearly that this dance had no *pas réglés,* that rather, as was so often the case in the time of Louis XIV, only the music and the general mood were prescribed, the details of execution being left to the dancer.

The ALLEMANDE is said to have been adopted at the court of Louis XIV as a kind of trophy from the annexation of Alsace. It did not reach its full flowering until much later. About 1760 a Parisian dancing master says that it is more popular in Paris than any other dance, and this is confirmed by the history of the public dance halls of the time, the *wauxhall* and the *Bal Champêtre*. This new French version had nothing in common with the old *allemande* of the sixteenth century and very little with the *Ländler*. The same dancing master, Guillaume, freely admits that everybody knew the *allemande* had come from Germany but that it was danced quite differently—every master taught it in his own way. The basic step seems to have been the *chassé,* the changing step to the side. What Guillaume and Dubois describe and what St. Aubin's beautiful picture of a ball (Plate 29) shows are the charming turns of the lady on the arm of the gentleman, the gliding of the gentleman under the arm of the lady, the passing of the partners back to back; in short, a succession of positions and attitudes full of that *grace et précision qui sert au développement de la belle nature,* but empty of all originality, power, and emotion—a last manifestation of the "art" which could scarcely conceal the poverty of the dance in that period.

The *allemande* in the French courtly form is said to have survived in Bohemia into the second half of the nineteenth century. Waldau describes it as one of the "most beautiful, most pleasant dances; but its figures are sometimes difficult to execute, if the beauty is not to be lost, for the particular charm of the dance lies in the fine carriage of the torso and in the graceful interlacing of the arms (the so-called *passes*). The dancers stand in couples or in a circle, one couple behind the other, or again two men between two women facing each other. The *allemande* has the triple time of the Austrian *Ländler;* it consists of three so-called *pas marchés* and is performed with glides, now forwards, now back."

Choral Dances

The CONTRE. The chief collection of English dances, which from 1650 ("1651") on was brought out in eighteen editions by the famous publisher John Playford under the title of *The English Dancing-*

Master or Directions for Country Dances, contains two broad types of choral dance: *rounds* and *longways.* The *round* is the *branle,* the circle dance with men and women alternating; the *longways,* a double file with the men and women in straight lines facing each other. In both, the dances are divided into a number of figures: groups of three, arches, stars, place changing, circling, moving and falling back, crossing over, hey, procession, swinging of partners right and left, and many others. The figures are manifold and their various combinations of the finding and losing of partners are inexhaustible—Playford's *English Dancing Master* describes in the eighteenth edition (1728) nine hundred country dances!

There is nothing specifically English about these dances. Circle and file are the basic forms of all choral dances and, with the majority of the figures, may be traced back to the culture of the Stone Age, indeed of the Early Stone Age. Even the arrangement of men and women in a double file facing each other and in couples has already been pointed out in a number of African tribes, among the Baila of Rhodesia, the Bergdama, and the Boloki of the Congo. The primitive, underlying theme is again the love combat with approaching and retreating, with separating and uniting. The North German folk movement has even preserved the old dance of coyness: in the figures *Damenstolz* (lady's pride) and *Herrenstolz* (gentleman's pride) the dancers move about haughtily with arms akimbo. Nor is England the only heir of the ancient dance property in the rest of Europe. Bohemia has a pure *longways* in its *chytavá,* and it is perhaps worth noting that a particular type of this Czech dance, the *motovidlo,* has the same meaning as the older English name for the "chain"—*reel.*

These figure chorals have been particularly developed in the court ballet. The participation of many dancers was important to the spectator here for only one reason. It supplied constant occupation and satisfaction for his eye through the variety of arrangement and movement of lines in geometrical designs, and indeed in significant successions of letters.

So holy creatures there within those lights,
Singing, flew to and fro, and made themselves
Now D, now I, now L, in figured flights.
They moved, singing to their own measure, till
One of these characters they had become,
Then for a little halted and were still.

DANTE, *Paradiso*, XVIII, 76 ff.
(Tr. Jefferson Butler Fletcher.)

Themselves they then displayed in five times seven
Vowels and consonants; and I observed
The parts as unto me they there seemed given.
Diligite iustitiam were massed
In the inscription as first verb and noun;
Qui iudicatis terram—were the last.
Then in the M of the fifth word they stayed,
Still duly ordered, so that Jupiter
Seemed to be silver there with gold inlaid.

Ibid., 88 ff.

Ballet chorals in figures were equally native to most countries; outside of the ballet, the classical territory of the figure choral was Spain. In his *Entremés del Carnaval,* Fumes y Villalpando describes in detail a Spanish marriage dance of the seventeenth century. The bride, with a female companion, enters and throws flowers into the air. Two young men join them and the four cross with *fleurets.* Two ladies increase the number to six and form a chain with the others, until the bridegroom and a friend make up the necessary eight.

> Then the eight with winged foot
> Cross and criss-cross gleefully,
> Turn their backs and turn their faces,
> Walk ahead and meet again

Play the game of sticks of love
Move with many turns ahead
As the custom may direct;
The *capona* sets the posture;
The *chacona* gives the leaps;
The *serdana* marks the measure,
And back again upon their places
Both the newly wedded sing
Seguidillas, rich of meaning,
And begin anew the dance.

Although the basic arrangement of the dancers is not given, we get a good picture: from the ancient motifs of the sword and group wooing dances with their weaving and unweaving, their movement forward and backward, the swinging of partners, the crossing, and intertwining, and the stick-tapping, a structure arises which is closely related to the Spanish church dances, on the one hand, and to the English *country* and *Morris dances* on the other.

This is by no means the only evidence. Theatrical spectacles like the *bailes* are full of precise indications for the execution of the social choral dance. Monteser's *El Gusto Loco,* published in 1668, contains as many as fifteen figures:

Bandas—bajando—cruzados—corro—cruzado—vueltas cruzadas de cuatro personas—cruzado y corro—arriba las cuatro mujeres—dos corros—vuelta cada uno con la suya—vueltas en sus puestos—bandas—las bandas deshechas—dos cruzados de á cuatro personas—por de fuera y acabar.

Some of these professional terms are obscure. But obviously a column dance (*arriba y abajo!*) of four couples, the men on one side, the women on the other, is indicated—otherwise the four women could not go *arriba* (up) together—with circle formation, crossing, procession, star, and *tour de mains.*

417

It must be understood that all these Spanish figure dances are *builes,* not *danzas*—folk dances, not court dances, just like the English *country dances.*

Consequently it would be difficult to explain why the courtly *contredanse* should have originated especially in England. The English *country dance* must have had some essential quality which the others, above all the Spanish figure dances, lacked. In fact it has one characteristic to be found nowhere else: the gradual entrance of couple after couple, the pleasing combination of the choral dance and the single couple dance.

But this, to be sure, is not an English invention either. The Rhodesian Baila leave the line in couples and dance together, and the Bergdama and Boloki do the same. In New Britain two rows of women dance opposite each other, and those at the end of the line move up past the others to the head. This keeps on until the original succession is restored. But in Europe the English alone seem to have applied this principle throughout. It is significant, too, that the English sword dance is so constructed that by clever planning and changing of couples each figure is repeated as many times as there are participants, until every dancer has had his turn.

Similarly in the *longways.* One after another the couples must move to the same melody, repeated over and over again, in the same figure pattern and keep on moving in it until all the couples have entered— unless the dance progressed beyond that. Ladies and gentlemen formed two opposite lines; the first couple danced a certain figure and changed places with the second; the second couple, having moved to the head of the line, performed the same figure and were once again in the second place, while the first couple, continuing in the dance, had moved into the third place, so that the third couple was now at the head of the line and entered into the dance. Thus the couples who had not yet begun to perform moved into the first place one by one, while those already dancing made their way on down the line and, overtaken by those coming after them, gradually got back to the head again. The pattern is

```
1
2   1
3   2   1
4   3   2   1   etc.
```

Instead of the individual couples, groups of two or three couples could enter the dance simultaneously, in a pattern something like this:

```
1   2                           1   2   3
    1   3                           1   2   4
2   3   1   4                           1   2   5
    2   4   1   5               3   4   5   1   2   6
3   4   2   5   1   6               3   4   5   1   2   7
    3   4   2   5   1   7               3   4   5   1   2   8
```

Besides this "minor set dance," there was the simpler "whole set dance": the first couple danced through the column, fell in line at the end, and was replaced by the second couple, which had now become the first; this couple in turn fell in line at the end and let the former third couple take first place. This kept up until all the couples had danced, and with the constant changing of places the original order was finally restored. The plan:

```
1   2   3   4   5   6
2   3   4   5   6   1
3   4   5   6   1   2
4   5   6   1   2   3
5   6   1   2   3   4
6   1   2   3   4   5
```

This required a good deal of time. No wonder that a *contre* in the cloister at Murano in Venice, mentioned by Casanova in 1775, lasted a whole hour.

A sure proof that England has the priority is the testimony of the Spanish poet Agustín de Rojas (born 1572) from about 1600. In his play *El Mejor Amigo el Muerto* the birthday of the queen is being described. She is celebrating it with a ball: "And here there is the custom that whoever will may enter into the *branle,* if he but wear a mask. What is the *branle?* It is a dance that the English people do." From this the situation is clear: the *bran = branle,* into which every new arrival may enter, is danced by the English. Esquivel Navarro definitely calls it the *bran de Inglaterra.* Its distinctive mark is apparently the possibility of adding to the *branle* any number of participants. Hence it is one of those dances "for as many as will." A scheme of figures in which all participate alike requires a fixed number of dancers and a simultaneous beginning. A choral dance in which as many as will may enter, early or late, each as he comes into the room, cannot use such a scheme; the only thing to do is to take up a position at the end of the line and wait patiently.

How England came by this dance can scarcely be ascertained, for the *country dance* was first a pure folk dance and hence cannot be traced historically. When it enters our historical vision—rather fleetingly at the end of the sixteenth century, and substantially with the appearance of the *Dancing Master* in 1650—it has already been accepted in the higher society. Even at the court, at least during the reign of Queen Elizabeth, it was danced by masters and servants together. Towards 1700 it begins its conquest of the Continent. Holland and France make the acquaintance of the *contre* about 1685. In 1688 the Parisian dancing master, Landrin, writes in an unprinted manual of the *contredanse* that three years before he had traveled to England to satisfy the Dauphin's wish for new *contres,* and had collected the rarest ones in that same school from which Sieur Isaac d'Orléans had formerly brought his to France. In 1706 the Parisian dancing master Feuillet publishes thirty-two *longways* in his *Recueil de Contredanses.* By 1714 the *contre* has reached Spain. Bonnet writes in 1723 that an English dance teacher introduced the *contre* twelve or fifteen years earlier, about 1710, and that by 1717 it is already "received almost everywhere." Indeed it is more than just "received." It is "next to the *minuet* the most popular dance at the court, at large balls, and at weddings." And in 1728 Dufort in his *Trattato del Ballo Nobile* describes, besides the *minuet,* only the *contre—non già perchè lo meriti,* "even if it does not deserve it."

One finds this judgment understandable: the chief essentials of all courtly dancing, the steps and body movements, had scarcely any part in it and it was far removed from the French ideal of *demi-coupés* and toe steps. *"Toute la plus grande perfection de ces contredanses, est de se bien tourmenter le corps, de se tirer en tournant, de taper des pieds comme des Sabotiers, & de faire plusieurs attitudes qui ne sont point dans la bien-séance."* (The whole art of these *contredanses* is in tossing the body about, twisting and turning, tapping their feet like clog dancers, and taking up positions which are not even decent.) The entire dance was based upon the smooth interweaving of the figures and the harmonious co-operation of the couples.

The rosy daughters of Neighbor Flamborough, whom Oliver Goldsmith introduces into his *Vicar of Wakefield* (1766), were thoroughly acquainted with the *jig* and the *round-about,* but entirely unfamiliar with *country dances.* It seems rather paradoxical that the rustic beauties knew how to dance the *round* but not the "rustic" *country dance.* On the Continent the *longways* had been transformed from a "rustic" *country dance* into a *counter dance,* a *contre.* The French language was more familiar in that age of gallantry than the English. The name *contre,* however, retranslated, as it were, into English, had like the dance itself lost the meaning of "rustic" there too.

At the beginning of the eighteenth century the other type of English *country dance,* the *round,* although discarded in England itself, was taken over by the French, at least in the form of the *round for eight.* But in France it was so completely transformed that it was called the *contredanse française;* it even received a special French name, the *cotillon,* "petticoat"—apparently from the beginning of a popular song:

Ma commère, quand je danse,
Mon cotillon va-t-il bien?

(My dear, when I dance,
Does my petticoat show?)

Under this name it soon returned to England: "Nae cotillion brent new frae France" (Robert Burns, *Tam O'Shanter*).

"In general," writes the dancing master Hänsel in 1755, "a *cotillon* consists mainly of a *minuet en Quatre* or *en huit* figures only in the second *entrée,* or if it consists of three *entrées,* it is varied. As far as the steps are concerned, they are all French. . . . *Cotillons* are very popular at large weddings, parties, and balls, and for variety are the most common, the gayest and the best next to the English dances." Or to put it a little more clearly, in the *cotillon* four couples arranged themselves in a square, they saluted with a procession at the first *entrée* and performed their figure to the second period of the music (*refrain*), in order to finish up at the same spot. Among the various figures employed in this dance *les ronds,* the *grande chaîne,* and the *moulinets* stand out. Under the name *les ronds* is concealed the ancient circular movement of one or all the dancers, clockwise or counter-clockwise. In the *grande chaîne,* all the dancers join hands, the ladies turn to the left, the gentlemen to the right, and all wind through the circle in this direction until the original couple come together again. In the *Dancing Master* the *chaîne* appears under the name of the *hey*—the English *hey* or *hay* comes from the French *haie,* "hedge," which with the same meaning was used in the sixteenth century to designate the last figure of the *danse des bouffons. Les moulinets* are the turning star of some or all of the participants, who all join the same hand and dance a *pas de gavote* around this central point in one direction.

The *cotillon* has several advantages over the *anglaise.* It could be broken off at any time and the tiresome waiting was done away with: all the couples started together. Yet it did not spread very quickly. I find the first mention of it in France in 1723, in Germany in 1741, and it seems not to have come to England until about 1770. This is quite natural since Great Britain had still her own *rounds*. Undoubtedly the constant alternation of the refrain with the same *entrée* over and over again was partly to blame for this. It produced a monotony different from that of the column dance but perhaps even more noticeable.

This monotony may account for the reconstruction of the *cotillon* in the course of the nineteenth century. What survived under the name of *cotillon* appeared in 1816 or 1817 as a dance in which variety was sought at any price, and which therefore degenerated.

"Oh, lengthiest and most curious of all dances! You are half play and half dance! Charming when you drive the various couples around in a circle, you are still more charming when you permit them, undisturbed and a little concealed to chat."

GUSTAV FREYTAG, *Soll und Haben*.

It was interspersed with *waltzes* and other turning dances, and also with social games, and enriched with all the convolutions of the old circle dances. The famous Parisian dancing master, Cellarius, has recorded "a hundred new *cotillon* figures" in his frequently reprinted and translated booklet.

Another branch which grew out of the old *cotillon* developed, in contrast to the latter, into a firmly fixed series of six figures, in the first half of the nineteenth century:

1. *Le Pantalon. Chaîne anglaise entière—Balancé—Chaîne des Dames—Demi-Promenade* (earlier: *Demi-queue du chat*).
2. *L'Eté. En avant deux—Traversé—Retraversé et balancé.*
3. *La Poule. Traversé—Balancé, quatre en ligne—En avant deux et en arrière—En avant quatre et en arrière.*
4. *La Trénis. Un cavalier et sa Dame—Le Cavalier traverse au milieu de deux Dames—Balancé et tour de main.*
5. *La Pastourelle. Un Cavalier et sa Dame en avant et en arrière,*

deux fois—En avant trois, deux fois—Le Cavalier seul—Demi-round à gauche.

6. *Le Finale. Chassé croisé huit—En avant deux—A droite et à gauche—Balancé et tour de main—Moulinet des Dames—Balancé et tour de main.*

Today we call this dance the *quadrille.* In the eighteenth century it was used for the square formation in riding tournaments, and in the ballet for the group entrance of an indefinite number of dancers. It was not yet very commonly used in connection with *contre* dances, however. Nevertheless, Pauli is familiar in 1756 with *quadrille* as the name of the *angloise entamée par quatre personnes* (English dance begun by four persons) and of the *cotillon à quatre.* Thus the *quadrille* of twelve couples in which Catherine II of Russia danced at St. Petersburg in 1741, appears to be closely related to ours. In 1767 the dancing master Chavanne differentiates between the *contredances françoises en cadrille* and the *colonnes angloises.* These names are distinguished later as the *contredanse française* and *quadrille* for the four-couple *contre* and as the *anglaise* for the double file *contre.* In contrast to the *contredanse française,* the *française* is, in the nineteenth century, a column dance like the *anglaise.*

The POLONAISE. We are familiar with Polish dance melodies since 1585; on account of their fresh rhythms the German dance collections of the next forty years gladly included them. They are double dances consisting of an introduction in two-four time and a conclusion in three-four time on the same theme, or introductory dance and afterdance on different themes. Neither the name nor the type of the *polonaise* appears among them. The Polish name *polonez* has probably come from the French.

The *polonaise* proper, with its stately gliding, is not mentioned until 1645. A French writer praises it in glowing terms:

"I know of no dance in which so much loveliness, dignity, and charm are united as in the *polonaise*. It is the only dance which becomes exalted persons and monarchs and which is suited to courtly dress. This dance is marked by poetic feeling and the national character, the outstanding trait of which is a ceremonial dignity. It does not express passion; it is a solemn procession."

Another Frenchman reports from Danzig in 1681 that the *danse polonaise* was *presque marchée* and preceded by the lackeys. And in 1719, at the marriage festival of the Electoral Prince at the Court of Saxony, the King "with the Queen opened the ball to the strains of magnificent music, to which a Polish dance was performed, *dames* and *cavaliers* couple after couple following the King. In front of the King walked four Marshals with their staffs, and since this took half an hour, the royal personages and their ladies round about sat down again; after this the Electoral Prince invited his bride to dance a *minuet*. . . . There were also English and German dances."

The *polonaise* is said to have been originally a triumphal march of the old warriors. Women did not come into the dance until later, and then in separate couples. Even the more recent *polonaise* with mixed couples was obviously a ceremonial choral, arranged according to age and dignity, in solemn gliding step. The stately procession was interrupted by courtly bending of the knee in front of the lady, by a promenade of the lady on the left side of the gentleman, and all sorts of figures out of the ancient choral dance. Adam Mickiewicz likens the *polonaise* to a shimmering, wriggling python. A special figure was the tagging of the lady; the foremost dancer had to give up his partner, and received the lady of the second couple, and so on, until he was left as "widower" in the end.

The use of the distinctive rhythm in the *polonaise* is apparently very recent. Not until the beginning of the eighteenth century does it seem to have freed itself from the duple time of the old, quiet, gliding "introductory dance." *Polonaise* rhythms, however, can be pointed out very early. In the fourteenth century we found *saltarelli* which differed from the *polonaise* rhythm only in beginning on the upbeat. Let us compare the *Lamento di Tristano* with Chopin's *Polonaise* in A major:

The tendency to triple time apparently comes from the same source which in the baroque period forced dances in triple time into the foreground almost exclusively and expanded old duple time dances into triple time. This explains how it was possible for Hans Leo Hassler occasionally to write so typical a four-four dance as the ceremonial *intrade* in three-four time against all tradition.

In the successor of the *saltarello*, the *galliard*, there are suggestions of the *polonaise* rhythm. In 1610 we find C. Simpson using that dotted note opening:

3/4

which is first recorded as *polonaise* rhythm in 1698. And in Biagio Marini we find

3/4

The opening figure, which gives such lightness and elasticity to the downbeat, has been pointed out by Arbeau as a drum accompaniment to the *pavane,* and it has been known in the Spanish dance for centuries, especially in the *seguidilla*.

Feldtenstein, who gives first place to the Polish dance "as far as grandeur and the rendering of a noble pride are concerned," describes its movement as the *pas de bourrée* (changing step) or one bending step and two straight steps—"with this difference, that the last of the straight steps at the end is more like a gliding step than a straight step." Each step gets one of the three quarter notes.

The German forms of the *polonaise* also kept to the old properties of the choral dance—chains, squares, arches, serpentine twists, and the like. But serious German masters turned against the debasement of

426

the dance, the dragging, the *pas comiques,* and the *tours puériles,* and pointed toward the *air grand et imposant* of the Polish nobility. The French did not become interested; Compan's dance lexicon does not record the *polonaise* at all.

The KRAKOWIAK, or *Cracow dance,* was the courtly after-dance to the *polonaise* and was danced, indeed, "in the manner of the *polonaise.*" Apparently it was in the beginning a choral dance for men, and only later were women admitted. Instead of a grave gliding dance, however, it was a merry skipping dance, and the couples added as a special feature spinning turns in one place.

1750–1900

THE AGE OF THE WALTZ

The Waltz

Goethe tells us that from his early youth his father gave him dancing lessons; he "instructed us most precisely in the positions and steps, and when he had brought us far enough to dance a *minuet,* played some pretty thing in three-four time on his *flûte-douce,* and we moved in time as best we could." He and Lotte swung round together in the *minuet,* and he persuaded her to dance the English *contre* and "even the *waltz.*" But as they "whirled round together like the spheres, it was certainly a little rough to begin with, because so few knew how to dance it." Even the daughters of the Strassburg dancing master, "who were always willing to dance a *minuet* to their father's little fiddle," found the *waltz* difficult. Out in the country, in Sesenheim, on the contrary, the *"allemande, waltz,* and *Dreher* were the beginning, middle, and end. All the people had grown up with this national dance."

A dozen years of Goethe's life mirror the fate of the dance between 1650 and 1800. In the patrician household of his father and in the home of the French dancing master in Strassburg he learned positions, steps, the *minuet* as the late representative of the courtly, periwigged world of the declining rococo. In the bourgeois society of about 1770 he found the English *contre* and even the German *waltz,* which had not yet been very generally mastered, but was danced in expert fashion at least by the German population of Alsace.

The eastern boundary of Germany rounds out the picture. On January 15, 1787, Mozart writes from Prague: "At six o'clock I went with Count Canal to the so-called *Breiten,* a rustic ball, at which the flower of the Prague beauties are in the habit of assembling. . . . I saw with wholehearted pleasure how these people jumped around with such sincere enjoyment to the music of my *Figaro,* which had been turned into all kinds of *contres* and *Teutsche* [*waltzes*]. . . ."

With the disappearance of that courtly world fashioned on the minnesinger ideals, the old society dance had lost its content and become an empty shell. The new bourgeois society borrowed the forms of the aristocracy, to be sure, but only until their own ideals had taken shape. The dance which it needed was not one of convention and ultimate stylization of artificial courtship, but the expression and, if you will, the release of youthful exuberance and youthful desire in the frame of communal festivity. Truth and simplicity are the insignia of this generation. Simple, natural lines replace the curves of the rococo, the idyll follows the tragic spectacle. The musical play in the vernacular supersedes the courtly *opera seria;* the song in the folk manner displaces the Italian aria. Again a folkloristic period dawns. Poets and musicians collect folk songs, the fairy tale attracts attention, and the bourgeoisie seeks its connections rather in rustic than in courtly culture.

The *contre,* which introduced the bourgeois epoch, is only an intermediary. By 1800 it was as much despised as it had been a hundred years earlier. The English dances are "nothing but a characterless tripping . . . the beautiful art has sunk to the level of ordinary physical exercises. They stamp around and leap to the rhythm and call that dancing."

Once more the time has come when fresh blood is needed, an inusion of the imitative style from the extravert side. "Every dance must have character! . . . Our figure dances without character and expression," we hear, are "the most artificial and ridiculous foot play. . . The empty changing of the sets, the alternation of these dead geometrical figures is nothing but sheer mechanism. . . ." The true dance "must have soul, express passion, imitate nature!" This is why the writers of the period sing the praises of the folk dances, which barely veil the wooing of the sexes in rhythmical movements, express passion, and imitate a small part of human nature. And this is also the reason that the same dance annual from which these words are taken has a long paragraph about the national dances of Europe and elsewhere. It was no ephemeral fashion which brought the folk dance to the last generation of the eighteenth century. It was the powerful impulse in this most impulsive of social pleasures to shake off all borrowed attitudes, all empty forms, and to mold the new bourgeois dance on the pattern of those dances in which the old forces still held sway: not studied and measured steps, but joyful, intensified movement, not stylized make-believe, but living actuality, not consciousness, but ecstatic rapture.

What the age was seeking it found in those close turning dances, jumping dances, *Ländlers*, or *waltzes* which had existed time out of mind in South Germany ready to burst forth from village and mountain valley when the hour struck. The *waltz*, which for more than a century has held undisputed sway in the ballroom, differs little from this folk dance. With smooth drawing-room floors and shoes without hobnails, it abandoned the slow tempo (even about 1900 the tempo for the *Ländler* was set at ♩ = M.M. 48!) and the *tours hardis*. The dancers no longer threw themselves from arm to arm; they gave up the skips and the turning under the arm, and forgot about the characteristic arrangement of the feet one behind the other in the third position on the fifth and sixth counts of the two-measure phrase. But by and large the *waltz* remained the same as the *Ländler*: a three-four rhythm with a strong accent on the first beat, to each two measures of which the couples in close embrace make a turn and at the same time follow a circular course, so that the dance resembles the twofold rotation of the heavenly bodies; the left foot strides out, the right follows gliding in a backward curve, and the left completes the half circle. In the second measure the same figure is repeated with the right foot leading.

Character, expression, spirit, passion—everything that the new era demanded from the dance, it found in the *waltz*. It might be wild enough. Ernst Moritz Arndt describes a waltz at a petty bourgeois affair in a village near Erlangen:

"The dancers held up the dresses of their partners very high so that they should not trail and be stepped on, wrapped them tightly in this shroud, bringing both bodies under one covering, as close together as possible, and thus the turning went on in the most indecent positions; the hand holding the dress lay hard against the breasts pressing lasciviously at every movement; the girls, meanwhile, looked half mad and ready to swoon. As they waltzed around on the darker side of the room, the clasps and kisses became still bolder. It is the custom of the country, and not as bad as it looks, they say: but I can now quite understand why they have forbidden the *waltz* in certain parts of Swabia and Switzerland."

But the *waltz* was not always on this plane. Higher ideals were embodied in the new dance. "I can imagine two enraptured, love-intoxicated beings, floating along in the ecstasy of joy," an unknown author writes of the *waltz* in 1801. And "never," confesses Goethe in the *Werther,* "have I moved so lightly. I was no longer a human being. To hold the most adorable creature in one's arms and fly around with her like the wind, so that everything around us fades away. . . ." For the first time in many years the dance has again become truly ecstatic: exaltation, surrender, and the extinction of the world round about.

With this knowledge the strange fate of the *waltz* becomes comprehensible: its hearty welcome and quick adoption in German bourgeois circles, its slow penetration of bourgeois society outside of Germany—

it was not accepted in England until 1812!—and the great and in some cases invincible reluctance of the courts, where there was no inclination to allow carefully guarded princesses "to float away intoxicated with love in an ecstasy of joy." The *waltz* was still prohibited at the court balls of the German imperial house in the reign of Wilhelm II.

But this is extremely significant: for the first time in centuries a dance conquers the world without the sanction of the powers that be, of courts, of dancing masters, or of France. The opinion of the teachers was summed up in the brief condemnation of J. M. de Chavanne in 1767: the *waltz,* he said, has *point de rapport avec la bonne danse* (nothing to do with good dancing). But this time it was not the dance teachers who had pointed out the way, and their disappointment over the "decline" of the art is reflected in all their books.

After many hundreds of years of leadership, France had to forego setting the dominant fashion. With the *quadrille* at the imperial court, which is so vividly depicted in a contemporary etching by B. Zix, we may compare what Vallentin tells of Napoleon: "When at a banquet in 1811 he noticed that the Count Henckel v. Donnersmarck was not dancing, and upon asking the reason was told that he was not acquainted with the French dances, Napoleon spat very close to the Count." A generation earlier a courtier could not possibly have been caught in this situation.

Meanwhile the *waltz* had gripped all Germany like an elementary movement. In that same Wetzlar of which Goethe has recorded the dance activities in the *Werther,* appears in 1782 the first book on the new dance: *Etwas über das Waltzen* by C. von Zangen. Fifteen years later it is the acknowledged favorite of all circles, and it soon becomes necessary to warn against excess. In 1797, Salomo Jakob Wolf's *Erörterung derer wichtigsten Ursachen der Schwäche unserer Generation in Hinsicht auf das Walzen* (Discussion of the most important causes of the weakness of our generation in regard to the *waltz*) was published at Halle and sold out so quickly that two years later a new edition was printed. The title of this new edition is more severe: *Beweis dass das Walzen eine Hauptquelle der Schwäche des Körpers und des Geistes unserer Generation sey. Deutschlands Söhnen und Töchtern angelegentlichst empfohlen* (Proof that the *waltz* is a main source of the weakness of body and mind of our generation. Most urgently recommended to the sons and daughters of Germany).

The recommendation was unavailing. Neither the children of Germany nor those of any other nation were influenced. At the end of 1791 an anonymous author in Berlin writes that "the *waltz* and the *waltz* only is now so fashionable that one sees nothing else at dances; if you just know how to *waltz*, everything goes fine." And six years later a journalist relates that the turning "is as common and contagious as a cold in the head." As early as 1790 the *waltz* comes from Strassburg to France—to a France where the dance madness can be gauged statistically from the fact that in the year 1797 there were six hundred and eighty-four public dance halls in the city of Paris alone. People shook their heads. "I can understand," exclaims L.-J.-B.-E. Vigée, "that the mothers like the *waltz*, but I cannot understand that they allow their daughters to dance it." Mothers and daughters remain unregenerate, and Ernst Moritz Arndt reports from France in 1804:

"People love these *waltzes* or genuine gliding dances—for they consist mainly of very light gliding—passionately, they alternate regularly with the *quadrille*, and still eyes and hearts cannot get enough of them. *Une walse! Oh encore une walse!* is the constant cry. This love of the *waltz* and the nationalization of this German dance is quite new. Only since this war has the *waltz* together with tobacco-smoking and other vulgar habits become common."

In the course of the nineteenth century the French created their own version, the skipping French *waltz*, and the Americans developed the slow, gliding *Boston* from the *waltz* about 1874. Even the Germans had a few variations, including the *Schottische* and the *two-step*. The *Schottische* arose from the incorporation of *waltz*-like turns in the *écossaise*. After the disappearance of the latter it lived on as a *waltz* in two-four time with the step pattern of that dance: starting in the

432

fourth position with the left foot forward, the right foot was thrust forward on the first count of the measure and the left foot skipped at the same time; on the second count both feet came together—the whole dance was performed on the toes with the legs stretched. The *two-step* or *balancé waltz* was light and airy: in three-four or two-four time the one foot flew forward, while the other took two skips (Plate 30).

The classical form, however, is and remains the Viennese *waltz*, which on the Danube was called the *Langaus*. The *waltz* in Vinzenz Martin's opera *Una Cosa Rara*, produced in Vienna in 1776, is regarded as the original model. But this opinion is contested. In 1797 a Breslau journalist writes in the elegant *Journal des Luxus und der Moden* that the ordinary *waltz* or turning dance "does not exclude all charm and grace in its slow, melting movement. But the Vienna *waltz* surpasses everything in wild fury; ordinarily the turning dance merges into it; rarely is it danced alone, and only a few females—those of an iron nature—give themselves up to its mad whirling. Most of them forego this bacchantic pleasure very unwillingly in response to the strict prohibition of mothers anxious for their health."

This increase of speed was, if not entirely, at least partly, the result of the transplantation to the smooth floor of the ballroom and the relegation of hobnailed shoes. It had its effect on the form of the melody and on the rhythm. In the heat of this rapid tempo with about two hundred quarter notes to the minute, the evenness of the three beats or the stamped accentuation of the second quarter of the measure, which gives a peculiar charm to many *Ländlers* and German *waltzes*, cannot be retained. In the Viennese *waltz* we have that overemphasis of the first beat and underemphasis of the second and at the same time that transparent floating and gliding which is suited to the lightness of urban dance dress and the smoothness of the floor. The urban influence makes itself felt also in the melodic line: the extreme leaps and wide intervals give place more and more to smooth progression—dance and music alike tend toward close movement. And finally we have a change of form: with the great increase in tempo the old familiar eight-measure period of the *Ländler* and the German *waltz* were altogether too short and were extended to sixteen measures.

This development did not come about at all suddenly. Even Josef Lanner calls his dances *Ländler* or *Deutsche* at first; not until his Opus 7 does he use the title *waltz,* and then not throughout. In his *Vermählungswalzer,* Op. 15 (about 1825), he begins to use the sixteen-measure period, which Weber had used earlier in his *Invitation to the Dance.*

The Polka and Related Dances

> To dance the *polka* men and women must have hearts that beat high and strong. Tell me how you do the *polka,* and I will tell you how you love.
>
> PERROT & ROBERT, 1845.

Not until 1825, or indeed really not until about 1830, does the absolute supremacy of the *waltz* in the field of the couple dance begin to wane. But the dances which come to contest this supremacy are rather deviations from the *waltz* than new additions. The only serious rival is the *polka.*

The polka is a turning couple dance in two-four time with the pattern

and the tempo ♩ = M.M. 88. The form in which we know it today is nothing but a poor remnant. Originally it consisted of ten figures, of which only five were used in the drawing room:

1. *Promenade.*
2. *Valse.*
3. *Valse à rebours* or *à gauche:* reverse *waltz* in close embrace, with turns on the right leg.
4. *Valse roulée* or *tortillée:* turning *waltz* with arms crossed; the gentleman always starts with the left foot; progressing forward

434

he turns the lady to the left, progressing backward, to the right.
5. *Pas bohémien:* the right leg does not rest in the usual manner on the fourth eighth, but makes a rapid heel-toe step.

All these figures were executed in the *polka* step; *valse* merely signifies turning dance. This step, however, was certainly not the pitiful *Gimpelgampel* of later times, but a lively movement in which the feet of both partners flew into the air and head, trunk, and arms moved no less vigorously. A contemporary colored lithograph by C. Vernier gives a beautiful picture of this dance (Plate 30).

The *polka* step itself was nothing new. Its simple pattern was a combination of the old *fleuret* and *pas de bourrée,* together with the so-called *schottische* step, with which the people of the time were familiar from the *écossaise.* This is why the *polka,* when it made its appearance in the German cities after 1830, was called the *Schottische.* The *polka,* however, has nothing to do with Scotland; it was altogether a possession of the peoples of central Europe. When in 1840 it was introduced with unexampled success in Paris, Perrot and Robert wrote: "The *polka* belongs to one country, which has the right to claim it always and everywhere, a country full of poetry . . . the old Germany." For the French of the nineteenth century, of course, Bohemia was a part of the Greater Germany. The Czech name *půlka,* "half" = semi- or chain-step, points to Bohemia, and it is said to have been a Bohemian peasant girl who was the first to dance a *polka* at the beginning of the eighteen thirties. The new dance was brought to Prague about 1835, to Vienna in 1839, and to Paris by a dancing master from Prague in 1840.

Contemporaneously with the *polka,* the *rejdovák* under the name *redowa* played a certain role in the more refined dance life of the European capitals. It was a Bohemian folk dance, executed as follows: "The dancer holds his lady as in the *waltz* and dances with her three measures forward turning to the left, then he dances one measure back turning to the right; now he dances three measures forward, this time, however, turning to the right, and one measure back turning to the left. With this the whole figure of the *rejdovák* is finished, and it is repeated as often as the dancing couple desires. Occasionally the waltzing pair inserts another figure: instead of turning they appear merely to sway to right and left. The *rejdovák* is in *waltz* tempo (three-four time), and the *rejdovačka* is for the most part in *polka* tempo (two-four time)."

The other couple dances of the time are also related to the *polka*. Among these are the *galop* and *Rutscher* (sliding dance), which are quick *polkas* wherein the couples gallop through the hall to a rapid two-four time, $\downarrow = $ M.M. 126, with the step pattern of the *polka;* the *Rheinländer* or the Bavarian *polka,* in contrast to the *galop,* is a slow *polka* with the step pattern

These dances came in about 1850. There is also the *polka-mazurka,* a *polka* in three-four time at $\downarrow = $ M.M. 144, fused with the *mazurka*.

Choral Dances

Frenchman: By the by, how do people dance in your country?
Creole: In our country? We jump, we flutter around, we laugh out loud, and cry a little.
Frenchman: Funny people! Why do you do that?
Creole: Because we're happy and we need to move our limbs.
Frenchman: Here we take four steps ahead and four steps back; after that we make a turn that is difficult because of our partner's dresses, then two or three geometrical bows. The cotton spinners in Poissy Prison make exactly the same motions.

TAINE

Here we have a strange reversal of the situation. In all previous centuries it was the couple dances which called for art and strict discipline and the chorals which with their freedom and primitivism gave release and recreation. Now it is just the opposite: the new couple dances, taken from old German and Slavic sources, more or less discard conventionalized style, and the choral dance, on the other hand, becomes the ceremonial, "learned" element, for the figures have to be thoroughly mastered if the dance is not to be tedious. Not that it is any more eagerly cultivated and studied on that account. On the contrary, its neglect is generally deplored by teachers and dancers. There is good reason for this neglect.

The decline of the choral dance is a cause and an indication of the social development. The choral dance, communal dances, demand a compact social order; they require an association in the dance which is something more than the mere correct execution of a series of figures and movements. The nature peoples—whose life is passed in the community of village and tribe to such an extent that the study of primitive psychology has established as their chief characteristic the predominance of the collective over the individual spirit—cultivate the couple dance but little and then only in the last stage of their development. The triumph of individualism in the nineteenth century inevitably raises the couple dance to the leading position and allows the choral dance to fall back. The latter is now devoid of content—a weak attempt to impose upon a chance gathering of a few dozen guests a communal feeling, the pretense of which is kept up for a few hours and dropped with the breaking up of the party. It is no wonder that it never realized any artistic depth. Even the names of the dances, of their figures and patterns, remain French; no vernacular translates them. People feel that they are being elegant when they dance these *écossaises* and *quadrilles,* but do not give themselves up to them. Consequently what success they had depended upon having a leader to call out the figures. And even then it was often dull and confused enough. New choral dances were scarcely invented any more, unless we wish to regard as new that *gallopade* and *hopsanglaise* in which E. T. A. Hoff-mann's educated monkey, Milo, "occasionally used to cut some strange capers" at *thés dansants,* and which "as a spurious form turns round and round eternally in a few extremely simple figures." "In such circumstances the dance is certainly poison for human beings; and in a case like this, one can thoroughly approve what Dr. Sponitzer says of the harmfulness of the dance in his little book *The Dance from the Pathological and Moral Point of View.*" Only the aristocracy and—although often only in revivals—the narrower circles of the small town and village prevented the complete degeneration of the choral dance. This was more than just the usual process of tenacious preservation of all cultural properties among nobles, petty bourgeois, and peasants; there was still something here of that communal feeling necessary for the life of the choral dance. Thus Tolstoi is able to describe for us in *War and Peace* an aristocratic ball in Russia at the beginning of the nineteenth century consisting entirely of *écossaises* and *anglaises.* The *anglaise* is simply the *contre* which has been discussed in the previous chapter.

In the *écossaise,* which flourished in the first third of the nineteenth century, gentlemen and ladies stand facing each other; every couple dances with every other couple a number of simple figures, such as the *moulinet, chaîne,* and *balancé.* The first couple dances the same two or three figures with the second couple, chassés down and back between the rows, and returns to the second place, while the second couple moves to the head of the line. The first couple now dances the same figures with the third couple, returns after the chassé to the third place, then dances with the fourth couple and so on, until it has danced with all the couples and has reached the foot of the line. This combination of couples is progressive: while the first couple dances with the fourth, the second and third couples dance together, and while the first couple dances with the sixth, the second and the fifth, and the third and the fourth unite.

```
1 + 2
1 + 3
1 + 4    2 + 3
1 + 5    2 + 4
1 + 6    2 + 5    3 + 4
1 + 7    2 + 6    3 + 5
1 + 8    2 + 7    3 + 6    4 + 5    etc.
```

Thus the *écossaise* is fundamentally the same as that old *contre* which went under the name of *anglaise* or *English*. But whereas the *pas* of the *anglaise* was executed like the medieval double step in which the one foot glides past the other, which is then drawn up to it, the *pas* of the *écossaise* was a changing step similar to the *pas de fleuret*, the *pas de bourrée*, and the *polka*. And while the *anglaise* was performed at a moderate speed, the *écossaise* had a quick, energetic tempo—usually in two-four rhythm. Only in this dance did the lady stand on the left of the gentleman, and even here this was not always the practice. As a rule there were only four figures. And even into these, *waltz*-like turns were finally introduced. Around 1833 the *écossaise* disappeared.

The *française* had a much quieter tempo. It was in six-eight time and the lady and gentleman were more independent. It must not be confused with the *contredanse française*, the *cotillon*, or the *quadrille*. In its simple form it had four figures; the double *française* had eight.

In Lion Feuchtwanger's *Success* we read: "The *française* was a country dance long out of fashion in the rest of Germany, but still popular in Bavaria, where it suited the temperament of the people and was considered the culminating attraction of all the balls. The dancers faced each other in long rows, and advanced towards each other, taking hands. Then they bowed, clasped each other close, and whirled madly round and round. The men braced their arms and lifted the women high off the ground, yelling loudly. They whirled their own partners, and then their neighbors' partners, shouting the directions of the complicated figures. They sweated and yelled with gleaming eyes. They revolved in giddy circles, supporting the women on their locked arms, the women's arms around their necks. They kissed and squeezed their partners, and then flung champagne down their throats, carried away by the torrent of sound from an enormous orchestra." (Tr. Willa and Edwin Muir.)

Besides English, Scottish, and French choral dances, there were also the Polish.

The *mazurek* or the *mazurka* is the only choral dance which goes back to the ancient circle in which the number of dancers was not limited. It far exceeds the other chorals in the number of its figures: Rosenhain describes fifty-six. Its step pattern has a good deal of latitude; the only characteristic steps are the stamping of the feet and the striking together of the heels. Strange to relate, the striking is done once the first time, twice the second time, and thrice the third time. Is there perhaps an old connection here with the *Siebensprung* (seven jumps)?

The last variation which we shall mention is again an English possession: the *quadrille à la cour* or, as it is usually called, *les lanciers,* with its five sets—*la Dorset,* six-eight; *Victoria,* two-four; *les moulinets,* six-eight; *les visites,* six-eight; *les lanciers,* four-four. The account of its invention by the Parisian dancing master Laborde in the year 1856 and its performance and introduction by the Prussian court ballet in lancer uniforms in the following year has been faithfully passed on from book to book. Actually it is considerably older. It appears to have been danced in Dublin as early as 1817. In any case a book by the dance teacher Hart, *Les Lanciers, a second set of Quadrilles for the Piano Forte* (1820), describes how it was danced in good society in the summer of 1819.

The *cancan* or *chahut* is the *enfant terrible* of this latest generation of choral dances. Leg thrust and leap are its most characteristic features; the best dancer is the one who can knock the spectator's hat off his head with her foot. A dancing master by the name of Chicard is said to have invented it. But what was there to invent in the *cancan?*

The old fertility motif of the woman throwing her leg high into the air—how often we have met it, in ancient Egypt, among primitive peoples, in Brittany! And the trick of knocking off the hat we saw not very far away from France as an important feature of the Catalonian *sardana*. But here we must seriously question the word "invention" and limit ourselves to the simple statement that the inciting *cancan* conquered the public ballrooms of the French capital in 1830 and lived on there for many decades (Plate 31).

This fact interests us as an example of those lapses into expanded movement which, even if widely separated, interrupt the close movement of civilized Europe. Even today we are experiencing in a late offspring of the *cancan*, in the musical revue, a new interruption. But if the *cancan* could still set the style for the public dance halls, if not for the society dance, today it is only the theatrical dance which interrupts the uniformity of close movement.

And with this our attention is directed to the exhibition dance, to the ballet.

The Exhibition Dance

> How mighty is a gesture! Convincing, exciting, lasting.
>
> Herder.

The rise of the *waltz* was a result of that longing for truth, simplicity, closeness to nature, and primitivism, which the last two thirds of the eighteenth century fulfilled. The dance, too, strove for character, soul, expression, passion. "Once more," we have written, "the time has come when fresh blood is needed, an infusion of the imitative style from the extravert side." Where could the new tendency have a more powerful and lasting effect than in that art form which had almost exclusively pointed Europe the way toward the imitative style, in the ballet?

Nature, character, soul, truth, and passion are the key words which meet us on every page of the *Lettres sur la danse et sur les ballets* (*Letters on Dancing and Ballets*). These were the high ideals which inspired their author, the great ballet master Jean-Georges Noverre (1727–1810), in his thoroughgoing reform, indeed revolution, of the exhibition dance. "Nature! Nature! And our compositions must be beautiful; let us renounce art, when it is not simple; it convinces only when it is concealed; it triumphs only when it is unrecognized and is taken for nature," he says. And again, "A beautiful painting is only a copy of nature; a beautiful ballet is nature herself, enhanced by all the charms of art." Consequently, "we must not merely practice steps; we must study the passions!" He despises nothing more than dancing for its own sake, for the sake of the steps. The earlier ballet had forgotten that the dance can speak to the soul—it was not even ballet at all, but at best a *divertissement*. The dancers must, if necessary, give up their prescribed movements in exchange for a soul, they must forget their feet and legs to concentrate on facial expression and gestures. Away with the old masks which had always banned the play of feature from the domain of the dancer; away with the long court dresses, which covered up the free play of the body; away with the classical symmetry of figures—it is against truth and destroys the illusion.

Noverre has been called the Shakespeare of the dance; it would have been better to call him the Gluck of the dance. Noverre's *Letters* of 1760 and Gluck's forewords to his operas *Alceste* (1768) and *Paris and Helena* (1770) have the same devout seriousness and the same passionate recognition of the dignity of art and its closeness to nature. The true ballet is for Noverre a drama of the stature and significance of spoken tragedy. As Gluck re-creates the *opera seria* as a work of art uniting music and drama, so Noverre, in the spirit of Balthasard Beaujoyeulx, transforms the old *divertissement* into a dance drama in which all the arts, music, costume and decoration, design and color, combine to send the spectator away from the theater in a state of emotional exaltation. No wonder that Noverre refers again and again in his correspondence to the antique pantomime of the Augustan Age.

For the first time in almost eighteen hundred years that imitative power, the steady decline of which has been the fate of the West, breaks through the crust of European civilization (Plate 28).

Following this reform the ballet undergoes for a second time a revival lasting a hundred and fifty years. But half of this period is decay and degeneration. After reaching a peak in the first third of the nineteenth century, the ballet falls back more and more into routine. Again the legs become more important than the spirit, again dancing for its own sake becomes the rule, and the dance drama sinks, as Noverre says, into a mere *divertissement*.

Once more the dying embers must be fanned into flame. Noverre's magnificent dream of a dance drama in which the poetic idea, in which music, costume, and decoration should unite in inspired naturalness with a technically finished but not self-sufficient dance—this great and beautiful dream is realized at the beginning of the twentieth century in the Russian ballet.

THE TWENTIETH CENTURY

THE TANGO PERIOD

Even before the end of the nineteenth century the dance teachers were trying to counteract the impoverishment of the society dance. *Minuet-* and *gavotte*-like figures, in Italy even *pavanes* of a sort, were to relieve the eternal uniformity of the *waltz* and the standardized *quadrille,* after the *polka, galoppe, Rheinländer,* and *mazurka* all had left the field.

It was a mistaken procedure based on a false estimate of the historical situation. A society which was more and more ceasing to be society in the old sense could not be fed on stale, warmed-over delicacies from the princely kitchen. To be sure, one could think of nothing better suited to the pseudo-rococo salons and the gilded palatial furniture of the bourgeois houses of about 1890 than these spurious *minuets* and *gavottes.* But they did not suit the people, especially not the young

443

people. For this generation was not throwing off the bourgeois stamp to move in the aristocratic and courtly direction.

Only two roads were open. The first was followed by those who were seeking a new order of society: the young, banded together in the youth movement, turned back to the communal dances of the people and of children, to which, at the turn of the century, Scandinavia and England had led the way. Rightly, since inner necessity pointed out this road, and successfully in most cases, though not in all, for many of these medieval choral dances had become too anemic and their spirit is often too narrowly circumscribed.

The amorphous "society," on the other hand, had taken over new dances from America. Ostensibly these dances came out of a foreign world; in reality, however, they had preserved, more faithfully than the European, that original state in which the dance arose out of an inner physical and spiritual need. The adoption of American Creole and Negro steps corresponds exactly to the assimilation of Spanish and Slavic dances in earlier centuries.

The discovery of the universal values of American Negro and Creole dances can in no sense be attributed to the bored and sensation-seeking snobs of the nineties. The *sarabande* and the *chacona* had been taken over more than three hundred years before. Two hundred years earlier, in 1789, Moreau de Saint-Méry writes with graceful pen an enthusiastic little book about the dance in the French West Indies; and thirty years later, in 1820, the famous Parisian dancing master Charles Blasis describes the Spanish and American Negro dances in a special chapter of his *Traité*. But it has to remain at the stage of mere admiration in the eighteenth and nineteenth centuries, until the store of movement of the European dance is exhausted.

Since the Brazilian *maxixe* of 1890 and the *cakewalk* of 1903 broke up the pattern of turns and glides that dominated the European round dances, our generation has adopted with disquieting rapidity a succession of Central American dances, in an effort to replace what has been lost to modern Europe: multiplicity, power, and expressiveness of movement to the point of grotesque distortion of the entire body. We have shortly after 1900 the *one-step* or *turkey trot;* in 1910, inspired by the Cuban *habanera,* the so-called "Argentine" *tango* with its measured crossing and flexing steps and the dramatic pauses in the midst of the glide; and in 1912 the *fox trot* with its wealth of figures. After the war we take over its offspring, the *shimmy,* which with toes together and heels apart contradicts all the rules of post-minnesinger Europe; the grotesquely distorted *Charleston;* in 1926 the *black bottom* with its lively mixture of side turns, stamps, skating glides, skips, and leaps; and finally the rocking *rumba*—all compressed into even movement, all emphasizing strongly the erotic element, and all in that glittering rhythm of syncopated four-four measures classified as *ragtime.* One can hardly imagine a greater contrast to the monotony of steps and melody of the latter part of the nineteenth century.

But the result of this blood transfusion is not satisfactory. There is little doubt that its success has not been permanent: in the first place there is the supercilious attitude of all dancers when asked about a dance that was in vogue two or three years before and has now been completely discarded, in the second place the anxiety regarding what is to be danced next winter, and in the third place the loss of character which all these dances have suffered on European soil. Properly the transformation should be a healthy, indeed a necessary process. For all imported dances must be adapted if they are to take root and flourish. But what we see here is not just a transformation but an inevitable disintegration of form through loss of content. A doctor who in the morning has performed critical operations, a lawyer or judge who has just done battle for the rights of a defendant, a merchant who must constantly worry over profit and loss—all these people who scarcely have time to change from their workaday clothes into evening dress appear incredible, ridiculous, indeed repulsive, in the positions and movements which among unencumbered nature peoples are meaningful, organic, and therefore in the deepest sense beautiful. Thus has our standardized civilization extracted from these foreign dances everything in them that is primitive, forceful, and ecstatic. In this rapid process of deterioration they lose their individual character and the power to interest those who dance them; after a few years they are abandoned or thrown together into new concoctions like the English *Yale,* which in 1927 was compounded of the *Charleston, fox trot,* and *tango* in arbitrary fashion.

Only the *tango* has continued to enjoy undiminished favor for more than twenty years in spite of polishing and refinement. To be sure, it is no pure Negro dance and owes its best qualities to the unusual dance talent of the Spaniards, who for four hundred years have made fruitful contributions to the European dance. When the *tango* made its appearance in the old world in 1910, it released a dance frenzy, almost a mania, which attacked all ages and classes with the same virulence. You may shake your head, smile, mock, or turn away, but this dance madness proves nonetheless that the man of the machine age with his necessary wrist watch and his brain in a constant ferment of work, worry, and calculation has just as much need of the dance as the primitive. For him too the dance is life on another plane.

But the rapid transformation which the *tango* and all the other American dances have undergone, the quick abandonment of the waving of arms and the shaking of shoulders, illustrates the universal socializing principle—civilization demands close movement. The final result of dance importation today is not, as one might think, the rejuvenation of intense emotion, but rather the rejection of all expanded movement and the preservation of those qualities only which lead inevitably toward closeness and restraint. Grotesque and exaggerated movement is discarded. The quiet glide replaces the old turning, and the restrained sliding step, the affected toe step. The original *two-step,* with one movement on each quarter note, quickly gives way to the *one-step,* with a single movement for a whole measure. In the *tango* the number and variety of steps is less important than the accentuation of certain of them. In spite of all the fluctuations in the development from the courtly glide through the *pas menus* of the *minuet* to the step, the tendency is always towards diminution and restraint of all movement. The dances of our modern ballroom are extremely quiet and reserved.

The twentieth century has rediscovered the body; not since antiquity has it been so loved, felt, and honored. Nobody really aware of what is taking place today needs to be told this. After a sleep of two thousand years the expressive imitative dance is awakening. Our generation does not find what it seeks in the ballet, in the world of dancing slippers, gossamer skirts, and artificial steps. It cries out, as Noverre once did, for nature and passion; again it desires, as he did, though perhaps too strongly, to exchange stereotyped movement for something genuinely of the soul.

As always, the new style begins not with the great performers, but with the people with ideas; as always, it turns back to the past to find not only form but courage to carry on. Isadora Duncan—and this shall be the only name we mention—breathes life into the statues of the Greeks. She frees the old Hellenic dance from the rigidity of sculpture, from its sleep in the museums. With insight and feeling she thaws out the movement and rhythm which the ancient sculptors had charmed into frozen calm. She is not the first and not the only one in the struggle against the ballet; but among her imitators at the turn of the century there was often too much egotism and too little ability. In the meantime the great and admirable technique of the ballet has come down to a generation of dancers who build freely on the happy consciousness of the body. What they dance is as manifold as their temperaments—serious and gay, stately and playful, earthbound and heaven-storming, simple and grotesque, crude and refined, human and demoniacal. They alternate from the romantic emphasis on feeling to the classic love of form. They have taken lessons from the ancient Greeks and from the nature peoples and have learned from the Oriental high cultures how to express spiritual states, moods, and dispositions with the greatest economy of means. One thing, however, they have not been able to acquire: the strength and stability of custom, the binding and sustaining power of communal tradition, the fusion of the individual in the universal or the typical. And this has been their salvation. In the midst of a period of conflict over new forms, where the other arts have floundered uncertainly, it has been their good fortune to express the joys and sorrows, the fears and hopes of mankind today in rapturous form. And yet not only of mankind today, but of men of all races and in all ages. For that to which they give living expression has been the secret longing of man from the very beginning—the victory over gravity, over all that weighs down and oppresses, the change of body into spirit, the elevation of creature into creator, the merging with the infinite, the divine.

Whosoever knoweth the power of the dance dwelleth in God.

Plates

Women's Dance Around the Man.
Paleolithic rock painting from Cogul, Spain

Paleolithic Mask Dancers

Cavern of Teyjat, Dordogne   Cavern of Trois Frères, Ariège

PLATE 1.

Toba Women in a Hypnotic Dance. Photo Oudheidkundige Dienst, Bandoeng

Corean Female Sword Dancers. Photo Galloway, N. Y.

PLATE 2.

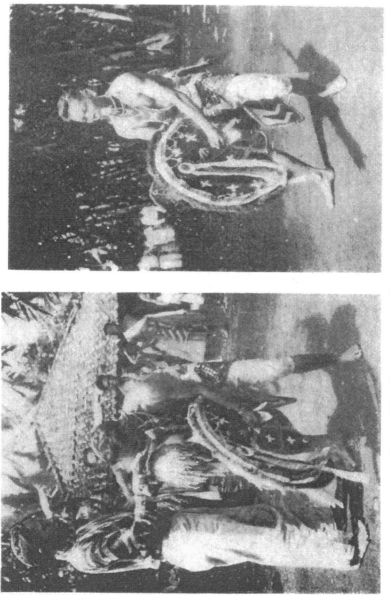

Javanese Horse Dancers. Photo Oudheidkundige Dienst, Bandoeng

PLATE 3.

Couple Dance on Mallorca

Bukovinian Hora. Photo Arhiva fonogramica, Bucureşti

PLATE 4.

New Mexico Dancers at Nambi Feast. Photo American Museum of Natural History, N. Y.

PLATE 5.

Tirinié—Women's Circle Dance, Brazil

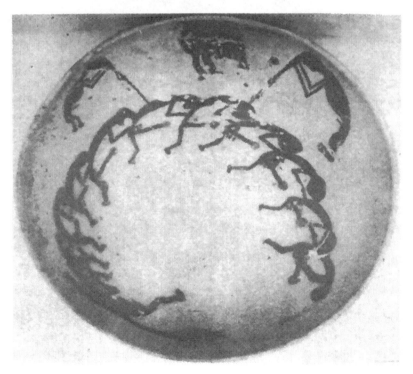

Phallic Rain Dance of the Hopi. Cup in the Ethnographical Museum, Berlin

PLATE 6.

Javanese Shadow Play Marionettes

Javanese Dances about 800 A. D. Temple at Borobudur

PLATE 7.

"Bridge," New Kingdom of Egypt. Pot fragment in the Torino Museum

Female Dancers from the New Kingdom of Egypt. Tomb painting at Shêkh 'Abd el Qurna. Photo British Museum

PLATE 8.

Old Kingdom, Tomb near Saqqāra. Photo Capart

New Kingdom, Egyptian Funeral Dances.
Relief in the Cairo Museum. Photo Borchardt

PLATE 9.

Dancing Siva. Medieval bronze in the Madras Museum. Photo Coomaraswamy

PLATE 10.

Greek Dancer with Breasts tied on. Vase in the Berlin Museum

Greek Horsemen's Dance. Vase in the Berlin Museum

PLATE 11.

Greek Leap Dancers. Vase in the Berlin Museum

Dancing Maenad. Late Neo-Attic Relief, Patras

PLATE 12.

Siamese Stage Dance. Photo Galloway

PLATE 14.

Stick Dance at Avila, Spain. Photo Laurent, Madrid

Stick Dance in Vendée. Photo Martel, Paris

PLATE 15.

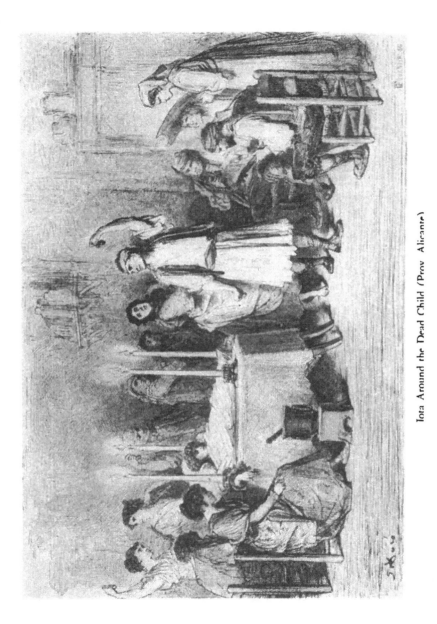

Iota Around the Dead Child (Prov. Alicante)

PLATE 16.

Late Greek Whirl Dance, Metropolitan Museum, N. Y., Gr. Msc. 139 f. 5 vo.

PLATE 17.

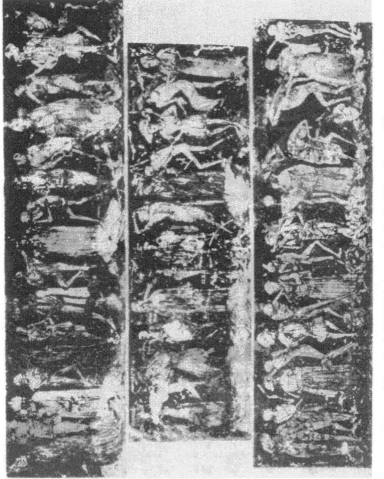

Dance of the Dead. Wall Painting in La Chaise-Dieu, France (fifteenth century)

PLATE 18.

Le Dit des Trois Morts et des Trois Vifs. *Heures* de Jean du Pré

Dance of the Dead. From Hartmann Schedel's *Weltchronik*, Nürnberg, 1493

PLATE 19.

Branle, Roman de Gicart de Nevers (fifteenth century)

Morisca. Innsbruck, Goldenes Dachl (c. 1500)

PLATE 20.

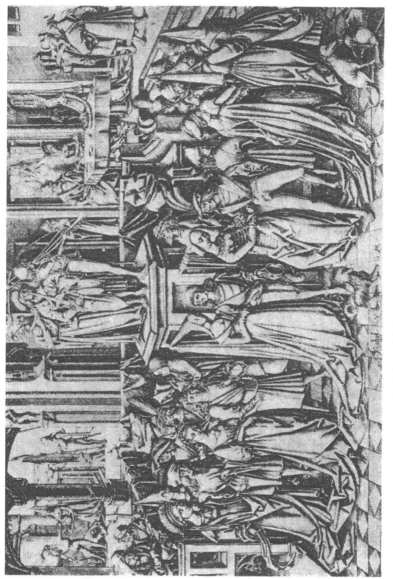

Israhel van Meckenem, Court Dance (c. 1500)

PLATE 21.

Pieter Brueghel, Sr. (1525-69), Kirmes, Vienna, Kunsthistorisches Museum

PLATE 22.

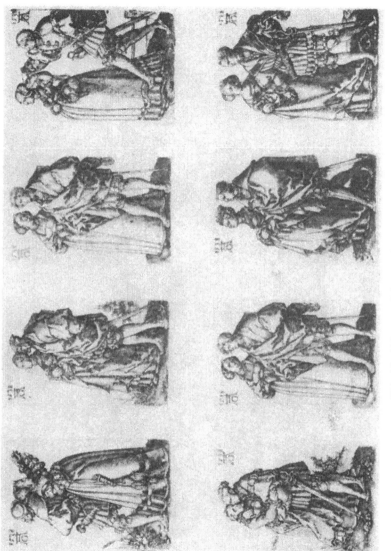

Heinrich Aldegrever, The Wedding Dancers, 1538

PLATE 23.

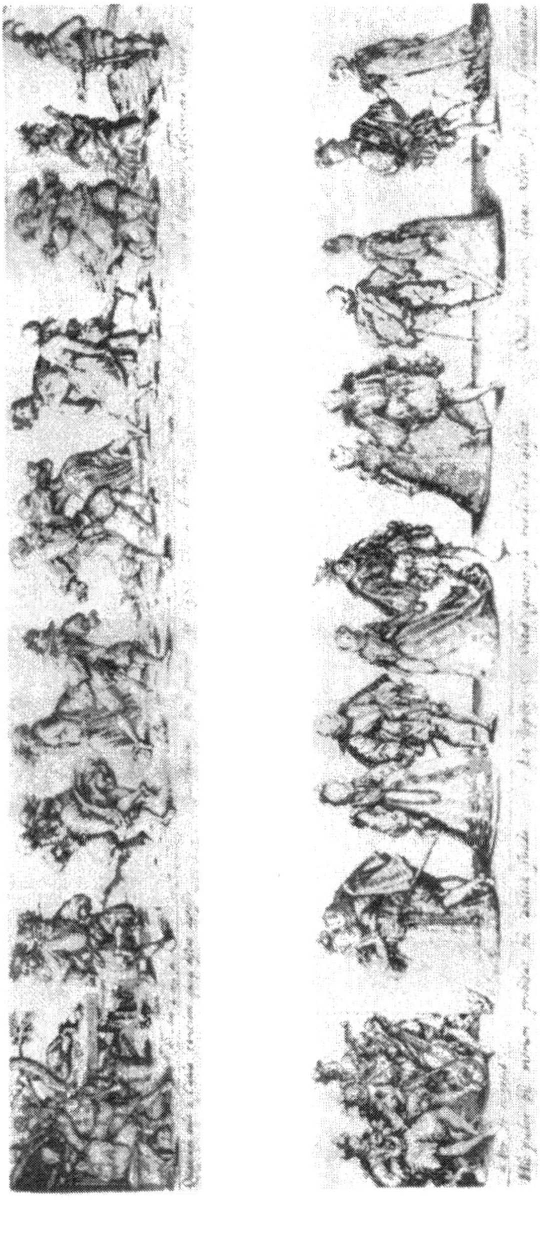

Théodore de Bry (1528–98), Peasants' and Court Dances

PLATE 24.

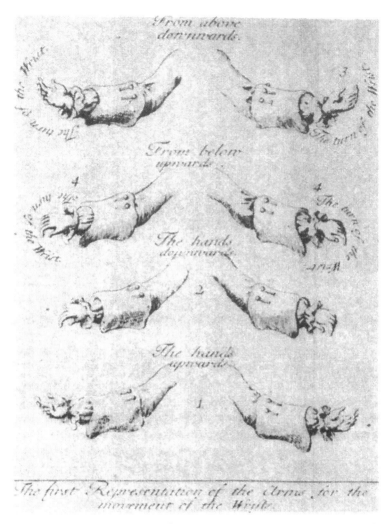

From the English Translation of Rameau, *Le Maître à danser* (Paris 1725)

PLATE 25.

L. Goupy, The Dance-Master Isaac

PLATE 26.

English Longways, 1698

PLATE 27.

Caricature of Noverre's Ballet *Jason et Médée*

PLATE 28.

Aug. de St. Aubin, *Le Bal paré*, Paris, 1773

PLATE 29.

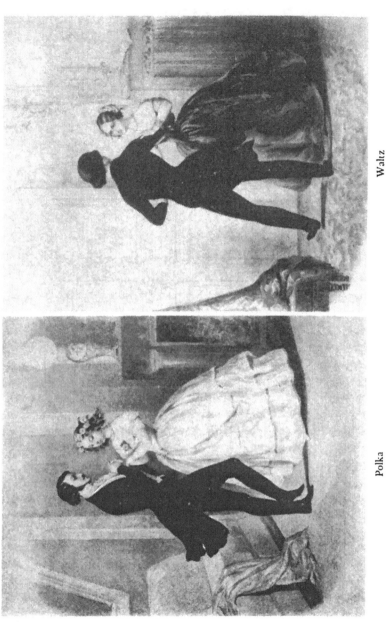

Polka

Anaïs Colin, *Le Maître à danser* (1844)

Waltz

PLATE 30.

Cakewalk

Cancan

PLATE 31.

Isadora Duncan, by Abraham Walkowitz

PLATE 32.

References

For more detailed references consult the German edition.

Page Line

9 14 Carl Appun, *Unter den Tropen*, p. 468f., Jena, 1871.

10 8 J. Maclaren, *My Crowded Solitude*, N. Y., 1926.

10 17 Wolfgang Kohler in *Psychologische Forschung*, I, pp. 33-35.

10 20 M. Moszkowski in *Zeitschrift für Ethnologie*, 43, p. 337, 1911.

11 11 Karl Groos, *Die Spiele der Menschen*, p. 113, Jena, 1899.

11 19 Richard Wallaschek, *Primitive Music*, N. Y., 1893.

11 28 Schebesta, *Bei den Urwaldzwergen von Malaya*, pp. 219, 266, Leipzig, 1927.

11 29 Friedrich Heinrich von der Hagen, *Minnesinger*, pp. 160, 183, Leipzig, 1838.

14 10 Paul and Fritz Sarasin, *Ergebnisse naturwissenschaftlicher Forschungen auf Ceylon*, Vol. III, "Die Weddas," pp. 512ff., Wiesbaden, 1887–1893.

15 6 A. R. Brown, *The Andaman Islanders*, pp. 129ff., Cambridge, 1922.

15 16 *id.*, p. 247.

16 3 Father Wilhelm Schmidt, *Der Ursprung der Gottesidee*, Part II, Vol. 3, "Die Religionen der Urvölker Asiens und Australiens," p. 126, Münster, 1931.

16 7 Harry Johnston, *The Uganda Protectorate*, II, p. 543, London, 1902.

16 19 Schebesta, *ibid.*, p. 219.

16 23 W. W. Skeat and Charles O. Blagden, *Pagan Races of the Malay Peninsula*, p. 131, London, 1906.

Page Line

16 27 Roland B. Dixon in *Bulletin of the American Museum of Natural History*, 17, part 3, 1905; 17, part 5, 1907.

17 6 *id.*, 1905.

17 25 Beck, *Die Ekstase*, p. 10, Sachsa, 1906.

18 15 Iden-Zeller, in *Zeitschr. für Ethnologie*, 43, p. 853, 1911.

18 33 Fritz Spellig in *Zeitschr. für Ethnologie*, 59, pp. 62f., 1927.

19 19 R. Parkinson, *30 Jahre in der Südsee*, pp. 237f., Stuttgart, 1926.

19 25 Augustin Krämer, *Hawaii, Ostmikronesien und Samoa*, pp. 379, 381f., Stuttgart, 1906.

20 6 W. Spies in *Kunst*, II, p. 456.

20 13 Beck, *ibid.*, p. 59.

21 3 J. W. Hauer, *Die Religionen*, p. 402, Stuttgart, 1923.

21 6 A. L. Kroeber in *Smithsonian Bulletin*, 78, p. 384, 1925.

23 13 M. Moszkowski, *Auf neuen Wegen durch Sumatra*, pp. 127f., Berlin, 1909.

24 23 George Groslier, *Danseuses cambodgiennes*, pp. 44f., Paris, 1913.

25 13 Beck, *ibid.*, p. 79.

27 21 Cyr. van Overbergh, *Les Mangbetu* (Congo Belge), p. 407, Bruxelles, 1909.

28 3 Matthias Josef Erdweg, in *Mitteilungen der Anthropologischen Gesellschaft*, 43, p. 304, Wien, 1902.

29 7 Kristof Bulat, in *Archiv. für slavische Philologie*, 37, p. 107, 1918.

451

REFERENCES

Page Line
30 2 Georg Schweinfurth, *Im Herzen von Afrika*, p. 328, Leipzig, 1918.

31 29 Ch. Blasis, *Traité élémentaire, théorique et pratique de l'art de la danse*, p. 101, Milan, 1820.

32 13 Paul-Louis Faye, in *Phoebe Apperson Hearst Memorial Volume*, p. 49, Berkeley, 1923.

32 15 Koch-Grünberg, *Zwei Jahre unter den Indianern*, I, p. 85, Berlin, 1910.

32 22 Thomas Winterbottom, *An Account of the Native Africans in the Neighborhood of Sierra Leone*, I, p. 108, London, 1803.

33 12 Karl Semper, *Die Palau-Inseln*, p. 57, Leipzig, 1873.

33 17 *id.*, p. 206.

34 10 Herbert Baldus, *Indianerstudien im nordöstlichen Chaco*, p. 106, Leipzig, 1931.

36 3 Hans Meyer, *Die Barundi*, Leipzig, 1916.

37 18 Adalbert v. Chamisso, *Gesammelte Werke*, II, p. 366, Leipzig, 1874.

38 10 J. W. Hauer, *ibid.*, p. 386.

40 3 Augustin Krämer, *ibid.*, pp. 315ff.

41 2 Rainer Maria Rilke, *Briefe aus den Jahren 1906-1907*, Leipzig, 1930.

45 8 J. W. Hauer, *ibid.*, p. 357.

46 6 Shway Yoe, *The Burman, his life and notions*, p. 2, London, 1882.

46 11 Carl Hagemann, *Spiele der Völker*, p. 122, Berlin, 1919.

46 13 Rougier, in *Anthropos*, 6, p. 174, 1911.

46 18 Harry Johnston, *ibid.*

47 9 Th.-B. van Lelyveld, *La danse dans le théatre javanais*, p. 89, Paris, 1931.

48 5 Heinrich v. Kleist, *Uber das Marionettentheater.*

51 25 C. G. Seligmann and Z. Brenda, *The Veddas*, pp. 134f., Cambridge, 1911.

52 12 Fritz Spellig, *ibid.*

52 30 Jaap Kunst, in *Driemaandelijksche Bladen*, 16, II, pp. 454f., 1916.

53 18 Karl Groos, *ibid.*, p. 112.

53 21 G. Catlin, *Letters and Notes on the*

Page Line
Manners, Customs, and Condition of The North American Indians, London, 1841.

54 6 Richard Andree, *Braunschweiger Volkskunde*, p. 198, Braunschweig, 1901.

58 33 C. G. Jung, *Psychologische Typen*, Zürich, 1930.

60 21 *id.*, p. 483.

60 23 Wilhelm Worringer, *Abstraktion und Einfühlung*, p. 32, München, 1918.

63 26 Paul Sébillot, *Le paganisme contemporain chez les peuples celtolatins*, p. 79, Paris, 1908.

67 22 Abbe H. Breuil, "L'âge des cavernes," *Revue arch.*, 19, 1912.

67 22 J. W. Hauer, *ibid.*, I, p. 182.

68 25 Walk, in *Anthropos*, 23, p. 875, 1928.

76 9 Günther Stahl, in *Zeitschr. für Ethnologie*, 57, p. 129, Plate 130, 1926.

76 23 J. W. Hauer, *ibid.*, p. 126.

78 7 Herbert Baldus, *ibid.*, pp. 106, 146, 148f.

81 12 R. Parkinson, *ibid.*, p. 143.

81 22 Roland B. Dixon, *ibid.*, p. 298.

81 29 Augustin Krämer, *Die Samoa-Inseln*, p. 319, Stuttgart, 1903.

82 17 Hans Flemming, *Tanzbeschreibungen oberbayrischer Schuhplattler*, pp. 3f., Berlin, 1925.

84 16 Curt Nimuendajú-Unkel, in *Anthropos*, 16, p. 382, 1921.

88 10 Edgar Hugo Meyer, *Badisches Volksleben im 18. Jh.*, p. 304, Strassburg, 1900.

89 14 Karl Theodor Preuss, in *Globus*, 86, I, p. 126, 1904.

89 30 Augustus Oldfield in *Transactions of the Ethnological Society of London*, p. 230, 1865.

91 17 Adolf Bastian, *Indonesien*, p. 110, Berlin, 1884.

92 4 Adam Wrede, *Eifeler Volkskunde*, p. 139, Bonn and Leipzig, 1924.

92 29 Koch-Grünberg, *ibid.*, I, p. 193.

452

REFERENCES

Page Line

93 14 Zache, in *Zeitschr. für Ethnologie,*
31, p. 73, 1899.

96 24 W. Lüpkes, *Ostfriesische Volks-
kunde,* p. 231, Emden, 1907. Benno
E. Siebs, *Die Norderneyer,* p. 128,
Norden, 1930.

97 14 August Ellrich, *Die Ungarn wie sie
sind,* p. 142, Berlin, 1831.

97 28 F. M. Böhme, *Geschichte des Tanzes
in Deutschland,* I, p. 190, Leipzig,
1886.

99 10 Johann Heinrich Fischer, *Beschrei-
bung der vorzüglichsten Volksfeste,*
I, p. 22, Wien, 1799.

100 19 Arved V. Schultz, *Die Pamirtad-
schik,* p. 85, Giessen, 1914.

104 16 Fritz Vormann, in *Anthropos,* 10, p.
172, 1915.

106 13 Leo Frobenius, *Und Afrika sprach,*
I, p. 200.

106 15 Yrjö Wichmann, *Volksdichtung und
Volksbräuche der Tscheremissen,* p.
51, Helsinki, 1931.

107 10 *Ungarischer oder dacianischer Simplicissimus, vorstellend seinen wun-
derlichen Lebens-Lauff,* p. 214, 1683.

109 11 R. Parkinson, *ibid.*

110 8 H. Klose, in *Globus,* 89, p. 13, 1906.

110 20 Lucian, *Von der Tanzkunst,* IV, p.
391, Leipzig, 1788.

111 4 *Die Vorsokratiker,* ed. W. Nestle,
pp. 172f., Jena, 1908.

111 14 J. S. Brandts Buys, in *Djawa,* 8, p.
123, 1928.

118 13 Siegfried Passarge, *Die Buschmän-
ner der Kalahari,* pp. 102f., Berlin,
1907.

119 27 Kurt Meschke, *Schwerttanz und
Schwerttanzspiel im germanischen
Kulturkreis,* Leipzig-Berlin, 1931.

120 23 *ibid., Rote Erde,* II, p. 178.

120 25 *ibid.,* p. 92.

121 27 Carl Hagemann, *ibid.,* p. 47.

125 17 James George Frazer, *The Golden
Bough,* N. Y., 1914.

126 12 Fritz Krause, *In den Wildnissen
Brasiliens,* p. 100, Leipzig, 1911.

126 29 Peekel, in *Anthropos,* 24, pp. 549ff.,
1929.

127 30 Rudolf Pöch, in *Mitt. d. Anthr.
Gesellschaft,* 35, p. 397, Wien, 1905.

128 17 O. Schellong, in *Globus,* 56, p. 83,
1889.

130 27 P. Martin de La Martinière, *Reise
nach Norden,* p. 68, Leipzig, 1706.

132 25 Roland B. Dixon, *ibid.,* part 5, p.
459, 1907.

133 9 Karl Theodor Preuss, in *Globus,* 90,
pp. 122, 124, 1906.

133 26 Wolfgang Köhler, *ibid.,* p. 35.

137 11 Friedrich Nietzsche, *Die Geburt der
Tragödie aus dem Geiste der Musik.*

138 3 Walter Siegfried, *Aus dem Bilder-
buch eines Lebens,* II, pp. 27ff.,
Zürich and Leipzig, 1926.

140 24 James Bonwick, *Daily Life and
Origin of the Tasmanians,* p. 38,
London, 1898.

142 5 Fray Bernardino de Sahagun, *Einige
Kapitel aus seinem Geschichtswerk
aus dem Aztekischen,* p. 293, Stuttgart.

143 23 A. L. Kroeber, *ibid.,* p. 304.

144 21 Teschauer, in *Anthropos,* 9, p. 34,
1914.

146 15 Georg Buschan, *Illustrierte Völker-
kunde,* II, p. 189, Stuttgart, 1926.

146 22 Teschauer, *ibid.*

148 31 Jacob Burckhardt, *Die Cultur der
Renaissance in Italien,* p. 203, Leipzig, 1899.

149 14 Translated by Jefferson Butler
Fletcher.

152 13 G. van der Leeuw, "In dem Himmel
ist ein Tanz,". . . , p. 21, München,
n.d.

153 24 Fray Bernardino de Sahagun, *ibid.,*
pp. 158f.

153 30 A. H. Fox Strangways, *The Music
of Hindustan,* p. 29, Oxford, 1914.

153 33 Elio Modigliani, *Un viaggio a Nias,*
p. 173, Milano, 1890.

158 14 Hahl, in *Ethnolog. Notizblatt,* 3, p.
99, 1902.

REFERENCES

Page Line

158 25 Rudolf Pöch, in *Zeitschr. für Ethnologie*, 39, p. 397, 1907.

159 22 Carl Ritter, *Die Erdkunde von Asien*, VIII, pp. 652f., Berlin, 1848.

160 18 Curt Nimuendajú-Unkel, in *Zeitschr. für Ethnologie*, 46, 1914.

161 23 Johannes Cadovius Müller, *Memoriale linguae frisicae*, p. 33, Norden-Leipzig, 1911.

161 33 Johann Heinrich Fischer, *ibid.*, p. 23.

164 21 F. Nork, *Etymologisch-symbolisch-mythologisches Real-Wörterbuch*, IV, p. 436, Stuttgart, 1845.

165 4 J. J. Bachofen, *Oknos der Seilflechter*, paragraph 2, 1859.

166 7 Fritz Böhme, *Masstäbe zu einer Geschichte der Tanzkunst*, II, p. 13, Breslau, 1927.

171 21 Peekel, "Lang-Manu," *Pater Schmidt Festschrift*, p. 551, 1927.

178 26 Curt Sachs, *Geist und Werden der Musikinstrumente*, p. 16, Berlin, 1929.

179 5 *id.*, p. 41.

179 9 *id.*, p. 44.

180 11 *id.*, p. 206.

183 29 Erich M. von Hornbostel, in Koch-Grünberg's *Vom Roroima zum Orinoco*, III, p. 416, Stuttgart, 1923.

188 5 Herbert Baldus, *ibid.*, p. 106.

189 2 Erich M. von Hornbostel, in *Anthropos*, 4, p. 1034, 1909.

190 23 Mieczyław Kolinski, in *Anthropos*, 25, p. 611, 1930.

191 6 Koch-Grünberg, *Vom Roroima zum Orinoco*, I, p. 54, Stuttgart, 1923.

193 24 Frances Densmore, in *Smithsonian Bulletin*, 75, p. 189, 1922.

196 32 J. Irle, *Die Herero*, p. 125, Gütersloh, 1906.

196 33 Villoteau, "De l'état actuel de l'art musical en Egypte," *Description de l'Egypte*, XIV, Paris, 1826.

197 20 Paul Wirz, *Die Marind-anim von Holl. Süd-Neu-Guinea*, IV, p. 3, Hamburg, 1925.

211 12 Oswald Menghin, *Weltgeschichte*

214 22 *id.*, p. 500.

222 23 François Bernier, *Voyages*, II, pp. 105f., Amsterdam, 1699.

225 16 Neuhauss, I, pp. 391ff.

226 12 G. Catlin, *ibid.*

226 20 *id.*

227 24 Karl Semper, *ibid.*, p. 251.

230 26 Adolf Erman, in *Zeitschr. für äg. Spr.*, 31, p. 71 (1893).

247 10 Lucian of Samosata, *On the Art of Dancing*.

252 13 Leo von Rozmital, *Ritter-, Hof- und Pilger-Reise 1465-1467*, Stuttgart, 1844.

253 8 Giraldus Cambrensis, *Itinerarium Cambriae*, Opera R. S., VI, 32.

253 28 *Strassburg Chronicle* of Kleinkawel, 1625.

254 30 J. W. von Goethe, *Über Italien 1788-89*.

255 18 Rainer Maria Rilke, *ibid.*

255 29 J. H. von Riedesel, *Voyage en Sicile et dans la Grande Gréce*, pp. 245-255, Lausanne, 1773.

256 18 J. W. von Goethe, *Der Rattenfänger*.

257 2 Sebastian Brant, *The Ship of Fools*.

259 1 Koch-Grünberg, *Indianermärchen aus Südamerika*, p. 208, Jena, 1921.

259 6 J. W. von Goethe, *Totentanz*.

259 13 Jacob Meydenbach, *Typographischer Totentanz*, Mainz, 1491.

268 18 A. Schultz, *Das höfische Leben zur Zeit der Minnesinger*, I, p. 544, Leipzig, 1889.

275 21 Joseph Bédier, in *Revue des Deux Mondes*, 135 (1896), pp. 156ff.

282 23 Pastor Neocorus, quoted in F. M. Böhme, *ibid*, I, 49.

289 13 Antonio da Tempo, pp. 117, 135.

291 22 J. Wolf, in *Die Tänze des Mittelalters*, I, 1918; P. Aubry, *Estampies et Danses royales*, Paris, 1907.

298 6 Hans Commenda, "Der Landla," in *Heimatgaue*, pp. 160-164, 1923.

299 27 Guglielmo Ebreo, *Trattato dell' Arte del Ballo*, Bologna, 1873.

REFERENCES

Page Line

300 25 Robert Coplande, *The Maner of dauncynge of Bace Daunces . . .*, ed. Furnivall, London, 1871.

309 7 Otto Kinkeldey, *A Jewish Dancing Master of the Renaissance*, New York, 1929.

318 5 Thoinot Arbeau, *Orchésographie*, p. 61, London, 1925.

319 15 E. Closson, *Le Manuscrit dit des Basses Danses . . .*, Brussels, 1912; H. Riemann, *Die rhythmische Struktur der Basses Danses*, Sammelb. d. Internat. Musikges. XIV, pp. 349ff.; F. Blume, *Studien zur Vorgeschichte der Orchestersuite*, Leipzig, 1925.

332 29 Father Marin Mersenne, *Harmonie Universelle*, p. 165, Paris, 1636.

334 4 Leo von Rozmital, *ibid.*, pp. 170, 178.

350 8 Rudolf Lothar, *Die Seele Spaniens*, pp. 297ff., München, 1923.

357 10 Michael Praetorius, *Terpsichore*, Wolffenbüttel, 1612.

359 10 Jules Ecorcheville, *Vingt suites d'orchestre*, pp. 49f., Berlin-Paris, 1906.

360 2 Simeone Zuccolo da Cologna, *La pazzia del ballo*, p. 20, Padova, 1549.

360 25 Thoinot Arbeau, *ibid.*, p. 52.

363 14 Thomas Platter, *A Montpellier*, pp. 219, 259, Montpellier, 1892.

370 26 Feuillet, *Recueil de danse*, Paris, 1709.

371 8 Gregorio Lambranzi, *New and Curious School of Theatrical Dancing*, ed. by Cyril W. Beaumont, London, 1928.

372 17 Compan, *Dictionnaire de danse*, p. 347, Paris, 1787.

375 20 Guillaume Bouchet, in Edmond Bonnafé, "Notes sur la vie privée à la Renaissance," (*La Revue de Paris*), 3, p. 380, 1896.

375 31 Brantôme, *La Vie des Dames galantes*, Discours III.

377 22 Federigo Zuccaro, *Il Passaggio per l'Italia*, pp. 40f., 1608, ed. by V. Lanciarini, Rome, 1893.

378 14 Bartholomäus Sastrow, *Herkommen, Geburt und Lauff seines gantzen Lebens*, Greisswald, 1824.

378 20 Felix et Thomas Platter, *Zur Sittengeschichte des XVI. Jahrhunderts*, pp. 219, 285, Leipzig, 1878.

379 24 Ernst Hamza, in *Zeitschr. des Deutschen und Osterreichischen Alpenver.*, 45.

380 1 *id.*, p. 123.

381 11 Grimmelshausen, *Der abenteuerliche Simplicius Simplicissimus*.

381 26 Johannes Bolte, in *Zeitschr. des Vereins für Volkskunde*, 35 (1925), 37 (1927); in *Alemannia* 18, 1890.

389 6 Zedler, *Gr. Universal-Lexicon*, X, p. 430 (1735).

392 7 Curt Sachs, *Barocke Tonkunst, Das Feuer* III, p. 191 (1922).

393 11 P. Rameau, *The Dancing Master*, London, 1931.

396 22 Giambattista Dufort, *Trattato del ballo mobile*, p. 119, Napoli, 1728.

397 7 Gottfried Taubert, *Rechtschaffener Tantzmeister*, p. 52, Leipzig, 1717.

397 12 *id.*, p. 572.

397 15 *id.*, p. 572.

398 3 J. M. de Chavanne, *Principes du Menuet*, Luxembourg, 1767.

398 9 Moreau de Saint-Méry, *De la danse*, Parme, 1803.

399 10 J. W. von Goethe, *Italien, Zweiter Aufenthalt in Rom*, 1788.

399 18 D. Moores, *Abriss des gesellschaftlichen Lebens und der Sitten*, p. 264, Leipzig, 1785.

400 11 J. M. de Chavanne, *ibid.*, p. 2.

402 1 Rameau, *ibid.*, p. 107.

402 18 Pompeo Molmenti, *La storia di Venezia nella vita privata*, III, p. 351, Bergamo, 1928–29.

406 23 Pécour et Feuillet, *Recueil de danse*, Paris, 1709.

407 18 D. Moores, *ibid.*, p. 141.

407 22 D. Moores, *ibid.*, p. 264.

410 22 Feuillet et Dezais, *Chorégraphie ou l'art de décrire la danse par caractères*,

REFERENCES

Page Line

figures et signes desmonstratifs, Paris, 1699.

411 5 W. Danckert, Geschichte der Gigue, pp. 17ff., Leipzig, 1924.

411 11 John Playford, The English Dancing-Master.

414 1 Guillaume, Caractère de la danse Allemande, Paris, 1760; Positions et attitudes de l'Allemande, Paris, 1768.

414 9 J. A. Dubois, Hindu Manners, Oxford, 1897.

414 28 Alfred Waldau, Böhmische Nationaltänze, I, p. 65, Prag, 1859, 1860.

416 7 Translated by Jefferson Butler Fletcher.

416 16 id.

421 2 Bonnet, Histoire generale de la danse, p. 135, Paris, 1723.

421 4 Christoph Gottlieb Hänsel, Allerneueste Anweisung zur Aeusserlichen Moral, Worinnen im Anhange die so genannten Pfuscher entdecket, Und überhaupt der Misbrauch der edlen Tanzkunst einem ieden vor Augen geleget wird, p. 169, Leipzig, 1755.

421 15 Rameau, ibid., p. 108.

422 12 Hänsel, ibid., pp. 167f.

423 19 Cellarius, 100 neue Cotillon-Touren, 9th Ed., Elfurt, 1898.

424 10 Charles Pauli, Elémens de la danse, Leipzig, 1756.

425 5 A. Simon, Poln, Elemente in der deutschen Musik, p. 30, Zürich, 1916 (Die Osterreichisch-Ungarische Monarchie in Wort und Bild).

425 15 Tobias Norlind, in Sammelbände der

Page Line

Internationalen Musikgesellschaft, 12, p. 514, 1911.

425 23 Adam Mickiewicz, Herr Thaddäus oder der letzte Einritt in Littauen, p. 269, Leipzig, 1882.

426 23 C. J. v. Feldenstein, Erweiterung der Kunst nach der Chorographie zu tanzen, p. 84, Braunschweig, 1772.

427 15 J. W. von Goethe, Aus meinem Leben, II, Buch 9.

427 19 J. W. von Goethe, Werther Buch I.

427 21 J. W. von Goethe, Aust meinem Leben, II, Buch 9.

427 24 J. W. von Goethe, Aus meinem Leben, III, Buch 11.

428 32 Tanzkalender, pp. 111ff., 1801.

430 21 Ernst Moritz Arndt, Reisen durch einen Teil Teutschlands, Ungarns, Italiens und Frankreichs, I, pp. 43ff., Leipzig, 1804.

432 26 ibid., IV, p. 198.

435 20 Perrot and Adrien Robert, La Polka ensiegnée sans maître, p. 9, Paris, 1845.

436 7 Alfred Waldau, ibid., pp. 36f.

438 4 E. T. A. Hoffmann, Kreisleriana, p. 4.

438 8 Journal des Luxus und der Moden, p. 289, 1797.

440 12 August von Rosenhain, Bermerkungen über das Tanzen, pp. 75ff., Schleswig, 1821.

442 12 Jean-Georges Noverre, Letters on Dancing and Ballets, Trans. and published by C. W. Beaumont, London, 1930.

444 27 Charles Blasis, Traité élémentaire, théorique et pratique de l'art de la danse, Milan, 1820.

Index

INDEX

INDEX

461

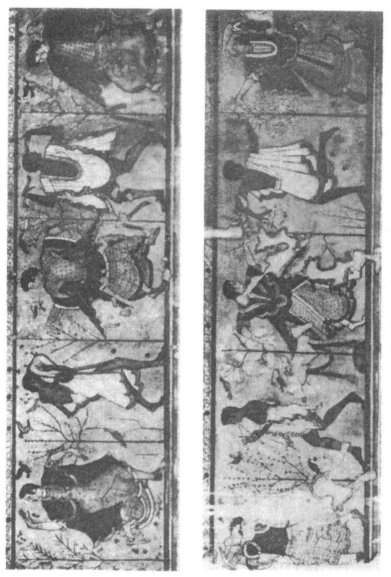

Etruscan Dances. Wall Painting, Metropolitan Museum, N. Y.

PLATE 13.

INDEX

463

INDEX

INDEX

INDEX

NORTON PAPERBACKS ON MUSIC